Palgrave Studies in Economic History

Series Editor
Kent Deng
London School of Economics
London, UK

Palgrave Studies in Economic History is designed to illuminate and enrich our understanding of economies and economic phenomena of the past. The series covers a vast range of topics including financial history, labour history, development economics, commercialisation, urbanisation, industrialisation, modernisation, globalisation, and changes in world economic orders.

More information about this series at
http://www.palgrave.com/gp/series/14632

Alfonso Díez-Minguela
Julio Martinez-Galarraga
Daniel A. Tirado-Fabregat

Regional Inequality in Spain

1860–2015

palgrave
macmillan

Alfonso Díez-Minguela
University of València
València, Spain

Julio Martinez-Galarraga
University of València
València, Spain

Daniel A. Tirado-Fabregat
University of València
València, Spain

Palgrave Studies in Economic History
ISBN 978-3-030-40483-3 ISBN 978-3-319-96110-1 (eBook)
https://doi.org/10.1007/978-3-319-96110-1

Library of Congress Control Number: 2018952080

Cover illustration: MELBA PHOTO AGENCY / Alamy Stock Photo

This Palgrave Macmillan imprint is published by the registered company Springer Nature Switzerland AG
The registered company address is: Gewerbestrasse 11, 6330 Cham, Switzerland

For all the people and places that made me.
Alfonso
For Jana, who joined us while we were writing this.
Julio
To Raquel, Dani, and Andrea.
Dani

Acknowledgements

This book is the result of years of work, during which time we received invaluable help from various colleagues and institutions. The debts we owe are numerous since a great many researchers provided comments and advice throughout the process, both informally and in seminars and conferences we shared. Much of the content to be found in the following pages comes from previous papers on which the authors collaborated with Rafael González-Val, Joan Rosés and Teresa Sanchis. It was and continues to be a pleasure to work with them. We would also like to thank those colleagues who selflessly shared their data and estimations, which in many cases are yet to be published but which enabled us to complete our analysis. Marc Badia, Emanuele Felice, Jordi Guilera and Pedro Lains let us have their most recent estimates for regional GDP for Portugal and Italy. Eduard Álvarez Palau, Jordi Martí Henneberg and Mateu Morillas Torné helped us with the mapping, and Peter Hall was always willing to work on the English, even against the clock when a deadline was approaching. The area of Economic History (EH-Valencia) of the Department of Economic Analysis at the University of València became a space that made the research task much easier and provided us with a permanent stimulus. And we must not forget the Department of Economic History, Institutions, Policy and World Economy at the University of Barcelona (UB), which is where the investigation that years later would result in the publication of this book began. Out of everyone at the UB we would most especially like to remember Francesc Valls, a colleague and friend who recently passed away. We would also like to express our gratitude to all the team at Palgrave Macmillan, for both the production and the publishing processes. Our thanks also go to Kent Deng (series editor), to two anonymous referees for their suggestions, and to Laura Pacey and Clara Heathcock for their patience, endless inspiration and excellent editing. Finally, we are grateful for the financial support received from the Ministry of Economy and Competitiveness via the ECO2012-39169-C03-02, ECO2015-65049-C12-1-P and ECO2015-71534-REDT projects.

Contents

List of Figures

List of Tables

1

Introduction

Why Is It Important to Study Regional Economic Inequality?

The world is a very unequal place from an economic point of view. The roughly 200 countries that today occupy the planet's surface present huge differences in income levels,[1] and there are big differences within the countries themselves, too. Yet it is only relatively recently that this territorial inequality has attracted the attention of academics, politicians and international organizations. The main reason for this, as has repeatedly been shown (Kanbur et al. 2005; Milanovic 2005; World Bank 2009), is the fact that the successful growth experiences of emerging countries like China and India have been accompanied by growing disparities, especially between coastal and inland regions.

The case of China is probably the most paradigmatic. Despite the rapid economic progress of the last few decades which has transformed it into a leading actor in the world economy, its income per capita lags behind that of the most developed countries. And with a gross domestic product (GDP) per capita of around 16,000 \$, China still has a long way to go to

[1] GDP per capita in Norway, currently one of the top-ranked countries in the world, is over 70,000 \$. This is more than 100 times greater than that of the poorest country, the Central African Republic, which barely reaches 680 \$ (international dollars, purchasing power parity [PPP]). IMF figures.

A. Díez-Minguela et al., *Regional Inequality in Spain*, Palgrave Studies in Economic History, https://doi.org/10.1007/978-3-319-96110-1_1

reach the almost 60,000 $ per-capita GDP of the US, occupying as it does a relatively modest position (79th) in the world ranking. Furthermore, this figure, which is a national aggregate, covers a wide range of realities. Provinces like Beijing, Shanghai and Tianjin have per-capita incomes of over 33,000 $, that is, close to those in what are considered developed countries such as South Korea and Spain. At the other extreme, however, Gansu, which is the poorest province, has a per-capita income that is only a quarter that of its counterparts, barely reaching 8000 $ (similar to Bolivia, which is ranked 120th in the world).[2] This contrast between coastal and inland areas is one of the basic characteristics of the developing Chinese economy.

Concern about territorial inequalities is also present in developed economies. Indeed the European Union (EU) plans to spend 352 billion euros on its cohesion policy over the period 2014–2020, a sum that represents virtually a third of its total budget. In particular, 182 billion euros will be allocated to regions with per-capita incomes below 75 per cent of the EU average.

The issue is not a minor one, and neither is the economic (and possibly political) reality to be dealt with. The Eurostat Regional Yearbooks (ERY) rate the question as a serious one and identify three characteristics of territorial inequality in Europe that need to be highlighted. The first is that there is a very high level of regional economic inequality. GDP per capita (GDPpc) in the richest NUTS2 region in the EU (Inner London) is over five times (5.8 in 2015) higher than the average for the EU-28. At the other extreme, the poorest regions have levels of GDPpc that are less than half the EU average. And these are not isolated cases—82 of the 276 NUTS2 regions that make up the EU-28 have a GDPpc below 75 per cent of the average. Another 45, however, exceed the EU average by at least 25 per cent.

The second is that regional inequality has a definite geographical profile in the form of a centre-to-periphery-type pattern. The ERY for 2017 points out that many of the rich regions of Europe can be found on a line

[2] Hunan, which occupies 16th position among the 31 provinces of China, has a per-capita GDP of around 13,000 $. Zhang and Zhang (2003) and Kanbur and Zhang (2005), among others, study the evolution of regional inequality in China.

that starts in northern Italy and crosses Austria and Germany before splitting into two branches of prosperity—one that goes through the Benelux countries towards southern England and another that heads off towards the Nordic countries. The equivalent line for poor regions starts in the Baltic republics, then heads south across Eastern Europe towards Greece, southern Italy and the southernmost parts of the Iberian Peninsula.

Third and finally, the same report highlight the growing importance of the NUTS2 regions in which the capitals of EU member states are located. With the exception of Germany and Italy, these regions top their respective national rankings in terms of GDPpc in all EU countries that comprise more than one NUTS2 region. This is true even when the state capital is an island of prosperity in a sea of relative poverty.

Bearing all these aspects in mind, Spain—a country of over 46 million inhabitants covering an area greater than 500,000 km^2 with a heterogeneity without parallel in Europe in terms of climate, geography, culture and language—serves as an excellent microcosm for analysing regional economic inequality. We would even argue that this inequality in Spain today reproduces on a smaller scale the same patterns identified by Eurostat for the European economy as a whole.

Considering the Spanish average to be 100, the GDPpc for Madrid, the richest NUTS2 region in Spain, was 136 in 2015. For Extremadura, the poorest, it was 69. To put it another way, the richest region enjoyed a per-capita income practically twice the size of the poorest. Although not of the same magnitude, regional differences in income levels are significant in a fair number of cases. In 2015, 3 of the 17 NUTS2 regions in Spain recorded a GDPpc below 80 per cent of the average (Andalusia, Extremadura and Castile-La Mancha). Another three, on the other hand, exceeded it by over 20 per cent (Madrid, Navarre and the Basque Country).

Apart from this, territorial inequality in Spain also forms a definite geographical pattern. In this case the richest regions are to be found in the north-eastern triangle of the Iberian Peninsula, with its vertices in Catalonia, the Basque Country and Madrid. The area covered by the triangle includes Aragon, La Rioja and Navarre, all of which have income levels higher than the Spanish average. Also forming part of the group are the Balearic Islands, located off the north-east coast of the Peninsula.

Meanwhile the poorest regions of Spain are located along a line running from the south-east of the Iberian Peninsula towards the north-west, cutting across Valencia, Murcia, Andalusia, Castile-La Mancha, Castile-Leon, Extremadura, Cantabria, Asturias and Galicia.

Finally, like in most EU countries, the Spanish NUTS2 region with the highest per-capita income is the one in which the state capital is located, Madrid, which, as already mentioned, has an income per capita over 35 per cent higher than the Spanish average. However, this was not always the case, as we will see in the course of the book. During much of the economic development process in Spain it was Catalonia and the Basque Country, the pioneers of Spanish industrialization, that frequently occupied the top places in the national ranking.

As can be imagined, the situation described in the previous paragraphs is a cause of social and political tension between territories, and in particular between traditionally rich regions that are losing ground and poorer regions that receive net transfer payments from the state. This transfer of resources forms part of a system of fiscal flows between autonomous communities and the state that tends to favour poorer regions and find funding in the richer ones. The financing model for the autonomous communities, that is, the criteria whereby the state decides what resources each territory should contribute or receive, is therefore a bone of contention causing disputes that can sometimes spill over into society and be taken up by the general public. Regional inequality and the funding of net payment transfers for the purposes of territorial rebalancing are weapons wielded by regional pro-independence movements at one end of the spectrum and those who want to recentralize power in the state at the other.

The best way of overcoming this situation, whether in Europe or Spain, is to make any actions designed to correct these inequalities more effective. However, evidence of this actually happening is thin on the ground. Various papers (Giannetti 2002; Puga 2002) have pointed out that, on a European scale, the economic integration process has achieved a certain level of convergence between member states in terms of income. Nevertheless, at least since the mid-1980s, this convergence has done little to close the gap between regions. On the contrary, regional inequality has continued to grow in spite of the huge resources allocated to the development of poorer regions through territorial cohesion policies. In the case of Spain, the situation is no different. Even with increased intervention and public spending aimed at territorial rebalancing in the context of integration within the EU, the gap between rich and poor regions has been growing since the mid-1980s.

With this problem in mind, the aim of this book is to search the past for the factors that determine regional inequality. The object is simply to identify and make visible those elements that need to be taken into account when designing public policies so that these policies can be more effective in getting to the root of the problem. We start from the premise that a knowledge of history, of the long-term evolution of territorial inequality, is a key element when it comes to understanding today's economic reality, especially if we consider that this reality is the result of a long and complex process, strongly influenced by technological and institutional change, geography and policies.

This introduction is followed by a brief overview of what the field of economics considers to be the main reasons that explain why inequality between territories exists and how it evolves over time. As we will argue later, whatever the economic reasoning used to explain the problem, it should be agreed that territorial inequality is caused by imbalances generated by the economic development processes and characterized by the integration of national markets, unequal technological advance, the speed of structural change and the varying degrees to which national economies are exposed to globalization processes. Understanding it therefore requires us to consider a great variety of elements together and carry out an empirical analysis covering a lengthy time period. At the end of the day, territorial inequality is to do with the movement of societies along pathways of growth that extend into the long term.

How Does Economics Explain the Existence of Regional Inequalities?

Studying the determinants and possible evolution of regional economic inequality has generally been approached from two different though very closely related economic viewpoints: international trade theory and economic growth theory. Given this context, the purpose of the following paragraphs is, first, to record which elements predominate in the various theoretical approximations carried out to explain the existence of economic inequality between territories, and second, to present the economic reasoning that provides the basis for hypotheses about the evolution of inequality during economic growth processes.

Various explanations for regional economic inequality have been put forward in the international trade literature. Neoclassical economic models, for example, have explained regional income disparities on the basis of spatial differences in the distribution of endowments (e.g. natural resources, factors of production and infrastructure) and technology. Differences in factor endowments would result in territorial specialization processes leading to marked differences in regional production structures. Thus regional specialization in sectors characterized by different productivity levels could be one explanation for territorial inequality.

With this analytical framework, the effect of removing obstacles to trade and the advance of market integration would favour the convergence of factor returns and living standards. The factor-price-equalization (FPE) theorem from the Heckscher–Ohlin (HO) model is optimistic about the consequences of market integration; the increase in trade and factor movements should lead to factor-price equalization across regions, an element that would encourage convergence between territorial production structures, thereby boosting GDPpc convergence. However, under the same HO framework, market integration could also lead to increasing regional specialization because regions still have different factor endowments, especially as regards accumulable factors like infrastructures and human capital. In this situation, the standard HO model allows FPE but not income equality (Rassek and Thompson 1998; Slaughter 1997). So, if we accept this economic reasoning, it makes sense for territorial cohesion policies to focus mainly on the public provision of infrastructures or human capital in more disadvantaged regions.

However, according to the new economic geography (NEG) literature, the neoclassical analysis is missing some relevant forces that can affect regional disparities and prevent convergence. NEG theoretical models suggest that the interaction between transport costs, increasing returns and market size under a monopolistic competition framework can lead to the spatial agglomeration of economic activity (Krugman 1991). Companies produce more efficiently and workers enjoy better welfare by being close to large markets, and therefore more companies and workers relocate to these areas. This creates a cumulative causation process that tends to increase income differences across territories. In other words the initial differences, far from becoming smaller with the advance of economic integration processes and production factor mobility, would tend to get bigger. Regions with the greatest market potential would probably see a concentration of economic activities subject to increasing returns, that is, those activities with the highest levels of productivity.

Bearing this in mind, if we accept that the elements detailed by the NEG provide an economic explanation for the existence of territorial inequality, then traditional territorial cohesion policies would not be effective. Indeed, rather than dedicate resources to providing the poorest regions with new infrastructures or human capital, these policies should boost the territory's connectivity, taking it economically closer to the big markets. The key to this, as suggested in the EU's Horizon 2020 programme, lies in designing transport and communications networks, essential aspects given the framework of today's technological revolution brought about by advances in information and communications technologies (ICT).

Nevertheless, it should be remembered that Puga (1999), extending the initial arguments of the NEG, pointed out that the relationship between the regional integration process and the degree of concentration of economic activity depends to a large extent on whether or not workers move across regions in response to income differentials. Industrial agglomeration tends to raise local wages in regions densely populated by companies. When higher wages lead workers to relocate from de-industrializing (poor) to more industrialized (rich) regions, agglomeration intensifies but wage differentials tend to collapse. In other words, market integration and industrial concentration should lead to income convergence. If workers do not move across regions, however, interregional wage differentials tend to persist and the relationship between integration and agglomeration is no longer monotonic. For example, in the case of further reductions in transport (transaction) costs, a new tendency towards dispersion can emerge as a result of congestion costs. Progressive market integration can thus eventually lead to income convergence, as predicted by traditional models. In other words, still within the NEG framework, the increasing integration of markets, especially the labour market, would eventually bring about a reduction in territorial inequality in the long term. This aspect, linked to the behaviour of the labour market, should therefore be included in any strategies followed by national or supranational governments in their fight to reduce territorial inequality.

Growth theory has also provided some insights into the causes of regional inequality. According to the Solow growth model, differences in capital per worker in a closed-economy context lead to slow income convergence across locations (Barro and Sala-i-Martin 2003). If cross-regional movements of capital are added to the model, convergence rates may increase due to the fact that capital moves from capital-abundant to capital-scarce regions following differences in relative returns (Barro et al. 1995). However, absolute convergence of incomes in this conceptualization would be slowed down if the poorest regions were also characterized by being endowed with few accumulable factors, that is, factors like human capital or infrastructures that make it possible to increase the productivity of the physical capital. Therefore, within the framework of neoclassical economic theory, public investment in these areas would to some extent be effective in promoting regional convergence processes.

A new strand of thinking known as endogenous growth theory also makes contradictory predictions about the impact of cross-regional integration. In the presence of increasing returns on activities that generate technical progress (e.g. R+D), the basic model (Romer 1986) predicts that increasing movements of capital will lead to regional divergence. This is because, if technology is not considered to be a public good and is therefore subject to the decision-making processes of individual agents and their desire for monopoly incomes, any increase in scale of the economy will have a positive lasting effect on growth, encouraging territorial inequality. With this conceptual framework, traditional cohesion policies would be ineffective. This has been taken into account in the EU's Horizon 2020 programme, which establishes that territorial cohesion policies should give precedence to investment in activities that generate knowledge and not only to the public provision of accumulable factors in less advantaged regions.

How Do We Expect Regional Inequality to Evolve in the Course of Economic Development Processes?

Judging from that brief review of the theoretical literature on regional income inequality, we can conclude that more empirical work is needed because the various models make conflicting predictions. However, it should be noted that economic history has traditionally argued that the early stages of modern economic growth, particularly when growth and regional market integration have increased in tandem, are associated with greater inequality in regional income per capita. Williamson (1965) studied income evolution in a cross-section of countries along with the long-term evolution of regional inequality in the US. His hypothesis was that regional inequality followed an inverted U-shape throughout the growth process, with increasing inequality being evident during the nineteenth century and then convergence afterwards. As far as the US is concerned, he argued that structural change and specialization increased inequality in the early stages of economic growth, but that the continuing process of structural change and integration in combination with associated increases in capital movements and internal migrations could explain any reduction in regional income inequalities.

Kim (1998) confirmed Williamson's findings, showing how regional inequality across regions in the US evolved following an inverted U-shaped pattern. He also argued that increased inequality during the second half of the nineteenth century could be explained by specialization and divergence in economic structures. Further advances in economic growth and national market integration in the twentieth century were accompanied by a decrease in regional income inequality, which was brought about by the homogenization of economic structures and convergence in productivity across states (also Kim and Margo 2004). Caselli and Coleman II (2001) went slightly further in their exploration of long-term regional inequality in the US, making a connection between regional convergence and decreases in agricultural employment in the poorest areas.

However, the inverted U-shape denoting the relationship between structural change, economic development and regional inequalities as suggested by Williamson (1965) had no theoretical framework to support it. To give it a solid economic foundation, Barrios and Strobl (2009) designed a model to support the hypothesis, building on the growth model based on technology diffusion developed by Lucas (2000). This makes it possible to trace the transition from pre-industrial stagnant economies to modern economies in the course of long-term economic growth. The dynamics of this transition depend on technology shocks or innovations which, from the very beginnings of industrialization, increase levels of productivity and speed up growth at national level.

At the start, these technology shocks are concentrated in particular areas because of their region-specific factor endowments (e.g. human capital, mineral resources) and/or institutions. Economic growth is therefore spatially localized, meaning that in the early stages of growth and industrialization there tends to be an increase in regional inequality. Although divergence forces are initially predominant, there comes a point when a process of technology diffusion from the leading region to other regions comes into play. The pace and timing of this diffusion depend on the technological capabilities of the other regions and the level of knowledge countrywide. Follower regions, which are all at different points in time as regards development, gradually adopt the leading region's innovations and move from stagnation towards growth. Regional convergence then begins. Other regions will eventually catch up either due to the spread of technology or as a result of factor flows (capital, labour). In these circumstances, the relationship between average income per capita across the country and regional inequalities becomes non-monotonic and traces an inverted U-shaped or bell-shaped curve over time. And thus the model supplies a theoretical framework to back up the Williamson hypothesis.

Research carried out by Barrios and Strobl (2009) also makes it possible to infer certain things about the forces that may affect regional income inequality during the economic development process. These authors argue that spatial inequalities would be greater if national markets were globally integrated. This would indicate the existence of a positive relationship between trade and regional economic inequality in any particular country.

Various studies have explored this relationship, in most cases going back as far as 1980 and analysing recent decades, and the evidence they provide suggests that trade has an effect that leads to greater regional inequalities.[3] Rodríguez-Pose and Gill (2006) and Hirte and Lessmann (2014) look at the effect that trade openness has on territorial inequality and include both developed and developing economies in their samples. The evidence found in these studies confirms that the effect does indeed exist. Rodríguez-Pose (2012) demonstrates that the effect is stronger in poorer countries. Likewise, Ezcurra and Rodríguez-Pose (2014) look at 22 emerging economies during the period 1990–2006 and again find that changes in international trade have given rise to a significant increase in interregional inequality and that the impact is strongest in the poorest countries. It would appear that greater exposure to trade, although it might benefit these emerging economies in aggregate terms, generates winners and losers among the regions.

However, if economic growth is considered to be endogenous and there are economies of scale in technology production, then public policies would be expected to channel funds into research and development (Baldwin and Martin 2004). Designing networks and reducing transport costs would also become important. NEG models provide a strong basis in this respect to explain the effect that declining transport costs and changes in market accessibility have on the geographical location of economic activity (Krugman 1991; Puga 1999; Fujita and Thisse 2002).

The presence of agglomeration economies could also prove to be an obstacle to regional income per-capita convergence.[4] Ciccone and Hall (1996) and Ciccone (2002) find an agglomeration effect that connects the density of economic activity with interregional differences in labour productivity, thereby making a link between economic density and agglomeration effects. Brülhart and Sbergami (2009) perform a Barro-type empirical analysis of economic growth determinants for a large sample of

---

[3] One exception would be Milanovic (2005), who analyses the five most populated countries in the world (China, India, the US, Indonesia and Brazil) between approximately 1980 and 2000, but finds no link between trade openness and regional inequality.

[4] On a related subject, NEG models provide ambiguous results concerning the impact of trade openness on a country's internal economic geography (Krugman and Livas Elizondo 1996; Paluzie 2001; Crozet and Koenig 2004; Hanson 2005). An overview of this literature is given in Brülhart (2011).

countries around the world and another sample comprising only EU member states for the period 1960–2000. Together with the explanatory variables traditionally used in this type of exercise, they introduce additional indicators for the spatial agglomeration of production and population. Their results indicate a positive relationship between the presence of agglomeration economies and growth in early stages of regional development. However, they also indicate that once a region reaches a certain level of income per capita, the relationship disappears or becomes negative. On this point they argue that their empirical analysis provides evidence to support the Williamson hypothesis.[5]

Another relevant dimension is the rate of change along the inverted U-shaped curve, an aspect also considered by Barrios and Strobl (2009). Region-specific factor endowments (physical and human capital) and public policies gain momentum as modern economic growth spreads across the regions. In an attempt to maintain territorial cohesion, the aim of such policies is to reduce regional disparities by financing the building of infrastructures, for example. In this regard, since 1986 the EU has given greater importance and dedicated more resources to regional policies designed to strengthen economic and social cohesion. A new high-level strategy (Europe 2020) was introduced under the Treaty of Lisbon, which for the first time included use of the term "territorial cohesion".

Two other elements from Barrios and Strobl (2009) are deserving of comment. If technological change is concentrated in specific sectors and therefore locations, then structural differences could increase the extent of regional income inequality. In other words it might be possible to see a direct relationship between regional production specialization and spatial income inequalities. This is particularly relevant because it is one of the main mechanisms explored by Kuznets (1955) and Williamson (1965). Also, the model allows for technology shocks (ICT revolution) and large-scale institutional change (supranational market integration),

[5] Gardiner et al. (2011) question Brülhart and Sbergami's (2009) results. They look at the relationship between agglomeration and growth in the EU-15 (1981–2007), but their results are inconclusive. They note that the relationship's existence lacks robustness when they introduce different agglomeration measures and change the size of the territorial units (NUTS1 or NUTS2). They also point out that the robustness of the results is reduced because only a limited period is studied (1960–2000).

and these could have a big impact on the long-term dynamics of regional inequality. If the ICT revolution or greater market integration benefits the richest regions most, for example, one would expect to see a rise in GDPpc inequality across regions.

Meanwhile Giannetti (2002) analyses the European experience, in which convergence among countries since the early 1980s has not been accompanied by convergence among regions. She argues that this may be partly due to sectoral specialization. Economic integration speeds up growth at country level but also increases within-country spatial disparities, since regions that specialize in high-tech sectors benefit most from knowledge spillovers while the opposite happens in regions that specialize in more traditional sectors.

How Has Regional Economic Inequality Really Evolved Over the Last 30 Years?

There is a growing body of empirical literature directed at testing the central hypothesis deriving from Williamson's (1965) seminal work and later studies such as that by Barrios and Strobl (2009). Indeed it was Barrios and Strobl (2009) who empirically tested their own model using parametric and semi-parametric techniques to check for the presence of an inverted U-shaped relationship between regional inequality and economic development. The sample they used was a panel of European countries for the period 1975–2000. They found strong evidence of a bell-shaped curve with an initial increase in regional inequalities and then, after a certain threshold, the beginning of convergence. The results are robust not only to changes in regional administration units and time periods, but also to the inclusion of control variables and non-European countries.

Lessmann (2014) also checks for the presence of an inverted U-shaped relationship between spatial inequality and economic development. To this end he uses a panel dataset of spatial inequalities in 55 countries at different stages of economic development during the period 1980–2009. He provides strong support for an inverted U-shaped relationship and, just as importantly, points out that regional inequality has recently been on the rise. This would suggest that there may be an N-shaped relationship between spatial inequalities and economic development.

Lessmann and Seidel (2017) carry out a similar exercise but expand the sample of countries with regional incomes on the basis of night-time -light satellite data,[6] which enabled them to cover 180 countries over the period 1992–2012. They, too, find evidence in support of the Williamson hypothesis. An analysis of the determinants of regional inequality leads them to suggest that trade openness brings with it an increase in regional inequality, but that this can be offset by regional transfers and investments in infrastructures and by making institutions more democratic. Importantly, at high income levels there is also a high degree of dispersion in regional incomes, which, as in Lessmann (2014), would indicate the presence of an N-shaped evolution. These papers argue that, although there are various forces that could possibly explain the presence of an N-shaped relationship between regional inequality and economic development, tertiarization currently seems to be the predominant trend in the most developed economies, that is, a structural shift away from industrial production towards a service base.

The N-shape hypothesis is in line with previous findings by Amos (1988). His study focused on the US during the period 1950–1983 and showed that the increase-decrease pattern discernible in the evolution of regional disparities that Williamson first drew attention to eventually turned into an increase-decrease-increase pattern, which would support the hypothesis that regional inequality increases in the later stages of development.[7] He attributed this new increase in regional inequality following completion of the Williamson curve to changes such as suburbanization and the transition to a service-based economy.[8] Ezcurra and Rapún (2006), however, questioned these results in a study covering 14 Western European countries over the period 1980–2002. Using nonparametric methodology and controlling through the use of additional

[6] This methodology is in line with Gennaioli et al. (2014), who worked with data for 83 countries covering recent decades. Depending on the availability of data, they found evidence of a regional convergence rate close to the 2 per cent generally seen in the growth literature. Magrini (2004) and Breinlich et al. (2014) contain reviews of the empirical literature on regional growth and convergence.

[7] He found that this was the case in 37 of the 50 US states by the early 1980s.

[8] See also List and Gallet (1999).

variables in the spirit of Barrios and Strobl (2009), they concluded that regional imbalances stabilize in the later stages of development.

In short, the existing empirical literature examines how regional inequality evolves over time and studies its main drivers. The question as to whether regional production specialization, openness, public expenditure, urbanization rates, market potential or economic agglomeration, for example, stimulate regional convergence/divergence can therefore be empirically tested. However, these empirical investigations only cover recent decades and fall short when it comes to considering a long-term perspective. Any analysis of the relationship between economic growth and regional inequalities should really take into account the entire economic development process, that is, starting with the earliest stages of modern economic growth, as in Kuznets (1955) and Williamson (1965). Given these conditions it is easy to understand why Lessmann (2014) himself noted that: "the major problem for this kind of research is that it is essential either to have historical data for single countries or to include poorer countries in a cross-country dataset, since the theories of Kuznets and Williamson point at the deep structural changes associated with the industrialization process".

And in the Long Term?

It is perhaps for this reason that the relationship between regional inequality and economic development has ultimately also attracted the interest of economic historians. Until recently the main problem was that, in most countries, reliable information on regional GDP for historical periods was practically non-existent. Fortunately, this situation has begun to change. Over the last few years several studies have supplied new regional GDP estimates at country level, and these make it possible to examine the long-term evolution of regional inequality. Most of these studies have been based on the work done by Geary and Stark (2002), in which the authors proposed a methodology for estimating historical regional GDP for the UK that has become the benchmark for other authors and countries (Wolf and Rosés in press).

With this new information, some investigations have provided further evidence for the existence of an inverted-U pattern. Crafts (2005), for example, found support for this hypothesis using new regional GDPpc estimates for the UK. He calculated that regional inequality increased after 1871 and reached its highest point in the early twentieth century, then declined until the 1970s. However, Geary and Stark (2015, 2016) have questioned these results, arguing that disparities had already started to diminish during the 1870s.

In the case of France, Combes et al. (2011) explored the long-term evolution of spatial inequalities across *départements*, observing an inverted U-shape in the manufacturing and services sectors stretching between 1860, 1930 and 2000. More recent studies, however, show a more complex view when GDPpc is used. While Caruana-Galizia (2013) finds an increase in regional disparities between 1840 and 1911, Bazot (2014), Díez-Minguela et al. (2016) and Rosés and Sanchis (in press) conclude that inequality in regional per-capita income began its downward trend at the turn of the century.[9]

For Portugal, Badia-Miró et al. (2012) provide empirical evidence to support the inverted U-shape and find that regional inequality peaked during the 1970s. In a related paper, Tirado and Badia-Miró (2012) analyse territorial inequality within the framework of the regions that make up the Iberian Peninsula as a whole. Their work also confirms the existence of an inverted U-shape for this supranational set of regions. Interestingly, it shows that the cluster of the poorest regions in the sample is to be found in the south-west of the peninsula in a geographical distribution that transcends state borders.

As regards Italy, Felice (2011) finds that regional disparities peaked in the aftermath of the Second World War. Since then, the dynamics have followed a pattern of convergence between northern and central regions but not between these and the *Meridionale*, and thus a noticeable north-south divide has arisen. In other words, leaving aside long-term evolution, the most striking element is that territorial inequality in Italy is characterized not so much by its magnitude as by the geographical polarization between a rich centre and north and a poor south. Daniele and

[9] For a critical review of the different estimates available for France, see Díez-Minguela and Sanchis (2017).

Malanima (2014) find a similar long-term evolution, but put forward a number of different regional GDP estimates for the post-unification period.

Other studies, however, do not fully support an inverted U-pattern over the long term. In their pioneering work, Barro and Sala-i-Martin (1991) demonstrated that differences between GDPpc across US states followed a steady downward trend between 1880 and the 1970s, except for the 1920s. They also showed that this trend stopped in the 1980s (see also Kim 1998; Mitchener and McLean 1999; Caselli and Coleman II 2001; Kim and Margo 2004). Along similar lines Enflo et al. (2014), working on the case of Sweden, observed a strong regional convergence spanning from the mid-nineteenth century up to the 1980s, followed by a subsequent upswing in the curve.

Finally, Buyst (2010, 2011) reveals another element of territorial inequality that merits analysis in its own right. His work shows that the most noticeable characteristic of regional inequality in Belgium is the reversal of fortunes between north and south in the course of the twentieth century. Regions that were rich in the nineteenth century have now become poor, while regions that were traditionally poor now enjoy higher levels of income.

Research Questions

Following the line of research that has studied the evolution and determinants of territorial inequality in different European states over the long term, this book provides an in-depth study of developments in the Spanish economy between 1860 and 2015, that is, we analyse how inequality has evolved over the entire trajectory of economic development in Spain. This trajectory is summarized in Chap. 2, which follows this introduction.

Chapter 3 presents the methodology used to construct the new estimates of regional GDPpc in Spain, breaking down the territory into NUTS3 and NUTS2 regions (provinces and autonomous communities respectively) and dividing sectors homogeneously into five production areas: agriculture, mining, manufacturing and public utilities, construction and services. The reason for constructing this new quantitative evidence is to enable the characterization and identification of key elements that have played a part in bringing about the scenario of regional inequality that exists today.

On the basis of this new evidence, the other chapters in the book aim to provide answers to a variety of research questions. Chapter 4 analyses the evolution of regional inequality over the long term in Spain. We provide a number of different indicators of inequality and study the patterns of convergence or divergence followed by Spanish regions from the mid-nineteenth century to the present. The results of this analysis enable us to establish a timeline showing the evolution of territorial inequality which we follow in the remaining chapters.

Chapter 5 explores how regional inequality has evolved in terms of mobility and persistence. In particular, we use different statistical methods to determine whether there has been a general trend whereby the richest regions have maintained their position over time or whether, on the contrary, any relevant changes can be seen in the positions occupied by the various regions in terms of income levels per capita. By doing this we hope to discover whether there has been a history of relative successes or failures among regions and at what point in time these have been most frequent.

Another element characteristic of territorial inequality is the presence of geographical patterns, that is, the grouping of geographically close regions into clusters of wealth or poverty. The text aims to identify when exactly the geographical patterns that characterize inequality in Spain today took shape. We should then be able to establish some hypotheses as to the causes (Chap. 6). We also analyse whether the clusters of poor or rich regions continue uninterrupted beyond national borders to include regions of Portugal.

Chapter 7 analyses the proximate causes of territorial inequality. To do this we start by breaking down the inequality in GDPpc into elements related to differences in regional labour markets (activity rates, unemployment) and elements linked to the presence of differences in labour productivity between regions. We then look at the factors that determine these differences in productivity by carrying out a number of quantitative exercises that will enable us to see whether or not they are in some way connected to the territories' different production structures or whether they are due to the different levels of productivity registered by each sector on a regional scale. This set of exercises is also used to establish which of the potential explanatory factors for regional inequality was most important in the various stages of the historical process of economic development in Spain.

Finally, as mentioned earlier, the case of Spain works as a microcosm that is extremely useful when it comes to analysing territorial inequality because it reproduces the basic characteristics that have been identified as applying to Europe today. Going into this aspect in greater depth, the book closes with Chap. 8 in which we analyse whether the evolution of regional inequality in Spain—in terms of the levels reached and characterization of the major stages involved in its growth or reduction—matches that seen in most of the south-western European economic area. To this end we provide new evidence on the historical evolution of territorial inequality in a significant area of Europe comprising all regions of Portugal, Spain, France and Italy. From the analysis performed it can be gathered that the main patterns observed in the evolution of inequality throughout the economic development process in Spain accurately reflect what happened in all four states as a whole.

References

Amos, O. J. (1988). Unbalanced regional growth and regional income inequality in the latter stages of development. *Regional Science and Urban Economics, 18*(4), 549–566.

Badia-Miró, M., Guilera, J., & Lains, P. (2012). Regional incomes in Portugal: Industrialisation, integration and inequality, 1890–1980. *Revista de Historia Económica, 30*(2), 225–244.

Baldwin, R., & Martin, P. (2004). Agglomeration and regional growth. In J. V. Henderson & J. F. Thisse (Eds.), *Handbook of regional and urban economics* (Vol. 4, pp. 2671–2711). Amsterdam: Elsevier.

Barrios, S., & Strobl, E. (2009). The dynamics of regional inequalities. *Regional Science and Urban Economics, 39*(5), 575–591.

Barro, R., Mankiw, G., & Sala-i-Martin, X. (1995). Capital mobility in neoclassical models of growth. *American Economic Review, 85*(1), 103–115.

Barro, R., & Sala-i-Martin, X. (1991). Convergence across states and regions. *Brooking Papers on Economic Activity, 1*, 107–182.

Barro, R., & Sala-i-Martin, X. (2003). *Economic growth* (2nd ed.). Cambridge: The MIT Press.

Bazot, G. (2014). Interregional inequalities, convergence, and growth in France from 1840 to 1911. *Annals of Economics and Statistics*, (113/114), 309–345.

Breinlich, H., Ottaviano, G. I. P., & Temple, J. (2014). Regional growth and regional decline. In P. Aghion & S. N. Durlauf (Eds.), *Handbook of economic growth* (Vol. 2, pp. 683–779). Amsterdam: Elsevier.

Brülhart, M. (2011). The spatial effects of trade openness: A survey. *Review of World Economics, 147*(1), 59–83.

Brülhart, M., & Sbergami, F. (2009). Agglomeration and growth: Cross-country evidence. *Journal of Urban Economics, 65*(1), 48–63.

Buyst, E. (2010). Reversal of fortune in a small, open economy: Regional GDP in Belgium, 1896–2000. *Rivista di Storia Economica, 26*, 75–92.

Buyst, E. (2011). Continuity and change in regional disparities in Belgium during the twentieth century. *Journal of Historical Geography, 37*(3), 329–337.

Caruana-Galizia, P. (2013). Estimating French regional income: Departmental per capita gross value added, 1872–1911. *Research in Economic History, 29*, 71–95.

Caselli, F., & Coleman II, W. J. (2001). The U.S. structural transformation and regional convergence: Reinterpretation. *Journal of Political Economy, 109*(3), 584–616.

Ciccone, A. (2002). Agglomeration effects in Europe. *European Economic Review, 46*(2), 213–227.

Ciccone, A., & Hall, R. E. (1996). Productivity and the density of economic activity. *American Economic Review, 86*(1), 54–70.

Combes, P. P., Lafourcade, M., Thisse, J. F., & Toutain, J. C. (2011). The rise and fall of spatial inequalities in France: A long-run perspective. *Explorations in Economic History, 48*(2), 243–271.

Crafts, N. (2005). Regional GDP in Britain, 1871–1911: Some estimates. *Scottish Journal of Political Economy, 52*(1), 54–64.

Crozet, M., & Koenig, P. (2004). Trade liberalization and the internal geography of countries. In T. Mayer & M. Mucchielli (Eds.), *Multinational firms' location and economic geography* (pp. 91–109). Cheltenham: Edward Elgar.

Daniele, V., & Malanima, P. (2014). Falling disparities and persisting dualism: Regional development and industrialization in Italy, 1891–2001. *Investigaciones de Historia Económica/Research in Economic History, 10*(3), 165–176.

Díez-Minguela, A., Rosés, J. R., & Sanchis, M. T. (2016). *Paris and the French desert revisited: Regional income polarization in France, 1860–2010.* Paper presented at the 56th European Regional Science Association Congress (ERSA), Vienna, 23–26 August.

Díez-Minguela, A., & Sanchis, M. T. (2017). *Regional income inequality in France: What does history teach us?* Paper presented at the XLIII Reunión de Estudios Regionales, Pablo de Olavide University, Seville, 16–17 November.

Enflo, K., Henning, M., & Schön, L. (2014). Swedish regional GDP 1855–2000: Estimations and general trends in the Swedish regional system. *Research in Economic History, 30*, 47–89.

Ezcurra, R., & Rapún, M. (2006). Regional disparities and national development revisited: The case of Western Europe. *European Urban and Regional Studies, 13*(4), 355–369.

Ezcurra, R., & Rodríguez-Pose, A. (2014). Trade openness and spatial inequality in emerging countries. *Spatial Economic Analysis, 9*(2), 162–182.

Felice, E. (2011). Regional value added in Italy, 1891–2001, and the foundation of a long-term picture. *Economic History Review, 64*(3), 929–950.

Fujita, M., & Thisse, J. F. (2002). *Economics of agglomeration.* Cambridge: Cambridge University Press.

Gardiner, B., Martin, R., & Tyler, P. (2011). Does spatial agglomeration increase national growth? Some evidence from Europe. *Journal of Economic Geography, 11*(6), 979–1006.

Geary, F., & Stark, T. (2002). Examining Ireland's post-famine economic growth performance. *Economic Journal, 112*, 919–935.

Geary, F., & Stark, T. (2015). Regional GDP in the UK, 1861–1911: New estimates. *Economic History Review, 68*(1), 123–144.

Geary, F., & Stark, T. (2016). What happened to regional inequality in Britain in the twentieth century? *Economic History Review, 69*(1), 215–228.

Gennaioli, N., La Porta, R., Lopez de Silanes, F., & Schleifer, A. (2014). Growth in regions. *Journal of Economic Growth, 19*, 259–309.

Giannetti, M. (2002). The effects of integration on regional disparities: Convergence, divergence or both? *European Economic Review, 46*, 539–567.

Hanson, G. H. (2005). Market potential, increasing returns, and geographic concentration. *Journal of International Economics, 67*, 1–24.

Hirte, G., & Lessmann, C. (2014). *Trade, integration, and interregional inequality.* CESifo Working Papers Series 4799.

Kanbur, R., Venables, A. J., & Wan, G. (2005). Introduction to the special issue: Spatial inequality and development in Asia. *Journal of Development Economics, 9*(1), 1–4.

Kanbur, R., & Zhang, X. (2005). Fifty years of regional inequality in China: A journey through central planning, reform, and openness. *Review of Development Economics, 9*(1), 87–106.

Kim, S. (1998). Economic integration and convergence: US regions, 1840–1987. *Journal of Economic History, 58*(3), 659–683.

Kim, S., & Margo, R. (2004). Historical perspectives on U.S. economic geography. In J. V. Henderson & J. F. Thisse (Eds.), *Handbook of regional and urban economics* (Vol. 4, pp. 2981–3019). Amsterdam: Elsevier.

Krugman, P. (1991). Increasing returns and economic geography. *Journal of Political Economy, 99*(3), 483–499.

Krugman, P., & Livas Elizondo, R. (1996). Trade policy and the third world metropolis. *Journal of Development Economics, 49*(1), 137–150.

Kuznets, S. (1955). Economic growth and income inequality. *American Economic Review, 45*(1), 1–28.

Lessmann, C. (2014). Spatial inequality and development: Is there an inverted-U relationship? *Journal of Development Economics, 106*, 35–51.

Lessmann, C., & Seidel, A. (2017). Regional inequality, convergence, and its determinants: A view from outer space. *European Economic Review, 92*, 110–132.

List, J. A., & Gallet, C. A. (1999). The Kuznets curve: What happens after the inverted-U? *Review of Development Economics, 3*(2), 200–206.

Lucas, R. E. (2000). Some macroeconomics for the 21st century. *Journal of Economic Perspectives, 14*(1), 159–168.

Magrini, S. (2004). Regional (di)convergence. In J. V. Henderson & J. F. Thisse (Eds.), *Handbook of regional and urban economics* (Vol. 4, pp. 2741–2796). Amsterdam: Elsevier.

Milanovic, B. (2005). Half a world: Regional inequality in five great federations. *Journal of the Asia Pacific Economy, 10*(4), 408–445.

Mitchener, K. J., & McLean, I. W. (1999). U.S. regional growth and convergence, 1880–1980. *The Journal of Economic History, 59*(4), 1016–1042.

Paluzie, E. (2001). Trade policy and regional inequalities. *Papers in Regional Science, 80*, 67–85.

Puga, D. (1999). The rise and fall of regional inequalities. *European Economic Review, 43*(2), 303–334.

Puga, D. (2002). European regional policies in light of recent location theories. *Journal of Economic Geography, 2*, 373–406.

Rassek, F., & Thompson, H. (1998). Micro and macro convergence: Factor price equalization and per capita income. *Pacific Economic Review, 3*(1), 3–11.

Rodríguez-Pose, A. (2012). Trade and regional inequality. *Economic Geography, 88*(2), 109–136.

Rodríguez-Pose, A., & Gill, N. (2006). How does trade affect regional disparities? *World Development, 34*(7), 1201–1222.

Romer, P. M. (1986). Increasing returns and long-run growth. *Journal of Political Economy, 94*, 1002–1037.

Rosés, J. R., & Sanchis, M. T. (In press). A long run perspective on French regional income inequalities, 1860–2010. In N. Wolf & J. R. Rosés (Eds.), *The economic development of Europe's regions: A quantitative history since 1900*. London: Routledge.

Slaughter, M. (1997). Per-capita income convergence and the role of international trade. *American Economic Review, 87*, 194–199.

Tirado, D. A., & Badia-Miró, M. (2012). New evidence on regional inequality in Iberia (1900–2000). *Historical Methods: A Journal of Quantitative and Interdisciplinary History, 47*, 180–189.

Williamson, J. G. (1965). Regional inequality and the process of national development: A description of the patterns. *Economic Development and Cultural Change, 13*(4), 1–84.

Wolf, N., & Rosés, J. R. (Eds.). (In press). *The economic development of Europe's regions: A quantitative history since 1900*. London: Routledge.

World Bank. (2009). *World development report: Reshaping economic geography*. Washington, DC: World Bank.

Zhang, X., & Zhang, K. H. (2003). How does globalisation affect regional inequality within a developing country? Evidence from China. *Journal of Development Studies, 39*, 47–67.

2

A Potted History: Spain 1860–2015

Regional economic inequality is an element characteristic of economic development processes. As we know, the improvement of an economy's level of development goes hand in hand with the increasing participation in its production and employment structure of economic sectors that show productivity gains and thus lead the aggregate growth of societies in terms of GDP per worker and GDP per capita. The advance of the leading sectors, however, is not distributed homogeneously across space. Indeed economic history has emphasized the regional character of these processes, exemplified by what happened in the context of the first industrial revolution (Pollard 1981).

With this reasoning in mind and following in the wake of Kuznets's (1955) characterization of inequality in income distribution during national development processes, Williamson (1965) provided a highly intuitive explanation of the mechanisms that generate regional differences. According to this author, the initial economic take-off experienced by sectors with the highest productivity (i.e. industry) would happen in a small group of territories. Because of this, the most dynamic sectors would carry the greatest weight in the production and employment structures in these places. Hence regional economic divergence would be

A. Díez-Minguela et al., *Regional Inequality in Spain*, Palgrave Studies in Economic History, https://doi.org/10.1007/978-3-319-96110-1_2

related to the uneven spread of industrialization. Specialization and divergence in economic structures would therefore explain the increase in inequality in the early stages of modern economic growth. Market integration, capital and, in particular, labour flows would strengthen and accelerate this process. Further progress and national market integration would later be accompanied by a reduction in regional disparities, which could be explained by the homogenization of economic structures and labour productivity convergence.

As we said in the introductory chapter, for a long time the Williamson hypothesis had no sound theoretical backing. However, Barrios and Strobl (2009), following the Lucas (2000) growth model, more recently proposed a theoretical framework for studying the evolution and determinants of regional economic inequality. In their model regional inequality emerges as a result of technology shocks (i.e. industrialization) concentrated in specific locations—they assume that, due to region-specific factor endowments and/or institutions, these technology shocks occur only in certain regions. These *lucky* regions will initially grow more rapidly, giving rise to spatial inequality. Other regions will eventually catch up, either through the spread of technology or as a result of factor flows (capital, labour). Barrios and Strobl (2009) thus give the Williamson hypothesis a theoretical foundation in line with classic contributions on regional economic growth, such as those that emerge from neoclassical growth theory (Barro and Sala-i-Martin 1991; Barro et al. 1995).[1]

The fundamentals in both cases would indicate that the forces behind the growth of regional inequality are the unequal spread of technological change and the advance of sectors with higher productivity gains in the production structures of just a few territories. However, there are other elements that may affect the dynamic that governs this inequality. The integration of the national goods and factor markets (capital and labour) can help consolidate the processes of regional production specialization, and international economic integration can involve greater exposure to technology change and thus affect the level of inequality. And, finally, public action in the shape of either market regulation or

[1] Barrios and Strobl (2009) also provide an economic foundation for the relative growth dynamics identified by the technology gap and catch-up literature (Abramovitz 1994).

regional equilibrium policies is another element that needs to be considered when analysing the path followed by regional inequality in the course of a society's economic development process.

Our objective here is to supply a synthetic view of the historical process of economic development in Spain broken down into major stages. Rather than try to analyse it from all angles, we concentrate on changes involving the elements described in the previous paragraphs, that is, the rate at which the Spanish economy advanced, the evolution of its production structure and sector employment, and the degree of integration of the goods and factor markets and the effects of this in both national and supranational terms. So as to give a stylized view of the process, the analysis will be carried out on the basis of four major stages into which we divide the relevant time period (Table 2.1). Generally speaking this division is the same as that used in historiography when studying the contemporary history of Europe. The first stage covers the second half of the nineteenth century and finishes on the eve of the First World War (1860–1910), the second basically covers the interwar period (1910–1950), the third the so-called Golden Age of capitalism (1950–1980) and, the fourth, the latest advance of globalization after the oil crisis of the 1970s (1980–2015).[2]

In the case of Spain, Prados de la Escosura (2003, 2016) has shown that the start of the growth process, understood as the sustained increase in per-capita GDP, can be traced back to the mid-nineteenth century. Between then and 2015 per-capita income has grown 16-fold at an average annual rate of 1.7 per cent. Prados de la Escosura also showed that there have been different stages with significantly different rates of

Table 2.1 Annual growth rates in Spain by major period (1990 Geary-Khamis $)

Period	GDP (%)	Population (%)	Per-capita GDP (%)
1860–1910	1.25	0.49	0.76
1910–1950	1.36	0.85	0.51
1950–1980	5.63	0.97	4.66
1980–2015	2.47	0.61	1.86

Source: Prados de la Escosura (2016)

[2] This division of time is broadly speaking the same as that used by Broadberry and O'Rourke (2010).

growth. The first covers the period 1850–1950 and involved a moderate growth rate. During the Golden Age, however, GDP grew by an annual rate of over 5 per cent, so despite rapid demographic growth, per-capita income increased considerably between 1950 and 1980. The final period, 1980–2015, was characterized by the growth rate slowing down again, with a decrease of around 11 per cent in per-capita GDP during the years of the Great Recession (2008–2013). Nevertheless, per-capita income in Spain doubled between 1974 and 2015.

Our period of study, 1860–2015, spans one and a half centuries and covers most of the Spanish economic development process. During this time the Spanish economy underwent a profound structural transformation that turned a predominantly agricultural society into a modern economy, with labour shifting away from agriculture to industry and the services sector and income per capita increasing accordingly. In order to summarize this lengthy period of Spanish economic development, we next analyse the characteristics of each of our four major stages.

The Early Stages of Modern Economic Growth, 1860–1910

The early stages of modern economic growth in Spain date back to the mid-nineteenth century. It was initially sparked by national market integration and the adoption of industrial innovations.[3] Before this time the national market was fragmented among various largely unconnected local and regional markets due to the continued existence of barriers and limitations to internal trade. Local tariffs and trade restrictions were widespread and weights and measures varied from region to region. Transport costs were also very high due to a lack of public investment in transport infrastructures, the use of traditional means of transport and the country's geography itself, which is extremely rugged and had no extensive system of water transport. As a result, regional commodity markets were barely integrated and prices were markedly different in different regions. While it is true that some interdependence in commodity prices

[3] See Rosés et al. (2010) for a detailed description.

had existed since the eighteenth century (Ringrose 1998), it was not until the second half of the nineteenth century that major advances in the integration of the national market took place. These involved the elimination of the institutional obstacles that hindered the free movement of goods and factors between regions and a decrease in transport costs deriving from the application of technological improvements to transport during the industrial revolution.

As far as institutional changes are concerned, political reforms in the nineteenth century strengthened property rights and reduced the transaction costs that got in the way of economic relations and impeded the free movement of goods within Spain. These reforms eliminated the main restrictions on trade (including tariffs and domestic customs duty), suppressed the guilds and the *Mesta* (a medieval association of cattle farmers), disentailed land (*desamortización*), abolished entailed estates (*mayorazgos*), and unified the system of weights and measures that had until then varied from region to region. Also, in 1868 a decree introduced by Treasury Minister Laureano Figuerola unified Spain's monetary system by basing it on a single currency: the peseta (in 1864, 84 different coins were in circulation). In addition to monetary unification, the banking system improved in a number of ways. Modernization began during the early 1840s and the process was completed in 1874 when the Echegaray Decree abolished the plural system based on various banks of issue and granted a monopoly to the Bank of Spain, which had also begun to open branches in provincial capitals.

Meanwhile improvements to the transport sector proved to be a determining factor in market integration. The construction of railways and advances in other modes of transport (roads and coastal shipping) brought about a decrease in transport costs. The first railway line was completed in 1848 and covered the 28 kilometres between Barcelona and Mataró. By 1866 the railway had connected all of Spain's main economic centres, and by 1901 all provincial capitals were part of the network (Wais 1987).[4] The country's infrastructure stock as a share of GDP rose from 4.27 per cent in 1850 to 27.2 per cent in 1900 (Herranz 2007). Thus transport

[4] In 1901 the rail network covered 10,827 km. By 1990 the length of the network had increased to only 12,560 km (Herranz 2005).

improvements, particularly the completion of the rail network, encouraged cheaper transport costs and the creation of a national market for the most important commodities during the second half of the nineteenth century.[5]

The outcome of all this was the gradual integration of the national goods market for the principal traded products, an integration that was characterized by the convergence of regional prices. Various studies have described the gradual convergence of regional grain prices from the start of the eighteenth century to its culmination in the second half of the nineteenth (Peña and Sánchez-Albornoz 1983; Barquín 1997; Matilla et al. 2008). The integration of capital and labour markets also led to great advances. In the case of capital markets, the main reforms affecting the monetary and banking systems (Tortella 1973; Sudrià 1982) led to a reduction in interest rate differentials across regions. Castañeda and Tafunell (1993) showed, for instance, that interregional short-term interest rate differentials declined sharply after 1850. Finally, the integration of Spain's labour market, measured in terms of the differences in real wage levels across regions, has also been extensively analysed. Rosés and Sánchez-Alonso (2004), for example, showed that PPP-adjusted rural and urban wages converged across different locations before the First World War, despite low rates of internal migration.

With the tariff reform of 1869, this internal market integration was accompanied by a gradual increase in economic openness towards neighbouring countries (Tena 1999). The reduction in protective tariffs was most notable at the end of the 1880s, when Spain signed various trade agreements with its main trading partners. Then the final decade of the century saw a huge change as regards the Spanish economy's integration with external markets. The gold convertibility of the peseta had already been abandoned in 1883, thereby debilitating Spain's position in the international capital markets, and then in 1892 the Cánovas tariff was introduced, signalling a return to protectionism and seriously threatening external integration (Serrano Sanz 1997). The return to protectionist policies, widespread across countries in the closing decades of the

[5] According to Herranz (2005), the introduction of the railway meant a reduction in haulage costs of up to 86 per cent in 1878.

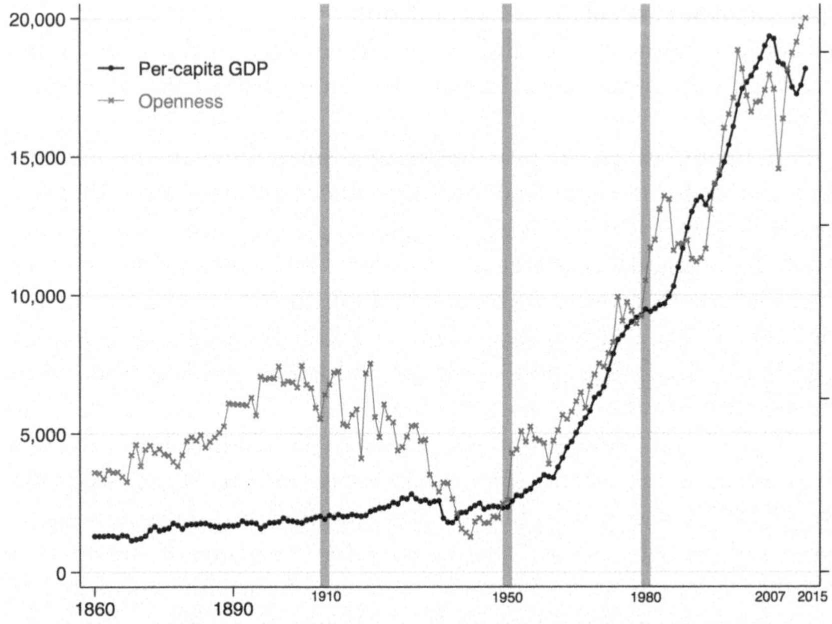

Fig. 2.1 Real per-capita GDP (left axis) and openness (right axis), Spain 1860–2015. Notes: Real per-capita GDP in 1990 in Geary-Khamis $; Openness defined as the share of exports and imports in GDP (current prices). Source: Prados de la Escosura (2016)

nineteenth century, was a reaction to challenges like the grain invasion caused by the first globalization. Around that time, many other countries also started adopting protectionist measures as part of a strategy to promote their own manufacturing sectors and compete with British goods in the international markets. Thus, the Spanish economy's rate of openness did increase during the second half of the nineteenth century. But this trend began to reverse in the 1890s, as can be seen in Fig. 2.1.

Advances in the integration of the national goods and factor markets in Spain brought about an intense process of regional specialization. From the mid-nineteenth century to the outbreak of the First World War, industrial production gradually became agglomerated in a small number of provinces, a development well documented by historiographers (Nadal 1973; Paluzie et al. 2004). While inland regions (apart from Madrid) underwent a substantial deindustrialization process, Catalonia and the Basque Country were the main areas in which industrialization continued (Nadal 1987).[6] By 1910 the contribution of these regions to Spanish industrial output was 31.6 per cent and 6.9 per cent, respectively, although their population represented only 10.5 per cent and 3.4 per cent (Tirado and Martinez-Galarraga 2008). The geographical concentration of manufacturing activities evolved over the period, with the general pattern being increased concentration of industry across Spain's provinces up to 1910 (Paluzie et al. 2004). This is a similar dynamic to that of other countries like the US (Kim 1995) and France (Combes et al. 2011), which also saw increasing agglomeration of industrial production during the early stages of national market integration and industrialization.

Nevertheless, internal migratory flows remained relatively low throughout most of the nineteenth century (Silvestre 2005). Due to the predominance of agricultural activities and their concomitant seasonality, many of these movements were temporary and involved short distances. Indeed, until the 1920s the number of permanent internal migrations remained small.[7] International migration, on the other hand, increased notably in the late nineteenth and early twentieth centuries, mainly in the direction of Latin America (Sánchez-Alonso 2000).

Until the First World War, however, the rate of economic growth rose only slowly and industrialization advanced with difficulty and was unevenly distributed across the geographical space. As a result, changes in the Spanish economy's production structure were virtually non-existent. In fact in 1910, as we can see in Fig. 2.2 and Table 2.2, about 60 per cent of the labour force were still employed in agriculture.

[6] In Catalonia the cotton industry, with a tradition that stretched back to the eighteenth century, gradually became mechanized in this period. In the Basque Country the iron and steel industry underwent rapid growth in the last quarter of the nineteenth century.

[7] The number of Spaniards residing outside their province of origin was fairly small, about 9.3 per cent in 1910 (Silvestre 2005).

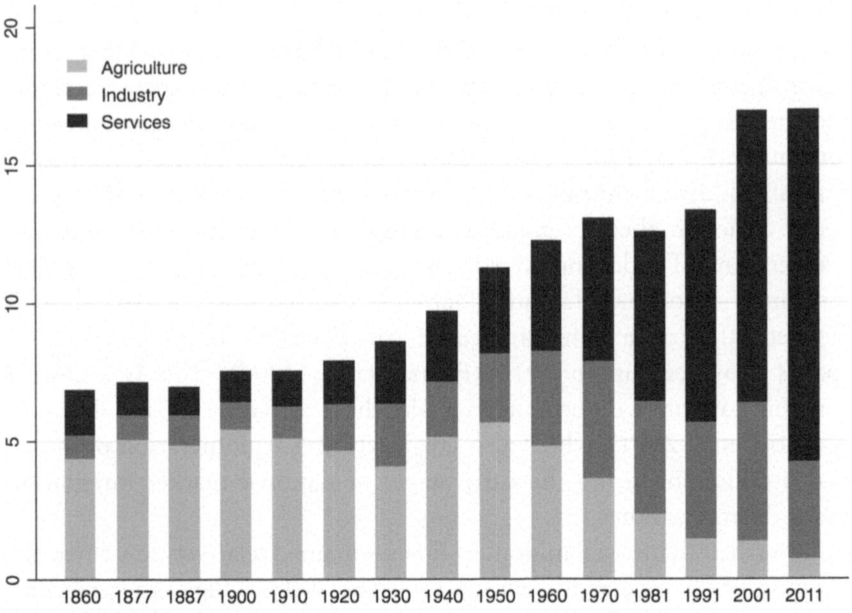

Fig. 2.2 Labour force by main economic activity in Spain, 1860–2011 (millions). Source: Population censuses

Table 2.2 Relative shares of employment and gross value added by major sector in Spain

	Agriculture		Industry		Construction		Services	
Year	Emp.	GVA	Emp.	GVA	Emp.	GVA	Emp.	GVA
1860	63.6	39.5	11.8	15.5	4.2	5.0	20.5	40.1
1910	58.1	27.8	13.5	27.3	4.4	3.4	24.0	41.4
1950	47.7	28.7	17.4	23.0	7.3	4.1	27.7	44.3
1980	17.1	6.8	24.8	29.5	9.6	9.5	48.5	54.1
2015	4.1	2.6	12.7	18.0	5.8	5.6	77.3	73.8

Source: Prados de la Escosura (2016)

The Interwar Years, 1910–1950

The period from the eve of the First World War to the end of the first ten years of autarky under the Franco dictatorship saw an increase in average economic growth rates. However, this was not the result of a steady advance but was shaped by major cycles corresponding to the different economic and political situations of the time. The First World War, for example, had a huge impact on the economy of a neutral country such as Spain. The general context of price increases brought opportunities for foreign trade and expansion to industrial sectors traditionally associated with producing for the national market (textiles, footwear). It was also a critical time for certain agricultural sectors, such as citrus fruits, that were geared towards export. This asymmetrical impact meant that, from an aggregate perspective, there was nothing in particular to boost the growth of per-capita GDP (Sudrià 1990).

Once the war was over, adjustments needed to be made to the Spanish economy to adapt it to a new situation in which prices returned to pre-war levels and extraordinary business opportunities disappeared. Oversized sectors that in some cases had grown through the intensive use of obsolete techniques had to be restructured, and labour and social conflict dominated the political scene in the years immediately after the war. In political terms the conflict was resolved by a change of regime, which meant abandoning the constitutional system in the form of a parliamentary monarchy that had been adopted after the Bourbon Restoration (1874) and establishing a disctatorship in 1923 (Primo de Rivera/Berenguer), which survived until the Second Republic was declared in 1931. During these years the annual growth rates of per-capita GDP speeded up considerably, settling at around 3 per cent (Prados de la Escosura 2016).

The period covering from the start of the Second Republic to the end of the first decade of the Franco dictatorship, which includes the Spanish Civil War (1936–1939), was characterized by the paralysation if not reversal of Spanish economic development. The years of the Republic (1931–1936), although they brought advances in social terms and as regards political and individual freedoms, did not see any economic progress because of the effects of the serious international crisis situation (Palafox 1991, 2012). The Civil War and the first decade of the Franco dictatorship brought the reversal of the lengthy economic development process, proof of which is the fact that per-capita GDP in Spain did not recover its pre-war level until 1954, 15 years after the conflict ended (Prados de la Escosura 2016).

Bearing in mind this great changeability, we carry out a review of what happened in various areas that may be related to the factors determining the evolution of territorial inequality. We divide this into two major stages: the period before the war and the period covering the war itself and the years up to 1950. The first stage saw the continued integration of the Spanish market, driven especially by a substantially bigger investment in infrastructures, particularly road improvements, which complemented the previous development of the railway network (Herranz 2005).[8] Increasing market integration was accompanied by large interregional migrations. People left declining regions, which were mainly rural and agricultural, to relocate in the richest regions, which were more urban and specialized in industry and services.[9] Rosés and Sánchez-Alonso (2004) describe how, once the market disruption caused by the First World War had been overcome, in the 1920s the Spanish economy again turned in the direction of the convergence of real regional wages that had begun in the mid-nineteenth century.

The growth of per-capita GDP was driven by the technological advances of the second industrial revolution. Sectors such as electricity, telecommunications and chemicals led industrial growth in a favourable political and economic climate. Public investment in infrastructures, including the burgeoning reservoir construction sector, and a legal framework that guaranteed returns for foreign investors encouraged big international corporations to enter the Spanish market in the sectors mentioned above, leading to productivity gains and changes in production structures and employment.

In parallel to this, structural change speeded up and the share of employment in agriculture decreased substantially while economic growth rates increased. Thus between 1910 and 1930 we see the start of a trend in which agriculture participates less in the GDP and employment structure. Notable progress in electrification offset the previous energy restrictions traditionally affecting industry in some regions, and

[8] The size of the road network increased from 36,300 km in 1900 to 109,176 in 1935. By 1960 the figure was 130,644 km and reached 162,298 km in 1990 (Gómez Mendoza and San Román 2005).

[9] These migratory flows did not, however, originate in the poor areas of southern Spain, since these provinces were far from the centres of industry (Silvestre 2005).

the location of industry extended to other areas, especially Madrid and Zaragoza. Industrial specialization spread to more territories because interprovincial migrations now made it possible to overcome any limitations that might be generated in the process by the local labour supply.

The second of our stages, which covers the Second Republic (1931–1936), the Civil War (1936–1939) and the first years of the Franco regime (1939–1950), posed a major setback to Spanish economic growth. Especially relevant to this study is the impact of the policy of autarky implemented following the Civil War. This went hand in hand with the strict regulation of the commodity and input markets, including state control of prices and quantities for most goods. The prices of agricultural and industrial goods, especially those considered essential for industrialization, were regulated and the distribution of some of them was partly centralized (Martínez-Ruiz 2008).

Foreign trade policy, designed to help achieve autarky, included stringent regulations on imported goods. A complex system of quotas and bilateral agreements along with a trade licencing mechanism governed both commercial and financial operations. In addition, the overvaluation of the peseta made exports difficult. The regulatory framework also blocked the possible entry of foreign capital through direct investments.[10] As a result, the Spanish economy lacked the foreign currency needed to import the raw materials and capital goods needed for economic recovery. Thus the inability to finance imports of capital goods and the ideological commitment to national industry that prevented foreign investment impeded the growth of the principal sectors of the second industrial revolution in Spain (Donges 1976; Catalan 1995).

Although price control policies created a false impression of price convergence, internal trade barely increased. And due to the lack of investment in infrastructure, transport costs remained unchanged during the 1940s and early 1950s. As for the factor markets, the Franco government limited increases in nominal wages and set them at a national level (Vilar 2004). The banking sector was also subject to very strict regulations, including those governing interest rates, which gave the appearance of

[10] Foreign investors were prohibited by law from owning more than 25 per cent of the equity of any company.

capital market integration, but in fact interprovincial credit flows were weak (Pons 1999).

As a result, economic growth and structural change ground to a halt. Employment in agriculture actually increased during the 1940s, and it took 20 years for per-capita income to return to pre–Civil War levels. Interprovincial migratory flows stopped and the increasing territorial concentration of industrial activity was checked.

The Road to Economic Modernity, 1950–1980

The mild economic liberalization introduced during the 1950s together with foreign aid eased the transition of the Spanish economy towards a new stage of economic development (Prados de la Escosura et al. 2012). This period was characterized by high rates of economic growth and the leading role played by the industrial sector in the country's economic activity. New investments in infrastructures such as roads, railways and communications networks led to further reductions in internal transport costs. Increasing confidence in the viability of Franco's dictatorship after the military and technology cooperation agreements between the US and Spain (1953) along with the regime's moderate economic reforms encouraged investment and innovation, and this contributed to more rapid economic growth (Calvo-González 2007; Prados de la Escosura et al. 2012).[11]

In 1959 an institutional reform known as the Stabilization and Liberalization Plan was introduced, the short-term aim of which was to put an end to the inflation and the trade deficit that were jeopardizing Spanish economic growth. Under the auspices of the World Bank and the International Monetary Fund (IMF), which provided a stabilization fund of 218 million dollars, the peseta-dollar exchange rate was devalued and various measures were put in place to stop the monetary expansion that

[11] What was known as North American aid, which was organized through various economic programmes and channelled via donations, loans and the entry of goods, lasted from 1953 to 1958. In aggregate terms it meant an influx of capital amounting to over 50 per cent of the foreign currency obtained by Spain from exports (Donges 1976).

was feeding the inflationary process.[12] Instead of the previous inward-looking development strategy, the new economic programme was directed towards increasing the country's presence in international markets, boosting exports and opening up the national market to imports. It also aimed to attract direct foreign investment by allowing foreign investors to own up to 50 per cent of a company's equity. Spain's membership of international organizations such as the General Agreement on Trade and Tariffs, the World Bank and the IMF and a more liberal approach to the regulation of international commodity and capital movements helped restore the confidence of foreign investors, and the economy was once again able to build its path to growth on the foundation of foreign savings.

Thus a new stage of economic growth opened up that would make it possible for the Spanish economy to participate as a latecomer in the Golden Age that reigned in Europe in the aftermath of the Second World War. Spanish GDP rose at an annual average rate of over 5.6 per cent and, despite rapid demographic growth, per-capita income levels more than doubled in this short period of time (1950–1975), as shown in Table 2.1. Growth was again driven by technological change and the gains deriving from the more efficient allocation of resources. After over 20 years of isolation, Spanish agriculture and industry suffered from a considerable technology gap, but this provided a catch-up potential that could be capitalized on in the new scenario of macro-economic equilibrium and economic liberalization. Hence it took only a very short period of time for agricultural production to be thoroughly mechanized and for an exponential advance to take place in those industrial sectors typical of the second industrial revolution, which in the case of Spain had only undergone a timid expansion during the interwar period.[13] These included artificial fibre manufacturing, the chemistry of petroleum derivatives, electric machine industries and electricity production itself.

This new phase of economic growth was also driven by the increasing integration of the Spanish national market and its integration into the international market. A new wave of growth began in the movement of

[12] Among other measures, interest rates were increased, the automatic pledging of public debt was cancelled and the advances that the Bank of Spain granted to public companies were stopped.

[13] According to the Statistical Yearbooks for Spain, the number of tractors and harvesters and the intensity of energy use per hectare increased more than fourfold in the space of 20 years.

goods, capital and labour both inside Spain and across its borders. Even so, the level of integration achieved by the Spanish goods and capital markets over this period still cannot be considered that of a truly open economy. In fact the integration of the Spanish economy in the international markets in the mid-1970s, measured by its rate of openness, was not very different from its integration at the end of the nineteenth century (Fig. 2.1).

Nevertheless, new investment in infrastructures such as roads, railways and communications networks led to further reductions in internal transport costs, giving rise to widespread production specialization. One of the most noticeable elements of this period was the growing mobility of the labour force, which was becoming increasingly concentrated in the big cities. The rural exodus towards urban areas and more developed European countries resulted in a substantial decrease in agricultural employment and an increase in the share of the manufacturing, construction and services sectors (Ródenas 1994; Bover and Velilla 1999; Bentolila 2001). Unlike during the previous stage in the 1920s, migrants from the southern provinces now played a key role and participated massively in migratory flows. However, although to a lesser extent than before, migrant destinations were still limited to a relatively small number of cities, mainly Madrid and Barcelona.[14] As for international migration, a new wave of out-migration flows took place over the period 1960–1973, with over 100,000 workers a year migrating to core European countries (see Table 2.3).

The result of all this was a far-reaching structural transformation of the Spanish economy. As can be seen in Fig. 2.2 and Table 2.2, the agricultural sector went from employing 48 per cent of the active population in 1950 to just 17 per cent in 1980. Industry, including the construction sector, reached its peak, generating around 40 per cent of employment and value added in 1980. However, the crisis of the 1970s, which in the case of Spain continued well into the 1980s, slowed down these upward trends and GDP growth rates were substantially reduced. The economic

[14] In 1930 almost half the population that lived in a province that was not their province of birth were living in Madrid (22.9%) or Barcelona (also 22.9%). In 1970 the proportions were similar, 23.8% and 23.7% respectively (Paluzie et al. 2009, 248).

Table 2.3 Emigration and internal migration rates (per 1000 people), Spain, 1887–1991

	Emigration	Internal migration	Internal migration
Period	[1]	[2]	[3]
1887–1900	3.43	2.00	na
1901–1910	5.52	2.90	na
1911–1920	6.17	2.80	na
1921–1930	3.84	4.30	na
1931–1940	0.99	2.80	na
1941–1950	0.96	na	na
1951–1960	2.22	na	na
1961–1970	3.01	na	9.80
1971–1980	1.39	na	6.50
1981–1991	0.51	na	5.00

Note: Column [2] refers to the annual rate (per 1000) among those born in another province during the intercensus period from 1877 to 1940. Column [3] refers to the annual rate (per 1000) among residents in another province (at the previous census date) during the intercensus period (García-Coll and Stillwell 1999). Thus columns [2] and [3] are not strictly comparable. See Paluzie et al. (2009) for more information

Source: Emigration: Sánchez-Alonso (1995), Bover and Velilla (1999); Internal migration: Paluzie et al. (2009, Table 1, p.255)

crisis had a serious effect on an economy which, having grown extremely quickly, was heavily in debt and highly energy-dependent. And as a result of its production specialization as part of the framework of European countries, Spain still had an excessively large proportion of the population employed in agriculture. More seriously, many were also employed in energy-intensive industrial sectors that faced great competition on the international markets, such as iron and steel, coal-mining and shipbuilding.

The severity of the crisis together with the political conflict that opened up in parallel with the end of the dictatorship (Franco died in 1975) meant that in the late 1970s and the early 1980s economic growth in Spain was very modest. The concentration of manufacturing industries decreased somewhat during these years, causing the spatial distribution to show a bell-shaped evolution over the long term (Fig. 2.3). Interregional migration rates also fell in the 1970s and early 1980s (Table 2.3), arguably as a result of the high levels of unemployment recorded during this period (Bentolila and Blanchard 1990; Bentolila and Dolado 1991).

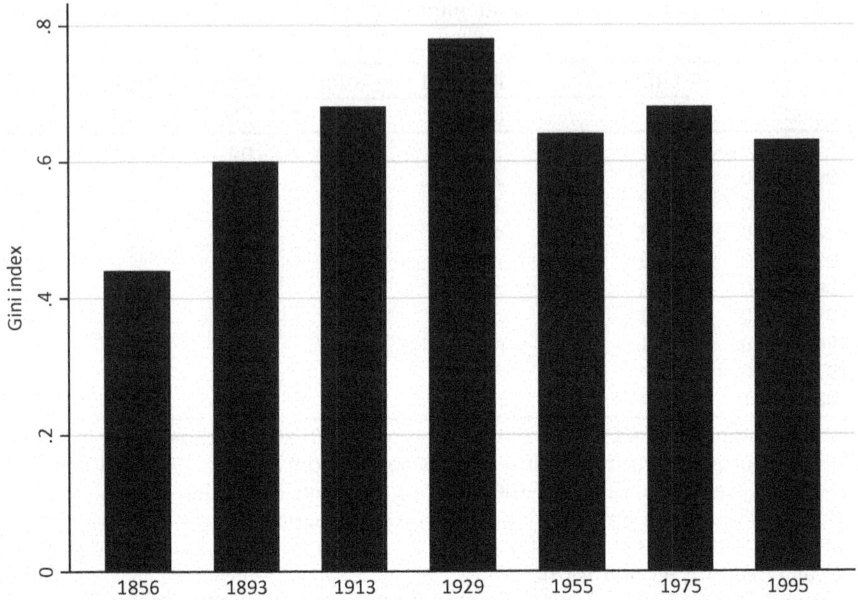

Fig. 2.3 Concentration in manufacturing at provincial level, Spain 1856–1995. Source: Paluzie et al. (2004)

From the Oil Crisis to the Global Economy, 1980–2015

With the death of Franco, Spain began a process of political transition towards a democratic regime in the form of a parliamentary monarchy. The return to democracy was especially difficult in a context of international economic crisis. Successive governments were forced to follow policies of macro-economic stabilization, overcome the severe crisis in the financial system and oversee the rationalization of the agricultural and especially industrial production structures.

The Spanish economy entered the 1980s with annual inflation of over 15 per cent and unemployment of 11 per cent, and the increase in oil prices had made the external deficit rise sharply. There were also outstanding structural reforms that needed to be tackled. The financial sector had to be put on a sound footing to cope with greater competition, and the more traditional industrial sectors were oversized and could not survive foreign competition. In short, the public sector had to take charge of far-reaching structural transformations.

The first governments of the democracy therefore made a special effort to lay the foundations of a new state which, while tackling serious macroeconomic problems, would also take the necessary steps to bring about structural reform. Indeed there was a continuous flood of reforms, planned in accordance with the so-called Moncloa Pact of 1977 and gradually implemented by the governments of the Union of the Democratic Centre (UCD: 1977–1982) and, in particular, the Spanish Socialist Workers' Party (PSOE: 1982–1986).[15] Of particular importance was the reform of a financial system that had lost 52 per cent of its bank branches between 1977 and 1985 (and 32.5 per cent of the sector's total assets).[16] Another task was the restructuring (or rationalization) of an industrial sector that had lost more than 800,000 jobs between 1975 and 1983.

Other measures were set in motion with the aim of repaying citizens for the efforts demanded of them by the adjustment programmes. The foundations of the welfare state were laid during these years, and in 1983 the law governing university reform was passed, allowing for more places to be provided and making access to university studies easier for a larger proportion of the population. In 1984 the unemployment benefit system created by the UCD government in 1980 was improved, in 1985 the law establishing free compulsory education until age 16 was passed, and in 1986 the Health Act was passed, which meant the universalization of the public health system.

However, perhaps the most important aspect of this period was the full incorporation of Spain into Western international institutions, in particular its membership of the European Economic Community, which came about on 1 January 1986. EEC entry and the subsequent developments associated with it, such as the Single European Act and the

[15] These early years included the Fiscal Reform of 1978. Led by the Treasury Minister Fernández-Ordóñez, this established a direct progressive tax on income that served to give the new state a certain degree of financial capacity.

[16] A detailed account of the banking and financial crisis can be found in Cuervo (1988).

Economic and Monetary Union (European Union), were the building blocks upon which Spanish economic growth during this period was based.

First, therefore, the economic support of the European Union was essential for financing the new wave of investments in infrastructure that helped to further reduce transport costs across Spanish regions and also across national borders. Huge amounts were invested in motorways, high-speed trains and telecommunications over this period, leading to major advances in the integration of the domestic market and its connections with international markets. Second, trade integration enabled the comparative advantages of the Spanish economy to be developed in the context of a large economy, which made it easier to take advantage of the economies of scale present in key sectors. Third, there was greater economic stability, making foreign investors more confident. And fourth, this was the ideal scenario for worker mobility, especially with the entry of large cohorts of emigrants into the labour market—mainly from the countries of Eastern Europe and Latin America—during periods of expansion, such as that between 1995 and 2008.

Once it had overcome the obstacles in connection with political transition and economic crisis, the Spanish economy therefore entered a new stage of economic growth that enabled it to advance along the path of economic development and changes in production structure. Structural change in this period was associated with the virtual disappearance of agriculture, which now occupied a marginal position in the composition of GDP and employment, and the decline of the industrial sector. Meanwhile the tertiary sector increased its participation in the production structure and in employment, especially in urban settings, which saw an agglomeration of population.

Internal and external migrations helped drive this process, which was now characterized by an increase in the dispersion of migratory flows. This dispersion was due to the fact that the sectors that attracted some of the largest cohorts of migrants in recent decades were construction and services, which are in principle less spatially concentrated than industry, at least in activities such as tourism that have a large presence in Spain (although less so in services of high value added, which do in fact tend to show greater spatial agglomeration). Growing congestion costs—such as rising property prices, the higher weight of amenities and other aspects related to quality of life, and the effect of redistributive policies—would also account for the greater dispersion of migratory flows over recent decades (Bover and Velilla 1999; Bentolila 2001).

Nevertheless, despite progress in the integration of the internal and external markets and in the flows of goods and factors that made production specialization possible, the growth rate of per-capita GDP between 1980 and 2015 was lower than that recorded during the Golden Age. The reason for this was that, in a context of extensive technological change in connection with information and communications technologies, much of the services sector that increased its participation in GDP and employment in Spain made no intensive use of these elements. The exception, affecting just a small group of territories characterized by their high urban density and higher income, is the agglomeration of services with high value added.

References

Abramovitz, M. (1994). Catch-up and convergence in the postwar growth boom and after. In W. J. Baumol, R. R. Nelson, & E. N. Wolff (Eds.), *Convergence of productivity: Cross-national studies and historical evidence* (pp. 86–125). Oxford: Oxford University Press.

Barquín, R. (1997). Transporte y precio del trigo en el siglo XIX: creación y reordenación de un mercado nacional. *Revista de Historia Económica, 15*(1), 17–48.

Barrios, S., & Strobl, E. (2009). The dynamics of regional inequalities. *Regional Science and Urban Economics, 39*(5), 575–591.

Barro, R., Mankiw, G., & Sala-i-Martin, X. (1995). Capital mobility in neoclassical models of growth. *American Economic Review, 85*(1), 103–115.

Barro, R., & Sala-i-Martin, X. (1991). Convergence across states and regions. *Brooking Papers on Economic Activity, 1*, 107–182.

Bentolila, S. (2001). *Las migraciones interiores en España*. FEDEA Working Papers, 2001–7.

Bentolila, S., & Blanchard, O. (1990). Spanish unemployment. *Economic Policy, 5*(10), 233–265.

Bentolila, S., & Dolado, J. J. (1991). Mismatch and internal migration in Spain. In F. Padoa (Ed.), *Mismatch and labour mobility* (pp. 182–236). Cambridge: Cambridge University Press.

Bover, O., & Velilla, P. (1999). *Migrations in Spain: Historical background and current trends*. Banco de España Working Paper, No. 9909.

Broadberry, S., & O'Rourke, K. H. (2010). *The Cambridge economic history of Modern Europe. Vol. 2, 1870 to the present*. Cambridge: Cambridge University Press.

Calvo-González, O. (2007). American military interests and economic confidence in Spain under the Franco Dictatorship. *The Journal of Economic History, 67*, 740–767.

Castañeda, L., & Tafunell, X. (1993). Un nuevo indicador para la historia financiera española: la cotización de las letras de cambio a corto plazo. *Revista de Historia Económica, 11*(2), 367–383.

Catalan, J. (1995). *La economía española y la Segunda Guerra Mundial*. Barcelona: Ariel.

Combes, P. P., Lafourcade, M., Thisse, J. F., & Toutain, J. C. (2011). The rise and fall of spatial inequalities in France: A long-run perspective. *Explorations in Economic History, 48*(2), 243–271.

Cuervo, A. (1988). *La crisis bancaria en España, 1977–1985*. Barcelona: Ariel.

Donges, J. (1976). *La industrialización en España*. Barcelona: Oikos-Tau.

García-Coll, A., & Stillwell, J. (1999). Inter-provincial migration in Spain: Temporal trends and age-specific patterns. *International Journal of Population Geography, 5*, 97–115.

Gómez Mendoza, A., & San Román, E. C. (2005). Transportes y comunicaciones. In A. Carreras & X. Tafunell (Eds.), *Estadísticas históricas de España: siglos XIX–XX* (pp. 509–572). Bilbao: Fundación BBVA.

Herranz, A. (2005). La reducción de los costes de transporte en España (1800–1936). *Cuadernos Económicos del ICE, 70*, 183–203.

Herranz, A. (2007). Infrastructure investment and Spanish economic growth, 1850–1935. *Explorations in Economic History, 44*(3), 452–468.

Kim, S. (1995). Expansion of markets and the geographic distribution of economic activities: The trends in U.S. regional manufacturing structure, 1860–1987. *Quarterly Journal of Economics, 110*(4), 881–908.

Kuznets, S. (1955). Economic growth and income inequality. *American Economic Review, 45*(1), 1–28.

Lucas, R. E. (2000). Some macroeconomics for the 21st century. *Journal of Economic Perspectives, 14*(1), 159–168.

Martínez-Ruiz, E. (2008). Autarkic policy and efficiency in the Spanish industrial sector. An estimate of domestic resource cost in 1958. *Revista de Historia Económica-JILAEH, 26*(3), 439–470.
Matilla, M., Pérez, P. A., & Sanz, B. (2008). La integración del mercado español a finales del siglo XIX. Los precios del trigo entre 1891 y 1905. *FUNCAS, Documentos de Trabajo* 391.
Nadal, J. (1973). The failure of the industrial revolution in Spain, 1814–1913. In C. M. Cipolla (Ed.), *The Fontana economic history of Europe* (pp. 533–626). Glasgow: William Collins.
Nadal, J. (1987). La industria fabril española en 1900: una aproximación. In J. Nadal, A. Carreras, & C. Sudrià (Eds.), *La economía española en el siglo XX: una perspectiva histórica* (pp. 23–62). Barcelona: Ariel.
Palafox, J. (1991). *Atraso económico y democracia. La Segunda República y la economía española.* Barcelona: Crítica.
Palafox, J. (2012). España y la crisis internacional de 1929. El papel de los desequilibrios internos. In P. Martín Aceña (Ed.), *Pasado y presente. De la Gran Depresión del siglo XX a la Gran Recesión del siglo XXI* (pp. 79–112). Bilbao: Fundación BBVA.
Paluzie, E., Pons, J., Silvestre, J., & Tirado, D. A. (2009). Migration and market potential in Spain over the twentieth century: A test of the new economic geography. *Spanish Economic Review, 11*(4), 243–265.
Paluzie, E., Pons, J., & Tirado, D. A. (2004). The geographical concentration of industry across Spanish regions, 1856–1995. *Jahrbuch Für Regionalwissenschaft, 24*(2), 143–160.
Peña, D., & Sánchez-Albornoz, N. (1983). *Dependencia dinámica entre precios agrícolas. El trigo en España, 1857–1890. Un estudio empírico*, Servicio de Estudios de Historia Económica, Banco de España, Madrid.
Pollard, S. (1981). *Peaceful conquest: The industrialization of Europe, 1760–1970.* Oxford: Oxford University Press.
Pons, M. A. (1999). Capture or agreement? Why Spanish banking was regulated under the Franco regime, 1939–1975. *Financial History Review, 6*, 25–46.
Prados de la Escosura, L. (2003). *El progreso económico de España.* Bilbao: Fundación BBVA.
Prados de la Escosura, L. (2016). Spain's historical national accounts: Expenditure and output, 1850–2015. *EHES Working Papers in Economic History, 103*, 1–145.
Prados de la Escosura, L., Rosés, J. R., & Sanz-Villaroya, I. (2012). Economic reforms and growth in Franco's Spain. *Revista de Historia Económica-JILAEH, 30*(1), 45–89.

Ringrose, D. (1998). *Spain, Europe and the "Spanish miracle", 1700–1900.* Cambridge: Cambridge University Press.

Ródenas, C. (1994). Migraciones interregionales en España (1960–1989): cambios y barreras. *Revista de Economía Aplicada, 2*, 5–36.

Rosés, J. R., Martinez-Galarraga, J., & Tirado, D. A. (2010). The upswing of regional income inequality in Spain (1860–1930). *Explorations in Economic History, 47*(2), 244–257.

Rosés, J. R., & Sánchez-Alonso, B. (2004). Regional wage convergence in Spain 1850–1930. *Explorations in Economic History, 41*(4), 404–425.

Sánchez-Alonso, B. (1995). *Las causas de la emigración española, 1880–1930.* Madrid: Alianza.

Sánchez-Alonso, B. (2000). Those who left and those who stayed behind: Explaining emigration from the regions of Spain, 1880–1914. *The Journal of Economic History, 60*(3), 730–755.

Serrano Sanz, J. M. (1997). Sector exterior y desarrollo en la economía española contemporánea. *Papeles de Economía Española, 73*, 328–330.

Silvestre, J. (2005). Internal migrations in Spain, 1877–1930. *European Review of Economic History, 9*, 233–265.

Sudrià, C. (1982). Desarrollo industrial y subdesarrollo bancario en Cataluña, 1844–1950. *Investigaciones Económicas, 18*, 137–176.

Sudrià, C. (1990). Los beneficios de España durante la Gran Guerra. Una aproximación a la balanza de pagos española, 1914–1920. *Revista de Historia Económica, 8*(2), 363–396.

Tena, A. (1999). Un nuevo perfil del proteccionismo español durante la Restauración, 1875–1930. *Revista de Historia Económica-JILAEH, 17*(3), 579–621.

Tirado, D. A., & Martinez-Galarraga, J. (2008). Una nova estimació retrospectiva del VAB regional industrial. Espanya (1860–1930). *Documents de treball de la Facultat de Ciències Econòmiques i Empresarials. Col.lecció d'Economia*, E08/192.

Tortella, G. (1973). *Los orígenes del capitalismo en España: banca, industria y ferrocarriles en el siglo XIX.* Madrid: Tecnos.

Vilar, M. (2004). La ruptura posbélica a través del comportamiento de los salarios industriales, nueva evidencia cuantitativa (1908–1963). *Revista de Historia Industrial, 25*, 81–126.

Wais, F. (1987 [1967]). *Historia de los ferrocarriles españoles.* Fundación de los Ferrocarriles Españoles, Madrid.

Williamson, J. G. (1965). Regional inequality and the process of national development: A description of the patterns. *Economic Development and Cultural Change, 13*(4), 1–84.

3

Methodology, Sources and New Evidence

Until recently the regional analysis of the Spanish economy over the long term has proved extremely difficult due to a lack of statistical data. The evolution of regional economic inequality in Spain has been well documented for the second half of the twentieth century, especially since 1955 when the Banco Bilbao Vizcaya (BBV 1999) started to publish regional macro-economic aggregates. However, although in itself extremely useful, this time period is not enough to enable us to fully understand the long-term evolution of regional inequality because the roots of this inequality date back to earlier times. Economic history has shown us that by the end of the Ancien Régime there were already appreciable differences between regions in Spain (Llopis 2004; Álvarez-Nogal and Prados de la Escosura 2007), and a key turning point that serves as a useful place to begin any study of regional inequality over the long term would be the introduction of industrialization processes and the start of modern economic growth (Kuznets 1966, 1971). In the case of Spain this would be the mid-nineteenth century.

With the arrival of modern economic growth—or, to put it another way, the transition from a Malthusian to a Solow-type growth economy—one would expect to see changes in regional development patterns,

A. Díez-Minguela et al., *Regional Inequality in Spain*, Palgrave Studies in Economic History, https://doi.org/10.1007/978-3-319-96110-1_3

possibly including an initial increase in regional inequality and ultimately a change in the long-term dynamics of divergence or convergence. The reason for this, as many authors have shown, is that industrialization and structural change do not reach all regions at the same time (Williamson 1965). Therefore only a historical perspective that goes back to at least the beginnings of modern economic growth will make it possible to take an all-encompassing view of how regional inequality has evolved and the changes that over time have given shape to the situation we have today. Thus a basic requirement of any exploration of regional inequality over the long term is for there to be easily accessible regional output data, ideally from at least the early stages of modern economic growth, that is, around the middle of the nineteenth century. In the case of Spain, however, as we mentioned at the start, the limited time coverage of regional GDP data has meant that studying regional inequality from a historical perspective has always been difficult.[1]

Given these circumstances, this book makes an important contribution by constructing a dataset of decadal figures for regional GDP from 1860 to 1930.[2] These estimates are then merged with data from a variety of sources for 1930–2015. For 1935–1950 we use the five-year figures provided by Alcaide (2003), for 1955–1979 we use the BBV's (1999) biannual figures and for 1980–2015 we use the official data published every year by the National Statistics Institute (INE—*Instituto Nacional de Estadística*). The data in all cases are for Spanish provinces, that is, NUTS3 in Eurostat terminology, and can therefore easily be aggregated to serve for NUTS2 regions (autonomous communities) or NUTS1 macro-regions.

Taken as a whole in combination with data on regional population, this information can give us a picture of regional inequality in per-capita

[1] For the nineteenth century and the first third of the twentieth, the only data available are those provided by Álvarez Llano (1986), who reports the distribution of GDP by autonomous community (NUTS2) for six different points in time. However, the fact that the exact method the author used to calculate these figures is unknown undermines their reliability. Among others, Carreras (1990), Martín (1992), Germán Zubero et al. (2001) and Domínguez (2002) have based their analyses of regional inequality in Spain on this dataset.

[2] The GDP estimates for Spain's provinces in 1860, 1900, 1910, 1920 and 1930 were calculated in collaboration with Joan Ramon Rosés (see Rosés et al. 2010). The estimates for 1870, 1880 and 1890 are from Díez-Minguela et al. (2016).

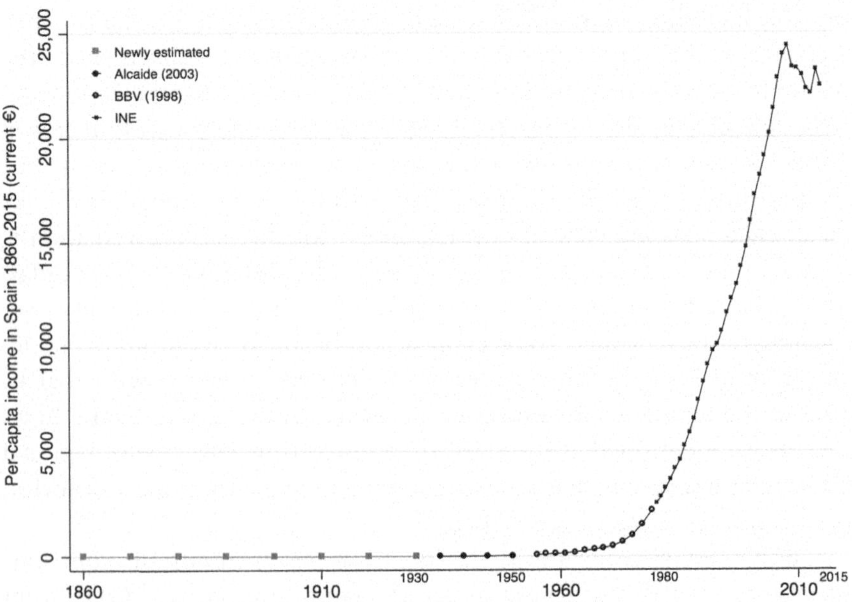

Fig. 3.1 Per-capita income in Spain (current €), 1860–2015. Source: Prados de la Escosura (2016, 2017) and main text

Table 3.1 Regional GDP, NUTS3 sources

Period	Source	Frequency	No. of sectors
1860–1930	Rosés et al. (2010) Díez-Minguela et al. (2016)	10 yearly	5
1935–1950	Alcaide (2003)	5 yearly	4
1955–1979	BBV (1999)	2 yearly	24
1980–2015	INE	yearly	7–11

Source: Main text

income in Spain over the long term, starting from the early stages of modern economic growth. Broadly speaking, we have data on regional GDP for different points in time starting from 1860. Although Table 3.1 and Fig. 3.1 show that the time frequencies of the figures vary over the course of Spain's economic development depending on the source used, we will generally present the data using intervals of ten and later five years. Because the sources for the period 1935–2015 are well known and have been widely described and used by Spanish economists, the first part of this chapter will concentrate on showing the procedure and sources used to produce a new set of estimates for Spanish regional per-capita GDP for the period 1860–1930.

Driven by a desire to gain a better understanding of economic phenomena, especially after the Great Depression of the 1930s, and helped by technological advances in data processing, a group of economists including Simon Kuznets devised an accounting system to measure the value of economic activity in the US. The end result of this collective effort was national accounting, a system whereby the value of the economic activity of any economy could be measured for a specific period of time. The GDP has been probably the best-known indicator for measuring the value of economic activity ever since.

After the Second World War the system of national accounting became more widely used due to the work carried out by the official statistics agencies in different countries which, in Europe at least, developed national accounts to varying degrees during the second half of the twentieth century. In many cases, however, the availability of regional accounts—equivalent to national accounts but territorialized—is limited to recent decades.[3] In Spain, publication of the first national accounts starting from 1954 began in the second half of the 1950s. Initially they were compiled by the Treasury (following the OECD's standardized system), but since 1965 they have been the responsibility of the INE. The first input-output table for the Spanish economy is for 1958. From a regional standpoint, the macro-economic aggregates provided by the BBV (1999) also date from the same period, starting in 1955.[4]

Ideally, GDP data for periods in the past should be obtained via the direct estimation of production in the same way that national and regional accounting is done in the present. However, the further back in time we go, the more difficult it is to find the statistical information needed to do this. Obviously this makes it difficult enough to reconstruct national accounts, but the problem is even greater when it comes to reconstructing regional accounts. Therefore, in the field of economic history and for the purposes of pinning down the time dynamics of regional growth,

[3] See Eurostat.

[4] These data series were compiled by researchers who played an active part in designing the national accounts and are therefore methodologically comparable.

researchers have generally been forced to use a variety of short-cut methods to carry out an indirect estimation of regional production. Regional input has sometimes been estimated using socioeconomic variables that are highly correlated with income, or by referring to fiscal information and statistics or by trying to determine the regional distribution of national input on the basis of information that in most cases is fragmented and limited.[5]

This state of affairs changed substantially with the appearance of a paper by Geary and Stark (2002). Aiming to analyse the economic performance of post-famine Ireland almost up to the eve of the First World War (1861–1911), they devised a methodology that would enable them to allocate UK GDP across England, Ireland, Scotland and Wales. This methodology, which involves distributing national GDP among territorial subunits on the basis of wage income, has a number of advantages. First, it has a solid theoretical foundation. Second, it produces robust results. When we compare official statistics for regional GDP recently compiled in the context of regional accounting with the results that would be obtained using the Geary-Stark methodology, any discrepancies fall within a reasonable margin. And third, crucially, this method of indirect estimation only needs a limited amount of statistical information, mainly active population and wages (by region and sector), which is often available for historical periods far back in time.[6] As pointed out in the introductory chapter, this methodology has enabled substantial advances to be made in the estimation of historical regional GDP over the last decade, especially where European countries are concerned. And this in turn has made it possible to analyse in much greater detail how the regional distribution of economic activity has evolved in a good many countries since the early stages of modern economic growth in Europe, which came about in parallel with the beginning of industrialization.[7]

[5] See, for instance, Good (1994) for the Habsburg Empire pre–First World War, Esposto (1997) for Italy 1870–1910, and Caruana-Galizia (2013) and Bazot (2014) for France in the nineteenth and early twentieth centuries.

[6] There would also be a need for historical data series of national GDP broken down by sector, since these are the basis for the territorial distribution of economic activity.

[7] Two exceptions of countries with historical income series compiled using methodology similar to direct estimation are the US (Easterlin 1957, 1960) and Japan (Fukao et al. 2015).

Another characteristic of the Geary-Stark methodology is that the regional distribution of national GDP is calculated separately for each of the main sectors of economic activity. In their original paper, this was done for three big economic sectors: agriculture, industry and services. In practice, however, the number of sectors considered can be greater, since this ultimately depends on the extent to which sectoral disaggregation has been carried out in the data series for national GDP that need to be distributed territorially.

For Spain we have complete series of historical national accounts from 1850 (recently updated as far as 2015) thanks to Leandro Prados de la Escosura (2003, 2016, 2017). These GDP data series for the Spanish economy with their sectoral disaggregation in combination with existing historical statistical data enable us to carry out an estimation of regional production between 1860 and 1930 in five sectors: (1) agriculture, (2) mining, (3) manufacturing and public utilities, (4) construction and (5) services. As explained later in the chapter, for some sectors we have been able to carry out what is reasonably close to a direct estimation of production. On some occasions we have had to resort to indirect estimation using the methodology proposed by Geary and Stark, while on others we suggest an alternative, such as the refinement made by Crafts (2005) to incorporate non-wage income into the estimations through the use of tax returns.

The resulting data series for regional GDP are nominal, at current prices and factor cost. Converting these to constant prices is done by applying the deflator for national GDP to the regional GDPs. Doing this is not without problems insofar as prices and their evolution can vary substantially over time, even between regions in the same state. For this study it was decided to consider national deflators as being representative of the evolution of prices on a regional scale rather than attempt to carry out an approximation of regional prices to correct any potential biases. It should therefore be noted that the estimated figures for regional per-capita GDP provide us with a good idea of the levels and evolution of productivity in the regions rather than the standards of living actually experienced in them.

There were two main reasons for this decision. The first concerns the difficulty involved in accurately estimating regional prices—especially for historical periods—due to the limited information available. The second is the fact that even today agencies like Eurostat use national deflators on their regional accounts. In any case, we should bear in mind the fact that the procedure followed to convert nominal values into real ones may generate a considerable bias, since it is obvious that there can be big differences between the cost of living in Paris (or Madrid or Milan) and the cost of living in Perpignan (or Badajoz or Salerno). Therefore the calculation of price levels on a regional scale should be considered a priority by the statistics agencies responsible for territorial accounting.[8]

The Territorial Units: Provinces (NUTS3), Autonomous Communities (NUTS2) and Macro-regions (NUTS1)

The transition from the Ancien Régime to the liberal state brought with it a reorganization of the territory. In the eighteenth century Spain was divided into approximately 30 administrative areas known as intendancies, which were later used as the basis for designating provinces. These in turn were created as administrative units in the 1830s following the territorial division designed by Javier de Burgos, Secretary of State for Public Works at the time. This division established the existence of 49 provinces based on historical and geographical criteria.[9] All these provinces were of a similar size and this territorial distribution has remained virtually unchanged up to the present day.[10] Conveniently for us, most of the existing historical statistics for Spain are based on this distribution, which is of enormous help when it comes to constructing regional macroeconomic variables.

[8] Although the estimation of purchasing power parities and regional deflators for the 155 years analysed lies outside the scope of this study, in Chap. 4, in order to test the robustness of the results, we provide a comparison between the evolution of regional inequality estimated with national deflators and the evolution that would be recorded if territorial price differences were taken into account.

[9] Although today there are 50 provinces in Spain, initially the Canary Islands (two provinces) were a single province and appear as such in statistics for the nineteenth and early twentieth centuries. In 1927 they were split into the two provinces we know today, bringing the total up to 50.

[10] To some extent this is an anomaly in the context of Europe, since most countries have seen changes in their internal and external borders over the course of history. An extreme example would be the changes that took place after the First World War (1914–1918).

Although the division into provinces may have remained stable, the state's political and territorial organization has changed significantly in other ways over the last century and a half. As in most European countries, the nineteenth century in Spain was a time of political and social upheaval. And there was also the "regional question". This already existed at the time of the Bourbon Restoration (1874–1923) and its presence has continued to a greater or lesser extent ever since, especially, though not exclusively, in Catalonia and the Basque Country.[11] Indeed, tension has surrounded the issue of what territorial organization the liberal state should adopt ever since it was created. This has given rise to moves not only in favour of centralization, for instance during the dictatorship of Primo de Rivera (1923–1930), but also in favour of (short-lived) federal projects such as those carried out during the First (1873–1874) and Second (1931–1936) Republics.

After the Civil War (1936–1939), General Franco's dictatorship set up a fascist-oriented regime characterized by, among other things, the extreme recentralization of the state as part of an ideology that defended the unity of the fatherland and the violent repression of those regions and collectives that had most loudly demanded greater levels of self-government. Despite this, at the start of the transition towards democracy after the death of Franco in 1975 it was clear that the old territorial demands had survived. It was intended that the aspirations of these peripheral regions should be included in Spain's Constitution of 1978, which laid down the conditions for creating a decentralized state. The territory was reorganized by grouping the provinces into 17 *comunidades autónomas* and two autonomous cities (Ceuta and Melilla) and recognizing the existence of "historical nationalities".[12]

Two aspects of the autonomous communities should be noted here. First, unlike provinces, they are of recent creation. They are territorial units with their own sense of history, but from a legal and administrative

---

[11] In some regions the Spanish language coexists alongside the local language (mainly Catalan, Basque or Galician). It is from these regions that demands have traditionally been made for a more federal view of the state, although this is not exclusively the case, as can be seen from the cantonalist movements in Murcia and Andalusia in the 1870s.

[12] This would refer to Andalusia, Aragon, the Balearic Islands, the Canary Islands, Catalonia, Valencia, Galicia and the Basque Country, all recognized as "historical nationalities".

point of view they have only a relatively short past going back just four decades.[13] And second, again unlike provinces, the autonomous communities vary enormously in size. Whereas Andalusia, for example, covers an area of around 87,000 km^2 (roughly 17 per cent of the total area of Spain), the autonomous communities of La Rioja and the Balearic Islands barely cover 5000 km^2 each (i.e. 1 per cent of the total).

In regional analysis today, territorial divisions follow the nomenclature used by Eurostat, the EU's statistics agency. Thus Spanish provinces correspond to NUTS3, while autonomous communities are NUTS2. Eurostat adds a third category—NUTS1 or macro-regions—which in the case of Spain are seven areas created by grouping autonomous communities together.[14] As mentioned earlier, the territorial unit we have chosen for estimating regional GDP in Spain is the province, the smallest of the three, which corresponds to NUTS3 in Eurostat terminology. However, as we progress with our analysis of regional inequality over the course of the book, we will be alternating between territorial units as necessary. Figure 3.2 shows the various administrative divisions in Spain today (NUTS3, NUTS2 and NUTS1).

A New Dataset of Regional GDP for Spain, 1860–1930 (Provinces/NUTS3)

The following pages describe the methodology used to estimate provincial GDP, mainly between 1860 and 1930. First we present the Geary-Stark methodology so that we can then explain the estimation strategies used for each of the five sectors considered (agriculture, mining, manufacturing and utilities, construction and services). The territorial basis for the estimation is the province (NUTS3), and GDP data are obtained for eight points in time: 1860, 1870, 1880, 1890, 1900, 1910, 1920 and 1930.

[13] This is relevant because we are carrying out a historical analysis and sometimes refer to the autonomous communities in periods that predate their creation. The regions' historical continuity makes this reasonable.

[14] The various different NUTS divisions in Spain are listed in Table A1 of the Appendix.

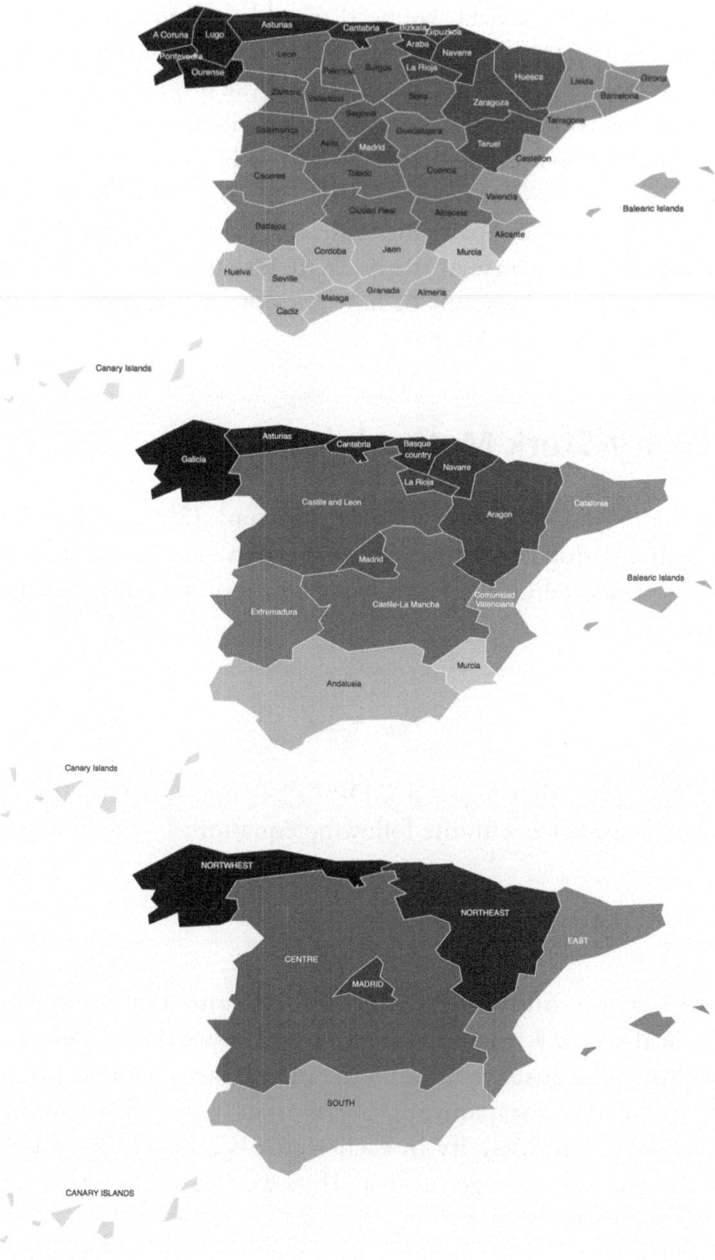

Fig. 3.2 Spanish provinces (NUTS3), autonomous communities (NUTS2) and macro-regions (NUTS1)

Once we have these data, we need to add the information obtained from other sources for the period 1935–2015. To make it possible to link these two sets of estimates, we have scaled all the original absolute figures for sectoral and regional GDP so that the provincial totals add up to the national total for Spain provided by Prados de la Escosura (2016, 2017). Thus we create a dataset of regional GDP that covers the entire economic development process in Spain and will serve as the basis for the analysis carried out over the course of the book. Before that, however, a detailed description needs to be given of how we obtained regional GDP estimates for the period 1860–1930.

The Geary-Stark Methodology

The methodology developed by Geary and Stark (2002) is based on the principle that national GDP is equal to the sum of all regional or provincial GDPs. The total GDP of the Spanish economy in algebraic terms is therefore:

$$Y_{ESP} = \sum^{i} Y_i \tag{3.1}$$

However, given that regional GDP (Y_i) is not available, this will be proxied in accordance with the following equation:

$$Y_i = \sum^{j} y_{ij} L_{ij} \tag{3.2}$$

where y_{ij} is the output or average added value per worker in each region i and sector j, and L_{ij} is the number of workers in each region i and sector j. Because we have no data for y_{ij}, this value is proxied by taking Spanish sectoral output per worker (y_j) and assuming that regional labour productivity in each sector is reflected by wages relative to the Spanish average (w_{ij}/w_j). Thus we can assume that regional GDP will be given by:

$$Y_i = \sum^{j} \left[y_j \beta_j \left(\frac{w_{ij}}{w_j} \right) \right] L_{ij} \tag{3.3}$$

where, as suggested by Geary and Stark (2002), w_{ij} is the wage paid in region i in sector j, w_j is the Spanish wage in each sector j, and β_j is a scalar that preserves relative regional differences but scales the absolute values so that the regional totals for each sector match the total for Spain. In the absence of regional output figures, Geary and Stark (2002) set out an indirect estimation model based on wage income, which makes it possible to estimate GDP by region at factor cost and current values. Broadly speaking, the basic data underlying this estimation procedure are national output per worker by sector and nominal wages and active population by sector and region.

This methodology provides us with a way of computing not only regional GDP but also values for the various industrial sectors in each of the 49 provinces considered. Geary and Stark (2002) distributed regional GDP among three sectors (agriculture, manufacturing and services), whereas we consider five (agriculture, mining, manufacturing and utilities, construction and services) given the availability of data. As we mentioned earlier, however, there are variations in the way these estimations by sector are carried out. In some cases there is enough information available for us to compute direct estimates of provincial aggregate production for some sectors, while in others we have to return to the Geary-Stark method or a variation of it.

Agriculture

For agriculture we have computed direct production estimates (nominal gross value added) for 1900, 1910, 1920 and 1930 by taking the production quantities of the different agricultural items found in GEHR (1991) and multiplying them by the relative prices and transforming coefficients calculated from the data provided by Simpson (1994). These real values were then converted into nominal values using the disaggregated agrarian prices in Prados de la Escosura (2003). Finally we scaled the absolute values so that the provincial totals for each sector would match the Spanish totals for agricultural value given in Prados de la Escosura (2003, 2016).

For the period 1860–1890 we used a modified version of the Geary-Stark method. A major problem with agricultural estimations is that we know the daily wage but not the number of working days in a year or the proportion of females working in the sector, and these are factors that are likely to vary greatly across regions. We therefore modified the initial estimates obtained following the original method by using a scalar computed by dividing our direct estimate for 1910 by that obtained with the Geary-Stark method. Consequently we assume that the number of days worked and the relative number of women working in each province remained constant between 1860 and 1910.

To carry out this strategy we first take provincial agricultural wages and the active male population in the sector and follow Geary-Stark methodology. Data on wages are from Bringas (2000)[15] and the active male population in agriculture is taken from the population censuses of 1860, 1877 and 1887 respectively. However, there are still a number of concerns to be dealt with. Using the statistical information available it is difficult to disentangle the size of the female workforce in agriculture and the number of working days per year and how these vary from province to province. We therefore rely on the direct estimates of agricultural production by province in 1910 (based on Simpson [1994] and GEHR [1991]) and divide them by the agricultural gross value added (GVA) obtained using the Geary-Stark indirect estimation method. The resulting scalar is used to correct our initial figures, assuming that the proportional size of the female workforce and the days worked per year in each province remained constant over the period 1860–1910. We then scale the values obtained so that the total agricultural GVA by province matches the total for Spain provided by Prados de la Escosura (2003, 2016). Given the absence of information for 1870, the agricultural GVA for that year was computed by interpolating the results for 1860 and 1880.

[15] For the 1880 estimation we use the closest available wage data, which are for 1887.

Mining

Mining production estimates were calculated using the production values disaggregated by province in the Spanish Statistical Yearbooks (*Anuario Estadístico de España*) for 1860, 1910, 1920 and 1930.[16] For 1870, 1880 and 1890, the Spanish Mining Statistics (*Estadística Minera de España*) provided an alternative source of data on mining production. The provincial values obtained were then used to distribute the country's total mining GVA at factor cost (Prados de la Escosura 2003, 2016). Given the absence of direct production data for 1900, we had to use an alternative methodology. This involved multiplying the provincial active population engaged in mining in 1900 by a productivity coefficient obtained from the data for 1920.[17] In other words we assume that labour productivity in mining for each province in 1900 was the same as in 1920.

Manufacturing and Public Utilities

To estimate regional industrial value added we begin by assuming the existence of a production function with constant returns to scale, where output is obtained via the contribution of two production factors: labour and capital.[18] The industrial gross value added (GVAmanuf) is defined as:

$$\text{GVAmanuf}_{it} = \alpha_{it}\left(\omega_{it} \times L_{it}\right) + \left(1 - \alpha_{it}\right)\left(r_{it} \times K_{it}\right) \tag{3.4}$$

where α_{it} is the share of wage income in industrial GVA in region i at time t, ω_{it} is the industrial wage in region i at time t, L_{it} is the total active population in industry in region i at time t, r_{it} is the returns to capital in industry in region i at time t and K_{it} is the capital stock in industry in

[16] We have taken the 1915 values for 1910 and the 1931 values for 1930.

[17] The year when more precise records of the mining workforce were first given in the population census (Foro Hispánico de Cultura 1957).

[18] For this sector we follow Crafts' (2005) refinement of the original Geary and Stark (2002) methodology and use tax data to allocate non-wage manufacturing income across regions.

region i at time t. For Spain information is available for each component in Eq. (3.4) except for r_{it}, which means we had to assume perfect capital mobility. Therefore

$$r_{it} = r_t \quad \forall i \tag{3.5}$$

The wage income included in Eq. (3.4) was estimated by first compiling the data series for employment in industry in each province using information from the population censuses for 1860, 1877, 1887, 1900, 1910, 1920 and 1930,[19] then collecting all available data on nominal industrial wages from a variety of sources.

Wages in manufacturing for 1860 are from Madrazo (1984),[20] who provides figures for ten categories of workers involved in road-building, six of which are quite well represented across provinces (apprentice, unskilled labourer, mason, bricklayer, carpenter and miner). The industrial wage for 1860 is calculated as a simple average of three categories based on levels of skill: bricklayers (skilled workers), unskilled workers and apprentices.[21] A number of problems still need to be tackled, however. There is high geographical coverage for bricklayers, but there are six provinces for which we have no wage information.[22] To fill the gap we use data for the closest comparable category in Madrazo (1984), that is, masons. Bricklayers' wages in these six provinces are therefore calculated from masons' wages and their deviation from masons' average wages nationwide, weighted by the industrial population of each province according to the 1860 population census. Meanwhile no wage figures are provided for any category of worker in Navarre, so these have had to be estimated. It would be reasonable to think that there might be a wage gradient influenced by geographical proximity. Indeed, all the other years available confirm that the industrial wage in Navarre is close to the aver-

[19] We aggregated the original data in the population census following Foro Hispánico de Cultura (1957) and the methodology used by Nicolau (2005) in her estimates of the national figures.

[20] "Jornales de los obreros de la construcción de carreteras durante el año 1860 en reales de vellón", Madrazo (1984, p. 208).

[21] We use a simple average given that no data on active population in each occupation are available and the average cannot therefore be weighted.

[22] Gipuzkoa, Lugo, Ourense, Oviedo, Bizkaia and Zamora.

age wage in neighbouring provinces. We therefore calculate the industrial wage in Navarre in 1860 as being the average wage in the neighbouring provinces.[23]

Industrial wages for 1900 are from Sánchez Alonso (1995),[24] who sourced them from IGE (1903). Simpson (1995) defines these as semi-skilled workers' wages and points out that the figures for two provinces—Pontevedra and Toledo—are excessively high.[25] The values in both cases have therefore been corrected by recalculating them as the average of the industrial wages in neighbouring provinces. Industrial wages for 1910, 1920 and 1930 are from the *Estadísticas de Trabajo y Jornadas de Trabajo*, published by the Ministerio de Trabajo (1927, 1931), and Silvestre (2003). The figures, which represent the nominal hourly wage, are weighted by the active population in each occupation according to different categories: skilled workers, skilled female workers, unskilled labourers and apprentices (male and female). For 1930 we use the hourly wage for 1925, since the average for subsequent years cannot be weighted by occupation due to the lack of available data. For 1910 we use the data for 1914. To overcome the fact that there are no data on industrial wages in the Canary Islands, it is assumed that in 1910 they were similar to the lowest industrial wage in the Spanish mainland provinces (0.28 ptas per hour). For 1920 and 1930 the increase in the industrial wage is assumed to be similar to the increase in the Spanish economy as a whole.

Finally, given the absence of wage data for 1880 and 1890, we make an interpolation using the figures available for 1860 and 1900. It was also assumed that the number of working days per year was identical in all provinces, and wage income was computed by multiplying wages by the size of the industrial working population.[26]

---

[23] To test this result we take wages for 1897, the nearest date available. In that year the industrial wage in Navarre was 3 per cent higher than the Spanish average weighted by the industrial population. If we apply this percentage to the Spanish value for 1860, the figure obtained almost exactly matches the figure we calculated at the start.

[24] "Jornales fabriles en las capitales de provincia (pesetas) en 1896–1897", Sánchez Alonso (1995), pp. 294–295. The original source is the Instituto Geográfico y Estadístico (1903), pp. XLVII–XLIX.

[25] Simpson (1995), pp. 190 and 199 respectively.

[26] The coverage provided by the wages dataset is far from perfect, which meant we had to make some assumptions. First, that the wages series, while not homogeneous over time, is representative

The data for constructing the capital income per province in Eq. (3.4) were drawn from various sources, some of which were fiscal. The main source was the *Estadística Administrativa de la Contribución Industrial y de Comercio* (EACI), which includes all statistical information on industry tax, with figures for total tax paid on industrial activity by province and industry. Introduced in 1845, the tax consisted of "a system of fixed rates per active unit of the main production means in each of the branches or productive processes established by the legislator" (Nadal and Tafunell 1992, p. 256). The rate was different for each type of machinery and branch of industry, and is therefore particularly useful when it comes to capturing provincial capital stock.

Nevertheless, a number of problems had to be dealt with when processing the data provided in the EACI. First, a limitation of the source is that it did not immediately adjust to changes in machine productivity. Second, the Basque Country (i.e. the provinces of Alava, Gipuzkoa and Bizkaia) and Navarre are not covered because they were exempt from paying this tax due to their special fiscal regime. Data for these provinces are instead taken from Parejo (2001), who used historical indices of production to estimate their contribution to Spanish industry in 1850 and 1900. Given that industry in the Basque Country expanded rapidly during the final decades of the nineteenth century, we make a geometric interpolation of Parejo's (2001) data to capture this trend, breaking the figures down using the active population in manufacturing in each of the three provinces as provided by the population censuses of 1860, 1877, 1887 and 1900. A linear interpolation is used in the case of Navarre.

The coverage of this tax had substantially changed by 1907. Joint stock companies, which were the largest in Spanish industry, were exempt from paying industry tax but had to pay a new corporate tax based on net profits (*Impuesto de Sociedades*). Over the years many companies were turned into joint stock companies in order to benefit from the lower rates payable under this new tax (Nadal and Tafunell 1992, p. 259). In 1921 this corporate tax became applicable to all types of companies, and thus many

of industry. And second, as regards the use of nominal wages, that there will be a bias given that price levels vary between regions (Geary and Stark 2002, pp. 933–934).

firms were exempted from paying the old industry tax. A consequence of all this is that after 1907 the information provided by the EACI is not representative of industrial activities. Fortunately Betrán (1999, pp. 674–675) reconstructed the industry taxes paid in each province in 1913 and 1929 using the data on both types of tax paid by industrial companies contained in the EACI and the *Estadística de la Contribución de Utilidades*. In short, provincial capital stock between 1860 and 1900 is obtained from the EACI,[27] while Betrán (1999) enables us to compute the regional participation in capital income for 1913 and 1929. For 1920, due to the absence of fiscal data, capital shares are interpolated using the figures for 1910 and 1930.

Once the provincial distribution of labour and capital income is obtained, we need to calculate the weight of each factor's income in the total industrial GVA. On this subject there is substantial international evidence showing that the output proportions of labour and capital remain relatively stable for long periods (Gollin 2002). We therefore chose to compute different factor shares for each industry, but not for each of our reference years. However, given that the industrial structure in each province varies over time, these factor shares vary in the different reference years at provincial level.

To calculate the factor shares in Eq. (3.4) we combine data from two sources. First, the provincial manufacturing structure based on data for nine manufacturing sectors is obtained from the same fiscal sources mentioned in the paragraphs above. The industry sectors considered are food, textiles, metal, chemicals, paper, wood, ceramic, leather and miscellaneous industries.[28] Second, the proportions of labour and capital used in these nine sectors at national level are obtained from the first-ever input-output table of 1958 (Andrés Álvarez et al. 1962).[29] On the basis of this information we constructed

[27] The years consulted are 1856, 1878–1979, 1890, 1893 and 1900.

[28] Due to lack of data, only seven industry sectors are considered for 1913 and 1929 (food, textiles and footwear, metal, chemicals, paper, wood and cork, and ceramic).

[29] The use of this source to construct factor shares and then apply them retrospectively means assuming that the intensity of factor use in 1958 is a good proxy for previous years. This assumption has also been made in previous estimations of industrial production indices for Spain (Carreras 1983; Prados de la Escosura 2003).

specific factor shares for each province and each reference year.[30] Taking all these components from Eq. (3.4) together, we can compute provincial manufacturing production. The share obtained for each province is then used to distribute the national GVA for manufacturing and public utilities provided by Prados de la Escosura.[31]

Construction

This sector comprises two subsectors: residential construction and public works. Data on residential construction were distributed across provinces, with figures for urban population (the percentage of people living in cities of over 5000 inhabitants) being drawn from Reher (1994). The urban population in 1870 is obtained by interpolating the information contained in the population censuses of 1860 and 1877. For public works we distribute national GVA across provinces using data on the provincial stock of infrastructures from Herranz (2008).[32]

Services

Many historical studies have suffered from the absence of information on wages in the service industries. Geary and Stark (2002: 923), who faced the same problem in their study of the British economy, calculated service sector wages as a weighted average of the series for agriculture and industry, in which the weights were each sector's share of the labour force. Our strategy is slightly different. In his historical national accounts, Prados de la Escosura (2003, 2016) supplies the GVA for 11 different branches of the Spanish services industry: transport, communications, trade, banking and insurance, housing, public administra-

[30] Given that no fiscal information is available, we assume a labour share similar to the Spanish total for the Basque Country provinces and Navarre.

[31] The lack of data for 1870 means we have had to obtain the provincial shares for manufacturing by interpolating the values for 1860 and 1880.

[32] Since Herranz's (2008) dataset only applies from 1870 onwards, the data for 1860 were based on urban population alone.

tion, education, health services, hotels and restaurants, domestic services and the liberal professions. Taking into account this level of disaggregation, we compiled the data for active population from population censuses, scaling the absolute values so that the provincial total for each sector would match the Spanish totals for the working population engaged in services, as provided by Prados de la Escosura. We then applied different wage figures depending on the skills and productivity levels of the workforce. To be specific, we used agricultural wages for domestic service, an unweighted average of skilled and unskilled wages in urban industry for commerce and hotels and restaurants, an unweighted average of agricultural and urban industry wages (skilled and unskilled) for transport and communications, and urban skilled wages for the remaining branches.[33]

A Long-term Dataset of Regional Economic Inequality, 1860–2015

This section presents the dataset we have constructed using the sources and methodology described above and which will serve as the basis for our work. In this initial approach to the data, our aim is to point out some of the stylized facts observed in the regional distribution of economic activity in Spain that will guide our analysis over the course of the book. We begin by looking at the long-term evolution of three variables: (a) the regional distribution of GDP (%), (b) the regional distribution of population (%) and (c) income per capita relative to the Spanish average (Spain = 1). In this stage, in order to make it easier to interpret the data provided, we will refer only to macro-regions (NUTS1) and autonomous communities (NUTS2) and a selection of years—1860, 1910, 1950, 1980 and 2015—which we will refer to as "benchmark years". The complete dataset can be found in Appendix,

[33] Wages were taken from the sources mentioned for the other economic sectors and from Rosés and Sánchez-Alonso (2004). For 1870 (given that no population census was published), the provincial values for the service sector were obtained as an average of 1860 and 1880.

which contains information on all the years that make up the dataset (rather than just a selection of decennial reference years).[34]

GDP and Population

A good place to begin would be to show the distribution of GDP in Spain for the first and last years of our study, that is, 1860 and 2015. In Fig. 3.3 the percentage for each of the seven macro-regions (NUTS1) represents the size of these economies and enables us to see their share of the national economy. This information, that is, the GDP, can be supplemented with the information on autonomous communities (NUTS2) shown in Tables 3.2 and 3.3. One of the noteworthy features is the fact that today half the national GDP is concentrated in MADRID (ES3) and EAST (ES5). In 1860 Madrid represented 5.5 per cent of national GDP, whereas this share had risen to 18.9 per cent by 2015. Meanwhile the EAST macro-region's GDP has risen from 22.6 per cent (Catalonia 12.2 per cent, Valencia 8.6 per cent and the Balearic Islands 1.8 per cent) to 30.9 per cent (Catalonia 19 per cent, Valencia 9.4 per cent and the Balearic Islands 2.5 per cent).

The shares of GDP for CENTRE (Castile-Leon, Castile-La Mancha and Extremadura) and SOUTH (Andalusia, Murcia), on the other hand, have fallen. Depopulation is a decisive factor in the first case because GDP is to a large extent related to population size, which is why Table 3.3 shows the relative weight of the autonomous communities in terms of population. In 1860, for example, about 26 per cent of Spain's population lived in the CENTRE macro-region, but by 2015 this had fallen to 12 per cent. Andalusia and Murcia, however, have maintained their relative weight in population. Indeed the weight

[34]Table A1 in the Appendix shows the NUTS1, NUTS2 and NUTS3 regions in Spain with the nomenclature currently used by Eurostat, which reproduces the official administrative nomenclature used in Spain. This nomenclature, however, is in Spanish and in some cases involves rather lengthy names (e.g. Comunidad Foral de Navarra, Principado de Asturias, Región de Murcia, Comunidad Valenciana). To simplify things we use shorter (and sometimes anglicized) versions throughout the main text when referring to the autonomous communities (i.e. Navarre, Asturias, Murcia, Valencia, etc.). The official denominations and equivalent versions we use in the text can be found in Table A2 in the Appendix.

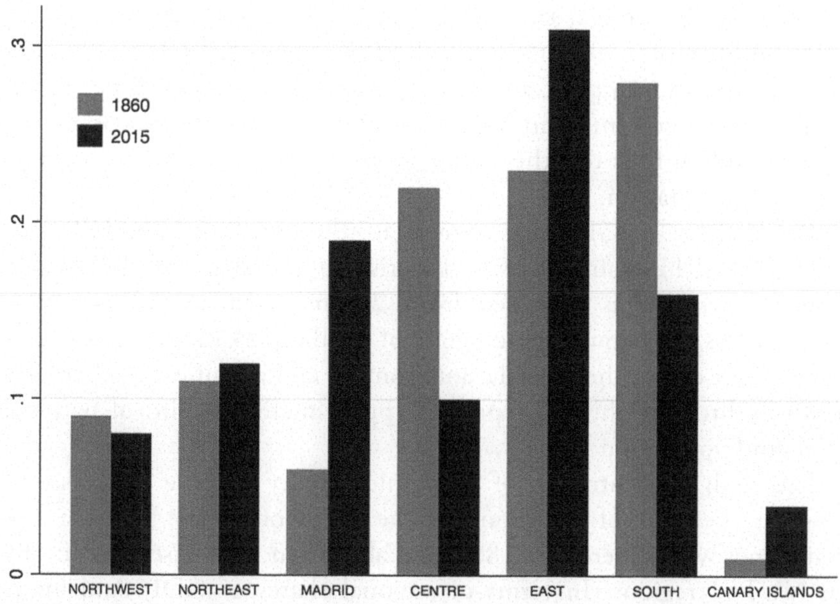

Fig. 3.3 Regional (NUTS1) shares of national GDP. Source: Main text

Table 3.2 Regional (NUTS2) GDP (%)

Region	NUTS2	1860	1910	1950	1980	2015
Galicia	ES11	5.6	6.3	6.9	6.0	5.2
Asturias	ES12	1.9	2.3	3.6	2.8	2.0
Cantabria	ES13	1.1	1.4	1.7	1.5	1.2
Basque Country	ES21	2.5	5.2	6.7	7.4	6.2
Navarre	ES22	2.0	1.4	1.6	1.7	1.7
La Rioja	ES23	1.0	0.8	0.9	0.8	0.7
Aragon	ES24	5.8	4.5	3.9	3.4	3.2
Madrid	ES30	5.5	6.7	9.6	14.8	18.9
Castile-Leon	ES41	11.4	9.5	9.5	6.2	5.0
Castile-La Mancha	ES42	7.5	6.0	5.4	3.6	3.5
Extremadura	ES43	3.4	3.3	2.9	1.7	1.6
Catalonia	ES51	12.2	20.2	17.9	19.2	19.0
Valencia	ES52	8.6	8.6	8.4	10.0	9.4
Balearic Islands	ES53	1.8	1.7	1.8	2.0	2.5
Andalusia	ES61	25.8	18.7	14.6	12.8	13.4
Murcia	ES62	2.5	2.1	2.1	2.4	2.6
Canary Islands	ES70	1.2	1.5	2.4	3.6	3.9
	Spain	**100.0**	**100.0**	**100.0**	**100.0**	**100.0**

of Andalusia is notable, as would be expected due its great size, and on both counts represents almost a fifth of the Spanish total (17 per cent of total area and 18 per cent of population). Catalonia (15 per cent), Madrid (14 per cent) and Valencia (11 per cent) are the other big regions and all four together today account for almost 60 per cent of the total population.

The weight in GDP has grown in the north (NORTHWEST, NORTHEAST) mainly due to the rise in the share of the Basque Country, which has increased from 2.5 per cent to 6.2 per cent. Nevertheless, the demographic weight of the Basque Country is still fairly low (4.7 per cent). The other 12 autonomous communities together have relatively little weight and represent approximately a third of national GDP and population.

This high concentration of economic activity that we see today is, however, the result of evolution over the course of history. We have seen that things were different in 1860, and also when we focused specifically on NUTS2 regions. In terms of regional shares of GDP, Andalusia's weight (25.8 per cent) used to be substantially greater than it is now, with levels accounting for up to a quarter of Spain's GDP. Catalonia (12.2 per cent) and Valencia (8.6 per cent) already occupied prominent positions in the past but with percentage shares smaller than today's. And the weight of Madrid (5.5 per cent) and the Basque Country (2.5 per cent) were comparatively much smaller than they are now.[35] Interestingly, these are not the only regions that stood out in 1860 because of their notable contribution to Spain's GDP. Other regions show comparable or even greater shares than those we have already mentioned, including Castile-Leon (11.4 per cent), Castile-La Mancha (7.5 per cent), Aragon (5.8 per cent) and Galicia (5.6 per cent). Table 3.3 enables us to compare these values with the relative weight of each autonomous community in terms of population.

The differences between our starting point in the mid-nineteenth century and the present would imply that different regions followed different patterns of behaviour over time. As a general illustration of

[35] The joint GDP share of these five autonomous communities in this case would have been around 55%, to a large degree due to the high participation of Andalusia in the mid-nineteenth century.

Table 3.3 Regional (NUTS2) population (%)

Region	NUTS2	1860	1910	1950	1980	2015
Galicia	ES11	11.5	10.4	9.6	7.5	5.9
Asturias	ES12	3.5	3.4	3.2	3.0	2.3
Cantabria	ES13	1.4	1.5	1.4	1.4	1.3
Basque Country	ES21	2.7	3.4	3.7	5.7	4.7
Navarre	ES22	1.9	1.6	1.4	1.4	1.4
La Rioja	ES23	1.1	0.9	0.8	0.7	0.7
Aragon	ES24	5.7	4.8	3.9	3.2	2.9
Madrid	ES30	3.1	4.4	6.5	12.4	13.8
Castile-Leon	ES41	13.3	11.9	10.3	6.9	5.3
Castile-La Mancha	ES42	7.7	7.7	7.3	4.4	4.4
Extremadura	ES43	4.5	5.0	4.9	2.9	2.4
Catalonia	ES51	10.7	10.5	11.5	15.8	16.0
Valencia	ES52	8.1	8.6	8.2	9.7	10.7
Balearic Islands	ES53	1.7	1.6	1.5	1.7	2.4
Andalusia	ES61	19.0	19.1	20.1	17.2	18.2
Murcia	ES62	2.4	3.1	2.7	2.5	3.2
Canary Islands	ES70	1.5	2.2	2.9	3.6	4.6
	Spain	**100.0**	**100.0**	**100.0**	**100.0**	**100.0**

this, we can categorize the autonomous communities into three large groups according to the evolution of their contribution to Spanish GDP. First we have a group of six regions that have increased their share over time, that is, between 1860 and 2015. Prominent among these is Madrid (up from 5.5 per cent to 18.4 per cent) with an increase that has also been continuous over time (and which, judging by its trajectory, seems likely to continue to grow in the future). There have also been substantial improvements in the cases of Catalonia (12.2 per cent to 19 per cent) and the Basque Country (2.5 per cent to 6.2 per cent), although both have experienced ups and downs at different points in time. Valencia's improvement has been more modest (8.6 per cent to 9.4 per cent), and the final additions to this group are island territories: the Balearic Islands (1.8 per cent to 2.5 per cent) and the Canary Islands (1.2 per cent to 3.9 per cent). It is interesting that, with the exception of Madrid, all the regions that make up this dynamic group that have increased their share of Spain's GDP are coastal areas, geographically on the periphery.

A second group would include those six regions whose contribution to national GDP has remained relatively stable over the last century and a half: Galicia (around 5.5 per cent), Murcia (around 2.5 per cent), Asturias and Navarre (around 2 per cent each), Cantabria (around 1.2 per cent) and the smallest region of all, La Rioja (around 1 per cent).[36] Apart from Murcia, however, over time these regions have steadily been losing demographic weight relative to Spain as a whole, as can be seen in Table 3.3.

Finally there is a group of five regions that have suffered a relative loss in their share of total Spanish GDP between 1860 and 2015. Indeed, in practically all these cases the reduction in size has been considerable, with some shares decreasing by over half. This group comprises Andalusia (down from 25.8 per cent to 13.4 per cent), Castile-Leon (11.4 per cent to 5 per cent), Castile-La Mancha (7.5 per cent to 3.5 per cent), Aragon (5.8 per cent to 3.2 per cent) and Extremadura (3.4 per cent to 1.6 per cent). In terms of population, the reduction is equally striking. With the exception of Andalusia, these are all inland regions and have not only been relatively less dynamic than other regions but have also experienced high levels of depopulation, as can be seen in Table 3.3.[37]

GDP Per Capita

Table 3.4 shows GDP per capita for the autonomous communities between 1860 and 2015 expressed in terms relative to the average for Spain (Spain = 1). A quick perusal of these figures lets us establish a comparison between the historical situation in 1860 and the current situation in 2015, leading us to pose some questions that we will try to answer in greater detail in the course of the book. For example, is inequality greater

[36] Within this group, Asturias and Cantabria are those that have probably experienced the most ups and downs in the course of their history.

[37] In fact these four regions that represented 31.2% of the population in 1860 represent only 15.3% today.

Table 3.4 Regional (NUTS2) GDP per capita (Spain = 1)

Region	NUTS2	1860	1910	1950	1980	2015
Galicia	ES11	0.48	0.61	0.72	0.80	0.89
Asturias	ES12	0.56	0.68	1.13	0.93	0.88
Cantabria	ES13	0.82	0.90	1.15	1.08	0.91
Basque Country	ES21	0.93	1.55	1.81	1.31	1.32
Navarre	ES22	1.05	0.87	1.17	1.28	1.25
La Rioja	ES23	0.90	0.87	1.12	1.16	1.09
Aragon	ES24	1.02	0.95	1.00	1.07	1.11
Madrid	ES30	1.77	1.52	1.48	1.19	1.36
Castile-Leon	ES41	0.85	0.80	0.92	0.90	0.94
Castile-La Mancha	ES42	0.97	0.78	0.74	0.82	0.78
Extremadura	ES43	0.75	0.66	0.60	0.58	0.69
Catalonia	ES51	1.14	1.93	1.56	1.21	1.19
Valencia	ES52	1.06	1.00	1.02	1.03	0.88
Balearic Islands	ES53	1.05	1.01	1.21	1.14	1.04
Andalusia	ES61	1.36	0.98	0.72	0.75	0.74
Murcia	ES62	1.03	0.67	0.77	0.95	0.81
Canary Islands	ES70	0.79	0.65	0.83	1.00	0.85
	Spain	**1.00**	**1.00**	**1.00**	**1.00**	**1.00**

Source: Main text

today than it was in the past? Is Spain more territorially unequal? If we look at the extremes, we see that the richest region today is twice as wealthy as the poorest (GDP per capita for Madrid is 1.9 times that of Extremadura), while in 1860 the richest region was three times wealthier than the poorest (in this case Madrid was 3.6 times richer than Galicia). The distance between the extremes has therefore shrunk. If we take all the regions together and construct a basic statistical indicator of dispersion such as the coefficient of variation, the results point in the same direction and show less regional inequality in the present (0.20) than in the mid-nineteenth century (0.30).[38] The extremes and comparisons between the starting and finishing points of the study are not the only areas of interest, though. Finding out about the journey from the point of origin to the present is one of the tasks of economic history, and to a large degree it is what we will be doing throughout the rest of the book.

[38] The coefficient of variation, which measures the relationship between the statistical average and the standard deviation, takes on values between 0 and 1. A value of 0 would indicate an absence of dispersion or inequality, and the more it increases, the more it reflects inequality.

Another interesting aspect of Table 3.4 is that we can see how individual regions evolve over time. Have things remained the same or have regions seen changes in their relative positions? In other words, have today's rich regions always been rich? Have the poor ones always been poor? Can we see any histories of success or failure in connection with reversals of fortune? And if we can, when did they happen? The results seem to indicate a certain amount of stability as regards the positions the regions have occupied. Among the rich regions, we see the continuous presence of Madrid, Navarre and Catalonia in both 1860 and 2015, while among the poor, Extremadura and the Canary Islands always seem to hover around the bottom of the ranking. However, the data show at least two clear examples that would point to reversals of fortune. The most obvious case is probably the marked decline of Andalusia, which has gone from being one of the leaders in 1860, occupying second position in terms of GDP per capita (1.36 relative to the Spanish average of 1.00), to being one of the stragglers today (0.74). The Basque Country, on the other hand, starting from a point below the Spanish average (0.93), has managed to transform itself into one of the regions with the highest income per capita in Spain (1.32). Detecting whether something is mobile or stable over time is one of the keys to analysing regional inequality, as is being able to detect when inequality may have become more extreme.

Finally, this first approach to the data on GDP per capita lets us highlight some elements of the economic geography of inequality in Spain. Today's differences follow a definite north-south pattern, or, to be more precise—as we mentioned in the introduction—they indicate the existence of a geographical pattern whereby the richest regions are located within a triangle in the north-east of the Iberian Peninsula with its vertices in Catalonia, Madrid and the Basque Country. This pattern was slightly different in 1860, partly due to the presence among the richest regions of Andalusia, the southernmost region of the Spanish mainland, and partly due to the relatively more prominent position of the Mediterranean arc in the east of Spain. As for the poorest regions, which today are mainly located in the south of Spain and close to the border with Portugal, the geographical pattern of the mid-nineteenth century more obviously included the north-western area of Spain (Galicia, Asturias and Cantabria). This being the case, at what point did the spatial structure of today's regional inequality take shape? What were the key stages in history? How quickly did the north-east of the peninsula take shape and establish itself as the area with the highest levels of income per capita? And importantly, taking all these aspects into account, is Spain a unique case or are the characteristics and evolution of regional inequality comparable to other countries in southern Europe? The comparative analysis we carry out that takes into account the nearby countries of France, Italy and Portugal may help provide answers to these questions.

Naturally these introductory paragraphs can serve only to briefly set out some of the aspects of regional inequality in Spain and its long-term evolution, based on a study of the new dataset of GDP and per-capita GDP we present here. And to pose questions. The purpose of these lines is therefore to set the stage for the analysis of regional inequality that we develop in the course of the following chapters.

References

Álvarez Llano, R. (1986). Evolución de la estructura económica regional de España en la historia: una aproximación. *Situación, 1*, 5–61.

Álvarez-Nogal, C., & Prados de la Escosura, L. (2007). The decline of Spain (1500–1850): Conjectural estimates. *European Review of Economic History, 11*(3), 319–366.

Alcaide Inchausti, J. (2003). *Evolución económica de las regiones y provincias españolas en el siglo XX*. Bilbao: Fundación BBVA.

Andrés Álvarez, V., et al. (1962). *Tabla input-output de la economía española. Año de, 1958*. Madrid: Organización Sindical Española.

Anuario Estadístico de España. (n.d.). Madrid.

Bazot, G. (2014). Interregional inequalities, convergence, and growth in France from 1840 to 1911. *Annals of Economics and Statistics*, (113/114), 309–345.

BBV. (1999). *Renta Nacional de España y su distribución provincial. Serie homogénea. Años 1955 a 1993 y avances 1994 a 1997* (Vol. I–II). Bilbao: Fundación BBV.

Betrán, C. (1999). Difusión y localización industrial en España durante el primer tercio del siglo XX. *Revista de Historia Económica, 17*(3), 663–696.

Bringas Gutiérrez, M. A. (2000). *La productividad de los factores en la agricultura española (1752–1935)*. Banco de España.

Carreras, A. (1983). *La producció industrial espanyola i italiana des de mitjan segle XIX fins a l'actualitat*. Ph.D. dissertation, Universitat Autònoma de Barcelona.

Carreras, A. (1990). Fuentes y datos para el análisis regional de la industrialización española. In A. Carreras & J. Nadal (Eds.), *Pautas regionales de la industrialización española (siglos XIX y XX)* (pp. 3–20). Barcelona: Ariel.

Caruana-Galizia, P. (2013). Estimating French regional income: Departmental per capita gross value added, 1872–1911. *Research in Economic History, 29*, 71–95.

Censo de Población. (n.d.). Madrid.

Crafts, N. F. R. (2005). Regional GDP in Britain, 1871–1911: Some estimates. *Scottish Journal of Political Economy, 52*(1), 54–64.

Díez-Minguela, A., Martinez-Galarraga, J., & Tirado, D. A. (2016). Why did Spanish regions not converge before the Civil War? Agglomeration economies and (regional) growth revisited. *Revista de Historia Económica/Journal of Iberian and Latin American Economic History, 39*(4), 417–448.

Domínguez, R. (2002). *La riqueza de las regiones. Las desigualdades económicas regionales en España, 1700–2000*. Madrid: Alianza.

Easterlin, R. A. (1957). State income estimates. In S. Kuznets & D. S. Thomas (Eds.), *Population redistribution and economic growth, United States, 1870–1950, vol. 1, Methodological considerations and reference tables*. Philadelphia: American Philosophical Society.

Easterlin, R. A. (1960). Interregional differences in per capita income, population, and total income, 1840–1950. In NBER (Ed.), *Trends in the American economy in the nineteenth century. Studies in income and wealth* (Vol. 24). Princeton, NJ: Princeton University Press.

Esposto, A. G. (1997). Estimating regional per capita income: Italy, 1861–1914. *Journal of European Economic History, 26*, 585–604.

Estadística Administrativa de la Contribución Industrial y de Comercio. (n.d.). Madrid.

Estadística Minera y Metalúrgica. (n.d.). Madrid.

Foro Hispánico de Cultura. (1957). *La población activa española de 1950 a 1957*. Madrid.

Fukao, K., Bassino, J. P., Makino, T., Papryzycki, R., Settsu, T., Takashima, M., & Tokui, J. (2015). *Regional inequality and industrial structure in Japan: 1874–2008*. Tokyo: Maruzen.

Geary, F., & Stark, T. (2002). Examining Ireland's post-famine economic growth performance. *The Economic Journal, 112*, 919–935.

GEHR—Grupo de Estudios de Historia Rural. (1991). *Estadísticas históricas de la producción agraria española, 1859–1935*. Madrid: Ministerio de Agricultura, Pesca y Alimentación.

Germán Zubero, L., Llopis, E., Maluquer, J., & Zapata, S. (Eds.). (2001). *Historia económica regional de España, siglos XIX y XX*. Barcelona: Crítica.

Gollin, D. (2002). Getting income shares right. *Journal of Political Economy, 110*(21), 458–474.

Good, D. (1994). The economic lag of Central and Eastern Europe: Income estimates for the Habsburg successor states, 1870–1910. *Journal of Economic History, 54*(4), 869–891.

Herranz, A. (2008). *Infraestructuras y crecimiento económico en España (1850–1935)*. Madrid: Fundación de los Ferrocarriles Españoles.

Instituto Geográfico y Estadístico. (1903). *Estadística de la emigración e inmigración de España, 1896–1900*. Madrid: Ministerio de Instrucción Pública y Bellas Artes.

Kuznets, S. (1966). *Modern economic growth: Rate, structure, and spread*. New Haven, CT: Yale University Press.

Kuznets, S. (1971). *Economic growth of nations: Total output and production structure*. Cambridge, MA: Harvard University Press.

Llopis, E. (Ed.). (2004). *El legado económico del Antiguo Régimen en España*. Barcelona: Crítica.

Madrazo, S. (1984). *El sistema de transportes en España, 1750–1850*. Madrid: Turner.

Martín, M. (1992). Pautas y tendencias de desarrollo económico regional en España: una visión retrospectiva. In J. L. García Delgado & A. Pedreño (Eds.), *Ejes territoriales de desarrollo: España en la Europa de los noventa* (pp. 133–155). Madrid: Colegio de Economistas de Madrid.

Ministerio de Trabajo, Comercio e Industria. (1927). *Estadística de salarios y jornadas de trabajo referida al período 1914–1925*. Madrid.

Ministerio de Trabajo y Previsión. (1931). *Estadística de salarios y jornadas de trabajo referida al período 1914–1930*. Madrid.

Nadal, J., & Tafunell, X. (1992). *Sant Martí de Provençals, pulmó industrial de Barcelona (1847–1992)*. Barcelona: Columna.

Nicolau, R. (2005). Población, salud y actividad. In A. Carreras & X. Tafunell (Eds.), *Estadísticas históricas de España: siglos XIX–XX* (pp. 77–154). Bilbao: Fundación BBVA.

Parejo, A. (2001). Industrialización, desindustrialización y nueva industrialización de las regiones españolas (1950–2000). Un enfoque desde la historia económica. *Revista de Historia Industrial*, (19–20), 15–75.

Prados de la Escosura, L. (2003). *El progreso económico de España 1850–2000*. Bilbao: Fundación BBVA.

Prados de la Escosura, L. (2016). *Spain's historical national accounts: Expenditure and output, 1850–2015*. EHES Working Papers in Economic History, No 103.

Prados de la Escosura, L. (2017). *Spanish economic growth, 1850–2015*. Palgrave Studies in Economic History, Palgrave Macmillan.

Reher, D. S. (1994). Ciudades, procesos de urbanización y sistemas urbanos en la Península Ibérica, 1550–1991. In M. Guàrdia, F. J. Monclús, & J. L. Oyón (Eds.), *Atlas histórico de las ciudades europeas. Península Ibérica* (pp. 1–30). Barcelona: Salvat—Centre de Cultura Contemporània de Barcelona.

Rosés, J. R., Martinez-Galarraga, J., & Tirado, D. A. (2010). The upswing of regional income inequality in Spain (1860–1930). *Explorations in Economic History, 47*(2), 244–257.

Rosés, J. R., & Sánchez-Alonso, B. (2004). Regional wage convergence in Spain 1850–1930. *Explorations in Economic History, 41*(4), 404–425.

Sánchez Alonso, B. (1995). *Las causas de la emigración española 1880–1930*. Madrid: Alianza Editorial.

Silvestre, J. (2003). *Migraciones interiores y mercado de trabajo en España, 1877–1936*. Ph.D. dissertation, Universidad de Zaragoza.

Simpson, J. (1994). La producción y la productividad agraria española, 1890–1936. *Revista de Historia Económica, 12*(1), 43–84.

Simpson, J. (1995). Real wages and labour mobility in Spain, 1860–1936. In P. Scholliers & V. Zamagni (Eds.), *Labour reward* (pp. 182–200). London: Edward Elgar.

Williamson, J. G. (1965). Regional inequality and the process of national development: A description of the patterns. *Economic Development and Cultural Change, 13*(4), 1–84.

4

Regional Income Inequality in Spain 1860–2015

According to data provided by the INE, income per capita for 2015 in Madrid, the richest autonomous community or NUTS2 region in Spain, was practically double that of the poorest, Extremadura. Since this is the territorial inequality that Spanish society has to face today, it would be reasonable to ask ourselves how it came about, how it evolved over the long term and what the current dominant trend is. These questions will be answered in the course of this chapter as we analyse how regional economic inequality evolved from 1860 to 2015, that is, over the complete trajectory of Spanish economic growth from its origins almost to the present. In particular we aim to identify the existence of a number of major stages in its evolution, and for this we employ indicators frequently used in the empirical literature on economic growth. These types of indicators have been used as tools for the empirical analysis of what is known as economic convergence between countries or between the regions of a single country (Barro and Sala-i-Martin 1991, 1992).

The concept of economic convergence refers to the hypothesis derived from certain models of economic growth theory, according to which, if countries (or regions) differ only in their level of initial per-capita income, in the real world we should observe a higher rate of growth in the poor economies than in the rich ones. The economic foundation for

A. Díez-Minguela et al., *Regional Inequality in Spain*, Palgrave Studies in Economic History, https://doi.org/10.1007/978-3-319-96110-1_4

this popular hypothesis is fairly intuitive. Given that the growth rate of per-capita income is directly related to the growth rate of per-capita capital, if it is believed that there are diminishing returns in the use of this production factor, it is deduced that a negative relation should arise between the initial income of an economy and its rate of long-term growth.[1]

The empirical analysis of whether or not this hypothesis is correct has given rise to the appearance of two definitions of convergence: β-convergence and σ-convergence. We say there is β-convergence if the poor economies grow more quickly than the rich ones, or, to put it another way, we would say there is β-convergence among a set of economies if there is an inverse relationship between the growth rate of income per inhabitant and its initial level. This concept is related to the concept of σ-convergence. We say there is σ-convergence if, given a set of economies, the dispersion or inequality in terms of income per inhabitant tends to decrease over time.

With this type of approach, the contribution of new evidence for the Spanish economy means we can try to determine the major stages in the evolution of territorial inequality within the framework of whether or not the hypotheses derived from the neoclassical growth literature are correct. This will serve to illustrate when exactly the factors highlighted in this body of literature as being determinants in the evolution of inequality have allowed the distance between regions in terms of per-capita income to close and when exactly those forces favouring the growth of inequality have predominated. Studying whether or not the β-convergence hypothesis is correct will also make it possible to identify which territories have followed growth trajectories further from the norm and to establish hypotheses as to why they have done so.

In presenting the evidence we have chosen to deal with different levels of territorial disaggregation. We provide information in connection with the highest level, that is, provinces (NUTS3), but where necessary we also provide indicators constructed on the basis of autonomous communities (NUTS2) or macro-regions (NUTS1). This is so we can extract as

[1] Under growth accounting, per-capita income growth results from labour productivity growth and changes in the labour force with respect to the total population. With this line of thinking, efficiency gains and capital deepening seem to be the main engines of labour productivity growth. In a world of diminishing returns, β-convergence may then arise.

much information as possible about the evolution of regional inequality and also analyse whether the results obtained are robust for the different territorial scales used in the analysis.

Finally, in our presentation of the results we refer to the major stages of the Spanish economy's development and integration process, defined on the basis of the historical economic evolution of Spain and other nearby countries. The chronology is broken down into four broad time segments—1860–1910, 1910–1950, 1950–1980 and 1980–2015—which correspond to the four major stages into which contemporary European economic history is usually divided and which to a large extent also serve as turning points in the progress of the Spanish economy as a whole. The first stage (1860–1910) roughly corresponds to the period before the First World War known in the international literature as the first globalization; the second (1910–1950) covers the interwar years; the third (1950–1980) corresponds to the Golden Age that followed the Second World War and came to an end with the oil crises of the 1970s; and the fourth and final stage (1980–2015) covers recent decades characterized by a new period of globalization and the technological revolution associated with information and communication technologies (ICT).

What Do We Know About the Evolution of Regional Economic Inequality in Spain?

The evolution of regional economic inequality in Spain has been well documented since 1955 thanks to the biannual series on regional income published by the Banco Bilbao Vizcaya (BBV 1999). In addition to this, since 1980 annual data based on Spanish regional accounting have been published by the National Statistics Institute. Both sources of information have been used in a great many studies on regional inequality, most of which have focused on analysing per-capita income.

Papers such as those by Mas et al. (1994) and De la Fuente (1996), among many others, have generally followed Barro and Sala-i-Martin's (1991) widely known methodology and obtained results that point to the existence of convergence (both β and σ) from 1955 to the 1970s, meaning that between those years there was a definite decrease in regional inequalities. According to these authors, the way the Spanish economy developed during the second half of Franco's dictatorship was driven by structural change and interregional migrations, which created the conditions that would favour a large reduction in territorial differences in per-capita income.

More recent papers, however, have extended the timescale of the analysis up to the end of the twentieth century and indicate that regional disparities in per-capita income in Spain passed through two clearly defined periods between 1980 and 2000. The first of these, which corresponded to the 1980s, saw a moderate reduction in disparities, with the highest degree of convergence being reached in 1988. From that year onwards and during the first half of the 1990s regional disparities very gradually began to grow; then in the second half they remained virtually stable (one might say stagnant). In the end the level of regional disparities in 2000 barely differed from the level of 1980, and so these papers conclude that the convergence process was very weak, if not non-existent, during these two decades (De la Fuente 2002; Cuadrado-Roura et al. 1999; Villaverde and Sánchez-Robles 2002; Tortosa-Ausina et al. 2005; Villaverde 2007; Cuadrado-Roura 2010). In other words, the economic progress that Spain experienced after it joined the European Union in 1986 was unaccompanied by any significant reduction in territorial inequalities.

As explained earlier, data on the geographical distribution of GDP for the period pre-1955 are scarce and therefore the study of regional economic inequality over the long term has been particularly difficult. Álvarez Llano (1986) provided regional GDP data for the nineteenth century and the early decades of the twentieth, but the reliability of his figures has been called into question because he did not explain the methodology he used in the estimations. Nevertheless, Carreras (1990) used these figures in an early attempt to analyse the evolution of regional inequality in Spain from a historical perspective. He found that it had followed a constant upward trend since 1800, reaching a peak around 1950 or 1960. Regional disparities then began to decrease, with inequality at a lower level in 1983 than it had been at the starting date of the study almost two centuries before.

More recently, however, new estimations of regional per-capita income for the period 1860–1930 have challenged this early view and pointed to the beginning of the twentieth century as the start of regional convergence in Spain (Rosés et al. 2010; Martinez-Galarraga et al. 2015; Díez-Minguela et al. 2016). Rosés et al. (2010) explored inequality in per-capita GDP for Spanish NUTS2 regions between the mid-nineteenth century and the 1930s. Using a battery of indicators, the authors found that the trend was towards increased inequality between 1860 and 1930. Their work would therefore indicate an absence of convergence among Spanish regions throughout the early stages of the economic growth process, with regional inequality reaching higher values before the Civil War (1936–1939) than at the start of the economic growth process in the mid-nineteenth century.

Research carried out to date identifies lengthy periods during which the trend was for territorial inequality to grow, other periods during which the tendency was for differences between regions with varying degrees of development to decrease, and yet others during which little variation in territorial inequalities was observed. This would mean that inequality did not follow a monotonic trend throughout the economic development process in Spain. In order to study this hypothesis in greater depth, we next use the dataset presented in the previous chapter to create a homogeneous overall picture of the evolution of territorial inequality for the period 1860–2015, that is, over the complete trajectory of economic growth in Spain.

How Has Regional Economic Inequality Evolved?

In order to visualize the evolution of regional inequality we constructed three indicators on different scales of territorial aggregation.[2] First to be calculated were the values for the simple coefficient of variation (SCV), an indicator widely used in the empirical literature on σ-convergence. It is defined as

[2] We also calculated other indices frequently used in the literature on inequality—the Gini index and the variance of logarithms, for example—and obtained results similar to those detailed here.

$$\mathrm{SCV} = \sqrt{\sum_{i=1}^{n}\left(\frac{y_i}{y_m} - 1\right)^2} \tag{4.1}$$

where y is per-capita GDP, i and m are regional and national values, respectively, and N is the total number of regions.

Second, in order to find out whether the biggest regions have followed a significantly different trajectory from the average, we calculated the weighted coefficient of variation (WCV), also known as the Williamson (1965, p. 11) index. This is calculated as

$$\mathrm{WCV} = \sqrt{\sum_{i=1}^{n}\left(\frac{y_i}{y_m} - 1\right)^2 \times \frac{p_i}{p_m}} \tag{4.2}$$

where y and p are per-capita GDP and population, respectively, i and m are the regional and national values, respectively, and n is the total number of regions.

And third, we decided to calculate an additional indicator of territorial inequality known as the Theil index. The reason for this was that one of its characteristics is that it enables data to be broken down, and we will make use of this later when we look at the determinants of territorial inequality. It is calculated as

$$T = 1/N\sum_{i=1}^{n}\frac{y_i}{y_m} \times \ln\left(\frac{y_i}{y_m}\right) \tag{4.3}$$

where y is again per-capita GDP, i and m are regional and national values, respectively, and N is the total number of regions considered.

Table 4.1 summarizes the results obtained for the benchmark years we have used to divide the economic development process into major stages. It shows the values calculated for the SCV, the WCV and the Theil index along with the maximum and minimum inequality ratios based on information on per-capita income levels for NUTS3 and NUTS2 regions in Spain.

Table 4.1 σ-convergence in Spain 1860–2015

Year	SCV	WCV	Max/min RATIO	Theil index
NUTS3—provinces				
1860	0.322	0.363	8.5	0.05
1910	0.400	0.478	5.3	0.07
1950	0.339	0.367	3.6	0.05
1980	0.244	0.213	2.9	0.03
2015	0.219	0.232	2.3	0.02
NUTS2—regions				
1860	0.301	0.299	3.7	0.04
1910	0.379	0.391	3.2	0.06
1950	0.313	0.341	3.0	0.04
1980	0.198	0.201	2.3	0.02
2015	0.209	0.228	2.0	0.02

Source: See main text

When we look at the figures in the table, the first thing that draws our attention is that territorial inequality in 2015 is lower than it was at the start of the economic development process in Spain in 1860. And this result is very robust. Regardless of the inequality indicator considered (SCV, SCW or Theil index) or the level of territorial disaggregation used in the calculation (NUTS2 or NUTS3), the value for 2015 is clearly lower than the value recorded for 1860.

At the same time it can also be derived from the figures in the table that changes in the level of territorial inequality have not followed a continuous downward trend between 1860 and 2015. Such continuity is only seen in the trajectory followed by the ratio between maximum and minimum levels of GDP per capita. The temporal evolution of the values calculated for the other indicators shows a marked increase in territorial inequality between 1860 and 1910, and this occurs independently of the level of territorial aggregation used. This means that any index of dispersion that takes into account the distribution as a whole indicates that territorial economic inequality in Spain increased during the first stage of the economic growth process, although this takes place in a context in which the distance between the distribution extremes may have decreased.

This trend changes from 1910 onwards. A new stage opened up in which a tendency for a continuous reduction in territorial economic inequality predominated, and this lasted throughout the periods

1910–1950 and 1950–1980. Here we are talking about a long period in which the hypothesis that emerged from neoclassical growth models, the σ-convergence, is proved correct. However, this statement needs to be qualified insofar as the rate at which territorial inequality decreases, at least if we follow the evolution of the values calculated for the SCW and the WCV, is higher during the period 1950–1980 than it is during the period 1910–1950. To put it another way, if we place ourselves within the framework provided by national economic history, we would agree that inequality decreased more markedly during the years of stability and growth under Franco's policy of economic development (desarrollismo) than it did during the highly unstable period that stretches from the First World War to the end of autarky, which includes the Great Depression of the 1930s and the Spanish Civil War.

The values calculated for the benchmark years 1980 and 2015 indicate a new change in trend. The higher values for some of the indices of dispersion would suggest that the hypothesis of σ-convergence between Spanish regions does not hold as far as this period is concerned. At least this is the dynamic we observe in the values calculated for the SCW and WCV indices constructed in line with territorial disaggregation at a NUTS2 level and the values for the WCV using data for NUTS3 regions. This means that the stage that begins with the Spanish economy's access to the EU and ends with the recovery of per-capita output levels after the Great Recession of 2008 is characterized by an increase in territorial inequalities.

It is possible to derive another element that merits consideration from the figures shown in Table 4.1, this being that the values calculated for the weighted index of inequality (WCV) tend to be higher than those for the unweighted index (SCW). This type of behaviour might indicate that the income levels recorded for the most populated territories in Spain are usually further from the average (and, as we will see later, often above it) than those for the least populated. This is an aspect that appears to merit special attention if we want to understand what has happened with regional inequality in Spain over recent decades.

In order to be even more precise with the timeline of territorial inequality in Spain as measured using different σ-convergence indices and to take advantage of all the information generated by our new dataset,

Figs. 4.1, 4.2 and 4.3 sketch out its evolution by presenting the results calculated for the different indicators in ten-year intervals between 1860 and 1940 and in five-year intervals from 1945 to 2015. Figure 4.1 shows regional income inequality in Spain at NUTS2 level between 1860 and 2015 using the values calculated for the SCW, WCV and Theil indices. The points marked on the graph show the values obtained and the lines sketch out how they change following a polynomial trend. To make comparison easier, all the indicators have been normalized at 1860 = 100.

As far as the points marked, that is, the values calculated, are concerned, we see that the levels of inequality estimated for the period 1860–1930 vary greatly, especially those for 1920. As we explained in the previous chapter, the reconstruction of data for territorial GDP per capita is subject to limitations deriving from the quality of the information available. Another limitation derives from the fact that in that particular year, 1920, the Spanish economy suffered serious fluctuations as a result of the First World War.

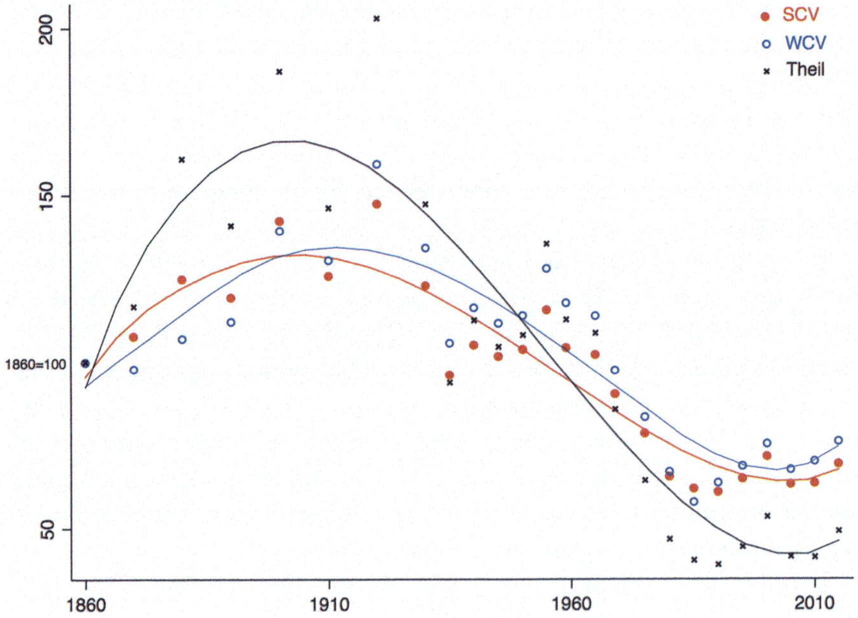

Fig. 4.1 Regional (NUTS2) per-capita income inequality in Spain (SCV, WCV, Theil) 1860–2015. Notes: 1860 = 100. Source: See main text

As for visible trends, the evidence presented in the graph confirms the non-monotonic evolution of regional income inequality over the course of these 155 years. We can see an upward trend that stretches from 1860 to 1920, the year in which all the indicators register their absolute maximum for the series. From then on, convergence across Spanish provinces predominates. However, this downward trend is particularly continuous and strong only between 1955 and the 1980s. The reason for this is that two strong fluctuations can be observed during the period 1910–1955. There is a dramatic reduction in inequality between 1930 and 1940, which might be explained by the decrease in average per-capita income in the context of the Great Depression and the Spanish Civil War. This is followed by the gradual recovery of the levels recorded in 1930, which continues up to 1955.

What can generally be considered a continuous reduction in levels of regional inequality came to a halt in the 1980s. From then on all indicators show a notable change in trend. The WCV values reach their absolute minimum in 1985, and those for the SCW and the Theil index in 1990. Since then they all show an increase in inequality as far as 2015. From a historical perspective it could be argued that the adjustment that the Spanish economy underwent as a result of the crisis of the 1970s, which in the case of Spain continued until the mid-1980s, and membership of the EU in 1986 marked the beginning of a new stage in which territorial inequality again starts to rise.

In short, if we view developments in terms of the tendencies observed in the lines sketched out by the three indicators, regional economic inequality in Spain has not followed a monotonic trend. Indeed, the changes would broadly correspond with the major stages marking the economic development process in Spain, that is, an increase in inequality in its early stages (1860–1910), stability and strong fluctuations (1910–1950), strong convergence and accelerated growth (1950–1980), and rising inequality as growth slows down (1980–2015). In other words, the trend in Spain has been for territorial inequality to mark out an inverted U-shape over time. However, the story of this trend does not finish when it reaches the end of this inverted U. It draws a picture of stagnation that could give rise to a change in trend, which means we might be witnessing the start of a turning point marking a new stage in which regional inequality again increases.

Figure 4.2 provides more noteworthy information in that the trends in the long-term evolution of regional income inequality are very similar for both NUTS2 and NUTS3. While the economic geography literature has stressed the importance of dealing with different spatial scales, in the case of Spain at least, the pictures that emerge at provincial and regional levels are very similar.[3] These main trends also appear when we consider alternative inequality indicators like the SCW or Theil indices, which are not plotted in this graph. So regardless of the territorial scale considered, the picture of inequality over time is similar to that sketched out earlier.

A serious difficulty in the literature is within-country comparisons. Supply-side indicators such as GDP make it possible for researchers to study the processes of labour productivity convergence or divergence.

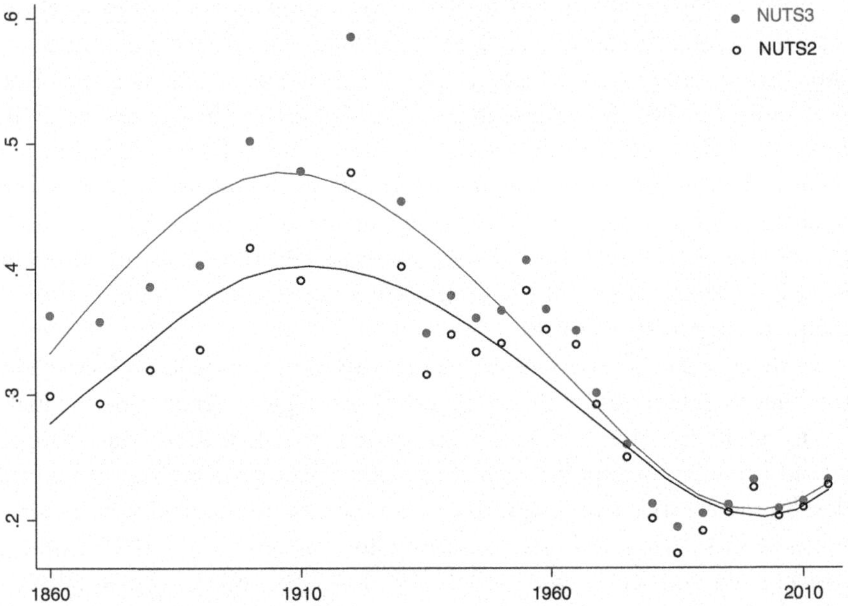

Fig. 4.2 Regional (NUTS2 v. NUTS3) per-capita income inequality in Spain (WCV) 1860–2015. Source: See main text

[3] Yamamoto (2008) deals with the issue of multiple spatial scales, using different territorial definitions in the analysis of the regional trajectories of spatial income inequality in the US.

But when per-capita GDP is used as a measure of living standards, interregional comparisons need to account for the existence of spatial price variation. In the absence of data on prices, nominal GDP has generally been adjusted using a national deflator which, in the presence of regional price variation, can bias interregional comparisons of per-capita income. Using a national deflator is still common practice today. Indeed Eurostat publishes annual regional data in terms of purchasing power standards (PPS), which are constructed at country level.[4]

In order to deal with any potential bias that might be generated by not taking spatial differences in prices into account, we have analysed the relationship between prices and income per inhabitant. In international economics it is generally accepted that there is a positive correlation between prices and income across countries, but this relationship has not been studied as much at regional level. In Spain, information on regional (NUTS3) prices and per-capita income between 2000 and 2010 has been published in the *Balance económico regional (autonomías y provincias). Años 2000 a 2010* (Alcaide-Guindo 2011), and it is on the basis of this that we estimate the linear relationship between prices and income per inhabitant using ordinary least squares in line with the following expression:

$$\ln(P_i) = \delta + \gamma . \ln(y_i) + \upsilon_i \tag{4.4}$$

$$\overline{P} = \sum_{i=1}^{n} \omega_i \times P_i = 1 \tag{4.5}$$

where P_i and y_i are the price level and nominal per-capita GDP of region i, and υ_i is the standard error term. National price level $\overline{P}$ is a weighted average of regional price levels. The results show that price-income elasticity varies between 0.128 and 0.233. In a similar vein using historical

[4]The EU acknowledges the importance of purchasing power parities (PPPs) (Regulation (EC) No 1445/2007). Eurostat requires spatial adjustment factors every six years to calculate PPPs using prices collected in various locations in each member state.

price information from the Instituto de Reformas Sociales, Gómez-Tello et al. (2018) have estimated provincial price levels in early twentieth-century Spain. Given this information and the historical estimates of per-capita GDP, price-income elasticity appears to be somewhat similar. Therefore, if we assume that the relation between prices and income per inhabitant is linear and constant, we can estimate regional prices for each period. Figure 4.3 enables us to compare the lines sketched using values calculated for the WCV based on regional nominal GDP data and values obtained based on GDP adjusted by regional prices as explained above, between 1860 and 2010.

Generally speaking, the long-term dynamics are fairly similar and dispersion is low. The graph in Fig. 4.3 thus reinforces the previous findings presented in Figs. 4.1 and 4.2. The evolution of regional inequality

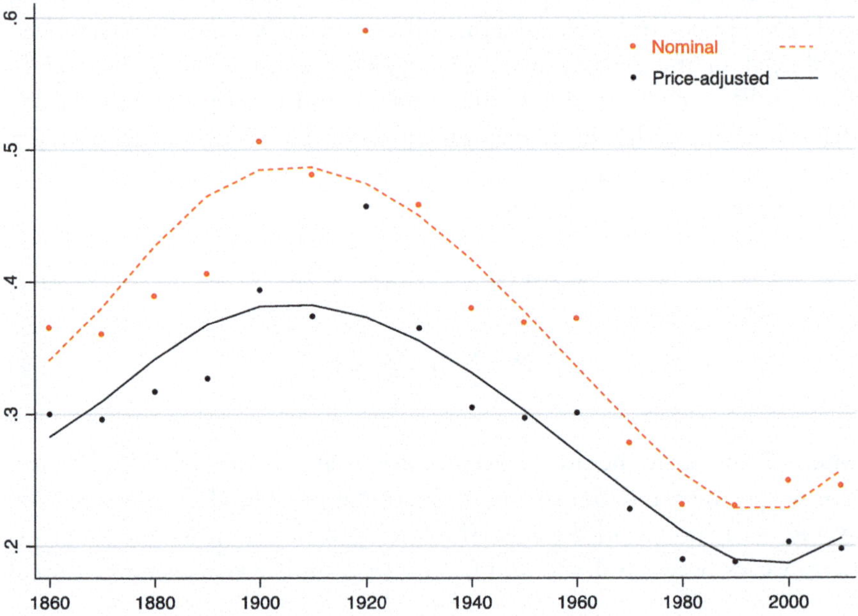

Fig. 4.3 Regional income inequality in Spain, 1860–2010. Note: Regional (NUTS3) prices are estimated using the parameters $\left(\hat{\delta},\hat{\gamma}\right)$ obtained for 2005 (3.712; 0.191). Price-income elasticity (0.191) therefore ranges between the minimum (0.128) and maximum (0.233) found. Source: See main text

exhibited an inverted U-shape between 1860 and 1980. However, since 1980 we see the beginnings of a new increase in inequality which is robust to the consideration of regional price differences and therefore appears to affect regional standards of living in the same way.

Is There a Relationship Between Initial Per-capita Income and Regional Growth Rates?

A complementary approach to σ-convergence methodology for investigating regional convergence processes is based on growth regressions in which the growth rate of per-capita income between two periods is explained by the initial level of per-capita income. A negative correlation between these implies a tendency for poor regions to catch up with rich ones. The convergence concept associated with these regressions is known as β-convergence.

Figure 4.4 relates the levels of regional (NUTS3) per-capita income in 1860 with the average annual cumulative growth rates for the same regions for the entire period 1860–2015. Each point shows this relationship for one Spanish province. To make it easier to interpret, the graph shows all the provinces belonging to the same macro-regions (NUTS1) using points of the same shape and colour. The exercise was carried out using data for nominal GDP per capita and its corresponding growth rate, and given that the GDP is nominal, the growth rates for each province include changes in prices. However, the absence of time series for prices in each province (NUTS3) prevents us from considering them in this analysis.

It can be seen from the information in Fig. 4.4 that the trend was for the poorer regions in 1860 to grow faster than the richer ones over the next 155 years (i.e. from 1860 to 2015). The value of R^2 is 0.6874, which would indicate that this relationship is significant. In line with other research, β-convergence appears to be strong during our period of study, which means that Spanish regions have undergone a process of β-convergence over the long term. However, further analysis is required (see Chap. 7) before we can know whether per-capita income growth is higher or lower as a result of economics, demographics or both.

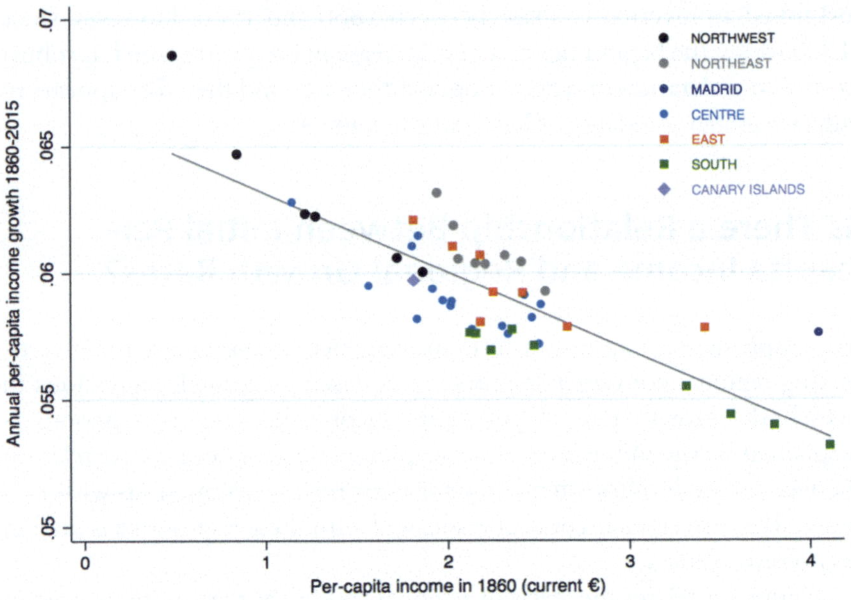

Fig. 4.4 *β*-convergence in Spain, 1860–2015. Notes: $R^2 = 0.6874$; $N = 49$. Source: See main text

Nevertheless, identifying the points representing the various regions enables us to make some additional observations. In 1860 regions with very high levels of per-capita income coexisted alongside others with markedly lower levels. And we can observe that the initially poor regions include a number of provinces in Galicia belonging to the NORTHWEST macro-region that have had a tendency to grow at above-average rate and thus converge with the average income for Spain.

However, among the provinces that were initially rich there are two different dynamics to be found. On the one hand, Madrid (MADRID) and Barcelona (EAST) have had much higher growth rates than would normally correspond to their initial levels of income, and this is why they have consolidated their privileged starting position in the course of these 155 years. And on the other, some Andalusian provinces (SOUTH) have had growth rates much lower—below the Spanish average—than should correspond to them given their initial income per capita, and the trend has therefore been for them to lose their privileged starting position over the long term. This type of evidence points to the existence of stories of relative success or failure among regions that have affected the relative positions they occupied among all the regions of Spain. This is an important element that is not normally considered in the literature on economic convergence, and we will look at it in more detail in Chap. 5.

In any case, it was deduced from the analysis of the temporal evolution of territorial inequality that this evolution did not follow a homogeneous trajectory over the entire period 1860–2015. In fact it followed a pattern that varied over the four periods into which we have divided the contemporary economic history of Spain: 1860–1910, 1910–1950, 1950–1980 and 1980–2015. Thus Fig. 4.5 presents new evidence as to whether or not the β-convergence hypothesis holds, but in this case distinguishing between the four relevant periods.

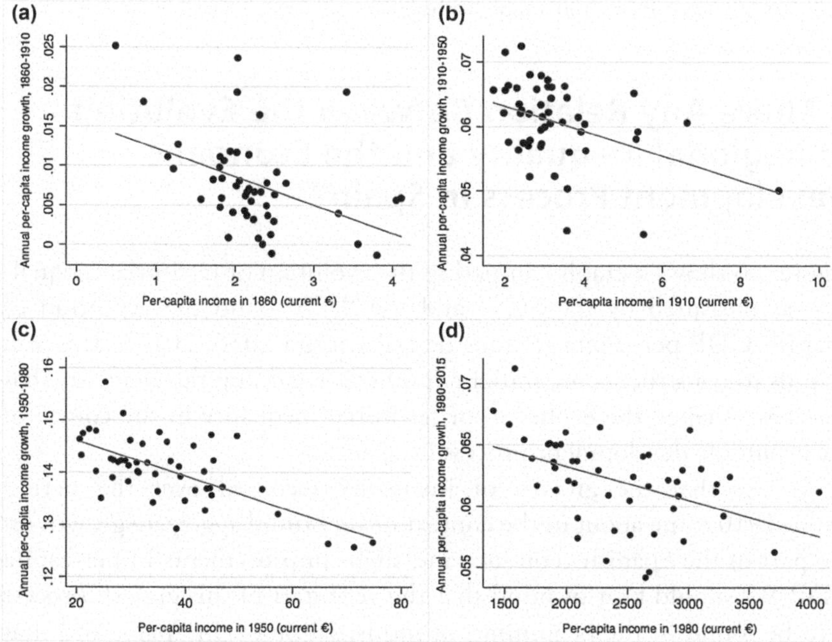

Fig. 4.5 β-convergence in Spain: (a) 1860–1910, (b) 1910–1950, (c) 1950–1980 and (d) 1980–2015. Notes: (a) 1860–1910: $R^2 = 0.1869$; $N = 49$. (b) 1910–1950: $R^2 = 0.1716$; $N = 49$. (c) 1950–1980: $R^2 = 0.4392$; $N = 49$. (d) 1980–2015: $R^2 = 0.2614$; $N = 49$. Source: See main text

The results indicate that of the four subperiods considered, only that covering between 1950 and 1980 shows a significant pattern of β-convergence (with the coefficient of determination, R^2, reaching a value of 0.44). The fact that the points marking the positions of the different provinces are highly dispersed would indicate that in none of the other three periods—1860–1910, 1910–1950 and 1980–2015—is there a significant relation between the initial level of regional income per capita and the subsequent growth rate (and this is supported by the low values obtained for the coefficient of determination). What this means is that the poorest regions in Spain in 1860 have tended to grow at a higher rate over the long term than the richest, but if we consider the existence of this relationship in each of the four major stages of Spanish economic development, the behavioural trend reaches a significant level only in the period 1950–1980. It is therefore confirmed that these are the years during which a real narrowing of the differences between regional levels of per-capita income in Spain can be found.

Is There Any Relation Between the Evolution of Regional Inequality and the Economic Development Process in Spain?

Figure 4.6 shows a graph comparing the evolution of territorial inequality—as measured by the SCW and the WCV—and the evolution of Spanish GDP per capita (Prados de la Escosura 2016, 2017). This will help us to construct some initial hypotheses regarding the elements that may have shaped the evolution of territorial inequality in the course of the economic development process in Spain.

We see that the growth of inequality recorded over the period 1860–1910 came about in the context of very timid aggregate growth on the part of the Spanish economy and slight improvements in per-capita GDP. We should bear in mind that the very start of this growth process is to be found in the beginnings of industrialization in Spain, and that this industrialization—as pointed out repeatedly in historical studies—was markedly regional in character, with Catalonia and the Basque Country being the main locations at this time. As a result, a high spatial

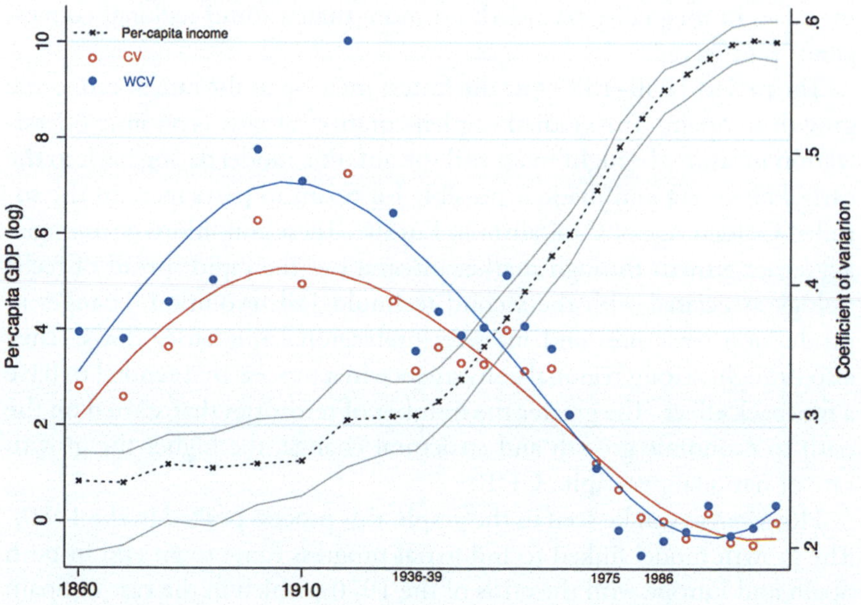

Fig. 4.6 Per-capita GDP and σ-convergence in Spain, 1860–2015. Source: See main text

concentration of industry was recorded, and this could explain the increase in regional inequality that came about in parallel with slow (because very spatially limited) national growth (Tirado-Fabregat et al. 2002).

The interwar years in Spain, which in our periodization fall between 1910 and 1950, saw the spread of the first industrialization and the beginning of the second technological revolution. At that time more regions began to participate in the process of technological and structural change that speeded up aggregate growth and kick-started the regional convergence process. This in turn was boosted by the increase in interprovincial migrations, which originated in the less-developed regions of the south-east and north-west of the peninsula and terminated in the centres of industrialization, which now included not only Catalonia and the Basque Country but also Madrid and Zaragoza. The considerable economic fluctuations that marked these years may in fact have acted to slow down this incipient dynamic since, despite there being no major increases in inequality recorded, no more than a timid regional convergence is observed.

The period 1950–1980 saw the fastest increase in the rate of economic growth in Spain. The gradual implementation of new economic liberalization measures brought to an end the autarkic model dating back to the early Franco era and made it possible for Spain to participate in the so-called Golden Age of Capitalism in Europe. These conditions encouraged aggregate growth through market integration, the rapid spread of technology associated with the second technological revolution, changes in production structures and massive interregional migratory flows. They also brought strong regional convergence in a process that tended to have a feedback effect. The greater the number of territories that started on the path to economic growth and structural change, the higher the growth rate of national per-capita GDP.

However, as can be seen in the graph, this process peaked in the 1980s. The growth model linked to industrial progress came to an end in both Spain and Europe with the crisis of the 1970s, which in the case of Spain was particularly severe and continued until the mid-1980s. The new stage that was opening up with the advance of European integration and international globalization was characterized by the boosting of economic growth through industrial and service sectors that were heavy users of ICT. Unfortunately much of Spain did not have the proper conditions to successfully embark on this stage. Only a few territories were able to participate fully in this new wave of technological change, and interregional factor flows—especially labour—no longer acted as a lever to drive efficient territorial allocation. As a result, aggregate growth again slowed down and territorial economic inequality began a new period of growth that continues throughout the last major stage analysed, 1980–2015.

To sum up, it has been shown that periods of slow aggregate growth have corresponded with increased territorial inequality, while accelerated growth, a sign that a greater number of territories are participating in the development process, has corresponded with a narrowing of the distance between rich and poor regions. The existence of a connection between the advance of the economic development process and the evolution of territorial inequality has been pointed out by various studies in economic history. These have shown that the earliest stages of economic development have a marked local or regional component (Pollard 1981) and that there is a link between the beginning of economic growth processes and the emergence of large-scale inequalities in the distribution of economic activity or population across the territory.

As mentioned in the introductory chapter, Williamson (1965) suggested that regional inequality followed an inverted U-shaped pattern over the course of the economic development process.[5] He observed that in the early stages of modern economic growth industrial activity was concentrated in specific locations, while the other regions remained largely agricultural. This in turn increased per-capita income inequality across regions, although over the long term these disparities eventually disappeared. Regional economic convergence was thus related to the uneven spread of industrialization. Market integration, capital and, above all, labour flows strengthened and speeded up this process. Specialization and divergence in economic structures would therefore explain the rise in inequality in the early stages of modern economic growth. Further progress and national market integration would then be accompanied by a reduction in regional disparities, which could be explained by the homogenization of economic structures and labour productivity convergence.

Figure 4.7 supplies evidence in support of Williamson's hypothesis for the case of Spain. It shows the levels of regional economic inequality calculated using the WCV and the corresponding levels of GDP per capita. It can be seen that regional income inequality rose in the early stages of economic development and then declined, which means that the Williamson (1965) hypothesis is largely compatible with the Spanish experience. However, with high levels of development a change of trend is observed. In chronological terms this would happen around the 1980s, and in development terms at the start of the current globalization process and with the spread of the third technological revolution. In other words, over the very long term the inverted U-shape propounded by Williamson

[5] Williamson (1965), inspired by Kuznets's (1955) seminal contribution on the dynamics of economic inequality, used regional data for the US and cross-country evidence for the late nineteenth and early twentieth centuries. After the Second World War regional studies gained ground, but data availability was still a serious limitation. Prominent among the pioneering studies that suggest the existence of a potential increase in regional income inequality in the early stages of economic growth are the classic works by Myrdal (1957) and Hirschman (1958).

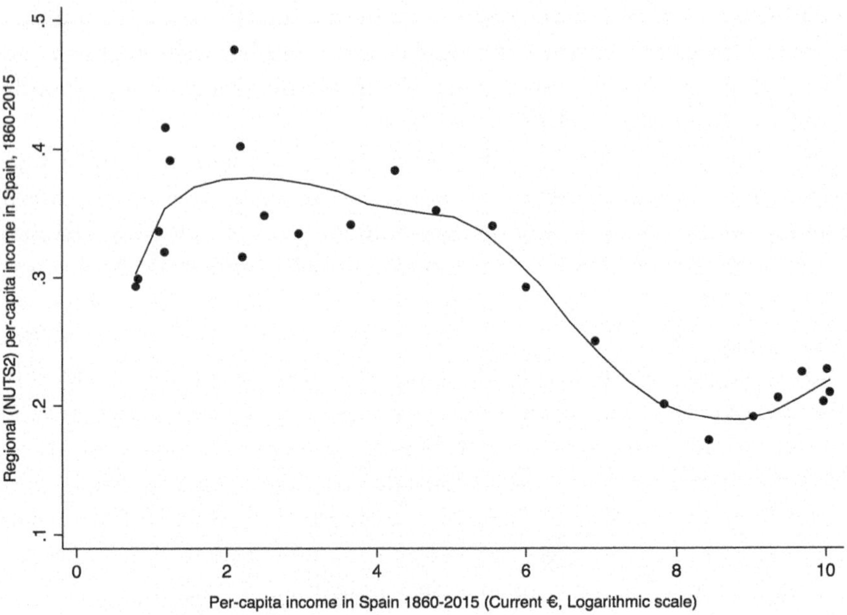

Fig. 4.7 Regional (NUTS2) per-capita income inequality in Spain (SCV, WCV, Theil) 1860–2015. Source: See main text

has turned into a curve in the shape of an elephant, to use the expression popularized by Milanovic (2016) in the case of personal income distribution. This dynamic presages the potential appearance of a new Williamson curve, which would mean that Spain would currently be entering a new segment of growth.

References

Alcaide Inchausti, J. (2003). *Evolución económica de las regiones y provincias españolas en el siglo XX*. Bilbao: Fundación BBVA.

Alcaide-Guindo, P. (2011). *Balance económico regional (autonomías y provincias) Años 2000 a 2010*. Madrid: Fundación de las Cajas de Ahorros (FUNCAS).

Álvarez Llano, R. (1986). Evolución de la estructura económica regional de España en la historia: una aproximación. *Situación, 1*, 5–61.

Barro, R. J., & Sala-i-Martin, X. (1991). Convergence across states and regions. *Brooking Papers on Economic Activity, 1*, 107–182.

Barro, R. J., & Sala-i-Martin, X. (1992). Convergence. *Journal of Political Economy, 100*(2), 223–251.

BBV. (1999). *Renta Nacional de España y su distribución provincial: serie homogénea años 1955 a 1993 y avances 1994 a 1997*. Bilbao: Fundación BBV.

Carreras, A. (1990). Fuentes y datos para el análisis regional de la industrialización española. In A. Carreras & J. Nadal (Eds.), *Pautas regionales de la industrialización española (siglos XIX y XX)* (pp. 3–20). Barcelona: Ariel.

Cuadrado-Roura, J. R. (Ed.). (2010). *Regional policy, economic growth and convergence: Lessons from the Spanish case*. Heidelberg: Springer.

Cuadrado-Roura, J. R., Garrido, R., & Mancha, T. (1999). Disparidades regionales y convergencia en España: 1980–2005. *Revista de Estudios Regionales, 55*, 109–137.

De la Fuente, A. (1996). Economía regional desde una perspectiva neoclásica. De convergencia y otras historias. *Revista de Economía Aplicada, 10*(4), 5–63.

De la Fuente, A. (2002). On the sources of convergence: A closer look at the Spanish regions. *European Economic Review, 46*(3), 569–599.

Díez-Minguela, A., Martinez-Galarraga, J., & Tirado, D. A. (2016). Why did Spanish regions not converge before the Civil War? Agglomeration economies and (regional) growth revisited. *Revista de Historia Económica/Journal of Iberian and Latin American Economic History, 34*(3), 417–448.

Gómez-Tello, A., Díez-Minguela, A., Martinez-Galarraga, J., & Tirado, D. A. (2018). *Regional prices in early twentieth-century Spain: A country-product-dummy approach*. DT-AEHE N°1802.

Hirschman, A. O. (1958). *The strategy of economic development*. New Haven: Yale University Press.

Kuznets, S. (1955). Economic growth and income inequality. *American Economic Review, 45*(1), 1–28.

Lorente, J. R. (1992). *La dispersión geográfica de los salarios*. Síntesis Mensual de Indicadores Económicos, Septiembre, Ministerio de Economía y Hacienda.

Martinez-Galarraga, J., Rosés, J. R., & Tirado, D. A. (2015). The long-term patterns of regional income inequality in Spain, 1860–2000. *Regional Studies, 49*(4), 502–517.

Mas, M., Maudos, J., Pérez, F., & Uriel, E. (1994). Disparidades regionales y convergencia en las comunidades autónomas. *Revista de Economía Aplicada, 4*, 129–148.

Milanovic, B. (2016). *Global inequality. A new approach for the age of globalization*. Cambridge, MA: Harvard University Press.
Myrdal, G. (1957). *Economic theory and under-developed regions*. London: Methuen & Co.
Prados de la Escosura, L. (2016). *Spain's historical national accounts: Expenditure and output, 1850–2015*. EHES Working Papers in Economic History, No. 103.
Prados de la Escosura, L. (2017). *Spanish economic growth, 1850–2015*. Palgrave studies in economic history. Palgrave Macmillan.
Pollard, S. (1981). *Peaceful conquest: The industrialization of Europe, 1760–1970*. Oxford: Oxford University Press.
Rosés, J. R., Martinez-Galarraga, J., & Tirado, D. A. (2010). The upswing of regional income inequality in Spain (1860–1930). *Explorations in Economic History, 47*(2), 244–257.
Sala-i-Martin, X. (1996). Regional cohesion: Evidence and theories of regional growth and convergence. *European Economic Review, 40*, 1325–1352.
Tirado-Fabregat, D. A., Paluzie, E., & Pons, J. (2002). Economic integration and industrial location: The case of Spain before World War I. *Journal of Economic Geography, 2*(3), 343–363.
Tortosa-Ausina, E., Pérez, F., Mas, M., & Goerlich, F. J. (2005). Growth and convergence profiles in the Spanish provinces (1965–1997). *Journal of Regional Science, 45*, 147–182.
Villaverde, J. (2007). Crecimiento y convergencia regional en España. (Algunas) causas del cambio. *Papeles de Economía Española, 111*, 240–254.
Villaverde, J., & Sánchez-Robles, B. (2002). Polarización, convergencia y movilidad entre las provincias españolas, 1955–1997. *Revista Asturiana de Economía, 20*, 7–26.
Williamson, J. G. (1965). Regional inequality and the process of national development: A description of the patterns. *Economic Development and Cultural Change, 13*(4), 1–84.
Yamamoto, D. (2008). Scales of regional income disparities in the United States, 1955–2003. *Journal of Economic Geography, 8*(1), 79–103.

5

Scratching Beneath the Surface: Distribution Dynamics

Why Should We Scratch Beneath the Surface?

Recent work by various economic historians has made it possible to share new evidence on regional per-capita GDP for various European countries.[1] In some cases this has opened a temporal window onto the second half of the nineteenth century.[2] With this new information researchers have not only been able to analyse how regional economic inequality has evolved in the course of different national development processes; they have also been given the opportunity to explore other territorial realities that have been brought to light and are worthy of attention.

In the case of Belgium, for example, Buyst (2010, 2011) has shown that the francophone areas of Hainaut and Liège, which today occupy the lowest positions in the per-capita GDP rankings by province, had income levels clearly above the average in 1896 (136 for Hainaut and 119 for Liège, with the Belgian average being 100). Today's wealthiest regions, on the other hand, are in the Flemish area of the country and did not occupy

[1] A compilation of investigations providing evidence for the period 1900–2010 for a sizeable set of European countries. See Wolf and Rosés (forthcoming).

[2] A number of researchers have provided retrospective estimates for regional GDP that go back as far as the sixteenth century (Enflo and Missaia 2018, for Sweden).

A. Díez-Minguela et al., *Regional Inequality in Spain*, Palgrave Studies in Economic History, https://doi.org/10.1007/978-3-319-96110-1_5

privileged positions at the end of the nineteenth century. A particularly noteworthy case according to Buyst's estimates would be Antwerp, which was below the national average in 1896 (91 out of 100) but exceeded it by over 15 points in 2000. And Brabant, with a per-capita income close to the national average in 1896, now occupies top position in the ranking with an income level over 40 per cent higher than the Belgian average. In other words, in the course of the economic development process there have been notable reversals of fortune which, in the case of Belgium, might help us to understand the origins of the political tension that exists between a historically prosperous but today relatively impoverished Wallonia, and Flanders, which was poor in the past but has become the richest territory in the country in the present.

Just as important are the public debate and political consequences of the north-south divide that confronts Italy. The work of reconstructing historical figures for regional per-capita income in this case has served to show that the deep north-south divide that characterizes the country today was less obvious at the end of the nineteenth century. The division has taken shape on the basis of regional histories with markedly different trajectories. Felice (2011) shows that some southern regions such as Sicily and Campania, with per-capita GDPs around 35 per cent below the Italian average in 2011, recorded values much closer to the average in 1871 (95 out of the average 100 for Sicily, and 109 for Campania), whereas currently prosperous regions such as the Aosta Valley in the north of the peninsula (with per-capita GDP of 136 out of 100 in 2011) were relatively poor in 1871 (with per-capita income 20 per cent below the Italian average).

In the case of France, Díez-Minguela et al. (2016) and Díez-Minguela and Sanchis (2017) have uncovered a different kind of reality involving the huge gap that exists in terms of per-capita income between the NUTS2 region in which the country's capital is located (Île-de-France) and the rest of the territory. In 2010 this region recorded a per-capita GDP over 60 points higher than the national average. However, according to the authors' estimates this gap was even larger in 1860 when the Île-de-France enjoyed twice the national average GDP. Given this state of affairs it is no surprise that in 1947 the greatest proponent of the need to take action on territorial economic inequality in France, Jean-François Gravier, published a book entitled *Paris et le désert français* (Gravier 1947)

Spain also has its share of realities such as these. Three of its 17 NUTS2 regions recorded a GDP per capita less than 80 per cent of the national average in 2015 (Andalusia, Extremadura and Castile-La Mancha), while another three exceeded it by more than 20 per cent (Madrid, Navarre and the Basque Country). However, the new evidence we provide here enables us to say that today's reality is a long way from the reality that existed in the early stages of Spain's economic development process, considered here to be 1860. It can be derived from the data that Andalusia, for example, a region that today occupies second last position among the 17 NUTS2 regions that make up Spain, was the second richest region in 1860 with a per-capita GDP 36 per cent higher than the national average. And the Basque Country, which today is the richest region after Madrid, occupied tenth position in the ranking in 1860 with a GDP per capita roughly ten points below the average.

It is these relative changes, which are only perceptible over the long term, that possibly have the greatest impact in national academic, social and political debates. At least that is the impression given by various recent academic papers such as that by Rodríguez-Pose (2018), who observes that "*persistent poverty, economic decay and lack of opportunities are at the root of considerable discontent in declining and lagging-behind areas the world over. Poor development prospects and an increasing belief that these places have 'no future'... have led many of these so-called 'places that don't matter' to revolt against the status quo. The revolt has come via an unexpected source: the ballot-box, in a wave of political populism with strong territorial, rather than social foundations.*"[3]

As far as these aspects are concerned, in the previous chapter we analysed how regional economic inequality evolved in Spain over the entire course of the historical development process. We used an approach based on the concept of convergence and the different ways that this has been explored in the neoclassical growth literature. Such an approach makes it possible to hypothesize about the determinants of the divergence-convergence process that characterized the evolution of regional inequality in Spain, at least between 1860 and 1980.

---

[3] Storper's (2018) thinking follows in the same vein. In his article he revives the statement published in The Economist (17, 2016): *Regional inequality is proving too politically dangerous to ignore.*

However, as has been shown repeatedly in the literature (Quah 1993, 1997), this approach cannot support the construction of hypotheses to explain realities such as those described in the preceding paragraphs. In the framework of the neoclassical growth literature it is difficult to give an economic foundation to phenomena like changes in leadership or the existence of stratification or polarization in the regional distribution of per-capita income. The economic foundation for poverty traps and convergence clubs is to be found in the corpus of theory that has come to be known as endogenous growth literature. With this type of models, the presence of increasing returns in certain knowledge-generating activities means that the scale of production becomes relevant in specialization processes, and these in turn generate long-term effects on regions' growth trajectories. Thus different endogenous growth models foresee the presence of multiple equilibria in national growth processes. They also provide an economic foundation for phenomena such as the poverty traps and convergence clubs described.[4]

The aim of this chapter is therefore to analyse the presence of realities of this type, characteristic of territorial economic inequality in Spain, and from a long-term perspective. We begin with a distribution dynamics approach (Quah 1993, 1997) to explore the shape of regional income distribution and how it changes over time, presenting box plots and kernel densities for the purpose. While box plots are a useful tool for assessing the degree of dispersion within a distribution and the presence of outliers, kernel densities allow us to graphically explore the form of the distribution for each decade. In general terms, the shape and height of the distribution inform us of the presence of stratification and polarization and the emergence of twin peaks or convergence clubs for each stage of economic development.

We then analyse other aspects of distribution dynamics such as mobility in order to find out how successful (or not) territories were over each period. Following Quah (1996), we examine transition probability matrices that estimate the likelihood of transition from one income class to another during a given period of time. To obtain more details we also

[4] On the economic foundation for the existence of poverty traps, see Azariadis and Stachurski (2005).

use these transition matrices to calculate the Shorrocks index (Shorrocks 1978). In addition, we compute Kendall's rank correlation coefficient (also known as Kendall's Tau) to study whether there were changes in the ranking and, if so, at what moments in time they were of the greatest magnitude.[5]

We can thus determine whether there has been a general trend in which the richest regions maintain their position over time, or whether on the contrary there have been notable changes in the positions occupied by the various regions in terms of income per capita. By doing this we hope to identify stories of relative success or failure among Spanish regions, discover when exactly these changes were most frequent and then, in the final part of this chapter, construct hypotheses about the economic and institutional conditions which led to the biggest changes in the map of regional inequality in Spain—an inequality that paradoxically would be considered unchanging when viewed from a short-term perspective.

Long-term Trends in Regional Income Distribution in Spain: Modality

To examine per-capita GDP inequality across Spanish regions in greater detail, we first use a distribution dynamics approach (Quah 1993, 1997). The level of territorial disaggregation will be provincial, that is, NUTS3 in Eurostat terminology. For each analytical exercise results will be provided for ten-year time intervals covering the period 1860–1930, which will subsequently be extended to cover the period 1940–2015, giving us a total of 17 intervals. Given the nature of our dataset and the type of exercises undertaken, we have normalized per-capita GDP for each decade, with the national average being equal to one (Spain = 1).

Box plots and kernel densities are presented in Figs. 5.1 and 5.2. The first of these shows income inequality at a NUTS3 scale in the form of box plots for each decade. A box plot is a graphic representation in which

[5] Yamamoto (2008) takes a similar approach in the study of territorial inequality in the US, 1955–2003.

values from the 25th to the 75th percentile of the distribution are grouped in a box. The 50th percentile is represented by a dividing line within the box. Two vertical lines appear at the upper and lower limits of the box, giving information about the adjacent values of the distribution. In other words they are order statistics that correspond to actual observations of the variable and cover the rank of observation that cannot be considered atypical.[6] Outliers are therefore outside the box (and marked by a black spot). Box plots are a useful tool for assessing the degree of dispersion within a distribution and the outliers.

As Fig. 5.1 indicates, differences in per-capita GDP across Spanish provinces have varied substantially over time. If we take a broad look at its evolution over the four stages into which we have divided the economic development process, a number of impressions begin to emerge. First, we see that the growth in inequality for the period 1860–1910 was driven by the behaviour of a small group of provinces that achieved income levels far above the average. For example, per-capita GDP for Barcelona (Catalonia) was over twice the national average from 1890 to 1910. Outliers are symptomatic of unequal economic growth, and this was a distinguishing feature in the early stages of industrialization. In Spain, for instance, some provinces (Barcelona, Madrid and the Basque provinces of Bizkaia and Gipuzkoa) had very high levels of per-capita GDP in the early twentieth century. The increase in average inequality would therefore be linked to the fact that a few regions took off economically and surged ahead of the distribution's central mass.

While dispersion was a distinguishing characteristic early on, the number of outliers decreased after 1910. At that point there were five provinces with per-capita GDP levels that should be considered as outliers, but by 1950 there were just two (Gipuzkoa and Bizkaia), and from that date the box plots show that income levels for all provinces fit within adjacent distribution values. And not only do the outliers disappear, but the boxes become more compressed after 1950. This would indicate that the average levels of inequality were decreasing over time, signalling the beginning of a convergence process that would continue until 1980.

[6] Of the interquartile rank, R (ξ.25), the upper adjacent value is defined as the actual value of the variable represented that is no larger than ξ.75 + 1.5R (ξ.25); the lower adjacent value would be the actual value of the variable represented that is no lower than ξ.25 − 1.5R (ξ.25).

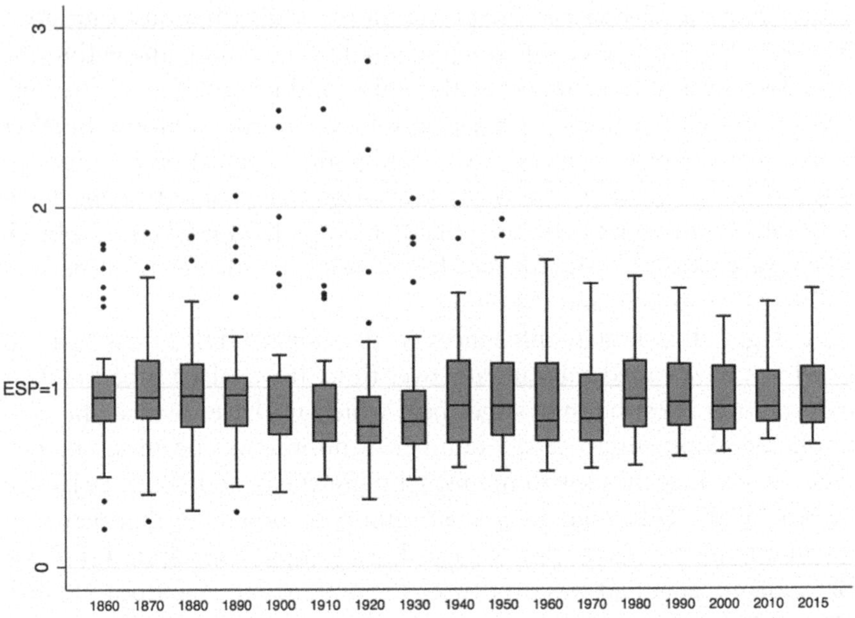

Fig. 5.1 Box plots of per-capita GDP by province, Spain 1860–2015 (Spain = 1). Source: See main text

The layout of the box plots for the period 1980–2015 enables us to characterize another element. The previous chapter showed that during these years there was an incipient increase in inequality as measured through the calculation of various synthetic indicators (SCW, WCV, Theil). The information in Fig. 5.1 indicates that this is not associated with a wider gap between the provinces located between the 25th and 75th percentiles of the distribution. In fact the size of the boxes has not followed a growth trend since the 1980s. The element driving inequality is the widening of the gap that exists between the income level of the regions situated in the 75th percentile and the income level corresponding to the adjacent value of the distribution. In other words, this distribution is starting to stretch upwards again.

In short, the economic convergence process of Spanish provinces that began during the interwar years (1910–1950) and became consolidated over the decades that followed (1950–1980) originated with the gradual closing of the gap between the small group of territories that had played leading parts in the first stage of national economic development (1860–1910) and average levels of income. However, in the last of the periods analysed we again catch a glimpse of this gap's tendency to widen, which would explain today's increasing territorial inequality.

To enable a more detailed discussion, we show kernel densities in Fig. 5.2. These allow us to graphically explore the modality of the distribution and its changes over time. The graph illustrates the kernel densities for each decade, treating each province (NUTS3) as an equal unit of observation. It also includes population-weighted kernel densities to take into account the different province sizes in terms of population.[7] As might be expected, changes in kernel distribution estimates are consistent with the evolution of overall inequality. However, these general trends are compatible with very different distributional shapes.

If we look first at the evolution depicted by the unweighted kernels, we see that during the initial period of relatively low inequality (1860) a large number of provinces were grouped around the Spanish average, as shown by the greater height of the distribution. However, between 1860 and 1910 the distribution shows a tendency towards there being a cluster of regions in the tails, especially the upper tail. While the lower tail gradually disappears, the upper tail stretches out as some provinces take off economically. In short, like the box plots did before, the unweighted kernels show that the regional distribution was characterized by a few regions forging ahead of the rest of the economy.

Two realities coexist in the second period analysed, which is 1910–1950. The upper tail is still stretching out until 1930, indicating the privileged positions attained by some provinces, mainly those that became industrialized during the stage characterized by market integration in Spain. These provinces reached values for per-capita income roughly twice the size of the Spanish average. Then, the shape of the distribution after the Civil War (1936–1939) shows a shortening of the upper tail that tallies with the story that emerges from the box plots.

[7] For simplicity's sake, we chose the Gaussian kernel with a width that minimized the mean integrated squared error (Silverman 1992).

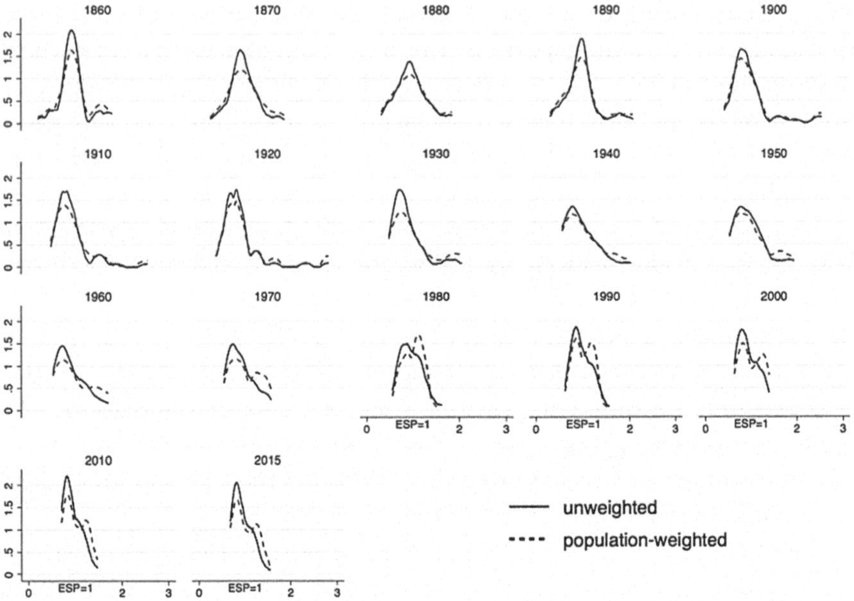

Fig. 5.2 Kernel densities for per-capita GDP by province, Spain 1860–2015. Source: See main text

In line with the advance of the regional economic convergence process over the period 1950–1980, the kernels show that the gap between the extremes of the distribution narrowed notably, and also that the decrease in inequality was accompanied by the virtual disappearance of that significant mass of provinces that formed the upper tail of the distribution. Finally, between 1980 and 2015 no very marked increase in the distance between the extremes of the distribution is observed, but there is a trend pointing to the formation of a relevant probability mass, that is, a relevant set of territories that tend to group together at income levels way above the average. An evolution of this kind could be an indication that territorial economic inequality over the last few years has been tending towards a bimodality or polarization scenario.

The information provided by the kernels calculated when the provinces are weighted by population reflects this trend more clearly. While the evolution during the second half of the nineteenth and the first half of the twentieth centuries is quite similar for both densities, there is a definite change from then onwards. The population-weighted kernels show that the more unimodal distribution typical of the early stages of economic development gradually become bimodal in the second half of the twentieth century. Hence the gradual disappearance of atypical values in the box plots would mean the emergence of a bimodal structure in provincial per-capita income distribution over the period 1950–2015.

Hence the element that characterizes the shape of the weighted distribution is bimodality. Nevertheless, it would be best to distinguish between two scenarios that correspond to the two subperiods into which we have divided this stage of the growth trajectory of the Spanish economy, 1950–1980 and 1980–2015. In the first, the bimodal distribution runs in parallel with an average reduction in inequality, which would signal a gradual closing of the gap between the peaks drawn by the kernels. However, the resurgence of bimodality between 1980 and 2015 runs in parallel with the new upswing in regional inequality. With these conditions, the second period would show increasing polarization between the income levels of two sets of territories grouped around averages that are moving further apart. In endogenous growth terminology this could be referred to as the formation of two convergence clubs.

Kernel diagrams have provided us with information about what the distribution as a whole looks like over different periods of time, but they tell us nothing about mobility within the distribution. The next section will therefore analyse other aspects of the distribution, particularly mobility within Spain, that is, how far provinces have risen or fallen since 1860. The aim is to find out the extent to which the regional rankings changed, or whether on the contrary the peaks and troughs of polarization were compatible with stability in the regions' positions across the national distribution.

Long-term Trends in Regional Income Distribution in Spain: Mobility

There are several exploratory tools for studying regional income mobility over time. Following Quah (1993, 1996), we look at transition probability matrices that provide the estimated probability, p_{ij}, of transition from income class *i* to income class *j* during given period of time S (Hammond and Thompson 2002). In this case we rank the 49 provinces (NUTS3) according to their per-capita GDP and then group them into five classes or quintiles (very poor, poor, average, rich and very rich) of the same size.[8] Our dataset contains provincial per-capita income in current pesetas, and hence the cut-offs vary over time.[9] Therefore, if y_t is a vector containing the income distribution in year *t*, then

$$y_{t+S} = P_{t,t+S} \times y_t \tag{5.1}$$

where $P_{t,\,t+S}$ is the transition probability that tells us how likely it is for a province to move from one income group to another. And in this way transition probability matrices enable us to study regional income mobility.

As an example, Fig. 5.3 shows the average probability, p_{ij}, that a province in the top or bottom quintile at the beginning of each period will remain in the same class at the end of that period. It would seem that persistence, especially in the upper part of the distribution, is an issue. The probability that a province in the top quintile will remain there has grown steadily from 60 per cent to 90 per cent between the periods 1860–1910 and 1980–2015. However, this finding is weaker when we look at the lower part of the income distribution, where there appears to be more mobility. To complete this information, Table A5.1 in the Appendix at the end of this chapter shows the transition probability matrices of all quintiles for all our periods of study (1860–1910,

[8] Regional (NUTS3) per-capita GDPs are ranked from highest to lowest for each year. Provinces are then classified into five equal income classes or quintiles. Each quintile contains 10 provinces, except for the bottom or "very poor" quintile, which has 9.

[9] Hammond and Thompson (2002) use the mean-adjusted log of relative per-capita income to create cut-offs, and thus income classes. These cut-offs are maintained over time.

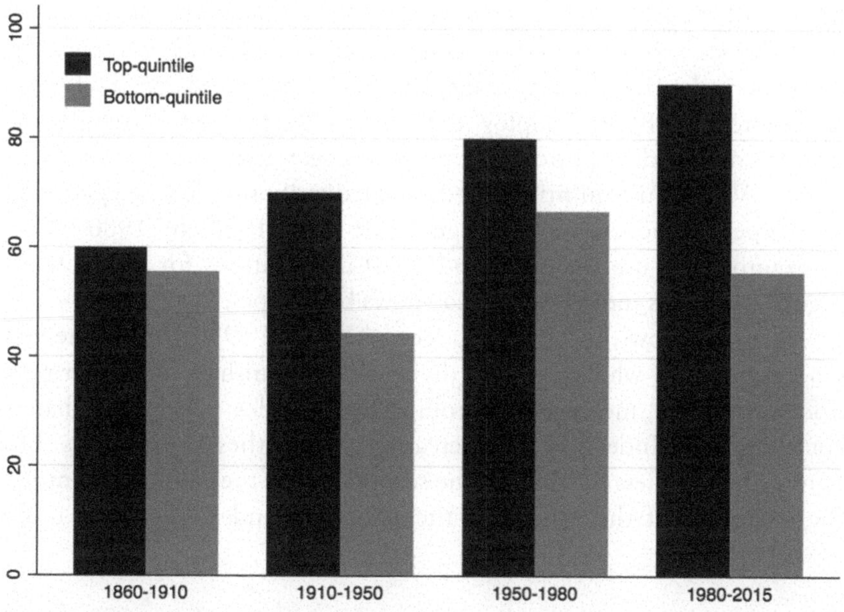

Fig. 5.3 Regional (NUTS3) income (class) mobility, Spain 1860–2015. Notes: The vertical axis indicates the probability that a province that was in the top or bottom quintile at the start of each period will remain in the same class. Source: See main text

1910–1950, 1950–1980 and 1980–2015), in which the diagonal p_{ii} shows the average probability of staying in the initial income class.

To provide further insight we use the transition matrices to calculate the Shorrocks index (Shorrocks 1978), namely SHI_{t+S}. This index condenses the information from the transition matrices into a scalar that in this case measures the mobility the Spanish provinces have undergone in terms of per-capita income over time. It is computed as:

$$\text{SHI}_{t+S} = \frac{\#\text{Classes} - \text{Trace}\left(\text{P}_{t,t+S}\right)}{\#\text{Classes} - 1} \tag{5.2}$$

where #Classes stands for the number of income classes. Since we have five equal income classes or quintiles, then #Classes = 5. Trace captures the sum of the elements in the diagonal of the transition matrix. Given that #Classes = 5, then SHI_{t+S} ranges from 0 to 1.25. The higher the Shorrocks index, the greater the mobility across income classes. Following Yamamoto (2008) we employ two methodologies. First we use the regional income distribution for the earliest year, that is, 1860, as "fixed-origin". We then use quintiles based on the distribution for the beginning of each period, hence "rolling-origin". For 1910–1920 and 1980–1990, for example, we use the 1910 and 1980 distributions for the "rolling-origin" Shorrocks index. Figure 5.4 shows both types.

As Fig. 5.4 shows, there are two scenarios. Until 1950, during the first two periods into which we have divided the Spanish economic growth process, mobility, measured as a rolling-origin index, was higher than it would be later. Indeed it was increasing during these early stages, but then seems trendless for most of the second half of the twentieth century. The evolution of the values for the Shorrocks index calculated using

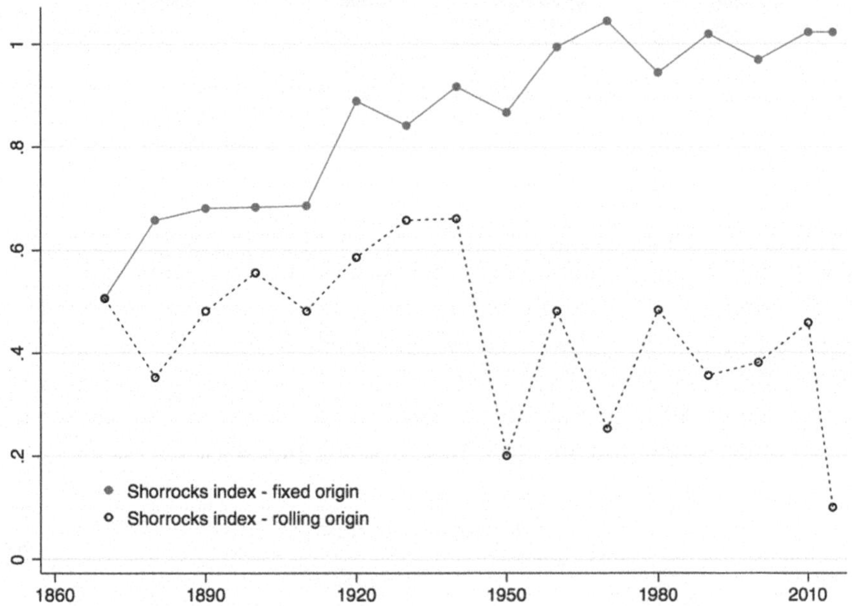

Fig. 5.4 Regional (NUTS3) per-capita GDP (class) mobility (Shorrocks indices), Spain 1860–2015. Notes: These are ten-year periods except for the last one, 2010–2015. Source: See main text

fixed-origin methodology provides similar evidence. The probability that a province will change quintile with the respect to the one it occupied in 1860 grows continuously, although the growth rate is more marked before 1950, after which the increase in probability is virtually insignificant. This kind of evidence strengthens the hypothesis that the biggest changes in the relative positions of Spanish regions came about in the early stages of the national economic development process. Since then the general rule has been for their positions to remain unchanged.

This would suggest that regional income mobility was noteworthy in the early stages of economic development. For example, the rise of the Basque Country in the final decades of the nineteenth century coincided with the decline of Andalusia, during a period in which market integration was taking place. Industrialization saw the appearance of new opportunities that stimulated economic growth in some provinces. As a result regional inequality increased, and with it mobility across income classes. Later we see a marked stability in regional income distribution. This, in turn, would point to the importance of history when it comes to explaining the varied fortunes of the regions, since it was in the first stages of development that there was greater mobility, giving rise to a scenario that barely changed in the following decades.

However, increased mobility across income classes does not necessarily imply changes in the rankings or relative positions of provinces. Similarly, low mobility, as measured by the Shorrocks index, could be associated with a high degree of positional change. To check our previous findings on mobility we compute Kendall's Tau coefficient, which considers the degree of concordance in the rankings of all pairs of observations for two variables. In our case the variables of interest would be per-capita GDP in the first and last years of the period. If two provinces have the same relative rankings in both periods, that pair is said to be concordant. But if their relative rankings change, then the pair is discordant. With N observations there are $(N^2 - N)/2$ possible pairwise comparisons. We therefore use Kendall's Tau to capture ranking as opposed to class mobility. It can be computed as follows:

$$\tau = \frac{PW_c - PW_d}{\left(N^2 - N\right)/2} \tag{5.3}$$

where PW_c is the number of concordant pairs and PW_d the number of discordant pairs. If all pairs are concordant, then $\tau = 1$, whereas if all pairs are discordant, $\tau = -1$. Thus high values for τ would reflect a low level of mobility in income ranking. Figure 5.5 shows the long-term evolution of Kendall's Tau. Again we use the rolling-origin and fixed-origin approaches.

Figure 5.5 also hints at the existence of two scenarios. The average value for Kendall's Tau statistic calculated following the rolling-origin method is lower during the period 1860–1950 than during the period 1950–2015. This means that the probability of a province changing position in the ranking was higher between 1860 and 1950. Kendall's Tau calculated using fixed-origin methodology reinforces this impression.

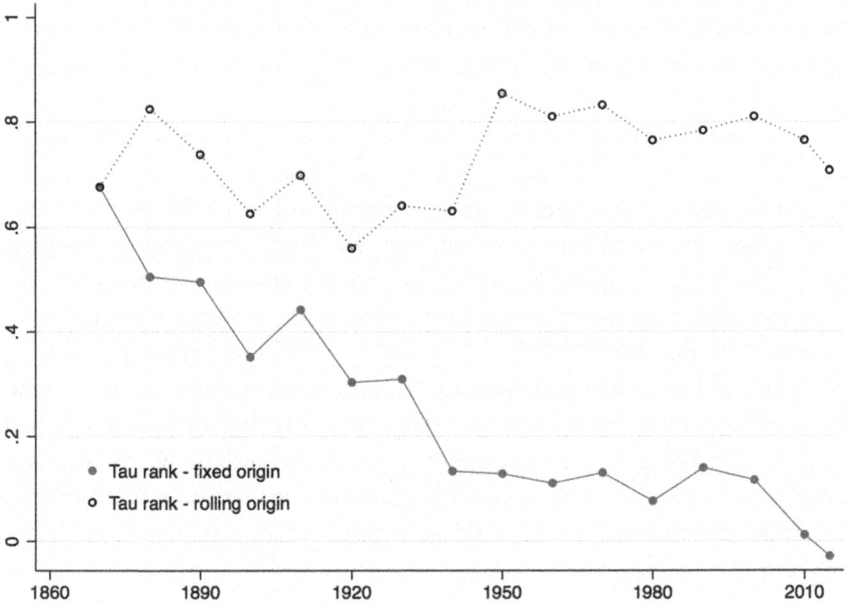

Fig. 5.5 Regional (NUTS3) per-capita GDP (ranking) mobility (Tau rank), Spain 1860–2015. Notes: These are ten-year periods except for the last one, 2010–2015. Source: See main text

The index's value falls continuously until 1950, but from that date to the present its evolution has been much more stable. In fact the only times that its value has dropped significantly were during the energy crisis of the late 1970s and as a result of the very recent Great Recession. Circumstances marked by serious crises can certainly have a significant effect on the positions occupied by different regions in the ranking, especially if some territories are more severely impacted than others. Next we will carry out a more detailed analysis of these regional experiences by studying specific cases of special interest.

Stories of Success and Failure

Now that two dimensions associated with regional inequality have been presented—the characteristics of per-capita GDP distribution and the degree of mobility—we can focus on an analysis of how the ranking for per-capita GDP evolved. We first evaluate the evolution of five provinces (NUTS3)—Barcelona, Bizkaia, Madrid, Seville and Valencia—which we have chosen because they are particularly relevant within the framework of the Spanish economy. With over two million inhabitants they represented approximately 15 per cent of the country's population in 1860, and they have been growing in importance over time insofar as they accounted for over 20 per cent of the population in 1950, and in 2015 their almost 15 million inhabitants represented over 30 per cent of the total. Indeed the capitals of these five provinces are five of the most populated cities in the country. In terms of their contribution to Spanish GDP their weight is even greater, jointly representing 22.5 per cent, 35.9 per cent and 44.4 per cent of the total in 1860, 1950 and 2015 respectively.

This select group of five also enables us to follow the trajectories of two provinces that played an important part at the start of the industrialization process in Spain, that is, Barcelona and Bizkaia. With the inclusion of Seville we can identify key moments in the history of a territory (Andalusia) characterized by its descent through the ranking in the course of these 155 years. And by studying the evolution of Valencia, the largest of the provinces that make up the NUTS2 region of the same name in our terminology, we will see an example of a territory that underwent industrialization at a later stage than the pioneering regions of Catalonia and the Basque Country. This territory also includes the third biggest city in Spain. Finally, Madrid is the province in which the country's capital is located, so including it as one of the provinces to be analysed will enable us to identify those points in history when being the capital was fundamental to its progress among the territories of Spain as a whole.

The graph in Fig. 5.6 summarizes the data on the subject, showing the different evolution of each of these five provinces in the Spanish ranking, out of the total of 49 provinces. In the first stage from 1860 to 1910 we see how Barcelona and Bizkaia break away into the top positions, with the latter's progress being particularly rapid. The provinces that had little participation in this first stage of Spanish industrialization, Seville and Valencia, saw no great changes in their positions over these years, although they did manage to remain in the top ten. Meanwhile Madrid, which at the start occupied the top position in the ranking but did not follow the

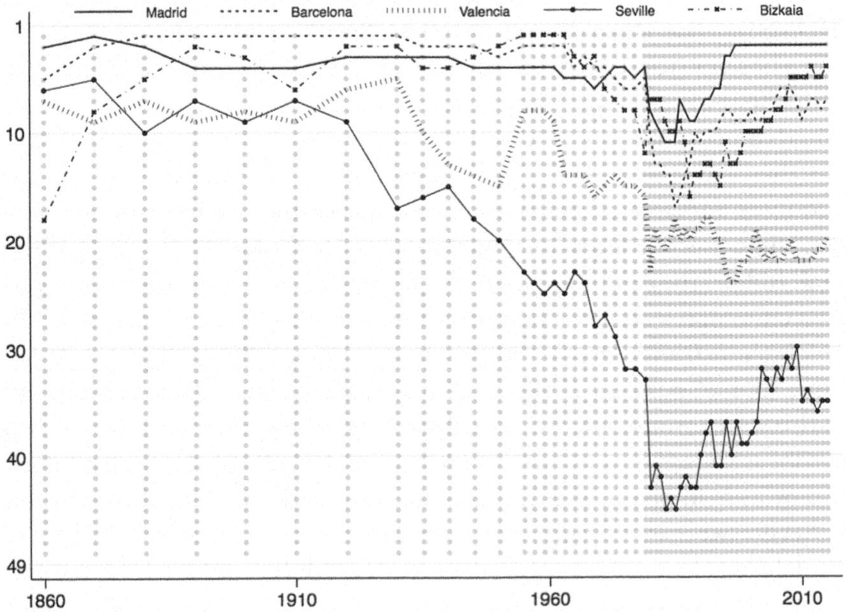

Fig. 5.6 Regional (NUTS3) per-capita GDP (ranking) mobility, Spain 1860–2015. Source: See main text

path of industrialization taken by the Catalan and Basque provinces, found itself in third place on the eve of the First World War.

There are no notable changes in the positions of Barcelona, Bizkaia and Madrid during the period 1910–1950. Valencia, on the other hand, reaches the peak of its historical trajectory in the ranking by the middle of this period, in 1930, but begins to lose ground during the years of Franco's autarky. No doubt the Spanish economy's isolation had a serious effect on an economy characterized by its agricultural sector, an incipient light industry and a very marked orientation towards the export market. However, the element that most attracts our attention is the beginning of a downward path for Seville's economy, which fell from seventh place in the national ranking to twentieth over this period. In a historical context that gradually saw more territories taking part in the transformation of Spain's economy into an industrial one, Seville's failure to industrialize would certainly have been one of the reasons that led to this dramatic drop in position.

The years between 1950 and 1980 are when Spain saw its greatest reduction in territorial inequality. This was helped by the spread of the industrialization process to more territories in such a way that the gap between the richest and poorest regions tended to become narrower. The strong progress made by some of these regions meant that all the territories analysed here lost relative positions when they were overtaken in terms of per-capita GDP by territories with less weight in population but with very dynamic behaviour at this time. Such would be the cases of the Basque province Gipuzkoa and Navarre, for instance, which rose from intermediate or already high positions to occupy the top places in the ranking in 1980. This setback was very limited in the cases of Madrid, Barcelona, Bizkaia and even Valencia, but it proved to be extremely serious in the case of Seville, which fell to 33rd position in the same year.

The relative positions of these provinces were greatly affected by the oil crisis, which had an impact on Spain that lingered until the 1980s. All the provinces analysed here lost ground during the first years of the interval 1980–2015. The most interesting element, however, is what happened after this shock. In a context that saw the beginning of a new period of territorial inequality accompanied by polarization, the three leading economies in the sample—Madrid, Barcelona and Bizkaia—

gradually recovered their positions and ended up in a cluster of rich regions. Valencia, on the other hand, followed a stable trajectory at around 20th position in the ranking, while Seville presented a dynamic of convergence from very low positions in the ranking towards a level that placed it in the middle of the table of provinces ranked in order of income. It could be suggested as a hypothesis that because Barcelona, Bizkaia and especially Madrid adapted better to the new paradigm of technology and international economic integration, they were able to regain prominent positions in the ranking after the obligatory production adjustment that marked the industrial crisis of the early 1980s. Such an adjustment does not seem to have been so successful in the cases of Seville and Valencia.

If we analyse the historical process in its entirety, Seville and Valencia would certainly represent two stories of relative failure. Seville dropped from sixth place to 35th, while Valencia fell from seventh to twentieth. A success story would be the case of Bizkaia, which occupied 18th place in 1860 but had become one of the country's richest provinces in 2015, occupying fourth place in the ranking.

The graph in Fig. 5.7 again presents the per-capita income ranking by province, but now the NUTS1 macro-regions to which each province belongs is represented by a different colour. The purpose of this is to include the provincial histories in a wider territorial context, in this case NUTS1, thereby making a first approach to the geographical aspects of territorial inequality.

If we look at the information the graph provides, we see that in 1860 there does not seem to be any pattern relating the positions of the provinces that comprise each NUTS1 region in the income ranking. The position occupied by each province thus appears not to be linked to the other territories that make up its macro-region. However, over the second stage of the economic development process in Spain, which takes place between 1910 and 1950, we see a few noteworthy territorial patterns begin to take shape. For example, various provinces in the NORTH and EAST NUTS1 regions along with MADRID (which is NUTS1, NUTS2 and NUTS3 all at the same time) close in on the top positions in the national ranking, while many of the provinces that make up the CENTRE, NORTHWEST and SOUTH macro-regions drop to lower positions.

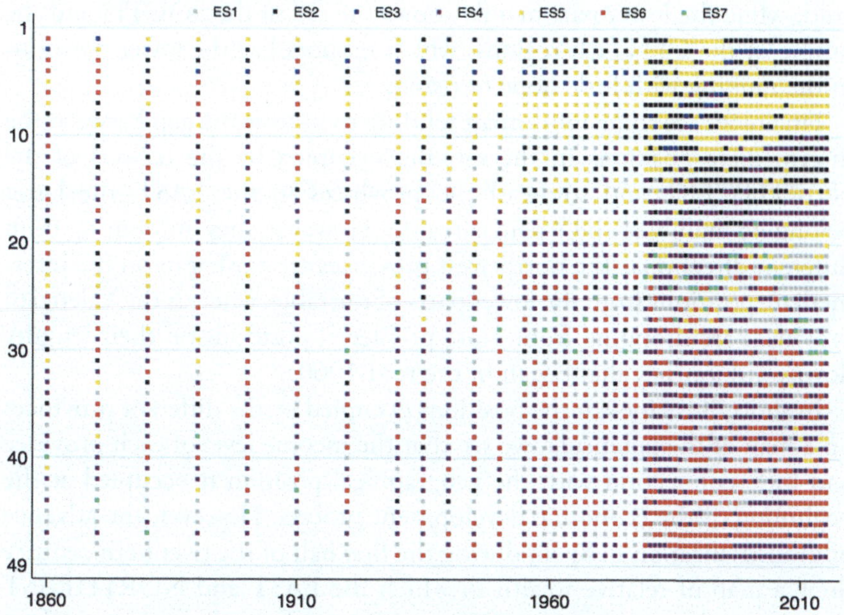

Fig. 5.7 Regional (NUTS3) per-capita GDP (ranking) mobility, Spain 1860–2015. Notes: ES1 = NORTHWEST; ES2 = NORTHEAST; ES3 = MADRID; ES4 = CENTRE; ES5 = EAST; ES6 = SOUTH; ES7 = CANARY ISLANDS. Source: See main text

In the period 1950–1980, which is a time of convergence for regional per-capita income in Spain, the map that was taking shape in the previous years is becoming more defined. However, we see that the EAST macro-region seems to be splitting in two. The southern part of this macro-region (Valencia) loses ground, while the northern and island sections (Catalonia and the Balearic Islands) hold on to their privileged positions. Elsewhere, the SOUTH and CENTRE regions are established as the poorest in Spain, while the NORTHWEST appears to be gradually rising towards the intermediate positions.

Since 1980 the new map of territorial economic inequality has taken on a more definitive shape. The MADRID and NORTH regions along with the northern part of the EAST are again occupying the top positions after making the necessary adjustment following the 1970–1980 crisis. The upper part of the graph in Fig. 5.7 is dotted with black, blue and gold, while the lower part mainly shows the red of the SOUTH and the purple of the CENTRE regions, which monopolize the lower positions in the ranking with little hope of rising.

Finally we see some movement tending to narrow the gap between the intermediate positions in the ranking occupied by the regions of the NORTHWEST and some of the provinces in the EAST, the latter belonging mainly to the Valencia region. However, they are coming from different directions. The north-west provinces are closing in on the intermediate positions from the lower parts of the table, whereas the Valencian provinces are dropping from more privileged positions on their lengthy downward journey that began in the mid-1960s.

In short, if we look at the positions occupied by the different provinces on a map of the peninsula, we see that the income level of each province had little connection with the geographical position it occupied at the beginning of the economic development process. However, the advance of industrialization in Spain during the first half of the twentieth century drew a map of relative wealth in which the EAST and NORTHEAST regions together with MADRID established themselves as the richest NUTS1 territories in the country, while the SOUTH, CENTRE and NORTHWEST regions tended to group together the poorest. This map evidently became more definite through the years of Franco's economic policy and saw no fundamental changes until the temporal division we position in 1980.

From then on, driven by the effects of the energy crisis, the MADRID and NORTHEAST regions have consolidated their leadership along with the northern part of the EAST NUTS1 region, which in the process has left the southern part behind. As far as the poorer regions are concerned, it would appear that the most northerly territories of the CENTRE region along with the NORTHWEST are heading towards levels of per-capita income typical of intermediate positions in the national ranking, leaving the SOUTH and the most southerly parts of the CENTRE NUTS1 regions at the bottom of the table.

To put it another way, today's map of relative wealth and poverty in the peninsula is beginning to show a north-south divide that did not exist in the mid-nineteenth century. The gradient of wealth then was located in the north-eastern triangle of the country (corresponding to the EAST and NORTHEAST NUTS1 regions) and poverty also affected large areas of the northern meseta and the extreme north-west of the peninsula. In order to go into the geographical aspects in more detail, Chap. 6 will focus on the in-depth study of the geography of territorial economic inequality.

Appendix

Table A5.1 Transition probability matrices by major period

	Q1	Q2	Q3	Q4	Q5	Total
1860–1910						
Q1	60.0	30.0	10.0	0.0	0.0	100.0
Q2	10.0	30.0	20.0	20.0	20.0	100.0
Q3	20.0	0.0	50.0	30.0	0.0	100.0
Q4	10.0	30.0	10.0	30.0	20.0	100.0
Q5	0.0	11.1	11.1	22.2	55.6	100.0
1910–1950						
Q1	70.0	20.0	10.0	0.0	0.0	100.0
Q2	20.0	30.0	20.0	10.0	20.0	100.0
Q3	10.0	20.0	50.0	20.0	0.0	100.0
Q4	0.0	30.0	10.0	40.0	30.0	100.0
Q5	0.0	0.0	22.2	33.3	44.4	100.0
1950–1980						
Q1	80.0	20.0	0.0	0.0	0.0	100.0
Q2	10.0	40.0	40.0	0.0	10.0	100.0
Q3	10.0	20.0	40.0	30.0	0.0	100.0
Q4	0.0	10.0	20.0	50.0	20.0	100.0
Q5	0.0	11.1	0.0	22.2	66.7	100.0
1980–2015						
Q1	90.0	10.0	0.0	0.0	0.0	100.0
Q2	10.0	60.0	10.0	20.0	0.0	100.0
Q3	0.0	30.0	40.0	10.0	20.0	100.0
Q4	0.0	0.0	40.0	40.0	20.0	100.0
Q5	0.0	0.0	11.1	33.3	55.6	100.0

Notes: Q1 refers to the top quintile and Q5 the bottom quintile of the regional income distribution

Source: See main text

References

Azariadis, C., & Stachurski, J. (2005). Poverty traps. In P. Aghion & S. N. Durlauf (Eds.), *Handbook of economic growth* (Vol. 1, pp. 295–384). Amsterdam: Elsevier.

Buyst, E. (2010). Reversal of fortune in a small, open economy: Regional GDP in Belgium, 1896–2000. *Rivista di Storia Economica, 26*, 75–92.

Buyst, E. (2011). Continuity and change in regional disparities in Belgium during the twentieth century. *Journal of Historical Geography, 37*(3), 329–337.

Díez-Minguela, A., Rosés, J. R., & Sanchis, M. T. (2016). *Paris and the French desert revisited: Regional income polarization in France, 1860–2010*. Paper presented at the 56th European Regional Science Association Congress (ERSA), Vienna, 23–26 August.

Díez-Minguela, A., & Sanchis, M. T. (2017). *Regional income inequality in France: What does history teach us?* Paper presented at XLIII Reunión de Estudios Regionales, Pablo de Olavide University, Seville, November 16–17.

Enflo, K., & Missaia, A. (2018). Regional GDP estimates for Sweden, 1571–1850. *Historical Methods: A Journal of Quantitative and Interdisciplinary History, 51*(2), 115–137.

Felice, E. (2011). Regional value added in Italy, 1891–2001, and the foundation of a long-term picture. *Economic History Review, 64*(3), 929–950.

Gravier, J. C. (1947). *Paris et le Désert Français*. Paris: Le Portulan.

Hammond, G. W., & Thompson, E. (2002). Mobility and modality trends in US state personal income. *Regional Studies, 36*(4), 375–387.

Quah, D. (1993). Empirical cross-section dynamics in economic growth. *European Economic Review, 37*(2–3), 426–434.

Quah, D. (1996). Twin Peaks: Growth and convergence in models of distribution dynamics. *Economic Journal, 106*(437), 1045–1055.

Quah, D. (1997). Empirics for growth and distribution: Stratification, polarization, and convergence clubs. *Journal of Economic Growth, 2*(1), 27–59.

Rodríguez-Pose, A. (2018). The revenge of the places that don't matter (and what to do about it). *Cambridge Journal of Regions, Economy and Society, 11*, 189–209.

Shorrocks, A. F. (1978). The measurement of mobility. *Econometrica, 46*(5), 1013–1024.

Silverman, B. W. (1992). *Density estimation for statistics and data analysis*. London: Chapman and Hall.

Storper, M. (2018). Separate worlds? Explaining the current wave of regional economic polarization. *Journal of Economic Geography, 18*, 247–270.
Wolf, N., & Rosés, J. R. (Eds.). (forthcoming). *The economic development of Europe's regions: A quantitative history since 1900*. London: Routledge.
Yamamoto, D. (2008). Scales of regional income disparities in the United States, 1955–2003. *Journal of Economic Geography, 8*(1), 79–103.

6

Spatial Patterns of Regional Income Inequality Then and Now

How Can We Explain the Spatial Pattern in Regional Income Inequality?

One of the elements highlighted by Eurostat when characterizing regional economic inequality in Europe is that it presents a definite geographical profile in the shape of a centre-to-periphery pattern. In fact, as we said in the introductory chapter, the Eurostat regional yearbook (ERY) for 2017 points out that many of the rich regions of Europe can be found on a line that starts in northern Italy and crosses Austria and Germany before splitting into two branches of prosperity: one that goes through the Benelux countries towards southern England and another that heads off towards the Nordic countries. The equivalent line for poor regions starts in the Baltic republics, then heads south across Eastern Europe towards Greece, southern Italy and the southernmost parts of the Iberian Peninsula. In this chapter we will try to verify whether the distribution of regional per-capita income follows a spatial pattern in the cases of Spain and the Iberian Peninsula as a whole, that is, Portugal and Spain together. And given the long-term character of the study, if there is a pattern we will analyse its evolution over time to enable us ultimately to outline some ideas as to its potential causes.

A. Díez-Minguela et al., *Regional Inequality in Spain*, Palgrave Studies in Economic History, https://doi.org/10.1007/978-3-319-96110-1_6

Referring back to Chap. 4, we will remember that regional economic inequality in Spain has taken on an inverted U-shape over time, or at least during the period that extends from the start of the growth and economic integration process in the mid-nineteenth century until the 1980s. This means that, after an initial period of growing inequality fuelled by the economic take-off of just a few regions, the basic characteristic of its evolution over the twentieth century was economic convergence, measured in terms of both σ and β-convergence.

A reasonable explanation for this type of evolution can be found in the neoclassical-type models for both international trade and economic growth. The initial advance of inequality would thus be explained by the specialization of a small group of regions in the sectors of highest productivity. This in turn would be explained by the relative abundance of factors such as physical and human capital. However, the economic integration of the territories that make up Spain ultimately encouraged the flow of goods and factors and their regional price convergence. Economic integration would therefore have contributed to the levelling of factor endowments and thus the convergence of production structures, productivity levels and finally territorial income.

Chapter 5, however, revealed the presence of other realities that also characterize territorial economic inequality in Spain, and it is more difficult to find an economic explanation for these if we limit ourselves to the same analytical framework. It was shown that some territories (e.g. Andalusia) have undergone a continuous process of relative decline in the course of Spain's economic history. Others (e.g. the Basque Country), which initially had low levels of income, have experienced continuous progress and positioned themselves permanently close to the top of the income ranking. In other words, at least during the first major stage of Spanish growth, the distribution of regional income was characterized by mobility between income groups. It was also shown how economic convergence was compatible with the appearance of clusters of regions grouped according to their relative levels of income, thus providing evidence of what Quah (1996) referred to as *twin peaks*.

Neoclassical trade and economic growth theories provide no solid economic explanation for this type of behaviour, but Quah (1996) reminds us that the existence of poverty traps or convergence clubs can be analysed by considering the ideas to be found in various endogenous growth models. With this kind of approach, the presence of increasing returns on certain knowledge-generating activities means that the scale of production is important in specialization processes, and that these processes have long-term effects on the growth trajectories of countries (or regions). Thus different endogenous growth models foresee the presence of multiple equilibria in national growth processes, thereby providing an economic foundation for phenomena such as *poverty traps* (Azariadis and Stachurski 2005) and *convergence clubs* (Quah 1997).

Nevertheless, in the final section of Chap. 5, which analysed the evolution in the income ranking of the provinces making up each Spanish macro-region (NUTS1), we noted the presence of a characteristic of regional economic inequality that had not yet been taken into account. Specifically, it was argued that the advance of Spanish industrialization could have given rise to a map of territorial inequality in which the location of the various provinces in the geographical space seemed to be a relevant in explaining income levels in the long term.

We saw how at the very start of the Spanish economic development process the level of income for each province bore no apparent relation to where the province was located. However, the advance of industrialization in Spain in the first half of the twentieth century sketched out a map of relative wealth in which the EAST and NORTHEAST NUTS1 regions along with MADRID established themselves as the richest territories in the country, while at the same time the SOUTH, CENTRE and NORTHWEST were forming a group of the poorest regions. Clearly a reality of this type must also be taken into account in any analysis of the causes of regional economic inequality in Spain, but the models and arguments presented so far provide no framework to enable a study of this type.

Nevertheless, the so-called new economic geography (NEG) does provide an analytical framework making it possible to explain the agglomeration of economic activity in the territory and how it relates to economic geography. It states that the existence of economies of scale in certain economic activities, mainly manufacturing in the pioneering models, forces companies to concentrate their production in a relatively small number of centres. If instead of this the aim were to minimize the costs of supplying consumers or stocking up from suppliers, the presence of high transport costs would act as a force favouring the dispersion of industry. Economic integration and lower transport costs a priori weaken this dispersion force and strengthen agglomerative tendencies.

The NEG includes another element that provides its models with a dynamic. From a theoretical point of view, the localization of end demand and input supply is not exogenous because there are cumulative causation mechanisms that tend to reinforce pre-existing industrial agglomerations. These include the *home market effect*, also known as *market access*. Although Fujita et al. (1999) provide a wide overview of the various agglomerative forces present in the NEG literature, in the seminal article by Krugman (1991) it is a combination of home market effect and labour force mobility that gives rise to the formation of centre-periphery-type patterns. Companies want to be located close to where the demand is in order to save on transport costs, and therefore industrial activities in which there are economies of scale are disproportionately concentrated in locations that have good market access. This disproportionate concentration of industry in these locations either brings about an increase in salaries or makes the location more attractive to workers migrating from other regions. Both these phenomena tend to lead to an even greater increase in the proportion of income and spending enjoyed by the already advantaged location. In this way the economic integration processes would be the driving force behind the appearance of geographical patterns like those described for the European Union or those which could potentially come about in the case of Spain.

The ideas contained in the NEG literature have also been backed up by recent developments in endogenous growth theory (with geography), thereby providing an economic foundation for the relationship between territorial differences in market access and regional growth. This body of theory posits that market size fosters growth because greater size leads to increasing returns on knowledge creation from investments in R&D and human capital training (Martin and Ottaviano 1999; Baldwin and Martin 2004). In this kind of model, market integration encourages larger markets to regionally specialize in activities characterized by the presence of increasing returns, thereby promoting growth. However, in the case of local R&D spillovers, the outcome could be the emergence of centre-periphery structures from a geographical point of view.

Now that we have described the economic foundation that enables us to construct hypotheses as to what causes geographical patterns to appear in the course of the development and economic integration processes, the next section will focus on supplying evidence for the existence and evolution of these patterns in the case of Spain.

Is There a Geographical Pattern of Territorial Inequality in Spain? Descriptive Evidence

As we already know, Spain's richest regions today are grouped inside the NORTHEAST, EAST and MADRID NUTS1 macro-regions. We also know that over the course of the Spanish economic development process there have been individual stories of success and failure and that, especially during the period 1860–1950, the distribution of regional income was characterized by the presence of significant interclass mobility. Given these conditions, we should ask ourselves when exactly the current map of inequality took shape and whether it has been stable over time.

A simple illustration of how regional income distribution has evolved spatially can be seen in the map in Fig. 6.1. The provinces (NUTS3) are shaded according to their ranking in a given year, with the darkest being the richest and the lightest the poorest. A rapid perusal gives us an initial idea of the existence of spatial patterns in the levels of per-capita income.

The maps show that in the first stage of the industrialization process, which we have dated between 1860 and 1910, there is no obvious geographical pattern to be seen as regards provincial levels of income. In fact, with the exception of the extreme north-west of the peninsula, we see that all the Spanish NUTS1 macro-regions contain a mixture of provinces with per-capita income levels in the upper and lower parts of the regional income distribution. This situation appears not to change to any great extent by the end of this period in 1910, when broadly speaking the same type of reality applies. The only noteworthy element would perhaps be that there are fewer provinces from the SOUTH macro-region continuing in the upper part of the distribution. Certainly the distribution of rich and poor provinces does not seem to follow any significant spatial pattern at the end of this early stage in the Spanish economic development process.

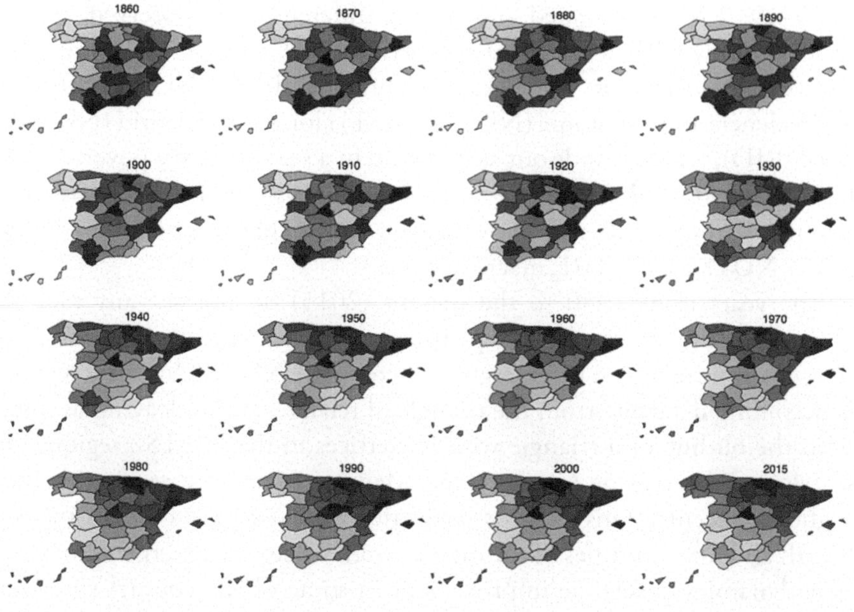

Fig. 6.1 Regional (NUTS3) per-capita GDP, Spain 1860–2010. Source: See main text

However, in the stage we have dated between 1910 and 1950 we start to discern the emergence of a geographical pattern in territorial inequality. Throughout this period the rich regions gradually seem to become grouped within the NORTHEAST, EAST and MADRID NUTS1 macro-regions, that is, in the territory occupied by the Mediterranean corridor, then extending along the Ebro valley towards the Basque Country. Madrid, the state capital, has no direct connection to this area, but it does have a level of income that places it in the top quintile. The poorest regions, on the other hand, are located along a line that crosses the peninsula from south-east to north-west. In other words the resulting pattern was characterized by a decreasing gradient of per-capita GDP running from the north-east to the south-west of Spain.

As would be expected, in the period 1950–1980, characterized as it was by strong regional convergence in a context of very little mobility between classes or quintiles, there are no major changes in the country's economic geography. The map that took shape during the period

1910–1950 is consolidated and no big differences are observed in the way it is drawn. The triangle of prosperity is still the one marked out by the vertices located in the Basque Country (NUTS1 NORTHEAST) and Valencia and Catalonia (NUTS1 EAST) along with Madrid (NUTS1 MADRID), which stands out as an island in a sea of relative poverty. The band of territory denoting the poorest provinces continues to cross the peninsula from south-east to north-west and includes various provinces of the NUTS1 CENTRE macro-region.

The years from 1980 to the present (2015) do not see any radical changes to the geography of Spanish territorial inequality. However, a new dynamic seems to be emerging whereby the NUTS2 Valencia region is becoming detached from the triangle of relative wealth, leaving us now with the outline of a triangle with its vertices in the NUTS2 regions of Catalonia, the Basque Country and Madrid. As for the areas with the highest concentrations of poor territories with per-capita GDPs in the fourth and fifth quintiles of the distribution, we see the emergence of two new dynamics: a relative improvement in some of the country's north-western provinces and a growing concentration of poor territories to the south of a line that cuts across the peninsula from east to west.

In short, it could be said that, at least since the 1950s, regional inequality in Spain has followed a spatial pattern. This would have taken shape in parallel with the advance of industrialization and the increasing number of territories that took part in it in the first half of the twentieth century. Since taking shape this pattern has undergone no radical transformations, and indeed changes of any kind were virtually non-existent between 1950 and 1980. However, although limited in size, changes do start to appear in the period 1980–2015 and the map of inequality seems to take on more of a north-south aspect than previously characterized the case of Spain.

Is the Pattern Significant? Analytical Evidence

The descriptive evidence provided by the maps does not, however, provide definitive confirmation of the existence of a spatial pattern in the distribution of per-capita GDP in Spain. In order to prove the existence of such a pattern, we now supply some spatial autocorrelation statistics. This type of indicator makes it possible to verify whether or not the income levels of the different regions are significantly associated with the levels reached by regions that are closer in a territorial sense.

To test for the presence of spatial clustering we use Moran's I spatial autocorrelation statistic, which can be defined as follows:

$$\mathrm{I} = \frac{\#\text{Provinces}}{\Sigma_i \Sigma_j \omega_{ij}} \frac{\Sigma_i \Sigma_j \omega_{ij} \left(Y_i - \overline{Y}\right)\left(Y_j - \overline{Y}\right)}{\Sigma_i \left(Y_i - \overline{Y}\right)^2} \tag{6.1}$$

where #Provinces is the number of provinces, Y_i is provincial per-capita GDP, $\overline{Y}$ is the average of Y, and ω represents the matrix of spatial weights.[1] We use two different matrices to compute the statistic: a contiguity matrix and an inverse distance squared spatial matrix (the distance being between provincial capitals).

According to Fig. 6.1, we should expect to see a positive spatial autocorrelation, at least from the end of the first half of the twentieth century. On the whole Moran's I statistic confirms our expectations, being significant at a level of either 1 per cent or 5 per cent for all years (see Fig. 6.2). The trajectories reveal that spatial autocorrelation was relatively low between 1860 and 1930, which would partly be due to the concentration of industry in certain non-contiguous provinces, for example, Barcelona and Bizkaia. It then increased rapidly between 1930 and 1950. Generally speaking, spatial clustering and decreasing regional inequality would indicate that high-productivity activities were spreading from the richest provinces to neighbouring or nearby provinces in the course of a process that continued throughout the second half of the twentieth century. However, spatial clustering occurred when income (class/ranking) mobility was very low, which would suggest that relative positions were consolidated.

The graph also shows that the maximum value of Moran's I is reached in around 2000, since when it seems to have started on a downward path. This evolution could be related to the new upsurge in inequality (see

[1] Subindex i denotes the province being studied, while j denotes the remaining provinces.

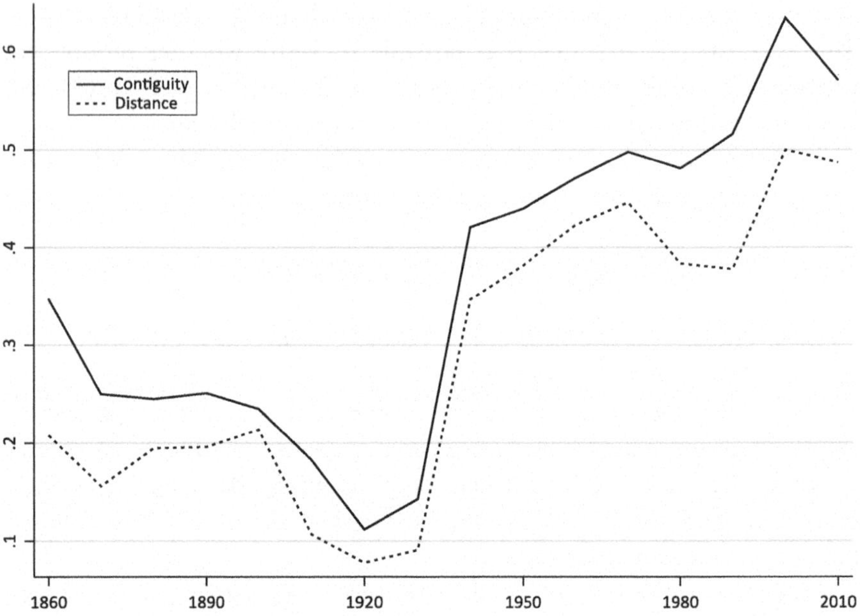

Fig. 6.2 Spatial clustering (Moran's I) of regional (NUTS3) per-capita GDP, Spain 1860–2010. Source: See main text. Note: All values are statistically significant at 1 per cent except for the years 1910, 1920 and 1930, for which values are significant at 5 per cent.

Chap. 4) in a context which sees the apparent reactivation of mobility between income quintiles (Chap. 5). Unfortunately there is not enough of a time perspective for us to categorically state that a new spatial pattern of regional inequality has begun.

To further analyse spatial clustering we present LISA maps of regional income inequality, LISA being local indicators of spatial association. These maps are useful for identifying the geographical position of rich (poor) provinces and the degree of spatial autocorrelation. The blue provinces denote clusters with low per-capita GDP, while the red ones are those with high per-capita GDP. As mentioned earlier, spatial clustering increased rapidly from 1930 onwards.

The map in Fig. 6.3 shows that by 1930 there were four major clusters with correlated levels of per-capita GDP, two of them (rich) in the EAST and NORTHEAST and two (poor) in Extremadura-Ciudad Real in the

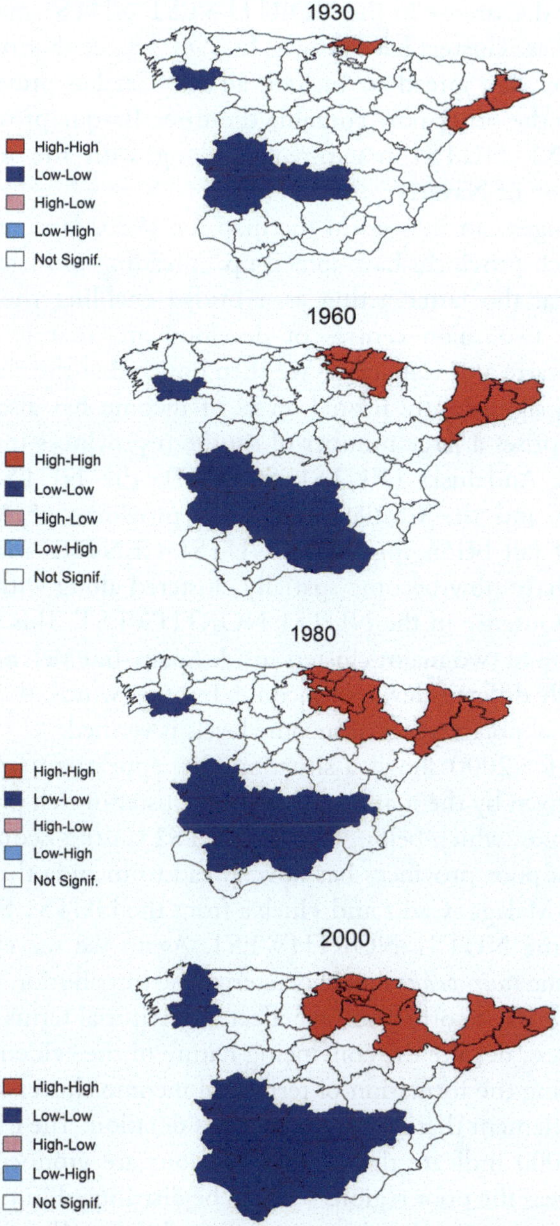

Fig. 6.3 Spatial clustering. LISA maps, 1930–2010. Source: See main text

CENTRE and Ourense in the NORTHWEST NUTS1 macro-regions. Since then these clusters have grown. In 1960 we see that one cluster of rich provinces has spread to include all the Catalan provinces in the EAST, while the other now contains the three Basque provinces of the NORTHEAST NUTS1 macro-region along with the neighbouring NUTS2 region of Navarre.

More changes can be seen in the map for 1980. First of all the two clusters of rich provinces have joined up, spreading to include La Rioja and Zaragoza, the latter acting as a bridge enabling the connection between the two main centres of development, that is, the Basque Country-Navarre and Catalonia. We then notice that the cluster of poor regions with significantly related levels of income has also grown. By 1980 it comprises a large number of southern provinces including four provinces of Andalusia (NUTS1 SOUTH), the NUTS2 region of Extremadura and the Castile-La Mancha provinces of Albacete and Ciudad Real (all belonging to the NUTS1 CENTRE macro-region). These areas have now become spatially clustered along with the distant province of Ourense in the NUTS1 NORTHWEST. This would point to the creation of two major clusters inside Spain, one rich and one poor, with markedly different levels of income. In other words, the existence of a strong spatial polarization of income levels is verified.

The map for 2000 shows a situation that appears to strengthen the impression given by the map for 1980. The cluster of rich provinces now includes Burgos, which belongs to the NUTS2 Castile-Leon region, and the cluster of poor provinces has now spread to include the Andalusian provinces of Malaga, Cadiz and Huelva from the NUTS1 SOUTH and Lugo from the NUTS1 NORTHWEST. Again we see evidence that bimodality, the *twin peaks* that characterize the distribution of provincial income levels, has a corresponding effect in territorial terms.

Nevertheless, despite the convincing nature of the evidence presented so far regarding the formation of territorial income clusters, this continues to be an element that merits special consideration. The LISA maps for 1980 and 2000 indicate that the rich regions are grouped in a single cluster, whereas the poor regions seem to be distributed in two territorial blocks, one in the south and one in the north-west. The reason behind this somewhat surprising fact becomes clear when we analyse regional inequality not just in Spain but in the Iberian Peninsula as a whole.

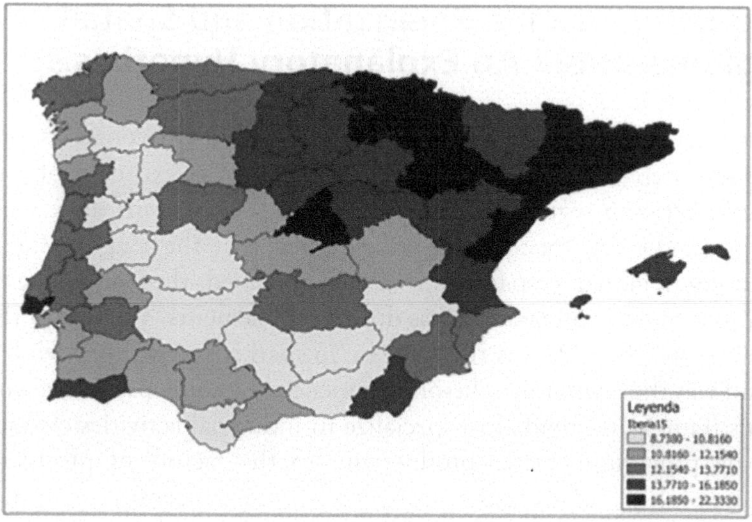

Fig. 6.4 Regional per-capita GDP in the Iberian Peninsula (2000). Source: Tirado and Badia (2014)

The map in Fig. 6.4 reflects territorial inequality in the whole peninsula, that is, Spain and Portugal together, in 2000. To create the map, per-capita GDP in 1990 PPP Geary-Khamis dollar was calculated for the NUTS3 regions of Spain and the historical districts of Portugal and then grouped in quintiles. Again, the darkest regions belong to the top or "very rich" quintile, while the regions from the bottom or "very poor" quintile are white.

The evidence the map provides enables us to see that the cluster of poor Spanish regions located in the SOUTH and CENTRE macro-regions actually connects with the cluster of provinces in the NORTHWEST via the regions of inland Portugal. Together they form a single band of poor regions that begins in the south-east of the peninsula and extends unbroken towards the west and north-west, taking in territories located on both sides of the Spanish-Portuguese border. In other words, the cluster of poor regions crosses the frontiers of the national states that make up the Iberian Peninsula.[2]

[2] An in-depth analysis of regional inequality in Iberia can be found in Tirado and Badia (2014).

Inequality, Income Polarization and Spatial Agglomeration: An Explanatory Hypothesis

Spanish economic history has supplied an explanatory hypothesis for the evidence offered in the previous section, that is, the existence of a relationship between regional income levels and the locations these regions occupy in the territory. It has been argued that the lengthy stage of increasing regional disparities that accompanied the early stages of Spanish economic integration was due to two elements. The first of these, as shown in Chap. 2, was the increase in market integration, while the second was the economic take-off experienced by some provinces which, in this framework, tended to specialize in industrial activities characterized by providing greater productivity to the factors of production. Because of this, and given the strongly territorial concentration of industry, the emergence of big differences in production structures across regions led to an upswing in regional economic inequality. As indicated in various investigations, the reason for this was that those regions that specialized in industrial production enjoyed higher levels of per-capita income.[3] The question that now needs to be answered is: how do we explain the fact that some territories and not others specialized in industrial activities in this context of economic integration and technological change? Is sector specialization related in any way to the location of territories in the geographical space?

Earlier in this chapter it was shown how NEG thinking provides a particularly suitable theoretical framework to answer questions of this type. It is therefore no surprise that various recent investigations have tested the empirical validity of the elements highlighted in the NEG literature as providing a plausible explanation for the patterns of territorial specialization observed in Spain. Economic historians have carried out detailed research into the roots and causes of this notable increase in the spatial concentration of manufacturing before the Spanish Civil War by exploring the two major explanatory theories in the literature: traditional

[3] This interpretation is provided in Rosés et al. (2010), for example.

trade theory (comparative advantage in a HO setting) and NEG. So how can the location of industry in Spain be explained?

Following Davis and Weinstein (1999, 2003), Rosés (2003) found evidence that the *home market effect* was the driving force behind early industrialization in Catalonia (around the 1860s). Rosés (2003) concluded that during the rise of Catalonia as a centre of industrial production in the first phase of Spain's industrialization two types of basic explanatory elements coincided: factor endowments, tied to the availability of human capital, and home market size, which resulted in advantages for the location of manufacturing around Barcelona. Tirado et al. (2002), in line with Kim (1995), identified economies of scale and market size as being determinants of Spain's industrial geography in the mid-nineteenth century. By the end of the century the explanatory power of these NEG effects had increased in parallel with the advance of the economic integration process.

More recently Martinez-Galarraga (2012), adopting the approach developed by Midelfart-Knarvik et al. (2002), confirmed and extended the previous findings of Tirado et al. (2002).[4] He found that as the domestic market became integrated and industrialization progressed in Spain during the second half of the nineteenth century, NEG forces grew to be the main determinant of Spain's industrial landscape. Although comparative advantage factors such as regional endowments of human capital or infrastructures were important in explaining regional industrial specialization, the scale effects suggested by Krugman (1991), captured by the interaction between economies of scale and market potential, played a decisive role. Industries with increasing returns tended to be concentrated in provinces with the best access to demand up to the 1930s.

From a different perspective, Martínez-Galarraga et al. (2008) analysed the existence of an agglomeration effect in Spanish industry over the

[4] This methodology has been used extensively in economic history: Wolf (2007) analysed reunified Poland during the interwar years after the First World War; Crafts and Mulatu (2005, 2006) studied the Victorian period in Britain; Klein and Crafts (2012) applied the approach when reexamining the manufacturing belt in the US between 1880 and 1920; Ronsse and Rayp (2016) studied the determinants of manufacturing location in Belgium between 1896 and 1961; Nikolic (2018) focuses on interwar Yugoslavia; and Missiaia (2018) analyses Italy in the period 1871–1911.

long term along the lines suggested by Ciccone and Hall (1996) and Ciccone (2002). Their paper provides evidence to support the existence of an agglomeration effect linking the spatial density of economic activity and interregional differences in industrial labour productivity in Spain. They showed that the estimated elasticity of employment with respect to labour productivity played a key role during the early stages of industrialization. The estimated elasticity between economic densities with respect to labour productivity in the industrial sector was about 5 per cent in the period 1860–1900 and 4.5 per cent in the interwar period (1914–1930), that is, close to the values for the US and Europe at the end of the 1980s provided by Ciccone and Hall.[5] Hence higher economic density in connection with greater market size brought about higher labour productivity in the provinces of Spain.

In the context of the Spanish economy, researchers have also tested another hypothesis emerging from the NEG literature, the verification of which will ultimately provide additional evidence of the explanatory potential of the elements highlighted by the NEG as playing a part in the shaping of Spanish industrial geography. Specifically, they studied the wage gradient, that is, the existence of higher wages in regions that have greater market potential resulting from the agglomeration of manufacturers in core regions (*backward linkages*), and the way these wages attract and generate migratory flows of workers (*forward linkages*). These are included among the centripetal forces highlighted by the NEG (Krugman 1991) as potentially being responsible for agglomeration in the early stages of economic development.

Following Hanson's (2005) influential research based on the Krugman wage equation, Tirado et al. (2013) examined the existence of a spatial structure in nominal industrial wages in Spain in the 1920s. The results verified that wages were higher in regions with greater market potential, and the authors confirmed the existence of a wage gradient centred on Barcelona, the main industrial centre of interwar Spain. Their work also showed that domestic market potential became more important as pro-

[5] Combes et al. (2011) carried out a similar analysis for France between 1860, 1930 and 2000. The parameters they estimated suggested that doubling employment density in a French *département* would result in labour productivity gains of around 5 per cent.

tectionism in the Spanish economy and main European markets increased during the 1920s, while the wage gradient centred on Barcelona declined.[6]

Likewise but following the NEG model in Crozet (2004), Pons et al. (2007) established a direct relationship between migration decisions and the host regions' market potential during the 1920s, thus verifying the presence of forward linkages in internal migrations between Spain's provinces in the interwar years. However, although Spanish workers were drawn to industrial agglomerations, this attraction was limited to relatively nearby areas. This would explain the apparently low intensity of internal migrations in Spain before the 1920s and the geography of the migrations of the interwar years. Migratory flows to the main industrial centres did not originate from the poorest regions furthest away from them in the south of the peninsula. The lower migration from these areas was due to migration costs that were proportional to the distance workers had to travel.

Recent investigations have also shown that the presence of NEG effects was not limited exclusively to industry. The impact of NEG-type mechanisms affected the Spanish economy as a whole in the early stages of economic development. There is evidence that proves that market access and agglomeration forces played an important part that helps explain the upswing in regional income inequality between 1860 and 1930. Martinez-Galarraga et al. (2015), following Ottaviano and Pinelli (2006), found a direct connection between market potential and regional economic growth in the early decades of the twentieth century. The provinces with the greatest market potential were those that experienced the highest growth, at least after the turn of the century. And Díez-Minguela et al. (2016), following Brülhart and Sbergami (2009), found that in line with NEG models, agglomeration economies in a context of market integration increased regional inequality in the second half of the nineteenth century and hindered its reduction during the early decades of the twentieth.

[6] This exercise thus contributed to the existing theoretical and empirical NEG debate on the effects of international integration on countries' internal geography (Hanson 1997; Krugman and Livas-Elizondo 1996; Crozet and Koenig 2004). A similar long-term analysis for Italy can be found in A'Hearn and Venables (2011).

To summarize, these investigations provide us with a foundation on which to base our explanatory hypothesis for the rise in regional economic inequality during the initial stages of Spanish economic development (Chap. 4) which, moreover, is compatible with the evidence on income polarization (Chap. 5) and the existence of a set of rich and poor regions that are not randomly distributed across the geographical space. This hypothesis is that, in a context of economic integration and reductions in transport costs, differences in regional market size magnified the industrial specialization of a small group of Spanish regions. This specialization helped these regions to benefit from increasing returns in manufacturing and allowed them to achieve higher levels of income, thereby creating an upsurge in regional economic inequality. Territorial inequality was related to the location of the regions in the geographical space. The cluster of rich regions was located in areas close to the big domestic and foreign markets. The grouping of poor regions was characterized by being located on the geographical periphery of Spain. A more detailed analysis of this hypothesis will be the focus of the next chapter.

References

A'Hearn, B., & Venables, A. J. (2011). Internal geography and external trade: Regional disparities in Italy, 1861–2011. *Quaderni di Storia Economica*, 12, Bank of Italy.

Azariadis, C., & Stachurski, J. (2005). Poverty traps. In P. Aghion & S. N. Durlauf (Eds.), *Handbook of economic growth* (Vol. 1, pp. 295–384). Amsterdam: Elsevier.

Baldwin, R., & Martin, P. (2004). Agglomeration and regional growth. In J. V. Henderson & J. F. Thisse (Eds.), *Handbook of regional and urban economics* (Vol. 4, pp. 2671–2711). Amsterdam: Elsevier.

Brülhart, M., & Sbergami, F. (2009). Agglomeration and growth: Cross-country evidence. *Journal of Urban Economics, 65*(1), 48–63.

Ciccone, A. (2002). Agglomeration effects in Europe. *European Economic Review, 46*(2), 213–227.

Ciccone, A., & Hall, R. E. (1996). Productivity and the density of economic activity. *American Economic Review, 86*(1), 54–70.

Combes, P. P., Lafourcade, M., Thisse, J. F., & Toutain, J. C. (2011). The rise and fall of spatial inequalities in France: A long-run perspective. *Explorations in Economic History, 48*(2), 243–271.
Crafts, N., & Mulatu, A. (2005). What explains the location of industry in Britain, 1871–1931? *Journal of Economic Geography, 5*(4), 499–518.
Crafts, N., & Mulatu, A. (2006). How did the location of industry respond to falling transport costs in Britain before World War I? *The Journal of Economic History, 66*(3), 575–607.
Crozet, M. (2004). Do migrants follow market potentials? An estimation of a New Economic Geography model. *Journal of Economic Geography, 4*(4), 439–458.
Crozet, M., & Koenig, P. (2004). Trade liberalization and the internal geography of countries. In T. Mayer & M. Mucchielli (Eds.), *Multinational firms' location and economic geography* (pp. 91–109). Cheltenham: Edward Elgar.
Davis, D. R., & Weinstein, D. E. (1999). Economic geography and regional production structure: An empirical investigation. *European Economic Review, 43*(2), 379–407.
Davis, D. R., & Weinstein, D. E. (2003). Market access, economic geography and comparative advantage: An empirical test. *Journal of International Economics, 59*(1), 1–23.
Díez-Minguela, A., Martinez-Galarraga, J., & Tirado, D. A. (2016). Why did Spanish regions not converge before the Civil War? Agglomeration economies and (regional) growth revisited. *Revista de Historia Económica/Journal of Iberian and Latin American Economic History, 34*(3), 417–448.
Fujita, M., Krugman, P., & Venables, A. J. (1999). *The spatial economy: Cities, regions and international trade.* Cambridge, MA: The MIT Press.
Hanson, G. H. (1997). Increasing returns, trade and the regional structure of wages. *Economic Journal, 107*, 113–133.
Hanson, G. H. (2005). Market potential, increasing returns and geographic concentration. *Journal of International Economics, 67*(1), 1–24.
Kim, S. (1995). Expansion of markets and the geographic distribution of economic activities: The trends in U.S. regional manufacturing structure, 1860–1987. *Quarterly Journal of Economics, 110*(4), 881–908.
Klein, A., & Crafts, N. (2012). Making sense of the manufacturing belt: Determinants of U.S. industrial location, 1880–1920. *Journal of Economic Geography, 12*(4), 775–807.
Krugman, P. (1991). Increasing returns and economic geography. *Journal of Political Economy, 99*(3), 483–499.

Krugman, P., & Livas-Elizondo, R. (1996). Trade policy and the Third World metropolis. *Journal of Development Economics, 49*(1), 137–150.

Martin, P., & Ottaviano, G. (1999). Growing locations: Industry location in a model of endogenous growth. *European Economic Review, 43*(2), 281–302.

Martinez-Galarraga, J. (2012). The determinants of industrial location in Spain, 1856–1929. *Explorations in Economic History, 49*(2), 255–275.

Martínez-Galarraga, J., Paluzie, E., Pons, J., & Tirado, D. A. (2008). Agglomeration and labour productivity in Spain over the long term. *Cliometrica, 2*(3), 195–212.

Martinez-Galarraga, J., Tirado, D. A., & González-Val, R. (2015). Market potential and regional economic growth in Spain (1860–1930). *European Review of Economic History, 19*(4), 335–358.

Midelfart-Knarvik, K. H., Overman, H., Redding, S., & Venables, A. J. (2002). The location of European industry. In European Commission (Ed.), *European economy: European integration and the functioning of product markets, 2/2002* (pp. 213–269). Brussels: Directorate-General for Economic and Financial Affairs.

Missiaia, A. (2018). *Old patterns die hard: Regional aspects of the Italian industrialization in the long run*. Paper presented at the Workshop on Economic Geography of Long-Run Industrialization, at the International Institute of Social History (IISH), 22–23 March.

Nikolic, S. (2018). Determinants of industrial location: Kingdom of Yugoslavia in the interwar period. *European Review of Economic History, 22*(1), 101–133.

Ottaviano, G., & Pinelli, D. (2006). Market potential and productivity: Evidence from Finnish regions. *Regional Science and Urban Economics, 36*(5), 636–657.

Pons, J., Paluzie, E., Silvestre, J., & Tirado, D. A. (2007). Testing the new economic geography: Migrations and industrial agglomerations in Spain. *Journal of Regional Science, 47*(2), 289–313.

Quah, D. (1996). Twin Peaks: Growth and convergence in models of distribution dynamics. *Economic Journal, 106*(437), 1045–1055.

Quah, D. (1997). Empirics for growth and distribution: Stratification, polarization, and convergence clubs. *Journal of Economic Growth, 2*(1), 27–59.

Ronsse, S., & Rayp, G. (2016). What determined the location of industry in Belgium, 1896–1961? *Journal of Interdisciplinary History, 46*(3), 393–419.

Rosés, J. R. (2003). Why isn't the whole of Spain industrialized? New economic geography and early industrialization, 1797–1910. *The Journal of Economic History, 63*(4), 995–1022.

Rosés, J. R., Martinez-Galarraga, J., & Tirado, D. A. (2010). The upswing of regional income inequality in Spain (1860–1930). *Explorations in Economic History, 47*(2), 244–257.

Tirado, D. A., & Badia, M. (2014). New evidence on regional economic inequality in Iberia (1900–2000). *Historical Methods: A Journal of Quantitative and Interdisciplinary History, 47*(4), 180–189.

Tirado, D. A., Paluzie, E., & Pons, J. (2002). Economic integration and industrial location: The case of Spain before World War I. *Journal of Economic Geography, 2*(3), 343–363.

Tirado, D. A., Pons, J., Paluzie, E., & Martinez-Galarraga, J. (2013). Trade policy and wage gradients: Evidence from a protectionist turn. *Cliometrica, 7*(3), 295–318.

Wolf, N. (2007). Endowments vs. market potential: What explains the relocation of industry after the Polish reunification in 1918? *Explorations in Economic History, 44*(1), 22–42.

7

What Explains the Long-term Evolution of Regional Income Inequality in Spain?

Over the previous chapters we have carried out a descriptive analysis enabling us to go more deeply into the main characteristics of regional inequality in Spain since the beginning of modern economic growth. We have seen, for example, that regional disparities in per-capita income have not disappeared despite more than 150 years of economic and political integration. Indeed, although they may be smaller than at other times in the past, they are still considerable today. On top of this, we have seen that the convergence process has not advanced since the 1980s and that we have entered a new stage marked by an (as yet slight) increase in regional inequality.

We have also seen how the history of Spanish regional inequality has fluctuated between periods of upsurges and downturns and diverse regional growth paths, which have led to an evolution in the shape of an inverted U-curve, that is, one major stage characterized by divergence followed by another characterized by convergence. In addition to this we know that there was relatively high mobility in the early stages of development and that a geographical pattern took shape over time that shows increasing polarization between the north, on the one hand, and the south and the territories along the border with Portugal on the other. And all this has happened since the start of the industrialization process

A. Díez-Minguela et al., *Regional Inequality in Spain*, Palgrave Studies in Economic History, https://doi.org/10.1007/978-3-319-96110-1_7

and in the course of two simultaneous economic integration processes: the construction of the national market, which began in the mid-nineteenth century, and Spain's integration into the international economy. Interestingly, this international integration has also been through several stages over these 150 years. After an unsuccessful start in the second half of the nineteenth century, it resumed in the middle of the twentieth century and then speeded up over later decades once Spain became a member of the European Union.

Now that we know what happened with regional economic inequality in Spain, the next step is to try and understand why. In this chapter we therefore present a number of empirical analyses to help us disentangle the basic forces behind the evolution of regional inequality in per-capita income.[1]

Income Per Capita, Labour Productivity and the Activity Rate: Which Matters Most?

One way of starting an analysis of regional differences in per-capita income is to carry out a simple decomposition exercise. This involves breaking down the GDP per capita (Y/N) into output per worker (Y/L) and the employment-to-population ratio (L/N) following this expression:

$$\frac{Y_{it}}{N_{it}} = \frac{Y_{it}}{L_{it}} \times \frac{L_{it}}{N_{it}} \tag{7.1}$$

where Y_{it} is GDP in region i in year t, N_{it} is the total population in region i in year t, and L_{it} is the total active population in region i in year t. Per-capita GDP is thus split between two terms: labour productivity and the economic activity rate. Simply put, this accounting exercise enables us to analyse the extent to which regional income disparities can be attributed to either differences in labour productivity or to demographic and institutional aspects affecting regional labour markets.

[1] Parts of this chapter are based on work carried out with Joan R. Rosés.

Identifying the role played by these two main components (aggregate productivity and labour markets) is no trivial issue but a matter of concern when designing regional policies (Esteban 2000; Ezcurra et al. 2005; LeGallo and Kamarianakis 2011). When regional imbalances are caused by disparities in regional labour markets, the effectiveness of public policies at regional level could be limited.[2] In contrast, if disparities in per-capita GDP are the result of differences in region-specific productivities, as in the EU in the late 1980s when productivity differentials explained almost two-thirds of the dispersion of GDP per capita (Esteban 2000), then public investment in infrastructures or human capital could be useful in reducing productivity gaps across regions and ultimately bring about convergence between less prosperous and more prosperous territories.

Figure 7.1 shows the long-term evolution of σ-convergence—or simply the coefficient of variation—for regional (NUTS2) GDP per capita, GDP per worker and the economic activity rate.[3] As we saw in earlier chapters, regional income inequality followed an inverted U-shaped pattern over the long term, with increasing inequality between 1860 and the early twentieth century followed by a long stage of decreasing inequality that in the case of income per capita lasted until the 1980s. Inequality in income per worker follows a trajectory similar to that for income per capita. However, the labour productivity convergence process does not come to a halt in the 1980s and the gap continues to narrow. Nevertheless, at different points in time, in both cases, the persistence of regional inequality seems to signal the end, at least temporarily, of this regional σ-convergence process.

The small differences in activity rates across regions over time show that regional disparities in per-worker income were the main factor contributing to the evolution of regional income inequality. However, in a context of decreasing labour productivity differentials since virtually the beginning of the twentieth century, the relative importance of aspects connected to the labour market has varied, despite the fact that its temporal evolution shows a certain stability. Interestingly, in the last of the

[2] This was the case in the US in the 1980s, for instance, where differences in employment rates across states were crucial (Browne 1989; Carlino 1992).

[3] The results and paths shown here are similar if the exercise is applied to other levels of territorial disaggregation (NUTS1, NUTS3).

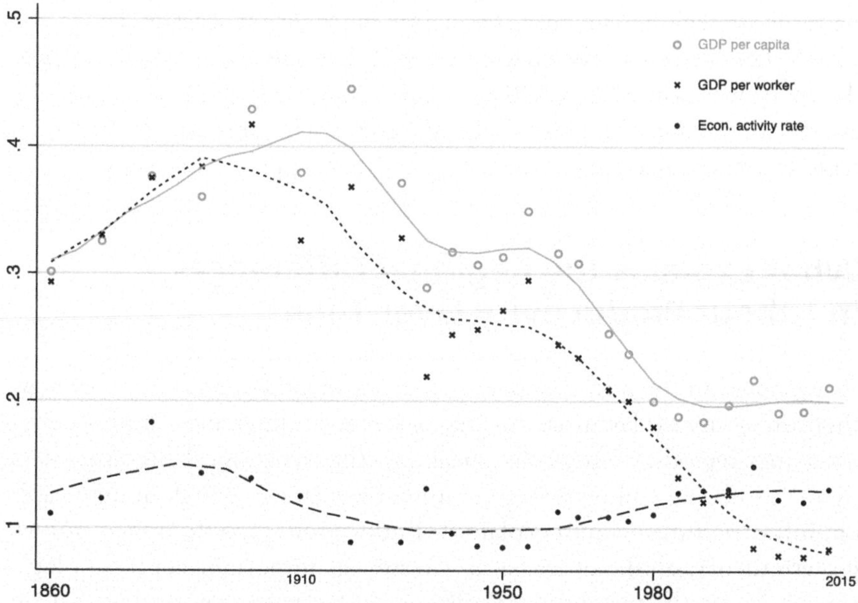

Fig. 7.1 Regional (NUTS2) inequality (GDP per capita, GDP per worker and economic activity rates). Note: Regional inequality is measured by a coefficient of variation. The solid and dashed lines are a polynomial smoothing. Source: See main text

major stages into which we have divided the long-term evolution of the Spanish economy, that is, 1980–2015, we see a trend towards a slight increase in the differences between regional activity rates. Also, since 1990 the coefficient of variation for these has been higher than that for regional differences in productivity. To put it another way, the gradual increase in regional inequality seen between 1980 and 2015 is due to increasing territorial differences in the labour market rather than the evolution of regional inequality in productivity. This is certainly an element to be highlighted when describing the determinants of growth in territorial inequality in recent times, since it calls into question the effectiveness of territorial cohesion policies aimed at reducing the gap between regional productivity rates.

From a broad temporal perspective, given the trajectory of these three components, it can be concluded that an analysis of the differences in regional labour productivity is essential for understanding the long-term patterns of regional income inequality in Spain, at least as far as the 1980s. For the rest of the chapter we will therefore focus on labour productivity as measured by GDP per worker, the aim being to explore those aspects that could be behind the differences in productivity between regions and their relative importance at different points in history.

What Explains the Regional Differences in Labour Productivity Over Time?

As we noted in the introductory chapter, from a theoretical point of view there are many explanations for the existence of differences in productivity across regions. Generically speaking, the neoclassical literature says that the unequal endowment of cumulative factors (capital, human capital, infrastructures) would explain it. Endogenous growth models or new growth theory, on the other hand, stresses the importance of technology, since it is also the technological differences between regions that explain the existence of regional inequality in terms of product per worker. And when we consider that the economy is made up of different sectors and that each sector has different levels of productivity, then territorial differences in the production structure become a prime factor for explaining regional inequality.

To get closer to the overall causes of differences in labour productivity across Spanish NUTS2 regions, we compute Theil's T index (Theil 1967) for different benchmark years on a decadal basis beginning in 1860.[4] This will enable us to measure regional inequality in labour productivity using GDP and employment figures at sector level, in line with the following equation:

$$T = \sum_{j=1}^{3}\sum_{i=1}^{n}\left(\frac{Y_{ji}}{Y}\right)\log\left(\frac{Y_{ji}/Y}{E_{ji}/E}\right) = \sum_{j=1}^{3}\sum_{i=1}^{n}\left(\log\left(x_{ji}\right)-\log\left(\bar{x}\right)\right)\frac{Y_{ji}}{Y} \quad (7.2)$$

[4]We follow Akita and Kataoka's (2003) approach. Martinez-Galarraga et al. (2015) present a decomposition exercise of this type for the period 1860–2000.

$$\overline{x} = \frac{Y}{E}$$

where Y is per-capita GDP, E is employment, j indexes the main sectors of the economy (agriculture, industry and services) and i the regions. The index is broken down into two components: within-sector inequality (T_W) and between-sector inequality (T_B). Equation (7.2) disaggregates into:

$$T = T_W + T_B = \sum_{j-1}^{3}\left(\frac{Y_j}{Y}\right)T_j + \sum_{j-1}^{3}\left(\frac{Y_j}{Y}\right)\log\left(\frac{Y_j/Y}{E_j/E}\right), \tag{7.3}$$

where

$$T_W = \sum_{j-1}^{3}\left(\frac{Y_j}{Y}\right)\sum_{i=1}^{n}\left(\log\left(x_{ji}\right) - \log\left(\overline{x}_j\right)\right)\frac{Y_{ji}}{Y} \quad \text{for } j = 1,2 \text{ and } 3, \tag{7.3a}$$

and

$$T_B = \sum_{j-1}^{3}\left(\frac{Y_j}{Y}\right)\log\left(\frac{Y_j/Y}{E_j/E}\right) = \sum_{i-1}^{3}\left(\log\left(\overline{x}_j\right) - \log\left(\overline{x}\right)\right)\frac{Y_j}{Y} \tag{7.3b}$$

where T_W is the weighted average of regional inequalities in labour productivity in each sector, and T_B is the inequality in labour productivity between sectors. The different Theil T indices are shown in Table 7.1 and Fig. 7.2 for the benchmark years that divide up our period of study.

As we can see from Table 7.1 and Fig. 7.2, overall regional inequality in per-worker GDP grew dramatically from 1860 to 1900, levelled off in the early decades of the twentieth century and then decreased. Regional disparities in labour productivity in the 1930s were fairly similar to those

Table 7.1 Theil T index, decomposition of labour productivity (NUTS2), Spain 1860–2015

	1860	1910	1950	1980	2015
Primary					
Inequality	0.031	0.012	0.009	0.020	0.006
GDP share (%)	39.5	27.8	28.7	6.5	2.6
Secondary					
Inequality	0.010	0.025	0.007	0.001	0.008
GDP share (%)	20.4	30.7	27.0	34.7	23.6
Tertiary					
Inequality	0.016	0.006	0.006	0.002	0.008
GDP share (%)	40.1	41.4	44.3	58.8	73.8
Within-sector inequality	0.021	0.013	0.007	0.003	0.008
Between-sector inequality	0.049	0.141	0.043	0.027	0.006
Overall inequality	0.070	0.155	0.050	0.030	0.014
Within-sector component (%)	29.7	8.6	13.7	10.8	59.8
Between-sector component (%)	70.3	91.4	86.3	89.2	40.2
Overall (%)	100.0	100.0	100.0	100.0	100.0

Source: See main text

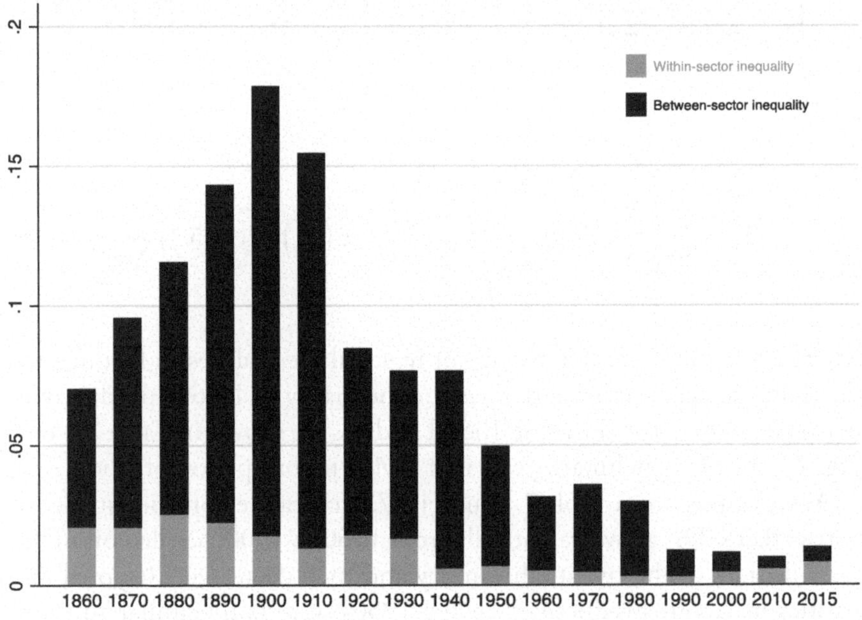

Fig. 7.2 Theil T index, decomposition of labour productivity (NUTS2), Spain 1860–2015. Source: See main text

prevalent in 1860. Then from 1940 onwards, regional convergence in per-worker GDP followed a downward trend until 1990, after which there has been little change. The values of the Theil index show us that inequality in regional income per worker in 2015 (0.014) was dramatically lower than it was in the early twentieth century, when it reached its peak (0.179).

So which aspect is the most important when it comes to explaining this evolution over time? As we can also see in Fig. 7.2, the between-sector effect accounts for the lion's share of regional inequality in output per worker. With the exception of the last three benchmark years considered (i.e. those in the twenty-first century), it explains more than two-thirds of the overall variation in labour productivity differentials. However, it could also be argued that the within-sector effect played a significant role in the first wave of economic integration and high regional inequality (with values close to 30 per cent in 1860). Indeed in more recent times its contribution has increased significantly to the point where it has overtaken the between-sector component in the most recent period. In fact the within-sector component would explain around 60 per cent of overall labour productivity in 2010 and 2015.

Taken together, these results strongly support the hypothesis that relates the upswing in regional inequality to the structural differences across regions that arose during the process of industrial concentration in the nineteenth century (Williamson 1965) and suggests that the convergence of sector shares across regions would have enhanced the regional convergence process. They also indicate that regional differences in within-sector productivity become more important in helping us understand inequality in those periods when the regional differences in productivity were smaller, that is, at the start of the growth process in the mid-nineteenth century and during the early years of the twentieth.

This is in line with the explanations offered by many of the studies that have analysed the determinants of regional inequality in Spain during the second half of the twentieth century. According to these investigations, the central role played by the convergence process in regional sector structures was a determinant of convergence in productivity and per-capita income in Spain during the period 1960–1985. They also argue that the end of the regional convergence process in the latter years of the twentieth century is linked to the exhaustion of the convergence process in sector structures and the persistence of significant differences in sector productivity levels across regions (Cuadrado et al. 1999; De la Fuente and Freire 2000). Our work complements this view, since the results presented above also allow for differences in productivity to be a cause of overall inequality in some periods, especially in the first benchmark year analysed and in the last decade. Now, in the twenty-first century, within-sector productivity differentials have become more important than differences in regional structures as determinants of regional inequality in aggregate labour productivity.

Table 7.1 also shows us the contributions of the different sectors to the within-sector component. Like the component itself, these have varied considerably over time. Surprisingly, the sector with the biggest regional differences in labour productivity in 1860 was the primary sector. Two factors could account for this: the big differences in relative land endowments and climate across Spanish regions, and temporary labour migrations across regions, which, although very important at harvest time (Silvestre 2007), are not considered in this type of exercise. The relative importance of the different sectors varied from 1910 until 1930, when industry became the main contributor to the within-sector component. This is in agreement with previous investigations that have stressed the presence of increasing returns in Spanish manufacturing during the period (Betrán 1999; Tirado et al. 2006; Martinez-Galarraga et al. 2008). It is also worth noting that over recent years it has been differences in productivity in the tertiary sector that have counted the most in explaining the within-sector component of the Theil inequality index, following a growth path from 1970 to 2015. It has been argued that this trend in recent decades would have been linked to the presence of agglomeration economies in the services sector (Paluzie et al. 2007).

Production Structure and Sector Productivity: Some Regional Histories

To focus on some individual histories in greater detail, we use a straightforward modification of the procedure developed by Hanna (1951) and subsequently employed by Kim (1998) to separate income-per-worker differences into industry-mix and sector productivity differentials.[5] This will enable us to explore each of the 17 NUTS2 regions to find out whether their situation in terms of aggregate per-worker income can be explained by a favourable production structure (and therefore specialization in the sectors with highest productivity) or by greater productivity in each sector.

The procedure involves constructing two hypothetical regional per-worker GDPs and comparing them with the real per-worker GDPs. The first assumes that all regions have identical industry-mixes and identical industry-per-worker GVA, both of which are set equal to the overall national average. The second assumes that regions have different industry-mixes but identical per-worker GVA, again equal to the national average. The difference between the two hypothetical incomes, which are based on industry-mix income and overall national GVA, provides a measurement of the GDP-per-worker disparities caused by divergence in regional industrial structures (the industry-mix effect). The difference between the actual GDP and the hypothetical industry-mix income is the variation in regional GDP per worker due to divergence in per-worker GVA (the productivity or wage-effect).[6] The results of this exercise are shown for our benchmark years in Table 7.2.[7]

The evidence presented in the table shows that variations in both industry-mix and labour productivity at a broad industry level are central to explaining the differences in GDP per worker. In most cases a direct correlation can be seen between the industry-mix and the wage-effect. This implies that a favourable industry-mix is accompanied by higher wages, while the reverse is also true. In order to detect additional facts, we

[5] Per-worker GVA in industry and region i is $GVA_i = (w_i \cdot L_i + r_i \cdot K_i)/L_i$. However, given the presence of perfect capital markets, $r_i \cdot K_i/L_i$ should be equal across all locations. Therefore w_i drives the differences in per-worker GVA across all regions.

[6] The use of a one-digit industrial classification in our calculations may conceal the importance of productivity in explaining regional differences in per-worker income more than it should. Regional per-worker GVA in manufacturing and services activities may be different due to variations in regional industrial structures at a finer industry level.

[7] Although one of our benchmark years used to divide the period of study into stages should be 1910, here we have decided to present the results for 1900 because this is the year that saw the greatest differences in income per worker, as can be seen in Fig. 7.2. This does not significantly change the results and allows us to explore the role played by the industry-mix and the wage-effect at the time of the highest productivity differential.

Table 7.2 Hanna-Kim decomposition (NUTS2), Spain 1860–2015

	1860	1900	1950	1980	2015
Galicia					
Industry-mix	−14.7	−35.5	−21.1	−28.8	0.6
Wage-effect	−69.4	−50.1	−17.5	−19.8	−8.4
Asturias					
Industry-mix	−15.4	−24.4	1.2	−5.3	1.3
Wage-effect	−47.8	−8.8	7.1	1.3	−6.3
Cantabria					
Industry-mix	−1.6	0.9	5.1	−5.0	1.8
Wage-effect	−19.3	−10.4	−2.6	1.5	−5.0
Basque Country					
Industry-mix	4.0	34.4	9.6	6.5	3.2
Wage-effect	−21.0	21.8	27.8	10.0	10.0
Navarre					
Industry-mix	3.8	−0.1	−2.4	1.3	3.8
Wage-effect	5.0	−10.5	4.3	5.8	5.0
La Rioja					
Industry-mix	2.2	7.3	−2.2	−3.7	2.9
Wage-effect	−3.2	6.6	2.5	4.2	−0.5
Aragon					
Industry-mix	−4.1	−3.3	−8.5	−1.4	1.3
Wage-effect	8.2	0.5	−3.7	2.0	0.5
Madrid					
Industry-mix	29.1	58.7	26.3	11.3	−1.2
Wage-effect	14.7	0.9	5.0	9.6	9.7
Castile-Leon					
Industry-mix	−1.6	−18.9	−9.2	−10.1	0.4
Wage-effect	−10.6	−0.3	2.0	−7.8	−4.0
Castile-La Mancha					
Industry-mix	2.8	−12.7	−16.3	−11.9	0.4
Wage-effect	6.3	9.6	−10.8	−12.4	−6.9
Extremadura					
Industry-mix	−3.8	−19.6	−27.3	−17.9	−2.6
Wage-effect	−18.2	−19.7	−22.3	−18.5	−13.1
Catalonia					
Industry-mix	9.8	30.8	15.1	7.1	1.6
Wage-effect	6.8	28.9	11.9	8.0	5.1
Valencia					
Industry-mix	−0.9	1.9	−2.9	2.7	1.4
Wage-effect	7.4	11.5	−0.4	−2.4	−6.0
Balearic Islands					
Industry-mix	−5.1	1.5	5.9	6.7	−0.7
Wage-effect	−19.5	−38.1	−0.5	−2.3	−0.8

(continued)

Table 7.2 (continued)

	1860	1900	1950	1980	2015
Andalusia					
Industry-mix	2.3	2.7	−7.4	−6.1	−3.0
Wage-effect	30.9	−6.7	−12.2	−8.1	−7.9
Murcia					
Industry-mix	0.8	−11.0	−6.1	−3.8	−1.9
Wage-effect	12.8	−18.5	−23.0	−10.2	−13.8
Canary Islands					
Industry-mix	−2.3	0.1	−10.0	1.8	−2.8
Wage-effect	−26.6	−46.7	−3.7	−3.5	−6.4

Source: See main text

now summarize the histories of three important regions—Catalonia, the Basque Country and Madrid—that serve as examples of success stories. These are followed by Galicia, Extremadura and Castile-La Mancha as examples of failed growth experiences in comparative terms, and Andalusia and Valencia, which are characterized as having experienced stages of both relative success and failure over the last 150 years.

Catalonia occupied one of the top three positions in the per-capita GDP ranking from 1860 until 1995, although its performance has been less successful over recent years. At first sight its high position in the ranking seems to have been due to both a favourable industry-mix and a productivity effect. Nevertheless, from the 1970s it appears that the region began to lose ground to Madrid and the Basque Country. Certainly its positive wage-effect fell behind those achieved by these two regions, and thus in the end Catalonia lost its privileged position.

The history of the Basque Country perfectly encapsulates the consequences of rapid industrialization and subsequent structural change. In 1860 it was not one of the top-ranking regions in terms of per-capita GDP.[8] Indeed it suffered a negative productivity effect (around 20 per cent below the Spanish average). However, only 40 years later (in 1900) with industrialization under way, the situation had changed dramatically. Now the region was outperforming Spain in both industry-mix and productivity effects by more than 34 per cent and 20 per cent respectively.

[8] A more optimistic view can be found in Carrión (2010) in his analysis of industry in Gipuzkoa in 1860.

The gap was still present in 1950, although the region's advantage due to industry-mix had decreased to less than 10 per cent. Nevertheless, the Basque Country maintained its lead throughout the second half of the twentieth century thanks to the contribution of a favourable industry-mix and its positive productivity effect, which has been the basis of its economy's success over recent decades after the tough industrial rationalization of the 1980s.

Madrid's position in the rankings for per-worker regional income is mainly due to its favourable industry-mix (in this case related to the pre-eminence of the services sector) during the first major stage of economic growth in Spain, that is, until around 1950. It has also managed to achieve an increasingly positive productivity effect, which has been particularly high since 1980. Overall, this first analysis shows that convergence of the economic structure across Spanish regions seems to have come about in such a way that only those regions with favourable, high-productivity effects have been able to maintain their top positions over the very long term.

In contrast Galicia, Extremadura and Castile-La Mancha have been among the lowest-ranking regions in per-capita GDP throughout the period. As would be expected, their industry-mix and productivity effects have been unfavourable; that is, they specialized in less productive economic sectors, and labour productivity was below the Spanish average in all of them. In general terms, however, the main negative effect for these regions during the period 1860–1950 was the industry-mix, but since then it has been the high, negative productivity effect that has been mainly responsible for keeping them at the bottom of the ranking.

The histories of Andalusia and Valencia, two of the most populated regions in Spain, are rather different. In 1860 Andalusia was the second richest region in the country, but then it went into decline. Its initial pre-eminence was due not to the region's industry-mix but to its positive productivity effect, which was based on mining and a relatively productive agricultural sector. Forty years later, in 1900, this advantage had disappeared and productivity was slightly below the average. Also, its industry-mix was not very different from the national average. From that time on, it seems fairly clear that the negative trend in both effects would explain its relative decline in GDP per worker.

Valencia achieved its highest position in the ranking for GDP per capita in 1930. Its rise to the top positions between 1860 and 1930 can be explained mainly by a positive productivity effect acting in the context of a regional production structure close to the national average. This dynamic was broken during the years of Franco's policy of autarky, which had a devastating effect on an economy that specialized in agricultural production for export and the manufacture of consumer goods. By 1950 it can be seen that Valencia was already in decline, and this decline has been growing ever since, mainly due to a negative productivity effect, possibly the result of its specialization in what might be considered a low-productivity tertiary sector, that is, tourism.

To sum up, it seems that the factors explaining the success or failure of regions in terms of per-worker GDP have changed in the course of Spain's experience of growth and integration over the long term. During the early stages it was the industry-mix that was the main factor determining the regions' relative positions (in line with what the Theil decomposition analysis suggested earlier). Later it was the convergence of economic structures that determined that the main explanation for a region's higher or lower position was linked to the presence of marked positive or negative productivity effects. This factor gradually gained more explanatory power during the growth experience of the twentieth century. Indeed Navarre, the region that most improved its ranking position in the course of the twentieth century (#11 in 1900 to #3 in 2000), has never had a particularly positive industry-mix effect, and its success is basically due to the presence of a positive, high-productivity effect. This would seem to be the key to sustained success over the long term.

Digging Deeper: Explaining Regional Labour Productivity Convergence

So far we have seen that the Spanish economy has undergone an extensive regional convergence process over the very long term, but that this did not follow a linear trajectory. In fact, measured by indicators such as β-convergence and σ-convergence, during the period 1860–1910 regional inequality followed a path characterized by divergence. However, from the second decade of the twentieth century onwards, it is convergence that has characterized the relative evolution of GDP per capita in the regions of Spain. This process was very weak in the years between the First World War and the beginning of the Franco dictatorship, then became much stronger during the Golden Age and has finally diminished or even reversed from the 1980s to the present. In order to complete our analysis, in this section we provide additional evidence on the factors that may have contributed to shaping this pattern.

If we adopt a dynamic perspective, there are other explanations for the relative performance of the regions during Spain's growth and economic integration processes. For instance, Solow-type neoclassical growth models highlight the importance of capital deepening as a key element for understanding convergence between the poorest and richest economies. These maintain that convergence comes about because the regions or countries that were initially the poorest with a low endowment of cumulative factors have higher marginal capital productivity, and this enables them to fuel higher economic growth rates than regions or countries that were initially richer. Another important aspect, this time singled out by endogenous growth models or new growth theory, is technological catch-up. Given that adopting technology is easier than developing it, poorer regions and countries can converge with richer ones by copying or adopting the technologies of the most advanced economies.

Other approaches, directly related to the arguments characteristic of development economics, emphasize the importance of the production structure and the changes it undergoes over the long term as an explanatory element for the regional convergence processes. Thus, for example, if we consider that the economy is made up of different sectors and that each of these sectors has different levels of productivity, the production structure will favour (or hinder) regional economic convergence if the reallocation of resources from traditional low-productivity sectors to modern high-productivity sectors comes about with greater intensity in the poor regions, or if the productivity levels of those sectors in which the poor regions specialize converge with the productivity levels of those sectors that carry the most weight in the rich regions.

Working to explore these aspects, Caselli and Tenreyro (2005) suggest a decomposition exercise of the convergence (divergence) at the mean levels of per-worker output of one region compared to that of the leading economy. This will enable us to identify the magnitude of the different forces identified by the theoretical literature. Following this approach, to investigate the sources of convergence in the output-per-worker ratio with a reference region we break down the overall catch-up into three components. The first, known as within-industry convergence, refers to the contribution of capital deepening and technological catch-up to the relative dynamic of the regions. The second identifies the role played by regional production structures in the regional convergence (divergence) process. This makes it possible to distinguish the effect generated by labour reallocation to high-productivity sectors and is a source of convergence very closely related to the third component (between-industry), which is driven by the convergence in productivity between the most common sectors of the leading region and those of the follower region.[9]

To make it easier to analyse the results, in this case we work at the NUTS1 regional level. And given that the decomposition exercise requires a benchmark region as a reference, we take the NUTS1 region of MADRID. The methodology then lets us examine whether labour productivity in Spanish NUTS1 regions converged with or diverged from that of MADRID, after which we can quantify the relative contribution of our three alternative components of convergence (divergence). The basic methodological approach is expressed as follows:[10]

$$\begin{aligned}&\text{Overall convergence in labour productivity}_{i,\text{Madrid}}\\&=\text{Within}-\text{industry convergence}_{i,\text{Madrid}}+\text{Labour reallocation}_{i,\text{Madrid}}\\&+\text{Between}-\text{industry}_{i,\text{Madrid}}\end{aligned}$$

Within-industry convergence can therefore be defined as each sector's catch-up in labour productivity to the labour productivity of the same sector in MADRID, weighted by the average labour share in that sector. The exercise allows us to present the contribution of the three main sectors

[9] Enflo and Rosés (2015) set out a similar exercise for Sweden.

[10] Caselli and Tenreyro (2005) present the detailed mathematical derivation of this.

(agriculture, industry and services) to the within-industry component, thereby identifying each sector's contribution to this source of convergence. The role played over time by the production structure and the changes it undergoes can be discovered by way of two elements. Convergence through structural change is captured through labour reallocation, which is labour moving from sectors characterized by low productivity to others with higher productivity, weighted by the sector's relative productivity. Convergence exists if the reallocation to more productive sectors happens faster in other regions compared to MADRID. Finally, between-industry convergence captures the contribution that comes from catch-up in productivities across sectors. This typically occurs when productivity in the sectors in which the latecomer regions had a higher share of the labour force converges with overall sector productivity in the benchmark region (Caselli and Tenreyro 2005). In all cases convergence is indicated by a positive sign and divergence by a negative.

Figure 7.3 shows the evolution of regional (NUTS1) productivity compared to that of the leading region (MADRID), illustrating the

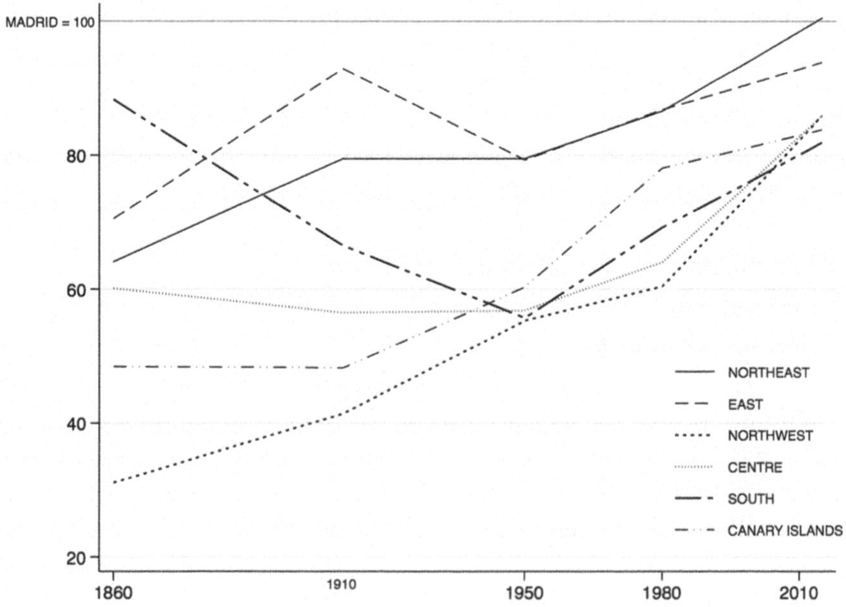

Fig. 7.3 Regional (NUTS1) gross value added (GVA) per worker in Spain, 1860–2015. Source: See main text

diversity of regional experiences over time. We can intuit a long-term common scenario predominated by the convergence in productivity of most regions with the values for the leader. Notable is the experience of SOUTH, comprising the NUTS2 regions of Andalusia and Murcia, which diverged between 1860 and 1950 and then began to catch up with MADRID in labour productivity.

Allowing a more detailed analysis of the determinants of this evolution, Table 7.3 shows the sources of convergence for the seven NUTS1 macro-regions for the whole period of study between 1860 and 2015. The first column shows the existence of convergence (positive sign) or divergence (negative sign) with respect to the benchmark macro-region, MADRID. The second column presents the within-industry convergence, which over the next three columns is broken down into the contribution made to it by each of the three main sectors of activity: agriculture, industry and services. The sixth column shows the contribution of labour reallocation, while the seventh and last presents the between-industry convergence.

Looking at the entire period it can be seen that—with the exception of SOUTH—all the NUTS1 regions have undergone a process of convergence in productivity with respect to MADRID. The bottom row of the table containing the totals for Spain shows that, generally speaking, practically half the overall territorial convergence is due to the within-industry component. We also see that this is due to productivity in the poorest regions in sectors such as services, which are tending to approach the level recorded by the richest region. This effect would be particularly relevant in cases such as NORTHWEST, CENTRE and CANARY ISLANDS. The other half is linked to the dynamic related to regional production structures. The convergence between productivity levels in agriculture (the most important sector in the poorer regions for much of the period) and those in industry and services, that is, the between-industry component, would also have significantly encouraged this secular convergence process between the average productivity of the lagging regions and the leader (see Fig. 7.2). Finally, the results of the decomposition indicate that labour reallocation seems not to have played a determining role in long-term regional convergence. Indeed, in some cases such as NORTHEAST and CENTRE it may even have acted as a source of divergence.

Table 7.3 Decomposition of regional income-per-worker convergence, 1860–2015

		Within-industry					
Region	Overall	All sectors	Agriculture	Industry	Services	Labour reallocation	Between industry
MADRID	–	–	–	–	–	–	–
NORTHEAST	0.3631	0.2399	0.0368	0.0338	0.1693	−0.0037	0.1270
EAST	0.2341	0.0810	0.0223	−0.0494	0.1082	0.0358	0.1173
NORTHWEST	0.5485	0.3999	0.1176	0.0000	0.2823	0.0097	0.1389
CENTRE	0.2576	0.2179	0.0135	−0.0267	0.2311	−0.0852	0.1249
SOUTH	−0.0637	−0.1916	−0.0519	−0.0916	−0.0480	0.0171	0.1108
CANARY I.	0.3540	0.2499	−0.0126	−0.0056	0.2681	0.0528	0.0514
SPAIN	**0.2696**	**0.1391**	**0.0183**	**−0.0330**	**0.1538**	**0.0242**	**0.1063**

This is certainly surprising given that structural change and the homogenization of regional production structures are usually singled out as being prime explanatory factors in a great deal of convergence research focusing on different periods of Spanish history. However, the period considered is very long and, as we saw in earlier chapters, the Spanish economy and regional inequality have undergone many different situations in the course of history. This would indicate that we should go beyond analysing the period as a whole and concentrate on a narrower time frame. Of the changes that have come about, one of the more important concerns the differences in absolute and relative sector productivity and how they vary over time (Fig. 7.4). Therefore dividing the period into subperiods will enable us to explore in greater detail the sources of convergence/divergence in each of the main stages of Spanish economic development.

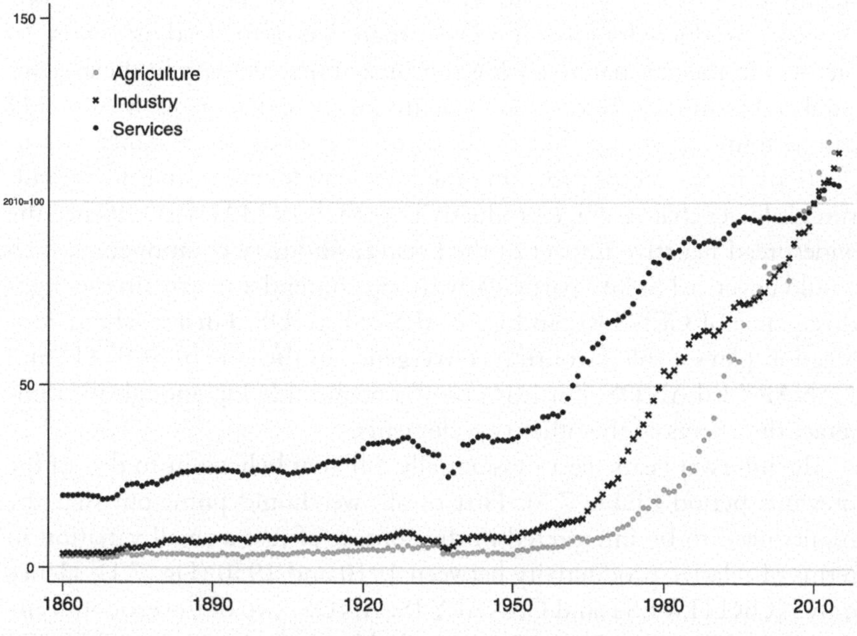

Fig. 7.4 Labour productivity by major economic activity in Spain, 1860–2015. Notes: Industry excluding construction. Source: Prados de la Escosura (2016)

Table 7.4 shows the results for the same exercise, but beginning with the initial period covering from 1860 to 1910. The first impression we get is that the north and south of the country behave differently. The north (NORTHEAST, EAST and NORTHWEST) converges with MADRID, while the south (mainly SOUTH and to a lesser extent CENTRE and CANARY ISLANDS) diverges. The second is that convergence in the northern regions is explained by the narrowing of the gap between the productivity of their production sectors and that of the leader (within-industry component)—particularly in the services sector—and by labour reallocation. However, the between-industry component shows a negative value, that is, it acts against convergence in all three cases. This may have something to do with the fact that productivity growth in the most common sector in these territories, which is still agriculture, is lower than that of average productivity in the leading region, MADRID, where its participation is lower (see Fig. 7.2).

Divergence in the regions of the geographical south is concentrated mainly in SOUTH. The main reason for this divergence is that the rate of sector productivity growth is lower than that of the leading region. In fact it is in the comparatively low advance of productivity in the agricultural and industrial sectors that the main source of divergence in SOUTH can be found. Also, just like in all the other regions, the advance of productivity in the sector providing the most employment, that is, agriculture, is lower than average productivity growth in MADRID. Hence the widespread negative impact of the between-industry component, which would nevertheless be a particularly strong contender to explain the slight divergence of CENTRE and CANARY ISLANDS. Finally, labour reallocation plays a role favouring convergence in the case of SOUTH and CANARY ISLANDS, but it is not of a magnitude big enough to counteract the effects of the other two elements.

The interwar years see a substantially different behaviour to that of the previous period (Table 7.5). First of all, we should point out that the results need to be interpreted in the context of just a small variation in terms of relative productivity between 1910 and 1950 (Fig. 7.1). Hence only NORTHWEST and CANARY ISLANDS, two of the economically slowest regions, manage to achieve a good level of convergence. SOUTH continues the steep decline already visible in the previous period, and

Table 7.4 Decomposition of regional income-per-worker convergence, 1860–1910

Region	Overall	Within-industry				Labour reallocation	Between-industry
		All sectors	Agriculture	Industry	Services		
MADRID	–	–	–	–	–	–	–
NORTHEAST	0.1534	0.1560	–0.0237	0.0304	0.1492	0.0608	–0.0634
EAST	0.2233	0.1493	–0.0189	–0.0082	0.1764	0.0960	–0.0221
NORTHWEST	0.1031	0.1884	0.0760	0.0094	0.1030	0.0241	–0.1094
CENTRE	–0.0362	0.0779	–0.0182	–0.0285	0.1246	–0.0257	–0.0885
SOUTH	–0.2180	–0.1956	–0.1086	–0.1247	0.0377	0.0263	–0.0488
CANARY I.	–0.0023	0.0132	–0.0086	–0.0843	0.1061	0.0545	–0.0700
SPAIN	**0.0388**	**0.0702**	**–0.0194**	**–0.0302**	**0.1198**	**0.0312**	**–0.0626**

Table 7.5 Decomposition of regional income-per-worker convergence, 1910–1950

Region	Overall	Within-industry					Between-industry
		All sectors	Agriculture	Industry	Services	Labour reallocation	
MADRID	–	–	–	–	–	–	–
NORTHEAST	0.0005	−0.0525	−0.0090	0.0225	−0.0660	−0.0862	0.1392
EAST	−0.1360	−0.1645	0.0003	−0.0444	−0.1204	−0.0500	0.0786
NORTHWEST	0.1394	−0.0239	0.0087	0.0118	−0.0443	−0.0817	0.2450
CENTRE	0.0035	−0.0725	−0.0434	0.0218	−0.0509	−0.1759	0.2519
SOUTH	−0.1081	−0.0993	−0.0827	0.0632	−0.0799	−0.1981	0.1893
CANARY I.	0.1212	0.1623	−0.0267	0.1488	0.0402	−0.2386	0.1975
SPAIN	**−0.0138**	**−0.0745**	**−0.0268**	**0.0207**	**−0.0684**	**−0.1096**	**0.1704**

while NORTHEAST and CENTRE barely show any convergence, the traditionally more dynamic EAST shows a relative lag with respect to MADRID in this period. This could be related to the relative loss of momentum in the industrial sector—and on an economic level in general—in regions bordering the Mediterranean in comparison to inland locations since the early decades of the twentieth century. Such a situation would have come about in connection with the adoption of a series of protectionist measures which, ever since the introduction of the Cánovas tariff in 1892, had been increasingly effective in shutting down the Spanish economy's links with the exterior (Tirado et al. 2013).

This is a period that, as we know, was characterized by the high volatility of growth in the years leading up to the Civil War, followed by a reversal in the pattern of economic development during the years of autarky. Given these conditions, the evolution of the various indicators is understandable. To begin with, the magnitude of the effects associated with the within-industry component is smaller than in the previous period. This is true for all three sectors into which activity is decomposed, regardless of sign. However, high values are recorded for the other two components, which are more closely linked to structural change and which also act with opposite trends to one another. Despite the differences between the periods before and after the Civil War, the negative signs for labour reallocation would indicate that structural change (which on a national level speeded up in the interwar years) took place with greater intensity in MADRID than in other regions. In other words, unlike in MADRID, in all the other regions employment grew proportionally more in the sector with the lowest productivity, that is, agriculture. Indeed in Chap. 2 we showed the reversal seen in the structural change process during the early Franco period. Nevertheless, in the context of the technology freeze characteristic of these years, productivity in the sectors of greatest weight in these territories grows (or falls) more quickly (slowly) than average productivity in MADRID, and this has a positive effect on regional convergence as shown by the between-industry component. In short, the small magnitude of the changes in sector productivity and the return to agricultural production, which was more intense in all regions than in the lead economy, would be the reason for the scant relevance of the relative changes recorded over these years.

A new scenario opens up in the period 1950–1980 (Table 7.6). Regional convergence with respect to the leading region becomes widespread and is of greatest magnitude in the lowest-income macro-regions, in line with the evolution of the β-convergence and σ-convergence indicators presented in Chap. 4. This dynamic is not explained by a tendency for sector productivity to grow at a higher rate in the follower regions. This really only happened—and in a dimension of little importance—in SOUTH, where productivity gains in the agricultural sector, in which intensification of energy use and marked capitalization was taking place, favoured greater productivity growth than in the benchmark region. The same thing happened, though to a lesser degree, in CANARY ISLANDS.

Therefore the convergence process that characterizes this period is to a large extent explained by elements linked to the production structures of the follower regions and their changes over time. On the one hand, the greater intensity of labour reallocation towards sectors of greater productivity in the lagging regions is the determining factor in the convergence process. And on the other, though still of much lower relative importance, the growth of productivity in industry and agriculture, which predominated in most of these regions, was higher than average productivity growth in MADRID, where the services sector carried more weight. This favoured regional convergence via the between-industry component associated with the sector structure of the regions.

The convergence process shows signs of exhaustion in the period 1980–2015. Nevertheless, the aggregate values of the overall convergence indicator in Table 7.7 still maintain a positive sign although they reach noteworthy values in only two regions, NORTHWEST and CENTRE, and to a lesser extent in NORTHEAST and SOUTH. In these macro-regions the within-industry component favoured convergence despite a widespread divergence in productivity in the industrial sector. To a larger degree, and depending on the region, structural-type elements like labour reallocation and the between-industry effect contributed to the convergence in productivity observed between the follower regions and the leader region, MADRID.

In short, the dynamic decomposition presented in the previous paragraphs strengthens the general identification of the determinants of the evolution of territorial inequality in Spain. The initial advance of the

Table 7.6 Decomposition of regional income-per-worker convergence, 1950–1980

		Within-industry					
Region	Overall	All sectors	Agriculture	Industry	Services	Labour reallocation	Between-industry
MADRID	–	–	–	–	–	–	–
NORTHEAST	0.0710	−0.0742	−0.0044	−0.0488	−0.0211	0.1280	0.0172
EAST	0.0751	−0.0452	−0.0065	0.0127	−0.0514	0.1022	0.0181
NORTHWEST	0.0507	−0.0423	−0.0640	−0.0117	0.0333	0.0845	0.0085
CENTRE	0.0713	−0.0297	−0.0408	0.0089	0.0021	0.0969	0.0042
SOUTH	0.1348	0.0204	0.0315	−0.0196	0.0085	0.1120	0.0024
CANARY I.	0.1782	−0.0788	0.0191	−0.0178	−0.0801	0.2618	−0.0048
SPAIN	**0.1147**	**−0.0261**	**−0.0163**	**−0.0052**	**−0.0045**	**0.1321**	**0.0087**

Table 7.7 Decomposition of regional income-per-worker convergence, 1980–2015

		Within-industry					
Region	Overall	All sectors	Agriculture	Industry	Services	Labour reallocation	Between-industry
MADRID	–	–	–	–	–	–	–
NORTHEAST	0.1383	0.0373	0.0149	0.0020	0.0204	0.0119	0.0891
EAST	0.0717	–0.0218	0.0079	–0.0318	0.0021	0.0295	0.0640
NORTHWEST	0.2552	0.0482	0.0655	–0.0400	0.0227	0.1407	0.0663
CENTRE	0.2190	0.0816	0.0407	–0.0279	0.0688	0.0779	0.0595
SOUTH	0.1277	0.0349	0.0141	–0.0263	0.0472	0.0596	0.0331
CANARY I.	0.0570	–0.0169	–0.0030	–0.0323	0.0184	0.0879	–0.0140
SPAIN	**0.1298**	**0.0223**	**0.0200**	**–0.0233**	**0.0256**	**0.0594**	**0.0481**

development process between 1860 and 1910 was marked by the productivity gains in industry and the growth of this sector's participation in the labour structure of a small number of territories. This dynamic brought divergence between the leader region and those regions that remained anchored in a backward economy in which the greatest weight corresponded to the agricultural sector and a traditional manufacturing sector that in terms of productivity was moving further away from modern manufacturing. Meanwhile the growth of modern manufacturing was based on higher capitalization and the incorporation of new technologies into the production processes. Nevertheless, the years between 1910 and 1950 saw no great relative changes, since the reversal of the development process characterized by the early years of the Franco regime, that is, the end of this stage, in a context of slow productivity growth in all sectors, had the effect of preventing the gap between the lagging regions and the leader from growing.

The main boost to convergence came about in the period between 1950 and 1980. During these years it was not linked fundamentally to capital deepening or to the closing of the technology gap with respect to the leader, but to the structural components that were the basis of the process. First, the transfer of resources from less productive sectors (agriculture) towards sectors such as industry became more intense in those regions that had more room for improvement in this respect. And second, these regions also benefited from productivity growth in agriculture and industry, whose production structures carried greater weight than their equivalent in the benchmark region, MADRID, which was already highly specialized in the services sector.

The last of these periods signals the end of a convergence process founded on structural change. We have shown how the weight of labour reallocation gradually decreased and how convergence in labour productivity was due to three effects in the period 1980–2015. However, its small magnitude is proof that this path to convergence was exhausted. The agricultural sector has seen its presence in the economy as a whole decrease dramatically, and the big differences in industrial productivity that came about in the course of the economic development process in Spain have become smaller with the passing of time; that is, there has been unconditional convergence in manufacturing productivity similar to that described by Rodrik (2016). With things as they are today, it is the differences in productivity growth rates in production sectors such as industry, in those activities with a greater technology component, and the services sector, especially services with high value added, that are the elements limiting the possibility of convergence of the poorest territories and that may even perhaps be the force behind a new stage of divergence.

To return to the beginning of the chapter, the widespread reduction of productivity differentials over the course of the economic development process in Spain means that differences today are very small, as we showed in Fig. 7.1. It also means that aspects linked to the labour market such as the economic activity rate and the unemployment rate, although their contribution to inequality in per-capita GDP has not changed substantially over time, have taken on greater relative importance in recent decades. This has consequences from the point of view of political implications in that once regional differences in productivity have decreased considerably, it is the way regional labour markets function that is the area in which public policies will need to be effective if the objective is to return to the path of decreasing regional economic inequality.

References

Akita, T., & Kataoka, M. (2003). *Regional income inequality in the post-war Japan*. ERSA conference papers ersa03p480, European Regional Science Association.

Betrán, C. (1999). Difusión y localización industrial en España durante el primer tercio del siglo XX. *Revista de Historia Económica, 17*(3), 663–696.

Browne, L. E. (1989). Shifting regional fortunes: The wheel turns. *New England Economic Review*, Federal Reserve Bank of Boston.

Carlino, G. A. (1992). Are regional per capita earnings diverging? *Business Review*, Federal Reserve Bank of Philadelphia, 3–12.

Carrión, I. M. (2010). Una aproximación a la intensidad industrial vasca: la industria guipuzcoana en 1860. *Investigaciones de Historia Económica, 6*(16), 73–100.

Caselli, F., & Tenreyro, S. (2005). *Is Poland the next Spain?* NBER Working Paper 11045, National Bureau of Economic Research.

Cuadrado, J. R., Garcia-Greciano, B., & Raymond, J. L. (1999). Regional convergence in productivity and productive structure: The Spanish case. *International Regional Science Review, 22*(1), 35–53.

De la Fuente, A., & Freire, M. J. (2000). Estructura sectorial y convergencia regional. *Revista de Economía Aplicada, 23*, 189–205.

Enflo, K., & Rosés, J. R. (2015). Coping with regional inequality in Sweden: Structural change, migrations, and policy, 1860–2000. *Economic History Review, 68*(1), 191–217.

Esteban, J. M. (2000). Regional convergence in Europe and the industry-mix: A shift-share analysis. *Regional Science and Urban Economics, 30*(3), 353–364.

Ezcurra, R., Gil, C., Pascual, P., & Rapún, M. (2005). Regional inequality in the European Union: Does industry-mix matter? *Regional Studies, 39*(6), 679–697.

Hanna, F. (1951). Contribution of manufacturing wages to differences in per capita income. *Review of Economics and Statistics, 33*(1), 18–28.

Kim, S. (1998). Economic integration and convergence: U.S. regions, 1840–1987. *Journal of Economic History, 58*(3), 659–683.

LeGallo, J., & Kamarianakis, Y. (2011). The evolution of regional productivity disparities in the European Union from 1975 to 2002: A combination of shift–share and spatial econometrics. *Regional Studies, 45*(1), 123–139.

Martinez-Galarraga, J., Paluzie, E., Pons, J., & Tirado, D. A. (2008). Agglomeration and labour productivity in Spain over the long term. *Cliometrica, 2*(3), 195–212.

Martinez-Galarraga, J., Rosés, J. R., & Tirado, D. A. (2015). The long-term patterns of regional income inequality in Spain, 1860–2000. *Regional Studies, 49*(4), 502–517.

Paluzie, E., Pons, J., & Tirado, D. A. (2007). Aglomeración y productividad del trabajo en las regiones españolas. In E. Reig (Ed.), *Competitividad, crecimiento y capitalización de las regiones españolas* (pp. 249–276). Bilbao: Fundación BBVA.

Rodrik, D. (2016). Unconditional convergence in manufacturing. *Quarterly Journal of Economics, 128*(1), 165–204.

Silvestre, J. (2007). Temporary internal migrations in Spain, 1860–1930. *Social Science History, 31*(4), 539–574.

Theil, H. (1967). *Economics and information theory*. Amsterdam: North Holland.

Tirado, D. A., Pons, J., & Paluzie, E. (2006). Los cambios en la localización de la actividad industrial en España, 1850–1936. Un análisis desde la nueva geografía económica. *Revista de Historia Industrial, 31*, 41–63.

Tirado, D. A., Pons, J., Paluzie, E., & Martinez-Galarraga, J. (2013). Trade policy and wage gradients: Evidence from a protectionist turn. *Cliometrica, 7*(3), 295–318.
Williamson, J. G. (1965). Regional inequality and the process of national development: A description of the patterns. *Economic Development and Cultural Change, 13*(4), 3–84.

8

Spain and Its Neighbours: An International Comparison

In previous chapters we assessed various dimensions of regional income inequality in Spain since the mid-nineteenth century. In this chapter we look at it from a supranational perspective, which should tell us whether inequality between Spanish regions reproduces on a smaller scale the trend followed by other nearby territories and countries. This will enable us to establish any similarities or differences, and these should provide us with the elements needed to gain a better understanding of the main mechanisms behind regional inequality.

In order to do this, it is essential that we have retrospective estimates of per-capita GDP for periods relatively far back in time, and, as we have already said, these are rather thin on the ground. In recent years, though, efforts have been made to correct this situation. Despite there being still only a limited number of countries for which such information is available, some international comparisons can be undertaken. In this chapter we therefore study the long-term evolution of regional income inequality in Spain and its closest neighbours in south-west Europe, that is, France, Italy and Portugal.[1] These four countries together cover a total surface

[1] Parts of this chapter are based on work carried out with Teresa Sanchis and Rafael González-Val.

A. Díez-Minguela et al., *Regional Inequality in Spain*, Palgrave Studies in Economic History, https://doi.org/10.1007/978-3-319-96110-1_8

area of 1,543,265 km^2, which is about 35 per cent of the surface area of the EU-28, and their 182 million inhabitants in 2010 (85 million in 1870) also represented roughly 35 per cent of the entire population of the EU-28.

First we give an overview of the economic evolution of our area of study by looking at the long-term dynamics of each individual country. The graph in Fig. 8.1 shows the evolution of per-capita GDP in the four countries that make up SW Europe measured in 1990 Geary-Khamis dollars. It can easily be seen that each country has followed a different growth pattern since the mid-nineteenth century. France stands out for having had the highest per-capita income since the first stages of development. It was an early participant in the industrial revolution and its lead over the other three countries in our study increased during the *Belle Époque* in the late nineteenth and early twentieth centuries. Despite the negative impact of the First World War, this lead continued to increase

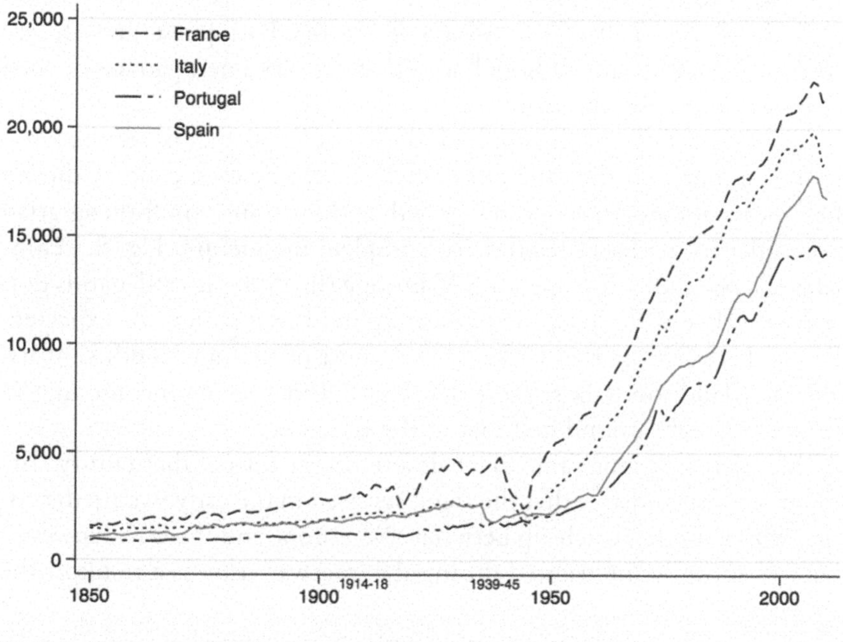

Fig. 8.1 Per-capita GDP by country (1990 Geary-Khamis dollars). Source: Maddison Project Database (Bolt and Van Zanden 2014)

over the interwar years and France has stayed ahead throughout the economic expansion of the *Golden Age* (1945–1973) and more recent decades.[2]

As regards Italy and Spain, which in the context of Western Europe were slow to industrialize, both follow a similar trajectory up to the Second World War. Growth in Italy speeded up during the so-called *Giolitti Age* (1901–1913), while Spanish economic growth did not reach its full potential until later in the twentieth century, especially after the First World War. However, Spain's per-capita GDP growth stagnated during the Civil War (1936–1939) and the subsequent period of autarky during the early decades of the Franco regime (1940s–1950s). Its economic growth then accelerated during the period from the late 1950s to the end of the Franco regime in 1975 (Prados de la Escosura 2003, 2016). Italy also experienced stronger growth in the aftermath of the Second World War (Felice and Vecchi 2015) and the same was true of Portugal, where economic growth before the First World War had been rather weak and began to increase slightly only in the interwar years (Lains 2003). Over the second half of the twentieth century Portuguese growth was similar to that of Spain, although in recent decades a new gap has opened up between the two countries.

Taken as a whole the information shown in Fig. 8.1 let us see the long-term evolution and the different paths followed by each country during the process of modern economic growth and the transition from agrarian economies to modern societies. To complete the picture, Fig. 8.2 compares the per-capita income for SW Europe (in 1990 Geary-Khamis dollars) with that of the UK, the pioneering industrial nation. As expected, the gap between the two widened over most of the nineteenth century, and the Maddison data suggest that by 1890 per-capita income in SW Europe was only around half that of the UK.

This relative decline came to a halt around the turn of the century. The Maddison data indicate that the trend reversed in the early twentieth century, with a modest catch-up between SW Europe and the UK. However, this was abruptly interrupted during the interwar years as a result of the

[2] On the long-term evolution of the French economy, see Toutain (1987) or Lévy-Leboyer and Bourguignon (1990).

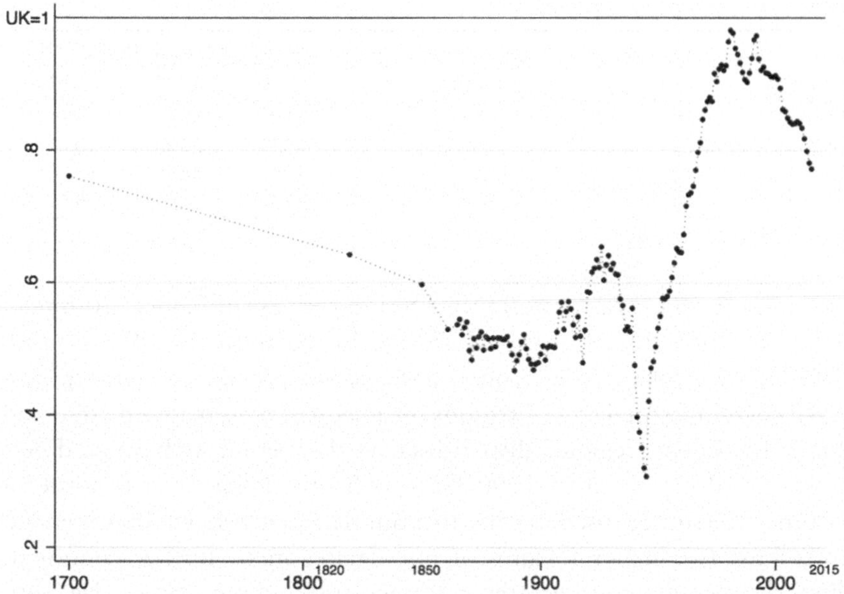

Fig. 8.2 South-west Europe v. the UK (per-capita GDP). Source: Maddison Project Database (Bolt and Van Zanden 2014)

Great Depression, the Spanish Civil War (1936–1939) and finally the Second World War (1939–1945). Historical estimates suggest that by 1950 per-capita income in SW Europe was again about half that of the UK. Catch-up primarily occurred between 1950 and 1981 and was the result of a combination of rapid economic growth in SW Europe and only moderate growth in the UK. By 1981, per-capita income in SW Europe had almost equalled that of the UK. However, recent decades have seen a new reversal of this trend, with SW Europe again lagging behind.[3]

In this chapter our aim is to focus on the regional dimension of these long-term national growth experiences from a supranational perspective. To do this, we have collected data on regional population and GDP for France, Italy, Portugal and Spain. This information has been gathered at the highest available level of territorial disaggregation, which varies from

[3] For an account of interwar and post-war economic growth in Western Europe, see Feinstein et al. (1997) or Crafts and Toniolo (1996).

Table 8.1 Descriptive statistics

Country	Number of regions	Average surface area (km²)	Average population (000)		
			1870	1950	2010
France	84	6691	439	493	715
Italy	20	15,103	1381	2358	3037
Portugal	18	5123	225	440	552
Spain	49	10,324	319	569	957

Source: See Appendix

case to case—84 *départements* (NUTS3) in the case of France, 20 *regioni* (NUTS2) for Italy, 18 historical *distritos* for Portugal and 49 *provincias* (NUTS3) for Spain. The result is a dataset of population and regional GDP covering a total of 171 regions on a decadal basis between 1870 and 2010. To evaluate regional disparities over this period we have used per-capita GDP expressed in 1990 Geary-Khamis dollars as a measure of income. The sources used to construct our dataset are shown in Appendix.

At least two major features of our dataset merit further comment. First, these regions vary greatly in surface area and population size, with the Italian regions standing out for having levels of population much higher than the average in the other countries, as can be seen in Table 8.1. And second, the departments of France predominate in our sample, accounting for almost half the 171 regions studied.

Bearing in mind this information about the countries and regions involved and the main characteristics and limits of our sample, we move on to the analysis of regional income inequality in SW Europe.

From Growing Regional Inequality to Income and Spatial Polarization

The Long-term Patterns of Regional Inequality in South-west Europe

Figure 8.3 shows per-capita GDP (black dots) for the regions of each country compared to average per-capita GDP for SW Europe as a whole (solid line) for 1860–2010. The grey bars represent all the regions of all

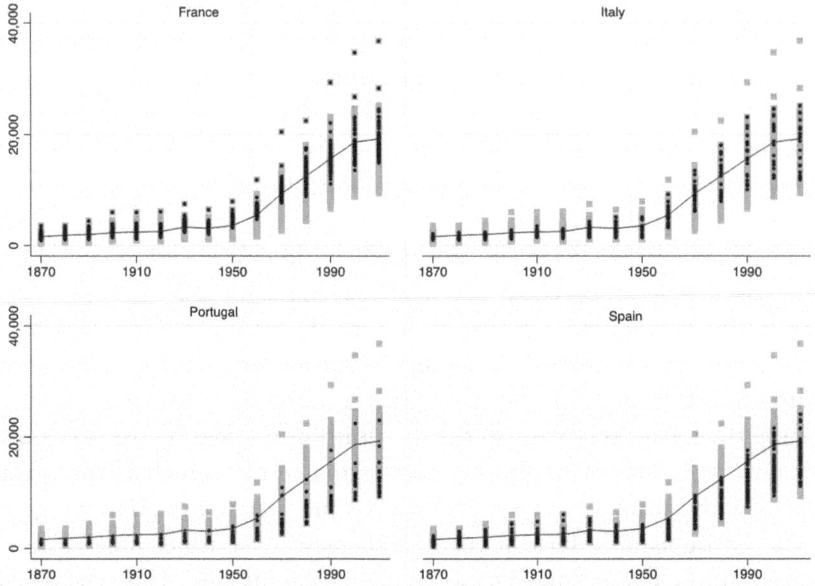

Fig. 8.3 Regional per-capita GDP (1990 Geary-Khamis $) by country, 1860–2010. Source: See Appendix. Note: Each black dot represents a region, while the solid line is average per-capita GDP for south-west Europe as a whole. The regions of all four countries combined are shown by grey bars.

four countries considered as a whole. We can see that the graphs show a more complex picture than that described previously at national level. In fact there are big differences within countries and there are regions in all countries with income levels both above and below the mean for SW Europe.

Most regions in France, for example, which is the wealthiest of the four countries, had values above the SW European average until the 1980s. Since then, however, the number of regions above the mean has decreased and a large group of French departments are currently below it, though still a long way from the bottom of the distribution of regions represented by the grey bars. The ever-increasing lead of the Île-de-France is also noteworthy. As regards the Italian regions, throughout the period of study they are fairly equally distributed above and below the solid line that marks the international mean, which is an indication of the traditional north-south divide. By 2010, the richest regions were some of the wealthiest in SW Europe (though far behind the Île-de-France), while the poorest were in the lower tail of the regional income distribution.

Like in the case of Italy, until the 1940s there were regions in Spain both above and below the SW European average. These provinces then dropped below the mean and occupied some of the lowest positions of all regions during the years of the Franco regime. Nevertheless, by the twenty-first century Madrid, the Basque provinces and Navarre had achieved a per-capita GDP above the average for SW Europe. And, finally, the Portuguese regions, excluding the capital region of Lisbon since 1940, have repeatedly fallen below the average per-capita GDP for south-west Europe and, together with a number of Spanish regions, occupy the lowest segments of the distribution marked by the grey bars.

Figure 8.3 throws up another interesting result, which is that in all four cases the absolute differences between the richest and poorest regions of the entire sample have tended to increase over time, indicating an increase in the dispersion of regional per-capita income. This type of evidence could mean that, in the case of SW Europe as a whole, one of the stylized facts of Spanish regional inequality may not be present, that is, the existence of a relationship between territorial inequality and economic development that forms an inverted U-shaped curve, at least over the period 1860–1980. Before we can test this hypothesis we need to analyse the relative position of the regions with respect to a mean that has also been growing over time.

To do this we pool together all 171 regions and broadly examine the spatial disparities between 1870 and 2010 using the analysis typical of the growth literature that we have already used in previous chapters (Barro and Sala-i-Martín 1991, 1992). To begin with, the dispersion of regional per-capita income is measured using both a single coefficient of variation (SCV) and a population-weighted coefficient of variation (WCV).

According to the graph in Fig. 8.4 there appear to have been four basic episodes. From the early stages of modern economic growth until the First World War, the trend was for regional disparities to increase. Thus the upward-rising section of the Williamson curve is clearly identified, particularly with the population-weighted coefficient of variation

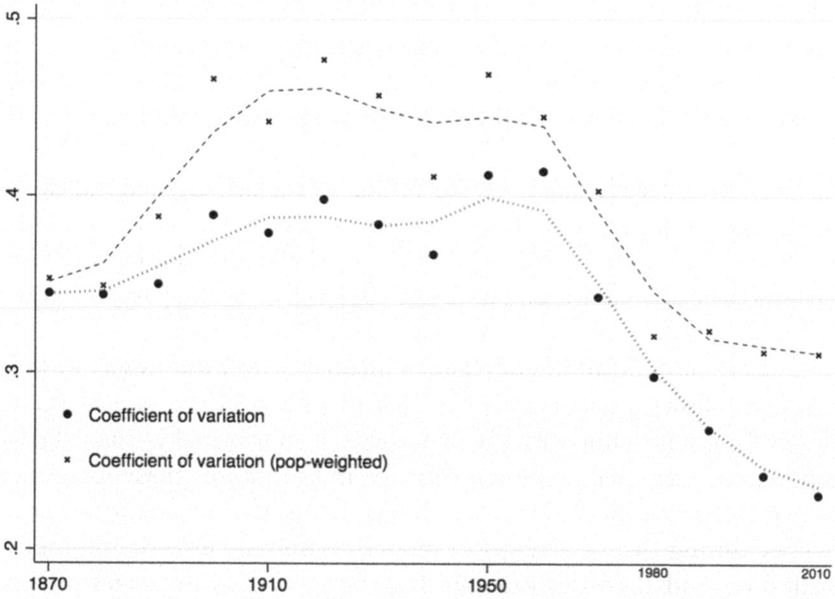

Fig. 8.4 Regional income inequality in south-west Europe, 1870–2010. Source: See Appendix

(WCV), which initially rises steeply in the graph. This indicates that the most populated regions experienced greater growth in per-capita income. In contrast, a markedly different evolution is seen for the period 1910–1950, with both curves following much flatter trajectories. Regional inequality reached a plateau in the interwar years, especially as far as WCV is concerned. Thus the big increase in regional inequality that started in the late nineteenth century came to an end in the early decades of the twentieth. From then on, regional disparities remained stable but relatively large until around 1950.[4]

[4] The fact that there were two world wars in the period 1910–1950 plus the disruption they caused may well have influenced the results. It would therefore be advisable to treat our findings with a certain degree of caution. The observation for 1950, for instance, only five years after the end of the Second World War, gives a high value that clearly influences the trend of the curve. Without this observation it could perhaps be argued that a convergence process would have begun several decades earlier and then continued through the Golden Age.

From 1950 onwards we see a marked regional economic convergence process that coincides with the higher growth rates recorded over the decades of the Golden Age (1950–1980). This process can be seen equally clearly through both the weighted (WCV) and unweighted (SCW) indicators. However, the rate by which regional inequality decreased during the final three decades analysed (according to the unweighted indicator) began to slow down, and if we take into account the evolution of the WCV we might even be talking about a trend reversal. To put it another way, since the crisis at the end of the 1970s hardly any decrease in income inequality has been recorded in the regions of SW Europe.

The long-term evolution of regional inequality over the area as a whole therefore follows a curve similar to that identified in the case of Spain. This evolution is in line with the hypothesis of an inverted U-shaped relation between regional income inequality and economic development of the type suggested by Williamson (1965) that is, that inequality tends to increase during the early stages of modern economic growth and industrialization and then decreases during the more mature stages of economic development. It is also noteworthy that the decrease in territorial inequality in the case of SW Europe came to a stop during the most advanced stages of the development process, which as far as we are concerned here starts around the 1980s.

In short, the historical evolution of regional inequality in SW Europe has a number of striking parallels with that of Spain. However, given that the type of evidence we have found so far shows only the relative position of the various regions with respect to the mean (σ-convergence), we will next look at the possible existence of a connection between the original levels of per-capita income and their subsequent rates of growth. In other words we will investigate the presence of β-convergence.

Figure 8.5 relates the levels of per-capita income of the regions of SW Europe in 1870 to the annual average cumulative rates of growth recorded for them over the whole period 1870–2010. The dots represent this relation for each of the 171 regions considered. To make the graph easier to interpret, all the regions belonging to each of the four countries are shown in the same colour. The exercise is carried out using data for per-capita GDP in PPP (Geary-Khamis $) and the corresponding rate of growth. We see in Fig. 8.5 that what were the poorer regions in 1870 tended to

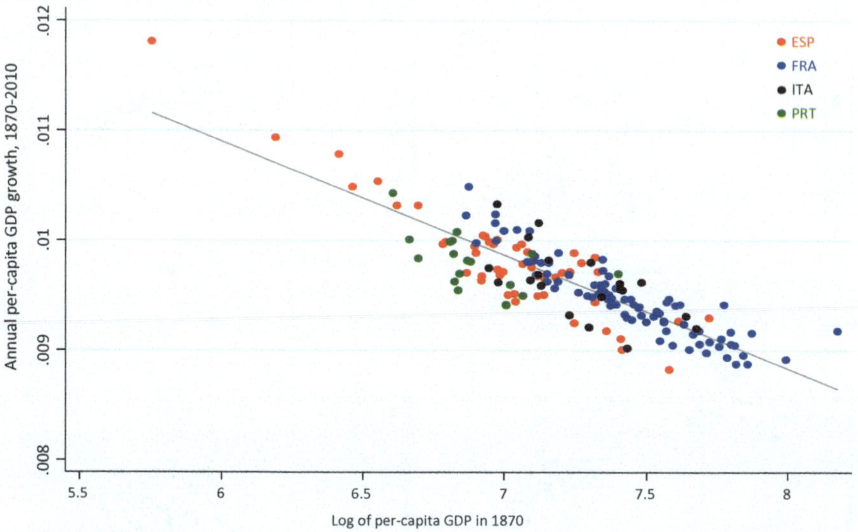

Fig. 8.5 *β*-convergence in south-west Europe (1870–2010). Source: See Appendix

grow faster than the richer regions over the next 140 years (i.e. from 1870 to 2010). The value of R^2 is 0.69, which would indicate that this relation is significant. This means that the regions that make up SW Europe have undergone a *β*-convergence process over the long term.

It can be deduced from the analysis of the temporal evolution of territorial inequality based on *σ*-convergence that this evolution did not follow a homogeneous trajectory over the entire period. In fact it followed a pattern that varied over the four major stages we outlined for both Spain and SW Europe, that is, 1870–1910, 1910–1950, 1950–1980 and 1980–2010. Figure 8.6 presents new evidence as to whether or not the *β*-convergence hypothesis is true, but in this case distinguishing between these four periods.

The results show that, of the four subperiods considered, only 1950–1980 shows a significant pattern of *β*-convergence (with the coefficient of determination R^2 reaching a value of 0.44). The high dispersion of the dots marking the positions of the various regions suggests that in none of the other three periods—1870–1910, 1910–1950 and

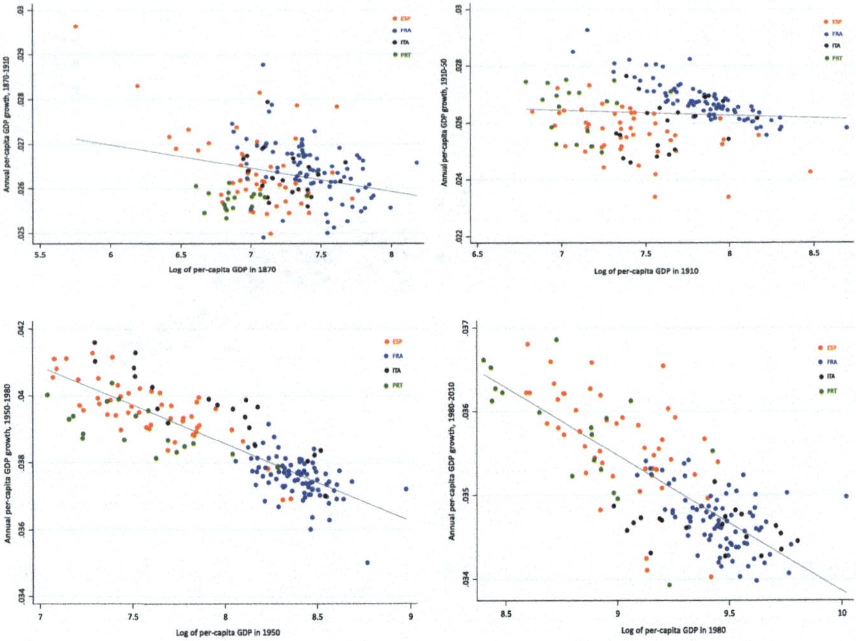

Fig. 8.6 β-convergence in south-west Europe (1870–1910, 1910–1950, 1950–1980, 1980–2010). Source: See Appendix

1980–2010—is there a significant relation between the original levels of regional per-capita income and subsequent growth rates (this being supported by the low values calculated for the respective coefficients of determination).

This means that over the long term the poorest regions of SW Europe in 1870 have tended to grow at a higher rate than the wealthiest regions at that date. However, if we consider the existence of this relationship in each of the four major stages into which we have divided the evolution of regional economic inequality, this behavioural trend is significant only for the period 1950–1980. It is therefore proven that, as in the case of Spain, it is during these years that a real narrowing of the gap between regional income levels in our sample of European regions is concentrated.

The Emergence of Twin Peaks in South-west Europe

As we explained in Chap. 5, if we want to gain a wider understanding of the spatial distribution of income, we need to consider it as a complex concept with different dimensions. For instance, it is important that we should study not only the dispersion but also the shape of the distribution and the potential presence of twin peaks or convergence clubs. We have therefore produced kernel densities of distribution (normalized with respect to the mean) for our dataset for SW Europe for each benchmark year, and these will enable us to graphically explore the modality of the distribution and its evolution decade by decade. Figure 8.7 shows these kernel densities between 1870 and 2010, with the regions being treated both equally and weighted by population size.[5]

It is interesting to see that for the first benchmark year (1870), which falls during the initial period of relatively low inequality, a large number of regions were grouped around the mean value for per-capita income in SW Europe. This is shown by the greater height of the distribution. However, over the period 1870–1910 there appears to have been an upsurge in inequality involving a higher concentration of regions in the tails of the distribution, especially the upper tail, which stretches out as some regions forged ahead of the others. This elongation contains the more developed regions of SW Europe, that is, those that industrialized in the early stages of modern economic growth and achieved levels of per-capita income considerably higher than the average. Hence kernel densities contribute to a better understanding of the patterns behind the increase in regional income inequality before the First World War.

Between 1910 and 1950 a new pattern emerges. The graphs in Fig. 8.7 show an evolution towards bimodality, which is even more evident once we make regional adjustments for population size. The unimodal distribution typical of the early stages of development has turned into a bimodal distribution by the end of this period. The result is a gradual disappearance of the upper tail and the gradual emergence of a bimodal structure. In other words, after an initial period that saw increasing

[5] Here, as in Chap. 5, we follow the distribution dynamics approach proposed by Quah (1993, 1996, 1997). For simplicity's sake we chose the Gaussian kernel with a width that minimized the mean integrated squared error, as suggested by Silverman (1992).

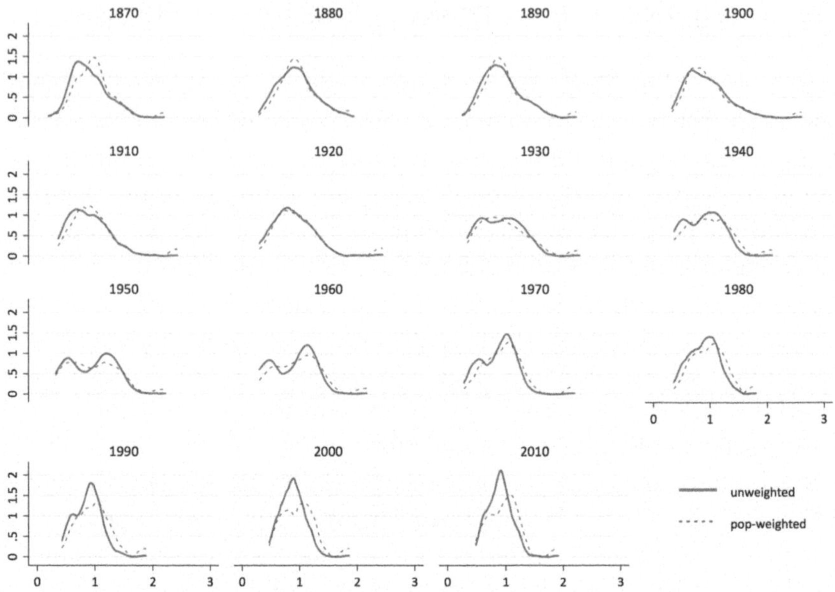

Fig. 8.7 Kernel densities, per-capita regional income, south-west Europe (1870–2010). Source: See Appendix

regional disparities in SW Europe, these disparities then remained steady during the interwar years. However, the polarization of regional incomes becomes increasingly pronounced.

In line with the advance of the regional economic convergence process, the kernels show that the distance between the extremes of the distribution narrowed considerably over the period 1950–1980. This decrease in inequality was accompanied by the virtual disappearance of the significant mass of provinces that comprised the upper tail, and the β-convergence process took place in parallel with the virtual disappearance of bimodality in the distribution. Not only are the regional per-capita GDPs situated closer to the mean for the sample over these years, the mode and the mean also tend to converge.

Finally, between 1980 and 2010 the kernels of the unweighted distribution show a probability mass accumulating around the mean income values. However, there is also a trend towards the formation of a large probability mass—that is, a large number of territories—at income levels much higher than the mean. An evolution of this kind could be a sign that territorial economic inequality has been evolving towards a scenario of bimodality or polarization over the last few years.

The information the kernels provide when we weight the regions of SW Europe by population more clearly reflects this trend. Whereas the evolution of per-capita income during the first three subperiods (1870–1910, 1910–1950 and 1950–1980) is fairly similar for both densities, there is a noticeable change in the fourth. The population-weighted kernels show that the more unimodal distribution of 1980 has become more bimodal in the observation for 2010. This means that, to use the terminology of endogenous growth models, we could be talking about the formation of two *convergence clubs* in the present. These characterized the shape of regional income distribution in 1950 and they do so again in 2010. It should also be pointed out that the bimodality of 2010 appears only in the weighted distribution. This would indicate that the regions that form the peak comprising the richest territories are also the most populated.

Mobility

Kernel diagrams provide information about income distribution in different periods. Now that we have noted the shape of the distribution, we can focus on the tails. To help us explore the main spatial patterns of per-capita income in SW Europe in greater detail, the rankings of all regions are shown in Fig. 8.8 and the top and bottom ten regions for the benchmark years are listed in Table 8.2a, b. First of all, it seems that by 1870 the Paris region (Seine) already had the highest per-capita income, twice the average for SW Europe. Second, it is clear that French regions, particularly those in the north, predominated in the upper tail of the distribution in the late nineteenth century.[6] Third, Madrid (#15) and Liguria (#19) were respectively the leading regions in Spain and Italy in 1870, whereas Lisbon, the richest region in Portugal, occupied a fairly low posi-

[6] While most of the top-ranked regions are located in northern France, there are exceptions such as Hérault and Rhône in the south-east and east.

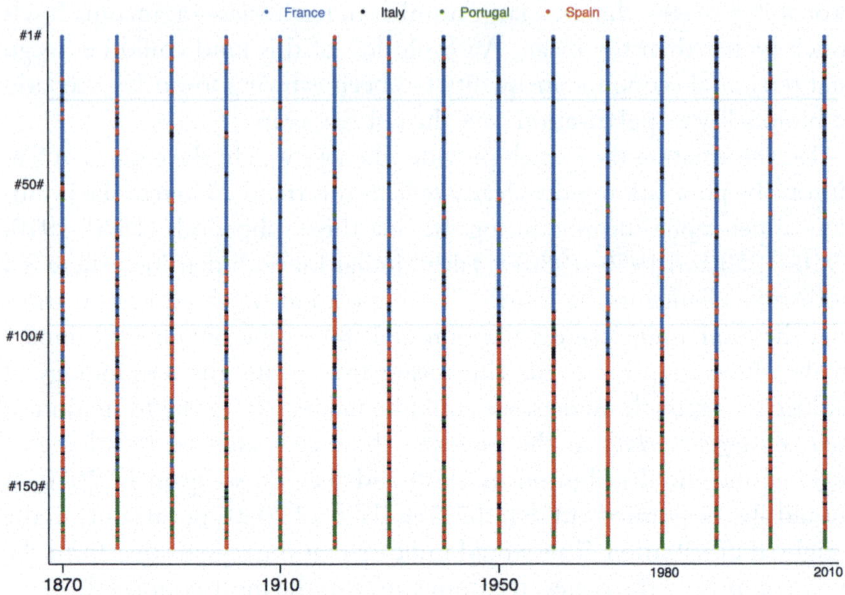

Fig. 8.8 Regional rankings for per-capita income, 1870–2010. Source: See Appendix

tion in the ranking (#83) with a per-capita income below the mean for south-west Europe.

In 1910 the top positions in the ranking were still dominated by French regions, with Paris (Seine) remaining on top, but some of the industrial regions of northern Spain had also risen to join them by this date. The case of Barcelona in particular stands out—not only did it have a per-capita income twice the average for south-west Europe, it was just behind Paris (Seine) at the top of the table. Gipuzkoa in the Basque Country also entered the top ten, occupying a position just above the top Italian region, Liguria (#11). In fact various Spanish and Italian regions improved their ranking positions during the early decades of the twentieth century.

It was again the French regions that occupied the top positions in the aftermath of the Second World War. Most striking is the decline of the Spanish provinces after the Civil War (1936–1939) and the subsequent period of autarky in the 1940s. The gap that opened up turned out to be

Table 8.2a Regional rankings for per-capita income in 1870, 1910, 1950, 1980 and 2010 (top ten)

Region	Country	1870	Region	Country	1910	Region	Country	1950	Region	Country	1980	Region	Country	2010
Seine/PR	FRA	1	Seine/PR	FRA	1	Seine/PR	FRA	1	Seine/PR	FRA	1	Seine/PR	FRA	1
Seine-Maritime	FRA	2	Barcelona	SPA	2	Haute-Saône	FRA	2	Valle d'Aosta	ITA	2	Rhône	FRA	2
Marne	FRA	3	Seine-et-Marne	FRA	3	Rhône	FRA	3	Marne	FRA	3	Valle d'Aosta	ITA	3
Eure-et-Loir	FRA	4	Rhône	FRA	4	Nord	FRA	4	Seine-Maritime	FRA	4	Haute-Garonne	FRA	4
Hérault	FRA	5	Oise	FRA	5	Seine-Maritime	FRA	5	Rhône	FRA	5	Savoy	FRA	5
Ardennes	FRA	6	Bouches-du-Rhône	FRA	6	Bouches-du-Rhône	FRA	6	Emilia Romagna	ITA	6	Bizkaia	SPA	6
Calvados	FRA	7	Aube	FRA	7	Meurthe-et-Moselle	FRA	7	Lombardy	ITA	7	Marne	FRA	7
Seine-et-Marne	FRA	8	Hérault	FRA	8	Seine-et-Marne	FRA	8	Trentino-Alto Adige	ITA	8	Trentino-Alto Adige	ITA	8
Bouches-du-Rhône	FRA	9	Seine-Maritime	FRA	9	Pyrénées-Orientales	FRA	9	Pyrénées-Atlantiques	FRA	9	Lombardy	ITA	9
Eure	FRA	10	Gipuzkoa	SPA	10	Isère	FRA	10	Loiret	FRA	10	Loiret	FRA	10
...			...			...			...			...		

Source: See Appendix

Table 8.2b Regional rankings for per-capita income in 1870, 1910, 1950, 1980 and 2010 (bottom ten)

Region	Country	1870	Region	Country	1910	Region	Country	1950	Region	Country	1980	Region	Country	2010
...			...			...			...			...		
A Coruña	SPA	162	Coimbra	PRT	162	Vila Real	PRT	162	Jaen	SPA	162	Guadalajara	SPA	162
Viseu	PRT	163	Leon	SPA	163	Ourense	SPA	163	Castelo Branco	PRT	163	Castelo Branco	PRT	163
Castelo Branco	PRT	164	Leiria	PRT	164	Lugo	SPA	164	Granada	SPA	164	Badajoz	SPA	164
Canary Islands	SPA	165	Guarda	PRT	165	Viseu	PRT	165	Ourense	SPA	165	Toledo	SPA	165
Faro	PRT	166	Ourense	SPA	166	Viana do Castelo	PRT	166	Badajoz	SPA	166	Braga	PRT	166
Oviedo	SPA	167	Viseu	PRT	167	Almeria	SPA	167	Viseu	PRT	167	Bragança	PRT	167
Ourense	SPA	168	Aveiro	PRT	168	Jaen	SPA	168	Guarda	PRT	168	Vila Real	PRT	168
Leon	SPA	169	Faro	PRT	169	Caceres	SPA	169	Viana do Castelo	PRT	169	Viseu	PRT	169
Pontevedra	SPA	170	Lugo	SPA	170	Granada	SPA	170	Bragança	PRT	170	Guarda	PRT	170
Lugo	SPA	171	Castelo Branco	PRT	171	Guarda	PRT	171	Vila Real	PRT	171	Viana do Castelo	PRT	171

Source: See Appendix

long-lasting and only in the final list (2010) do we again see a significant presence of Spanish regions in the upper positions of the table.

The rankings also reveal that there were no Portuguese territories among the 20 most advanced regions before 2010, and even then the only region to win a place in this select club of the wealthy was Lisbon (#13), the country's capital. As for the Italian regions, we can see from Fig. 8.8 that they only started to become established in the upper positions after 1940. Liguria (#15) and the Aosta Valley (#16) both appear in the top 20 by 1950, and after 1980 we see that Emilia Romagna (#6), Lombardy (#7), Trentino-Alto Adige (#8) and Piedmont (#12) are some of the regions with the highest per-capita income in SW Europe. Spanish regions, on the other hand, reappear as a significant presence only in 2010, in this case in the shape of Bizkaia (#6), Madrid (#12) and Alava (#14).

Turning our attention now to the bottom of the ranking, Fig. 8.8 and Table 8.2a, b show us that the lower tail of the distribution contained only Portuguese and Spanish regions. In 1870 the poorest regions were mostly in the north-west of the Iberian Peninsula. Portuguese regions had a greater presence in the lowest positions in the 1910 ranking, but by 1950 the composition had changed and, with Spanish regions again occupying many of the bottom positions, the very poorest in terms of per-capita income were those located in the south (Andalusia) and near the Portuguese border. Thus by the mid-twentieth century, Andalusia had definitively lost the prominent position it had once held.

Only in the rankings for 1870 and 1910 do any French regions appear in the lower tail, that is, Corrèze in 1870 (#152) and Lozère in 1910 (#156), though by 1950 they had risen up through the rankings, with the lowest per-capita income being recorded for Lozère (#98). Italy, on the other hand, underwent the same process in reverse. No Italian regions appear in the bottom 20 positions of the ranking for 1870 or 1910, but in the 1950 benchmark year Basilicata (#158) had become the poorest region in Italy—followed closely by Calabria (#157)—with a per-capita income of around 40 per cent of the mean for SW Europe. Other southern Italian regions had average incomes ranging between 50 per cent and 60 per cent of the European average (in increasing order these were

Molise, Sicily, Abruzzi, Sardinia, Puglia and Campania), but none of them appeared among the 20 poorest regions in the table.

There are no great changes to the 1950 map of regional poverty in the benchmark years of 1980 and 2010. Thus it appears that this reality that had been taking shape during the first stage of the industrialization and economic development process in SW Europe has become a constant. In 1980 and 2010 it is basically the regions of the south and west of the Iberian Peninsula that form the greatest cluster of poverty. Beyond these, only the territories of Sicily, Calabria and Campania in the south of Italy occupy positions among the 20 poorest regions in the table in 2010.

To summarize, a study of the rankings of the richest and poorest regions of SW Europe points to the existence of a certain mobility in the years between 1870 and 1950. However, from this time onwards the regional rankings are characterized by their stability, indicating very low mobility at both the top and the bottom of the distribution. Also, if we analyse what regions have occupied the extreme positions in the table, there appears to be a relationship between the income levels of these regions and their locations in geographical terms, with a concentration of the wealthiest regions to the north and a majority of relatively impoverished regions in the south and west. The exception to this is the presence among the richest regions in the sample of Lisbon and Madrid (home to the capitals of their respective states) in the final benchmark year analysed.

Did a Geographical Pattern Emerge?

Figure 8.9 shows the spatial distribution of regional per-capita income in SW Europe and makes it possible for us to easily explore the main geographical patterns. The regions are grouped in quintiles for each benchmark year. As usual, black indicates "very rich" areas and light grey "very poor" areas. The information contained in the maps shows how the uneven economic development of SW Europe has gradually given shape to a geography that places the southern regions of Italy and most of the regions in the south-west of the Iberian Peninsula at the bottom of the income distribution ranking. Meanwhile many of the rich regions are

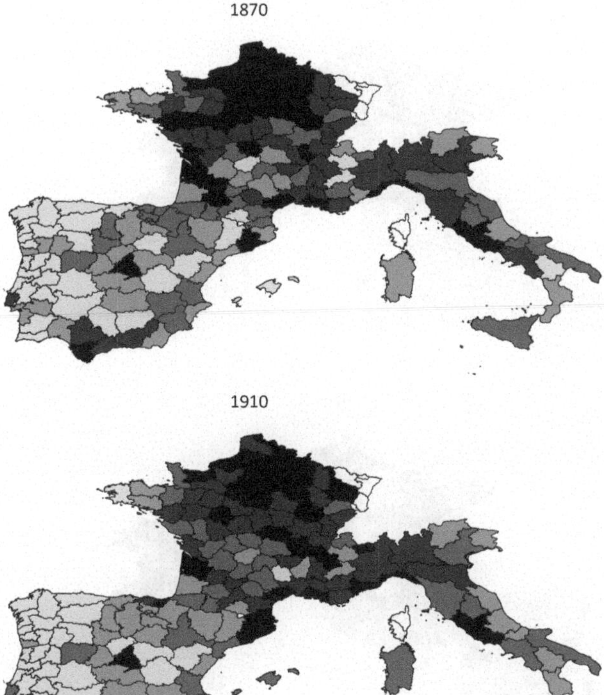

Fig. 8.9 Maps of regional per-capita income in south-west Europe (quintiles). Source: See Appendix

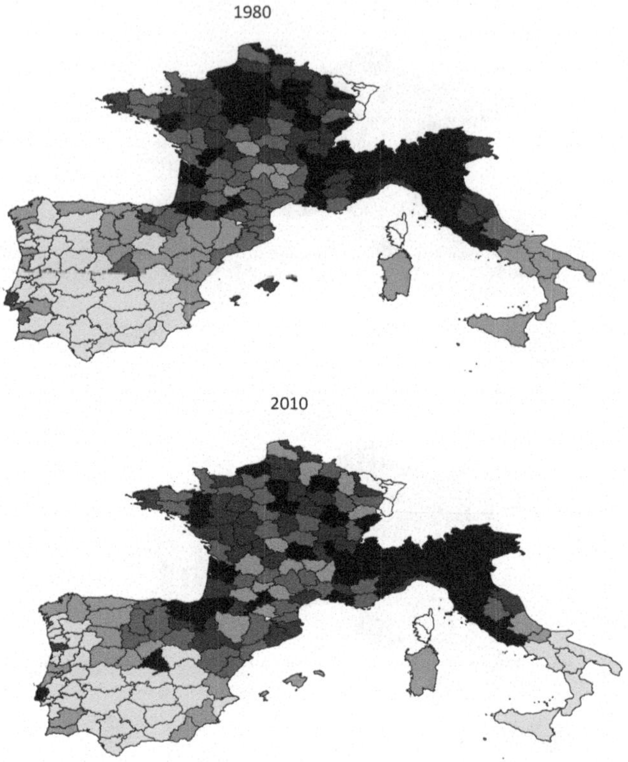

Fig. 8.9 (continued)

clustered in the north of France around Paris (Seine), the north of Italy and, to a lesser extent, north-eastern Iberia. In short, it seems that the geography of regional inequality in SW Europe has formed a core-periphery pattern.

The makings of the geographical groupings into which today's poorest regions are laid out were already visible in the map for the benchmark year 1950. Since then there have been no great changes. The poorest geographical areas in that year (southern Italy and the south-west of the Iberian Peninsula) are still the poorest in 2010. However, some changes can indeed be identified in the geographical positions occupied by the richest regions. The map for 1950 shows a strong territorial polarization whereby these regions have grouped together to form a gradient that starts in the north of Italy and crosses France towards Paris. In recent years (1980–2010) this cluster of wealth has lost definition because some of the regions of central-eastern France have dropped away. Also, over these same years a notable increase can be observed in per-capita income levels for the regions in which the capital cities of Spain (Madrid) and Portugal (Lisbon) are located, both far away from the gradient described above.

Nevertheless, it can still be said that regional inequality in SW Europe today continues to follow the spatial pattern that took shape in the period 1870–1950. This developed in parallel with the advance of industrialization, which began in just a small group of territories. Later, this group gradually grew bigger during the first half of the twentieth century and, once the pattern was drawn, it has undergone no radical changes. In fact, changes were virtually non-existent between 1950 and 1980. However, they do appear to a certain degree in the period 1980–2010, although they are very limited in size. What is noticeable about today's map of regional inequality is that it shows a more definite north-south divide in Italy and the Iberian Peninsula than in previous periods. We can also see that the cluster of rich regions has been losing definition, which can be explained by the drop in position of various French departments and the economic take-off of spatially isolated centres of wealth corresponding to national capitals (particularly Madrid and Lisbon).

Industrialization, Economic Development and Regional Inequality

The previous sections enabled us to identify four different stages in the evolution of regional income inequality in SW Europe. The period 1870–1910 was characterized by the spread of industrialization and the first wave of globalization (Pollard 1981; O'Rourke and Williamson 1999), then between 1910 and 1950—a period roughly corresponding to the interwar years—opportunities arose due to new energy sources such as electric power, but in the context of a globalization backlash.

During the first period regional disparities increased mainly because a handful of regions in France and Spain stretched the upper tail of the distribution. In the second period, however, this inequality flattened out due to the participation of more regions in modern economic growth, particularly those in northern Italy (Liguria, Lombardy, Piedmont), Spain (Madrid) and Portugal (Lisbon). The fact that only a few regions industrialized in these years led to the appearance of a "twin peaks" or bimodal distribution that clearly deserves further thought and consideration.

The third period (1950–1980) saw a rapid convergence process take place between the relative income levels of the regions in SW Europe. It also saw most of the income becoming concentrated around a single mean. However, despite this convergence process it has been shown that there were no great changes in the composition of the regions occupying the top and bottom positions of the income ranking, nor in the territorial map they drew. This dynamic could be related to the spread of the industrialization process and structural change to an ever-increasing number of regions. This would certainly have been encouraged by the size of the migratory flows from poor regions to richer ones in a context of increasing, but limited, international economic integration.

Finally, in the last of the periods some interesting changes can be observed. On the one hand the regional convergence process seems to come to a halt, while on the other there again appears a concentration of regions at two income levels significantly different from the mean. Also, the map of inequality starts to show a more marked north-south division, in which only those regions that are home to national capital cities experienced economic take-off. Indeed the growth dynamic of these regions was significantly higher than the average and they went on to join the select group of wealthy regions in the sample. Certainly the uneven effects of the crisis of the 1970s contributed to the slowing down of the convergence process. In addition, the new international economic context that opened up in the 1980s—characterized by the spread of a new wave of technological change, increasing international integration of the goods and factor markets, and a less active role for national regional development policies—would have laid the foundations for a possible new stage of increasing territorial inequality involving main actors and geography that are not the same as the ones we have seen before.

Finally, the study of regional economic inequality in south-west Europe, including its evolution and the identification of its main characteristics (shape, mobility and geography), enables us to construct some hypotheses about the key factors needed to understand it. Just as we saw in the case of Spain, there seems to be a relationship between economic development and regional disparities resembling the hypothesis constructed by Williamson (1965). However, the outline of this inverted U-shaped curve appears to come to a halt around 1980. From then on we see a new stage that could signal the start of a timid increase in the growth of inequality involving greater polarization between regional income levels, a certain mobility in the positions the regions occupy in the income rankings and a spatial design with a marked north-south profile.

For the purpose of verifying that the evidence matches Williamson's hypothesis relating the level of regional inequality with the advance of the

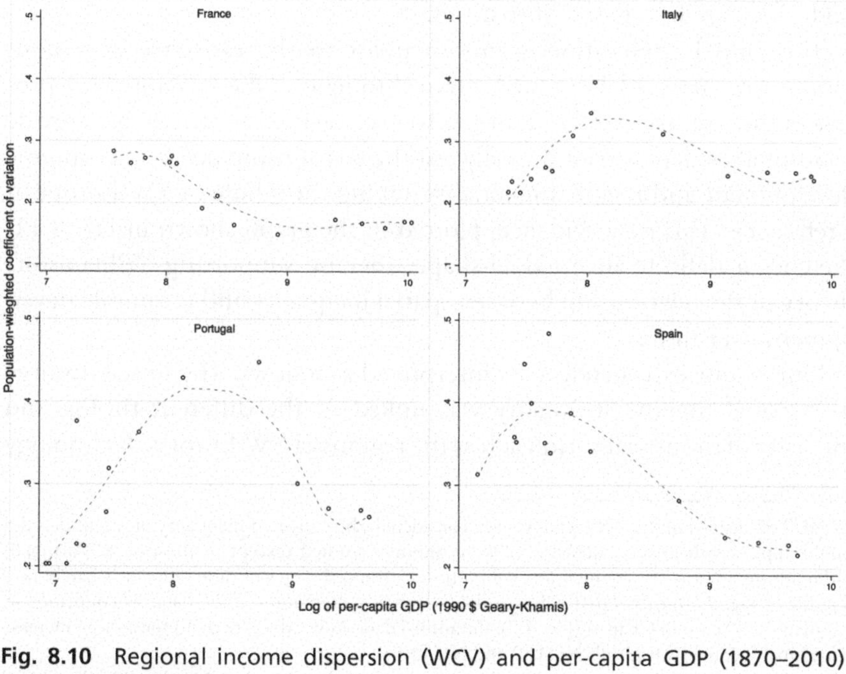

Fig. 8.10 Regional income dispersion (WCV) and per-capita GDP (1870–2010). Source: See Appendix

economic development process, Fig. 8.10 presents the outline corresponding to this relationship for each of the four countries studied. The *y*-axis shows the values calculated for the WCV, while the *x*-axis shows the real levels of GDP per capita (expressed in logarithms). Each observation corresponds to one of the benchmark years analysed.

From the information presented in the graphs it can be deduced that the inverted U-shaped relationship between development and regional inequality suggested by Williamson is plainly identified for each country. However, there are some country-specific features that merit comment. First, in the case of France the upward trend of the inverted U-curve does not show. It might be argued that this is because modern economic growth in this early-industrialized country started before 1870, the first year for which estimates of per-capita GDP are available. The curve also appears to be flatter than for the other countries. Second, the Iberian countries recorded the highest levels of regional inequality in the past, while France recorded the lowest. Finally, the convergence process came to a halt in the later stages of development, and this has given rise to a slight increase in regional disparities.[7]

This initial exploration seems to point to the existence of a non-monotonic inverted U-shaped curve throughout the development process in the countries of SW Europe. To investigate this further, we provide additional evidence to empirically test the relationship between economic development and regional inequality, taking the whole of SW Europe as a reference. This new evidence, plotted in the graph shown in Fig. 8.11, sketches a definite inverted U-shape, thereby supporting Williamson's theory of the relationship between spatial inequality and economic development over time.

Our results can therefore be interpreted as follows. The initial upsurge in regional income inequality was linked to the different timing and intensity of industrialization across the regions of SW Europe. Technology

[7] If NUTS2 instead of NUTS3 regions were considered, the increased inequality of recent decades would appear with greater intensity in the economies studied (except in the case of Portugal). Although the increase in regional inequality in the advanced stages of development is barely perceptible in Fig. 8.10, this is partly due to the decennial presentation of the data. As confirmed in the analysis of Spain in Chap. 4 (Fig. 4.2), the annual data show a definite trend towards an increase in regional inequality, for both NUTS2 and NUTS3.

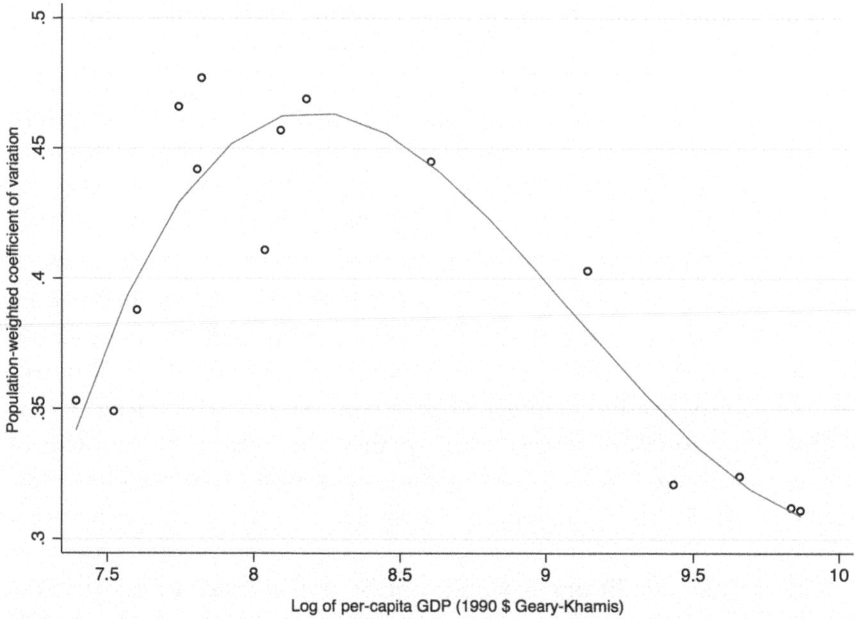

Fig. 8.11 Regional income dispersion (WCV) and per-capita GDP in south-west Europe (whole sample, 1870–2010). Source: See Appendix

shocks occurred with the adoption of the new technologies that characterized the first and second technological revolutions. This led to an increase in regional inequality between 1870 and 1910, with inequality remaining at maximum levels until the 1950s, after which a convergence process began. The spread of new technologies and production sectors to a greater number of regions was responsible for this decrease in regional inequality. However, convergence came to an end in the 1980s. The last three decades represent a period of high income levels and a more far-reaching tertiarization process in the most advanced regions of the sample. The new technology shock arising from the third industrial revolution, associated with ICT, was the cause of current uneven regional growth.[8]

[8] This interpretation of the causes of the current increase in territorial inequality (especially at a NUTS2 territorial scale) is also found in Lessmann (2014).

Indeed throughout the process of economic development, the structural transformation of the regional economies has taken place in a context characterized by changing conditions affecting, among other things, international trade and public policies. Clearly the different degrees of international economic integration of the four economies along with the national policies of territorial equilibrium affecting each of them will no doubt have contained or encouraged the increase in territorial inequality.[9] Nevertheless, the effects have not been so great as to change the long-term trend. This was shaped by the unequal territorial impact of the regional production specialization processes in the context of the first and second technological revolutions. Neither do these effects appear to have counteracted the start of a new pathway of growth in territorial inequality, this time in the context of a new technology shock affecting some economies that are characterized by their high degree of integration into the international economy.

Given these conditions it would not be out of place to say that the long-term analysis of the patterns of regional economic inequality in SW Europe should serve as a warning as to its potential future evolution. Seemingly increasing inequality, polarization of income levels and the geography of regional economic development are elements that, like in the 1950s, are again characterizing regional economic inequality in the Europe of today, and its containment should be made a priority on the political agenda. If not, we may have to wait various decades, as in the past, for the economic development process itself to correct the territorial imbalances it generates.

---

[9] On the elements that can extend or contain the increase in territorial inequality throughout the development processes, see for example Barrios and Strobl (2009), Lessmann (2014) and Ezcurra and Rodríguez-Pose (2014). Díez-Minguela et al. (2017) contains a detailed statistical analysis of the determinants of regional economic inequality in SW Europe, which confirms the existence of an N-shaped relationship between the level of economic development and territorial inequality taking into account other potential explanatory elements.

Appendix

Regional Data

GDP and Population:

France:

The data for the 84 NUTS3 regions come from various sources. The *départements d'outre-mer* are excluded, as is Corsica in 1860, 1900 and 1930. Furthermore, because Alsace, Lorraine and a small area of the Vosges were part of the German Empire between the Franco-Prussian War (1870–1871) and the First World War (1914–1918), for the sake of consistency we have excluded the Alsace departments (Bas-Rhin and Haut-Rhin) and the territory of Belfort (included in Haut-Rhin), which remained part of France. The Treaty of Frankfurt (1871) established that most of the Moselle department in Lorraine was to be German, along with some parts of Meurthe. The remains of these departments formed a smaller version of the former Lorraine under the name Meurthe-et-Moselle. Hence we exclude Moselle but include Meurthe-et-Moselle. Finally, we have merged Seine and Seine-et-Oise to form Paris (Seine). We assumed that the regional shares in 1860 were equivalent to those in 1870. We then computed our values for 1880 and 1890 based on the work by Guillaume Bazot. No data are available for 1940, so we make an interpolation.

1860 (1870), 1896, 1930:	Combes et al. (2011)
1880, 1890:	Bazot (2014)
1911, 1921:	Díez-Minguela and Sanchis (2017)
1954, 1962, 1975:	Rosés and Sanchis (forthcoming)
1982:	Eurostat
1990, 2000, 2007:	INSEE, Comptes régionaux. Base 2010

Italy:

The data for the 20 NUTS2 regions with current borders come from Felice (2015, Table A.2.3). Although today Italy comprises 21 NUTS2 regions, in the dataset Bolzano is merged with the region of Trentino-Alto Adige. GDP data are provided on a decadal basis for years ending in 1, from 1871 to 2011 (with the exception of 1938 for 1940/1941). We would like to thank Emanuele Felice for kindly sharing data with us.

Portugal:

The data for the 18 historical district regions between 1890 and 1980 were calculated on a decadal basis (excluding Madeira-Azores). These were compiled from the original dataset in Badia-Miró et al. (2012). We would like to thank Marc Badia-Miró, Jordi Guilera and Pedro Lains for kindly sharing data with us and also for providing us with estimates for 1990–2010. For these later years the authors distributed the GDP for Portuguese NUTS2 regions among the historical districts on the basis of population size and the NUTS2 regions to which the municipalities comprising these districts belonged. Regional historical GDP estimates for 1870 and 1880 are not available, so we assume that the shares of regional GDP in 1870 and 1880 would have been equivalent to those for 1890, the first year for which estimates are available.

Spain:

The data for the 49 NUTS3 regions or provinces between 1860 and 2010 were compiled on a decadal basis (excluding Ceuta and Melilla) but computing the two Canary Island provinces as one, which gives us the current 50 provinces. The data are from various sources: see Rosés et al. (2010), Martinez-Galarraga et al. (2015) and Tirado et al. (2016).

National Data

GDP Per Capita:

Maddison Project Database (Bolt and Van Zanden 2014).

Population:

1850–1950: Maddison: http://www.ggdc.net/maddison/oriindex.htm.
1950–2010: Total Economy Database: https://www.conference-board.org/data/economydatabase/.

References

Badia-Miró, M., Guilera, J., & Lains, P. (2012). Regional incomes in Portugal: Industrialisation, integration and inequality, 1890–1980. *Revista de Historia Económica/Journal of Iberian and Latin American Economic History, 30*, 225–244.

Barrios, S., & Strobl, E. (2009). The dynamics of regional inequalities. *Regional Science and Urban Economics, 39*(5), 575–591.

Barro, R. J., & Sala-i-Martín, X. (1991). Convergence across states and regions. *Brookings Papers on Economic Activity, 1*, 107–182.

Barro, R. J., & Sala-i-Martín, X. (1992). Convergence. *Journal of Political Economy, 100*, 223–251.

Bazot, G. (2014). Interregional inequalities, convergence, and growth in France from 1840 to 1911. *Annals of Economics and Statistics*, (113/114), 309–345.

Bolt, J., & Van Zanden, J. L. (2014). The Maddison project: Collaborative research on historical national accounts. *Economic History Review, 67*(3), 627–651.

Crafts, N. F. R., & Toniolo, G. (Eds.). (1996). *Economic growth in Europe since 1945*. Cambridge: Cambridge University Press.

Díez-Minguela, A., Gonzalez-Val, R., Martinez-Galarraga, J., Sanchis, T., & Tirado-Fabregat, D. A. (2017). *The long-term relationship between economic development and regional inequality: South West Europe, 1860–2010*. EHES Working Papers in Economic History 119.

Ezcurra, R., & Rodríguez-Pose, A. (2014). Trade openness and spatial inequality in emerging countries. *Spatial Economic Analysis, 9*(2), 162–182.

Feinstein, C. H., Temin, P., & Toniolo, G. (1997). *The world economy between the World Wars*. Oxford University Press.

Felice, E., & Vecchi, G. (2015). Italy's growth and decline, 1891–2011. *Journal of Interdisciplinary History, 14*, 507–548.

Lains, P. (2003). Catching-up the European core: Portuguese economic growth, 1910–1990. *Explorations in Economic History, 40*(4), 369–386.

Lessmann, C. (2014). Spatial inequality and development. Is there an inverted-U relationship? *Journal of Development Economics, 106*, 35–51.

Lévy-Leboyer, M., & Bourguignon, F. (1990). *The French economy in the nineteenth century: An essay in econometric analysis*. Cambridge: Cambridge University Press.

O'Rourke, K. H., & Williamson, J. G. (1999). *Globalization and history: The evolution of a nineteenth-century Atlantic economy*. Cambridge, MA: MIT Press.

Pollard, S. (1981). *Peaceful conquest: The industrialization of Europe, 1760–1970*. Oxford: Oxford University Press.

Prados de la Escosura, L. (2003). *El progreso económico de España*. Bilbao: Fundación BBV.

Prados de la Escosura, L. (2016). Spain's historical national accounts: Expenditure and output, 1850–2015. *EHES Working Papers in Economic History, 103*, 1–145.

Quah, D. (1993). Empirical cross-section dynamics in economic growth. *European Economic Review, 37*, 426–434.

Quah, D. (1996). Twin peaks: Growth and convergence in models of distribution dynamics. *The Economic Journal, 106*(437), 1045–1055.

Quah, D. (1997). Empirics for growth and distribution: Stratification, polarization, and convergence clubs. *Journal of Economic Growth, 2*(1), 27–59.

Silverman, W. B. (1992). *Density estimation for statistics and data analysis*. London: Chapman and Hall.

Toutain, J. C. (1987). *Le Produit Intérieur Brut de la France de 1789 à 1982*. Grenoble: Économies et Société.

Williamson, J. G. (1965). Regional inequality and the process of national development: A description of the patterns. *Economic Development and Cultural Change, 13*(4), 1–84.

9

Conclusions

The electoral victories of Donald Trump in the US and the advocates of Brexit in the UK are not just a reflection of a growing economic inequality and social polarization. They also show definite spatial patterns. These political responses on the part of the electorate are linked to factors of various types. From an economic perspective they can be seen both as a defence of class interests stemming from a perception of increased inequality in personal income and as a reaction to changes in the relative wealth of territories. One example of this spatial pattern would be the relative decline experienced by areas that were once prosperous and dynamic, such as the industrial north of England and the manufacturing belt of the US—especially the Detroit area, birthplace of the automotive industry—which have suffered a severe economic downturn over recent decades. Voters in both of theses territories opted for Brexit and Trump, respectively, in the hope of radically changing the status quo.

The relative impoverishment of traditionally wealthy regions and the widening income gap between the most prosperous and the most disadvantaged regions have fuelled the widespread perception that, in today's context of technological change and globalization, there are territories

A. Díez-Minguela et al., *Regional Inequality in Spain*, Palgrave Studies in Economic History, https://doi.org/10.1007/978-3-319-96110-1_9

that "don't matter", and this has led to "political revenge" (Rodríguez-Pose 2018). In Europe, this territorial issue presents other aspects that give rise to additional areas of tension that go beyond the economy alone. It is one of a variety of reasons behind the rise of political movements demanding profound changes in territorial structures and political decision-making in a number of countries such as the UK itself (with the Scottish independence referendum in 2014), Spain (the Catalan independence movement) and Belgium (the Flemish independence movement).

Due to its possible economic, social and political consequences, the issue of regional inequality is therefore a cause for concern because, just like the evolution of interpersonal inequality, it has been gradually increasing over the last few decades. This has been especially evident in Europe. The trend began at the end of the 1970s after the oil crisis, evolving in an economic setting which, as time passed, underwent changes in the foundations that had underpinned economic growth (and regional convergence) during the Golden Age following the Second World War.

Technological progress since the 1980s, based especially on developments in ICT, has had a particular impact on the advanced services sector and the financial sector, that is, high wage activities, which have tended to become concentrated in large urban areas and in addition attract skilled workers from other less prosperous regions. Thus the big urban agglomerations of Europe have managed to act as magnets for the most innovative activities and the most skilled jobs, thereby encouraging knowledge spillovers between workers. And the regions where the national capitals are located, which play the role of political and administrative centres, have been especially favoured in recent decades, increasing their ability to become areas of attraction and economic growth.

More traditional manufacturing activities, on the other hand, have seen that the advance of technological change has in many cases been labour-saving, with the automation of production processes bringing about a reduction in semi-skilled and unskilled jobs that has had the greatest impact in those regions that specialized in these sectors (usually capital-intensive industries typical of the second industrial revolution). Therefore, while regions in industrial decline or located on the periphery of Europe experience a deteriorating economic situation that in some cases has already lasted decades, other metropolitan regions enjoy economic dynamism and productivity gains as a result of incorporating new technologies.

These changes have come about in an economic setting characterized by ever-increasing globalization which, among other things, has given rise to the creation of global value chains and the relocation of some of the production process, especially, but not exclusively, in the industrial sector. So as to reduce production costs in global markets that are more and more competitive—and in which transport costs have already fallen substantially—companies have transferred production to other areas of the planet in search of lower salaries. This relocation has been concentrated mainly in the countries of south-east Asia, making the most of the opportunities offered there (such as cheap labour or a flexible labour market) of globalization. From a European perspective, this has created problems in the generation of employment in certain regions, especially those specializing in traditional sectors with lower productivity that have been unable to fight off international competition.

Overall, these changes to the world economy have tended to be much more advantageous to big metropolitan regions than to lagging, peripheral regions, thus giving rise to increased territorial inequality. On top of this, the Great Recession that began in 2008 only strengthened these trends and widened the territorial divide in Europe (Fratesi and Rodríguez-Pose 2016; Cuadrado-Roura et al. 2016). In this context, long-term structural changes—along with the situational changes typical of the turn of the century—pose a serious challenge when it comes to mitigating regional inequalities through public policies and managing to do so without affecting the efficiency and aggregate economic growth of the various economies (Iammarino et al. 2018). And these are inequalities that attract a large part of the European Union budget in the shape of territorial cohesion policies.

It is in this context that the book has carried out a detailed analysis of regional inequality in one of these economies, Spain, not just for recent decades but throughout the entire economic development process. The purpose of this was to help us understand the current situation by learning from history, construct hypotheses as to its future evolution and suggest elements that should be taken into account when dealing with the problem, bearing in mind that it is not an issue that arose overnight. On the contrary, throughout the text we have argued that the current situation is the result of a long, complex process in which geography, technology, institutions and public policies have all played a part.

The first conclusion we can draw is the importance of technology and, therefore, productivity. Regional inequality in Spain reached its peak at the beginning of the twentieth century, in a context that saw the increasingly rapid integration of the domestic market, due to technological change in a limited number of sectors and territories. A considerable gap opened up between those regions (Catalonia, the Basque Country) that specialized in the industrial sectors that were more likely to introduce new technologies (textiles, iron and steel) and those that were still committed to traditional sectors (agriculture, livestock farming). It would therefore not be out of place to say that if new technologies are located in territories that are already dynamic and prosperous, which is what happens, the differences will continue to increase.

In a similar vein, the second conclusion we can draw from the case of Spain is that the slowing down and/or stagnation of regional income convergence in the 1980s was caused by the growing differences in labour markets rather than by labour productivity, which continued to converge until the start of the new century. Regional income convergence in the US has also slowed down over the last three decades (Ganong and Shoag 2017), coinciding with an increase in property prices in more prosperous locations which, according to the authors, could alter the traditional composition of labour flows. A peculiarity of the Spanish economy is the importance of property assets. This preference for bricks and mortar could strengthen the way housing is linked to territory, thereby affecting the size and composition of labour flows. If the least skilled workers stay where they are while the most skilled are drawn to the most dynamic, prosperous places, then one would expect to see a continuous increase in territorial inequality.

Thirdly, it has been shown that the territorial imbalances that came into being during periods of great technological change and economic integration are enduring. Levels of inequality take time to decrease and the relative positions of the regions and economic geography, once they have taken shape, tend not to change over time. Therefore the problems associated with unbalanced regional development, far from disappearing, survive. The forces that drive production specialization also involve aspects linked to the territories' geoeconomic position. Prosperity and poverty are not distributed randomly across the geographical space, but form clusters that group together territories with different income levels and can create areas of great dynamism or give rise to spatial traps. This is certainly an element that influences the perception that spatial effects exist, with positions being shared by neighbouring territories.

In Spain the most striking stories of relative success (the Basque Country) and failure (Andalusia) are the result of profound changes that open up new growth possibilities for some territories and have the opposite effect for others. Both elements, relative success or failure, can create tension between those territories and individuals that believe the institutional framework is perfect for making political decisions and those who directly oppose the status quo. Given the multifaceted nature of the elements that characterize territorial inequality, studying the case of Spain illustrates the many dimensions that need to be taken into account by public policies aimed at solving the problems described here.

The first element to consider is their relevance. The need for public intervention and where it should be directed are considered differently depending on the economic theory. Broadly speaking, the more traditional view associated with neoclassical growth models trusts in the good functioning of the markets to correct spatial imbalances through factor mobility. Therefore, since regional convergence will be the expected outcome due to the existence of mechanisms of growth diffusion from the richest regions to the poorest, this approach sees no need for economic intervention through public policies. Although it might be argued that the mechanisms of diffusion worked relatively well during the Golden Age, this does not seem to have been the case in recent decades, at least not in Europe, where, as we have already pointed out, territorial inequality continues to be a problem.

Many academics, in particular those working in the areas of urban economics and new economic geography, argue that investing in poor regions implies a trade-off between efficiency and cohesion—with significant implications for the aggregate growth of the economy—resulting from the existence of agglomeration economies in the production processes, and this would make public intervention inadvisable. However, this is not a widespread view. Various studies have shown that the aggregate effect of the density of economic activity on labour productivity is relatively limited (Ciccone 2002). Others have shown the existence of a relationship between the agglomeration of production and growth, but point out that it may not be monotonic throughout the development processes (Brülhart and Sbergami 2009). It has also been argued that the result of this type of exercise is highly sensitive to the territorial units on which the study is based or to the indicators of agglomeration and density used. This being so, it has been suggested that policy makers should be cautious about basing any policy assumptions on a trade-off between national growth and regional inequality (Gardiner et al. 2011), or that the problem should be overcome as part of the design of territorial policies (Iammarino et al. 2018).

Our results support the need for caution. It has been argued in the text that the presence of agglomeration effects may perhaps make it possible to give a well-founded explanation for the increasing territorial concentration of industry and output during the first stage of Spanish economic development, which acted as a driving force for aggregate growth. Nevertheless, we have also shown that the increasing growth rates of the Spanish economy during the years of the Golden Age were compatible with a redistribution of activity across the territory. In recent decades, however, convergence between regions has come to a halt, and this has meant that many of the characteristics of regional inequality that have been taking shape since the start of the economic development process are persisting and even growing.

Hence the north-east of the peninsula, that is, the triangle joining Madrid, the Basque Country and Catalonia, is today in a better relative position to face the future both economically and geographically that other territories. The economic strength of this area, as we have seen over the previous pages, is a result of the evolution that has taken place in the course of the entire economic development process. Its geographical advantage comes from its greater proximity to the higher-income markets in the heart of Europe. In contrast the south of the peninsula, the areas close to the Portuguese border (on both sides) and the interior of Spain, which have undergone a severe depopulation process in recent decades, today start from a position of disadvantage in both economic terms—this position having become ever more firmly established since the early stages of the Spanish economic development process—and geographical terms—due to their relative remoteness on the southern periphery of the continent. What all this means is that much of the peninsula is facing a serious challenge if it does not want to remain perpetually in the same situation of relative backwardness, with the difference in income compared to the more dynamic regions of the centre of Europe growing steadily and, worse still, all this happening in the complex context of intense technological change and global markets that exist today.

Given these conditions, the question remains: what would be the best policies to halt the advance of territorial inequality? In recent decades the European Union has implemented territorial cohesion policies designed basically to encourage factor accumulation in the poorest regions and improve the connectivity of the most peripheral areas with the economic (and geographical) centre of the continent, mainly through investing in the construction of infrastructures aimed at improving transport. Bearing this in mind and not intending to cover every angle, we have characterized the explanatory potential of various elements that underlie interregional differences in income. Understanding them may be useful when it comes to deciding what types of measures are needed and the political and territorial settings that should be targeted in order for them to be most effective.

So, it has been argued that territorial inequality is an intrinsic characteristic of the growth processes, but it has also been shown that its containment can be traced back to changes in regional production structures, which in turn come about through the integration of regional labour markets. Today, however, the predominant characteristic is the low territorial mobility of labour, both nationally and internationally. The absence of movements of any size makes it possible for significant differences, sustained over time, to arise between activity rates and/or unemployment rates, and these become explanatory factors for territorial differences in per-capita income. Therefore, although they have not traditionally been seen as aiding cohesion, policies aimed at encouraging interregional labour mobility might today be a key element for keeping regional income inequality in check.

However, it can be derived from the study that the role played by regional disparities in the labour market has only been important at very specific moments in Spanish economic history, mainly in recent times. In historical terms it is the regional differences in productivity that have formed the bulk of our explanation of territorial inequality. And although it may have been shown that these have been modest in recent times, the Spanish experience indicates that, in today's context of technological change and globalization, it would not be going too far to say that they could well increase again in the future. In fact this dynamic can already be seen in the industrial and services sectors. Given these conditions, the Spanish experience points to the importance of policies aimed at reducing inequality in productivity between regions, that is, territorial cohesion policies, but at the same time warns that, when it comes to designing them, it is essential to understand the elements on which they should be based.

Although we do not address every question, in the text we identify four elements that are not always given the importance they deserve in the design of territorial cohesion policies. Two of these are widely known. First we have shown that, during the period dominated by economic convergence between regions, the fact that the gap between the average levels of productivity in agriculture, industry and services on a national scale became narrower was very important, indeed more important than the narrowing of the gap between the productivity levels of each separate province and those of the leading region. This type of evidence would indicate that it was not the greater provision of cumulative factors in poor regions that drove the regional convergence process. Second, another important part of the convergence process was linked to the rapidity with which the lagging regions travelled the path of structural change. This would point to the ineffectiveness of cohesion policies aimed at maintaining levels of production or income in sectors of low productivity.

Nevertheless, it is the second two elements deriving from the long-term study of Spain that are the most striking. The first of these is that our understanding of the elements that favour or hinder the regions' relative development varies greatly. Experiences are different in different regions, during both stages of divergence and convergence. Therefore the one-size-fits-all character of cohesion policies—those recipes that rely on homogeneity in action without taking into account the peculiarities of each territory—are doomed to failure. This diversity also calls into question the appropriateness of designing these policies in a single political setting, be it national or supranational, and suggests that there should be proximity between the political authority where decisions are made and the sources of knowledge of the particular characteristics of each territory.

This scenario begs another question, which involves our fourth element. The administrative units involved in cohesion policies are not immune to change. Neither autonomous communities (NUTS2) nor provinces (NUTS3) seem to be the most suitable administrative units for assessing and/or correcting current challenges. Many of today's problems either spill out beyond these units of analysis (supraregional or supranational clusters of territories) or conceal the dynamics of inequality present within themselves (urban areas v. rural areas or areas with low population density). All types of problems should therefore be dealt with through policies designed from a perspective that transcends traditional territorial scales.

Finally, and to conclude, the work we have done at least shows that there is less inequality today than there was a century ago. Over the long term, whether due to the invisible hand or the visible workings of public policies, we have seen a decrease in territorial imbalances. Nevertheless, the time the process has taken can by no manner or means be considered limited. Territorial inequality was, has been and still is a question of time and space.

References

Brülhart, M., & Sbergami, F. (2009). Agglomeration and growth: Cross-country evidence. *Journal of Urban Economics, 65*(1), 48–63.

Ciccone, A. (2002). Agglomeration effects in Europe. *European Economic Review, 46*(2), 213–227.

Cuadrado-Roura, J. R., Martin, R., & Rodríguez-Pose, A. (2016). The economic crisis in Europe: Urban and regional consequences. *Cambridge Journal of Regions, Economy and Society, 9*, 3–11.

Fratesi, U., & Rodríguez-Pose, A. (2016). The crisis and regional employment in Europe: What role for sheltered economies? *Cambridge Journal of Regions, Economy and Society, 9*, 33–57.
Ganong, P., & Shoag, D. (2017). Why has regional income convergence in the U.S. declined? *Journal of Urban Economics, 102*, 76–90.
Gardiner, B., Martin, R., & Tyler, P. (2011). Does spatial agglomeration increase national growth? Some evidence from Europe. *Journal of Economic Geography, 11*(6), 979–1006.
Iammarino, S., Rodríguez-Pose, A., & Storper, M. (2018). Regional inequality in Europe: Evidence, theory and policy implications. *Journal of Economic Geography*. https://doi.org/10.1093/jeg/lby021.
Rodríguez-Pose, A. (2018). The revenge of the places that don't matter (and what to do about it). *Cambridge Journal of Regions, Economy and Society, 11*, 189–209.

Appendix

Table A1 Territorial units (NUTS), Spain

Code	NUTS1	Code	NUTS2	Code	NUTS3
ES1	Noroeste	ES11	Galicia	ES111	*A Coruña*
				ES112	*Lugo*
				ES113	*Ourense*
				ES114	*Pontevedra*
		ES12	Principado de Asturias	ES120	*Asturias*
		ES13	Cantabria	ES130	*Cantabria*
ES2	Noreste	ES21	País Vasco	ES211	*Araba/Álava*
				ES212	*Guipuzkoa*
				ES213	*Bizkaia*
		ES22	Comunidad Foral de Navarra	ES220	*Navarra*
		ES23	La Rioja	ES230	*La Rioja*
		ES24	Aragón	ES241	*Huesca*
				ES242	*Teruel*
				ES243	*Zaragoza*
ES3	Comunidad de Madrid	ES30	Comunidad de Madrid	ES300	*Madrid*

(*continued*)

A. Díez-Minguela et al., *Regional Inequality in Spain*, Palgrave Studies in Economic History, https://doi.org/10.1007/978-3-319-96110-1

Table A1 (continued)

Code	NUTS1	Code	NUTS2	Code	NUTS3
ES4	Centro	ES41	Castilla y León	ES411	*Ávila*
				ES412	*Burgos*
				ES413	*León*
				ES414	*Palencia*
				ES415	*Salamanca*
				ES416	*Segovia*
				ES417	*Soria*
				ES418	*Valladolid*
				ES419	*Zamora*
		ES42	Castilla-La Mancha	ES421	*Albacete*
				ES422	*Ciudad Real*
				ES423	*Cuenca*
				ES424	*Guadalajara*
				ES425	*Toledo*
		ES43	Extremadura	ES431	*Badajoz*
				ES432	*Cáceres*
ES5	Este	ES51	Cataluña	ES511	*Barcelona*
				ES512	*Girona*
				ES513	*Lleida*
				ES514	*Tarragona*
		ES52	Comunidad Valenciana	ES521	*Alicante/ Alacant*
				ES522	*Castellón/ Castelló*
				ES523	*Valencia/ València*
		ES53	Illes Balears	ES531	*Eivissa i Formentera*
				ES532	*Mallorca*
				ES533	*Menorca*
ES6	Sur	ES61	Andalucía	ES611	*Almería*
				ES612	*Cádiz*
				ES613	*Córdoba*
				ES614	*Granada*
				ES615	*Huelva*
				ES616	*Jaén*
				ES617	*Málaga*
				ES618	*Sevilla*
		ES62	Región de Murcia	ES620	*Murcia*
		ES63	Ciudad Autónoma de Ceuta	ES630	*Ceuta*
		ES64	Ciudad Autónoma de Melilla	ES640	*Melilla*

(*continued*)

Table A1 (continued)

Code	NUTS1	Code	NUTS2	Code	NUTS3
ES7	Canarias	ES70	Canarias	ES703	*El Hierro*
				ES704	*Fuerteventura*
				ES705	*Gran Canaria*
				ES706	*La Gomera*
				ES707	*La Palma*
				ES708	*Lanzarote*
				ES709	*Tenerife*

Table A2 Official nomenclature and equivalent used, NUTS2

Code	NUTS2	Equivalent
ES11	Galicia	Galicia
ES12	Principado de Asturias	Asturias
ES13	Cantabria	Cantabria
ES21	País Vasco	Basque Country
ES22	Comunidad Foral de Navarra	Navarre
ES23	La Rioja	La Rioja
ES24	Aragón	Aragón
ES30	Comunidad de Madrid	Madrid
ES41	Castilla y León	Castile-Leon
ES42	Castilla-La Mancha	Castile-La Mancha
ES43	Extremadura	Extremadura
ES51	Cataluña	Catalonia
ES52	Comunidad Valenciana	Valencia
ES53	Illes Balears	Balearic Islands
ES61	Andalucía	Andalusia
ES62	Región de Murcia	Murcia
ES70	Canarias	Canary Islands

Table A3 Gross domestic product (%), NUTS3

Code	Province	1860	1870	1880	1890	1900	1910	1920	1930
ES111	A Coruña	2.69	2.39	2.08	1.83	2.15	2.51	1.98	2.33
ES112	Lugo	0.59	0.68	0.78	0.75	1.04	1.17	1.21	1.36
ES113	Ourense	1.27	1.24	1.25	1.17	0.92	1.15	0.73	0.92
ES114	Pontevedra	1.04	1.12	1.14	1.14	1.62	1.46	1.01	1.47
ES120	Asturias	1.93	2.01	2.00	2.12	3.18	2.35	3.02	3.19
ES130	Cantabria	1.15	1.20	1.15	1.24	1.46	1.36	1.45	1.74
ES211	Araba/Álava	0.53	0.69	0.83	0.67	0.81	0.49	0.42	0.39
ES212	Gipuzkoa	0.91	1.29	1.71	1.84	2.57	2.13	1.52	2.03
ES213	Bizkaia	1.08	1.39	1.68	2.51	3.26	2.62	4.46	3.77
ES220	Navarra	2.02	2.23	2.36	1.73	1.38	1.37	1.75	1.43
ES230	La Rioja	0.99	1.07	1.11	1.03	1.10	0.83	0.63	0.72
ES241	Huesca	1.61	1.55	1.48	1.34	1.11	1.02	1.09	0.88
ES242	Teruel	1.43	1.30	1.18	1.14	1.05	0.94	0.82	0.63
ES243	Zaragoza	2.76	2.80	2.80	2.59	2.34	2.57	3.14	2.72
ES300	Madrid	5.52	6.25	6.56	6.63	6.79	6.71	8.22	10.55
ES411	Ávila	0.96	0.96	0.94	0.98	0.81	0.87	0.68	0.65
ES412	Burgos	1.74	1.84	1.90	1.56	1.67	1.39	1.50	1.09
ES413	León	1.09	1.08	1.05	0.99	0.97	1.12	1.51	1.29
ES414	Palencia	1.27	1.24	1.19	1.04	1.00	0.82	0.67	0.67
ES415	Salamanca	1.49	1.78	2.06	1.64	1.82	1.72	1.39	1.11
ES416	Segovia	1.00	0.93	0.84	0.82	0.70	0.62	0.54	0.58
ES417	Soria	0.77	0.79	0.81	0.86	0.61	0.65	0.50	0.46
ES418	Valladolid	1.73	1.70	1.64	1.61	1.47	1.40	1.21	1.06
ES419	Zamora	1.37	1.27	1.16	1.47	1.08	0.93	0.93	0.75
	ESP	**100.0**	**100.0**	**100.0**	**100.0**	**100.0**	**100.0**	**100.0**	**100.0**

(*continued*)

Table A3 (continued)

Code	Province	1935	1940	1945	1950	1955	1957	1959	1961
ES111	A Coruña	2.99	2.87	2.85	2.78	2.47	2.44	2.42	2.37
ES112	Lugo	1.39	1.29	1.15	1.13	1.07	1.11	1.09	1.01
ES113	Ourense	1.11	1.08	1.16	1.07	0.90	0.87	0.85	0.84
ES114	Pontevedra	2.09	2.01	2.00	1.95	1.82	1.83	1.81	1.79
ES120	Asturias	3.57	3.76	3.67	3.61	3.52	3.55	3.49	3.42
ES130	Cantabria	1.51	1.49	1.54	1.67	1.66	1.66	1.69	1.66
ES211	Araba/Álava	0.60	0.60	0.59	0.52	0.61	0.60	0.62	0.65
ES212	Gipuzkoa	2.52	2.50	2.65	2.56	2.48	2.44	2.42	2.44
ES213	Bizkaia	2.89	2.91	3.12	3.64	4.18	4.13	4.11	4.16
ES220	Navarra	1.68	1.59	1.59	1.60	1.54	1.53	1.54	1.55
ES230	La Rioja	1.05	1.04	1.01	0.93	0.86	0.87	0.86	0.85
ES241	Huesca	0.93	0.87	0.83	0.80	0.78	0.81	0.83	0.82
ES242	Teruel	0.68	0.58	0.57	0.57	0.58	0.58	0.54	0.50
ES243	Zaragoza	2.60	2.71	2.54	2.52	2.35	2.38	2.38	2.40
ES300	Madrid	8.44	9.13	9.22	9.62	11.84	12.13	12.34	12.83
ES411	Ávila	0.74	0.71	0.71	0.69	0.49	0.51	0.48	0.46
ES412	Burgos	1.66	1.47	1.46	1.39	1.21	1.20	1.14	1.08
ES413	León	1.59	1.48	1.58	1.77	1.61	1.64	1.57	1.53
ES414	Palencia	0.96	0.87	0.94	0.96	0.72	0.68	0.66	0.64
ES415	Salamanca	1.24	1.19	1.31	1.30	1.11	1.11	1.10	1.08
ES416	Segovia	0.67	0.58	0.68	0.75	0.64	0.63	0.58	0.53
ES417	Soria	0.61	0.58	0.56	0.52	0.42	0.42	0.37	0.35
ES418	Valladolid	1.29	1.20	1.26	1.25	1.23	1.18	1.13	1.12
ES419	Zamora	0.83	0.82	0.87	0.86	0.76	0.74	0.71	0.68
	ESP	**100.0**	**100.0**	**100.0**	**100.0**	**100.0**	**100.0**	**100.0**	**100.0**

(continued)

Table A3 (continued)

Code	Province	1963	1965	1967	1969	1971	1973	1975	1977	1979
ES111	A Coruña	2.38	2.32	2.36	2.35	2.41	2.40	2.41	2.48	2.52
ES112	Lugo	0.98	0.92	0.91	0.85	0.79	0.76	0.72	0.75	0.78
ES113	Ourense	0.83	0.81	0.76	0.77	0.74	0.76	0.72	0.70	0.71
ES114	Pontevedra	1.83	1.85	1.92	1.86	1.94	1.95	1.99	2.04	2.07
ES120	Asturias	3.33	3.24	3.25	3.22	3.08	3.03	3.05	2.91	2.88
ES130	Cantabria	1.63	1.59	1.57	1.54	1.51	1.42	1.40	1.40	1.41
ES211	Araba/Álava	0.71	0.80	0.82	0.89	0.89	0.91	0.95	0.95	0.94
ES212	Gipuzkoa	2.53	2.67	2.63	2.67	2.66	2.63	2.62	2.50	2.32
ES213	Bizkaia	4.25	4.27	4.20	4.20	4.05	4.01	4.05	3.80	3.49
ES220	Navarra	1.62	1.58	1.60	1.56	1.57	1.55	1.54	1.53	1.50
ES230	La Rioja	0.86	0.83	0.81	0.77	0.75	0.73	0.70	0.71	0.74
ES241	Huesca	0.81	0.75	0.72	0.71	0.71	0.66	0.69	0.66	0.66
ES242	Teruel	0.51	0.46	0.45	0.45	0.39	0.37	0.37	0.37	0.36
ES243	Zaragoza	2.43	2.41	2.37	2.36	2.27	2.27	2.23	2.26	2.28
ES300	Madrid	13.09	13.95	14.23	14.48	14.75	15.36	15.95	15.91	16.07
ES411	Ávila	0.46	0.42	0.39	0.40	0.37	0.35	0.35	0.34	0.34
ES412	Burgos	1.12	1.10	1.06	1.04	0.99	0.96	0.95	0.96	0.94
ES413	León	1.52	1.47	1.42	1.31	1.27	1.18	1.13	1.11	1.14
ES414	Palencia	0.63	0.60	0.55	0.54	0.50	0.46	0.46	0.48	0.48
ES415	Salamanca	1.05	0.98	0.93	0.90	0.86	0.80	0.76	0.75	0.75
ES416	Segovia	0.50	0.45	0.43	0.42	0.40	0.38	0.37	0.36	0.35
ES417	Soria	0.35	0.33	0.30	0.30	0.27	0.26	0.24	0.23	0.21
ES418	Valladolid	1.20	1.23	1.24	1.29	1.29	1.33	1.34	1.35	1.33
ES419	Zamora	0.68	0.65	0.59	0.54	0.50	0.47	0.44	0.42	0.42
	ESP	**100.0**	**100.0**	**100.0**	**100.0**	**100.0**	**100.0**	**100.0**	**100.0**	**100.0**

(*continued*)

Table A3 (continued)

Code	Province	1980	1981	1982	1983	1984	1985	1986	1987	1988
ES111	A Coruña	2.53	2.57	2.70	2.57	2.52	2.47	2.44	2.40	2.34
ES112	Lugo	0.86	0.89	0.90	0.93	0.95	0.85	0.79	0.77	0.81
ES113	Ourense	0.72	0.76	0.76	0.71	0.75	0.77	0.72	0.71	0.73
ES114	Pontevedra	1.91	1.94	1.90	1.87	1.86	1.90	1.85	1.79	1.81
ES120	Asturias	2.80	2.83	2.87	2.79	2.75	2.85	2.86	2.71	2.68
ES130	Cantabria	1.47	1.52	1.48	1.47	1.46	1.40	1.32	1.30	1.36
ES211	Araba/Álava	1.10	1.16	1.16	1.13	1.04	1.04	1.02	0.98	0.97
ES212	Gipuzkoa	2.45	2.46	2.41	2.35	2.20	2.28	2.21	2.21	2.18
ES213	Bizkaia	3.89	3.94	3.95	3.84	3.77	3.72	3.70	3.44	3.33
ES220	Navarra	1.74	1.79	1.74	1.70	1.67	1.65	1.64	1.71	1.66
ES230	La Rioja	0.78	0.80	0.80	0.83	0.83	0.90	0.80	0.76	0.76
ES241	Huesca	0.66	0.60	0.61	0.58	0.62	0.68	0.65	0.60	0.63
ES242	Teruel	0.47	0.50	0.51	0.49	0.53	0.42	0.41	0.38	0.41
ES243	Zaragoza	2.30	2.25	2.26	2.43	2.39	2.38	2.39	2.43	2.49
ES300	Madrid	14.81	14.82	15.12	15.32	15.13	14.79	15.47	15.56	15.43
ES411	Ávila	0.41	0.38	0.35	0.36	0.36	0.37	0.37	0.36	0.37
ES412	Burgos	1.03	1.01	1.03	1.03	1.04	1.09	1.07	1.11	1.04
ES413	León	1.17	1.20	1.24	1.27	1.31	1.30	1.25	1.20	1.13
ES414	Palencia	0.54	0.49	0.48	0.52	0.53	0.48	0.46	0.50	0.48
ES415	Salamanca	0.74	0.71	0.77	0.78	0.78	0.82	0.79	0.79	0.80
ES416	Segovia	0.36	0.35	0.39	0.37	0.36	0.39	0.39	0.38	0.38
ES417	Soria	0.25	0.23	0.26	0.25	0.27	0.27	0.27	0.25	0.27
ES418	Valladolid	1.29	1.25	1.33	1.28	1.26	1.30	1.32	1.31	1.33
ES419	Zamora	0.46	0.41	0.43	0.42	0.45	0.49	0.45	0.45	0.46
	ESP	**100.0**	**100.0**	**100.0**	**100.0**	**100.0**	**100.0**	**100.0**	**100.0**	**100.0**

(*continued*)

Table A3 (continued)

Code	Province	1989	1990	1991	1992	1993	1994	1995	1996	1997
ES111	A Coruña	2.40	2.30	2.28	2.32	2.33	2.30	2.43	2.38	2.34
ES112	Lugo	0.76	0.75	0.73	0.72	0.73	0.70	0.76	0.74	0.70
ES113	Ourense	0.69	0.67	0.67	0.68	0.71	0.69	0.67	0.64	0.62
ES114	Pontevedra	1.81	1.81	1.81	1.80	1.77	1.79	1.78	1.80	1.81
ES120	Asturias	2.66	2.57	2.54	2.57	2.54	2.52	2.43	2.37	2.30
ES130	Cantabria	1.38	1.33	1.31	1.33	1.31	1.31	1.25	1.24	1.22
ES211	Araba/Álava	0.94	0.91	0.92	0.89	0.89	0.89	0.94	0.98	0.98
ES212	Gipuzkoa	2.21	2.17	2.10	2.07	2.06	2.08	2.09	2.10	2.10
ES213	Bizkaia	3.38	3.35	3.36	3.31	3.30	3.25	3.29	3.19	3.19
ES220	Navarra	1.72	1.66	1.66	1.65	1.63	1.62	1.71	1.73	1.74
ES230	La Rioja	0.75	0.76	0.76	0.76	0.76	0.76	0.77	0.76	0.77
ES241	Huesca	0.59	0.60	0.59	0.58	0.60	0.60	0.56	0.54	0.53
ES242	Teruel	0.44	0.39	0.41	0.40	0.39	0.39	0.38	0.38	0.38
ES243	Zaragoza	2.49	2.47	2.46	2.45	2.42	2.42	2.35	2.37	2.38
ES300	Madrid	15.46	15.68	15.75	15.83	15.89	15.96	16.80	16.86	17.01
ES411	Ávila	0.38	0.37	0.37	0.36	0.38	0.37	0.36	0.35	0.33
ES412	Burgos	1.00	0.98	0.95	0.95	0.96	0.96	1.04	1.05	1.03
ES413	León	1.16	1.10	1.09	1.08	1.10	1.08	1.14	1.09	1.07
ES414	Palencia	0.46	0.45	0.45	0.44	0.46	0.43	0.45	0.45	0.43
ES415	Salamanca	0.79	0.79	0.79	0.77	0.80	0.83	0.76	0.76	0.73
ES416	Segovia	0.37	0.37	0.37	0.36	0.37	0.37	0.38	0.35	0.36
ES417	Soria	0.26	0.25	0.24	0.24	0.25	0.24	0.25	0.25	0.25
ES418	Valladolid	1.27	1.23	1.26	1.28	1.29	1.25	1.35	1.34	1.31
ES419	Zamora	0.44	0.43	0.42	0.43	0.45	0.43	0.40	0.39	0.36
	ESP	**100.0**	**100.0**	**100.0**	**100.0**	**100.0**	**100.0**	**100.0**	**100.0**	**100.0**

(*continued*)

Table A3 (continued)

Code	Province	1998	1999	2000	2001	2002	2003	2004	2005	2006
ES111	A Coruña	2.31	2.26	2.16	2.14	2.18	2.19	2.20	2.21	2.20
ES112	Lugo	0.68	0.64	0.66	0.66	0.64	0.63	0.63	0.65	0.65
ES113	Ourense	0.60	0.60	0.59	0.60	0.61	0.60	0.58	0.58	0.58
ES114	Pontevedra	1.80	1.82	1.77	1.76	1.72	1.73	1.75	1.74	1.77
ES120	Asturias	2.30	2.20	2.22	2.21	2.19	2.16	2.14	2.15	2.16
ES130	Cantabria	1.23	1.23	1.23	1.23	1.23	1.21	1.20	1.20	1.19
ES211	Araba/Álava	1.01	1.01	0.97	0.98	0.99	0.98	0.99	1.00	1.03
ES212	Gipuzkoa	2.11	2.09	2.09	2.13	2.07	2.02	2.01	2.00	2.03
ES213	Bizkaia	3.22	3.26	3.26	3.15	3.12	3.10	3.07	3.07	3.01
ES220	Navarra	1.73	1.73	1.73	1.71	1.71	1.70	1.69	1.69	1.67
ES230	La Rioja	0.77	0.76	0.76	0.75	0.74	0.75	0.74	0.74	0.74
ES241	Huesca	0.51	0.51	0.51	0.53	0.53	0.53	0.52	0.51	0.51
ES242	Teruel	0.36	0.35	0.35	0.35	0.35	0.34	0.33	0.34	0.33
ES243	Zaragoza	2.34	2.27	2.24	2.22	2.26	2.26	2.27	2.27	2.28
ES300	Madrid	17.40	17.55	17.74	17.85	17.89	17.88	17.92	17.92	18.05
ES411	Ávila	0.33	0.32	0.32	0.31	0.30	0.29	0.30	0.29	0.29
ES412	Burgos	1.02	0.98	0.96	0.92	0.92	0.92	0.92	0.92	0.89
ES413	León	1.04	1.06	1.01	1.00	0.98	0.96	0.94	0.95	0.94
ES414	Palencia	0.42	0.41	0.40	0.39	0.40	0.41	0.40	0.40	0.38
ES415	Salamanca	0.71	0.66	0.68	0.69	0.69	0.69	0.68	0.66	0.65
ES416	Segovia	0.35	0.37	0.36	0.35	0.35	0.35	0.35	0.35	0.34
ES417	Soria	0.24	0.23	0.22	0.21	0.22	0.22	0.22	0.20	0.20
ES418	Valladolid	1.27	1.27	1.24	1.22	1.22	1.19	1.18	1.18	1.16
ES419	Zamora	0.35	0.37	0.35	0.34	0.34	0.34	0.34	0.32	0.33
	ESP	**100.0**	**100.0**	**100.0**	**100.0**	**100.0**	**100.0**	**100.0**	**100.0**	**100.0**

(continued)

Table A3 (continued)

Code	Province	2007	2008	2009	2010	2011	2012	2013	2014	2015
ES111	A Coruña	2.24	2.26	2.31	2.33	2.30	2.27	2.29	2.24	2.27
ES112	Lugo	0.63	0.62	0.61	0.63	0.63	0.64	0.64	0.65	0.66
ES113	Ourense	0.57	0.58	0.57	0.58	0.59	0.60	0.60	0.58	0.57
ES114	Pontevedra	1.79	1.81	1.78	1.75	1.71	1.70	1.73	1.74	1.73
ES120	Asturias	2.16	2.16	2.11	2.12	2.11	2.07	2.02	1.99	1.97
ES130	Cantabria	1.19	1.19	1.19	1.19	1.18	1.17	1.15	1.15	1.13
ES211	Araba/Álava	1.04	1.06	1.02	1.01	1.03	1.03	1.05	1.07	1.07
ES212	Gipuzkoa	2.03	2.00	1.97	2.00	2.02	2.04	2.03	2.02	2.02
ES213	Bizkaia	2.97	3.03	3.05	3.08	3.06	3.08	3.05	3.08	3.09
ES220	Navarra	1.67	1.68	1.69	1.70	1.71	1.70	1.71	1.72	1.73
ES230	La Rioja	0.74	0.74	0.74	0.74	0.74	0.74	0.74	0.74	0.73
ES241	Huesca	0.53	0.55	0.54	0.55	0.55	0.54	0.56	0.54	0.52
ES242	Teruel	0.34	0.34	0.33	0.33	0.33	0.33	0.33	0.33	0.31
ES243	Zaragoza	2.31	2.31	2.31	2.32	2.30	2.27	2.30	2.30	2.28
ES300	Madrid	18.06	18.16	18.56	18.38	18.66	18.89	18.89	18.88	18.92
ES411	Ávila	0.29	0.29	0.30	0.29	0.30	0.30	0.29	0.29	0.28
ES412	Burgos	0.90	0.91	0.90	0.90	0.91	0.92	0.90	0.88	0.87
ES413	León	0.94	0.92	0.95	0.94	0.93	0.93	0.91	0.89	0.87
ES414	Palencia	0.39	0.39	0.39	0.38	0.39	0.38	0.38	0.37	0.37
ES415	Salamanca	0.64	0.63	0.65	0.62	0.63	0.62	0.61	0.61	0.61
ES416	Segovia	0.34	0.33	0.32	0.33	0.32	0.31	0.31	0.31	0.31
ES417	Soria	0.20	0.20	0.20	0.21	0.21	0.20	0.20	0.20	0.20
ES418	Valladolid	1.16	1.13	1.13	1.16	1.15	1.14	1.14	1.15	1.16
ES419	Zamora	0.33	0.32	0.32	0.33	0.33	0.34	0.33	0.32	0.32
	ESP	**100.0**	**100.0**	**100.0**	**100.0**	**100.0**	**100.0**	**100.0**	**100.0**	**100.0**

(*continued*)

Table A3 (continued)

Code	Province	1860	1870	1880	1890	1900	1910	1920	1930
ES421	Albacete	1.33	1.53	1.75	1.61	1.38	1.22	1.27	1.33
ES422	Ciudad Real	1.74	1.61	1.45	1.65	1.43	1.57	1.44	1.25
ES423	Cuenca	1.22	1.06	0.88	1.03	0.98	0.77	0.74	0.69
ES424	Guadalajara	1.30	1.16	0.96	0.90	0.83	0.71	0.55	0.54
ES425	Toledo	1.92	1.93	1.95	2.15	1.78	1.71	1.59	1.22
ES431	Badajoz	2.08	2.06	2.10	1.93	2.01	2.07	1.76	1.80
ES432	Cáceres	1.30	1.36	1.44	1.28	1.12	1.19	0.86	1.04
ES511	Barcelona	6.93	8.09	9.26	10.62	14.40	14.59	17.81	15.65
ES512	Girona	1.76	1.83	1.87	1.83	1.72	2.42	1.32	1.35
ES513	Lleida	1.58	1.60	1.64	1.49	1.24	1.28	1.30	1.09
ES514	Tarragona	1.96	1.91	1.93	2.05	2.14	1.85	2.06	1.68
ES521	Alicante/Alacant	2.36	2.34	2.29	2.24	2.18	2.19	2.29	2.59
ES522	Castellón/Castelló	1.69	1.71	1.80	1.70	1.74	1.44	1.37	1.41
ES523	Valencia/València	4.58	5.01	5.52	4.67	5.08	4.93	5.38	5.65
ES530	Balears, Illes	1.80	1.42	1.07	1.17	1.38	1.66	1.31	1.91
ES611	Almería	2.19	1.86	1.78	1.38	1.40	1.27	1.16	0.97
ES612	Cádiz	4.62	4.16	3.70	3.68	2.78	3.50	2.01	2.03
ES613	Córdoba	2.13	1.93	1.79	2.26	1.80	1.87	1.95	1.99
ES614	Granada	4.72	3.92	3.26	2.72	2.07	2.65	2.47	2.11
ES615	Huelva	1.07	1.07	1.18	1.63	1.24	1.33	0.89	1.22
ES616	Jaén	2.26	2.04	1.82	2.17	1.89	1.97	1.61	1.38
ES617	Málaga	4.44	3.81	3.27	3.24	2.11	2.66	1.68	2.10
ES618	Sevilla	4.39	4.15	3.91	3.92	3.28	3.43	3.18	3.16
ES620	Murcia	2.51	2.70	2.85	2.70	1.91	2.07	2.06	2.37
ES700	Canarias, Islas	1.20	1.00	0.80	1.29	1.16	1.46	1.55	1.67
	ESP	**100.0**	**100.0**	**100.0**	**100.0**	**100.0**	**100.0**	**100.0**	**100.0**

(*continued*)

Table A3 (continued)

Code	Province	1935	1940	1945	1950	1955	1957	1959	1961
ES421	Albacete	0.95	0.90	0.99	0.97	0.82	0.84	0.80	0.79
ES422	Ciudad Real	1.42	1.35	1.43	1.49	1.32	1.28	1.23	1.24
ES423	Cuenca	0.85	0.86	0.86	0.88	0.72	0.77	0.74	0.68
ES424	Guadalajara	0.61	0.59	0.57	0.55	0.49	0.52	0.50	0.45
ES425	Toledo	1.55	1.39	1.45	1.54	1.20	1.24	1.21	1.15
ES431	Badajoz	1.92	1.80	1.86	1.85	1.62	1.74	1.71	1.59
ES432	Cáceres	1.11	1.08	1.09	1.05	1.01	1.02	1.01	0.96
ES511	Barcelona	12.52	13.46	13.24	13.58	15.45	15.00	15.17	15.62
ES512	Girona	1.71	1.59	1.58	1.61	1.52	1.48	1.51	1.61
ES513	Lleida	1.46	1.39	1.37	1.24	1.00	1.08	1.11	1.21
ES514	Tarragona	1.85	1.70	1.61	1.47	1.44	1.46	1.49	1.49
ES521	Alicante/Alacant	2.38	2.30	2.28	2.18	2.33	2.27	2.30	2.37
ES522	Castellón/Castelló	1.08	1.12	1.12	1.07	1.22	1.26	1.28	1.22
ES523	Valencia/València	5.55	5.53	5.39	5.18	5.62	5.72	5.82	5.62
ES530	Balears, Illes	2.02	2.21	2.00	1.82	1.86	1.83	1.90	1.90
ES611	Almería	0.70	0.78	0.76	0.74	0.66	0.67	0.69	0.67
ES612	Cádiz	2.00	2.03	2.11	1.99	1.91	1.88	1.92	1.91
ES613	Córdoba	1.84	2.00	1.94	1.94	1.96	1.87	1.87	1.73
ES614	Granada	1.80	1.60	1.58	1.50	1.43	1.38	1.36	1.36
ES615	Huelva	1.20	1.15	1.15	1.13	1.03	0.99	0.95	0.90
ES616	Jaén	1.79	1.86	1.64	1.52	1.41	1.39	1.47	1.39
ES617	Málaga	1.82	1.80	1.86	1.86	1.70	1.71	1.73	1.78
ES618	Sevilla	3.76	3.76	3.82	3.89	3.45	3.35	3.26	3.27
ES620	Murcia	2.16	2.09	2.10	2.08	1.84	1.85	1.87	1.96
ES700	Canarias, Islas	2.28	2.34	2.34	2.39	2.14	2.39	2.38	2.37
	ESP	**100.0**	**100.0**	**100.0**	**100.0**	**100.0**	**100.0**	**100.0**	**100.0**

(*continued*)

Table A3 (continued)

Code	Province	1963	1965	1967	1969	1971	1973	1975	1977	1979
ES421	Albacete	0.80	0.73	0.70	0.67	0.67	0.64	0.63	0.64	0.64
ES422	Ciudad Real	1.23	1.18	1.10	1.09	1.02	1.06	1.03	1.00	0.96
ES423	Cuenca	0.65	0.58	0.55	0.49	0.47	0.50	0.49	0.47	0.45
ES424	Guadalajara	0.44	0.42	0.41	0.42	0.41	0.42	0.39	0.40	0.39
ES425	Toledo	1.11	1.03	1.03	1.09	1.10	1.13	1.09	1.07	1.06
ES431	Badajoz	1.43	1.34	1.25	1.18	1.14	1.13	1.05	1.02	1.01
ES432	Cáceres	0.92	0.86	0.85	0.81	0.77	0.76	0.72	0.72	0.74
ES511	Barcelona	15.51	15.72	15.84	15.80	15.90	15.70	15.68	15.61	15.39
ES512	Girona	1.64	1.61	1.58	1.61	1.59	1.56	1.59	1.62	1.64
ES513	Lleida	1.25	1.18	1.12	1.18	1.15	1.13	1.08	1.03	1.02
ES514	Tarragona	1.46	1.45	1.49	1.53	1.49	1.53	1.69	1.69	1.68
ES521	Alicante/Alacant	2.46	2.52	2.58	2.62	2.65	2.73	2.78	2.86	2.96
ES522	Castellón/Castelló	1.18	1.13	1.13	1.11	1.13	1.14	1.16	1.19	1.20
ES523	Valencia/València	5.48	5.39	5.35	5.35	5.42	5.49	5.48	5.62	5.66
ES530	Balears, Illes	1.93	1.97	2.08	2.16	2.23	2.24	2.22	2.26	2.36
ES611	Almería	0.67	0.65	0.67	0.67	0.71	0.75	0.78	0.86	0.84
ES612	Cádiz	1.88	1.87	1.93	2.01	2.04	1.98	1.97	2.05	2.03
ES613	Córdoba	1.64	1.63	1.54	1.48	1.46	1.39	1.32	1.34	1.35
ES614	Granada	1.35	1.30	1.30	1.29	1.28	1.26	1.21	1.23	1.23
ES615	Huelva	0.89	0.86	0.85	0.89	0.97	1.02	1.06	1.01	0.96
ES616	Jaén	1.33	1.28	1.25	1.20	1.15	1.13	1.09	1.08	1.08
ES617	Málaga	1.83	1.92	1.98	1.98	2.05	2.06	2.01	2.04	2.09
ES618	Sevilla	3.23	3.20	3.29	3.20	3.24	3.19	3.08	3.07	3.05
ES620	Murcia	1.99	1.97	2.00	2.02	2.05	2.06	2.04	2.05	2.11
ES700	Canarias, Islas	2.42	2.47	2.63	2.72	2.96	3.01	2.92	3.08	3.39
	ESP	**100.0**	**100.0**	**100.0**	**100.0**	**100.0**	**100.0**	**100.0**	**100.0**	**100.0**

(*continued*)

Table A3 (continued)

Code	Province	1980	1981	1982	1983	1984	1985	1986	1987	1988
ES421	Albacete	0.68	0.64	0.65	0.65	0.65	0.70	0.62	0.63	0.63
ES422	Ciudad Real	1.02	0.99	1.00	1.02	1.03	1.04	1.04	1.07	1.06
ES423	Cuenca	0.45	0.42	0.44	0.41	0.41	0.43	0.42	0.40	0.40
ES424	Guadalajara	0.41	0.40	0.40	0.39	0.41	0.43	0.41	0.42	0.47
ES425	Toledo	1.05	1.09	1.03	1.01	1.01	1.10	1.02	1.09	1.11
ES431	Badajoz	0.97	0.95	0.93	0.91	1.01	1.00	0.96	0.99	0.99
ES432	Cáceres	0.69	0.68	0.71	0.72	0.90	0.96	0.89	0.91	0.96
ES511	Barcelona	14.33	14.07	13.57	13.26	13.44	12.85	13.19	13.46	13.69
ES512	Girona	1.62	1.61	1.55	1.57	1.63	1.64	1.69	1.70	1.71
ES513	Lleida	1.21	1.20	1.19	1.20	1.22	1.17	1.15	1.16	1.16
ES514	Tarragona	2.00	1.97	2.04	2.11	2.06	2.20	2.29	2.17	2.20
ES521	Alicante/Alacant	3.19	3.23	3.11	3.17	3.15	3.16	2.98	3.01	2.99
ES522	Castellón/Castelló	1.35	1.35	1.33	1.33	1.29	1.32	1.38	1.35	1.31
ES523	Valencia/València	5.47	5.70	5.53	5.57	5.73	5.72	5.56	5.56	5.55
ES530	Balears, Illes	1.98	2.07	2.12	2.17	2.24	2.40	2.34	2.38	2.38
ES611	Almería	0.83	0.91	0.89	0.88	0.94	0.91	0.93	0.98	0.94
ES612	Cádiz	2.18	2.16	2.25	2.18	2.12	2.18	2.27	2.24	2.22
ES613	Córdoba	1.32	1.28	1.34	1.37	1.32	1.36	1.26	1.34	1.31
ES614	Granada	1.33	1.35	1.36	1.37	1.42	1.32	1.33	1.38	1.39
ES615	Huelva	1.03	0.98	0.96	0.98	1.03	1.04	1.11	1.02	1.01
ES616	Jaén	1.20	1.20	1.17	1.30	1.17	1.26	1.19	1.17	1.23
ES617	Málaga	2.06	2.07	2.17	2.19	2.19	2.29	2.28	2.37	2.32
ES618	Sevilla	2.89	2.84	2.86	2.81	2.83	3.04	2.97	3.06	3.07
ES620	Murcia	2.41	2.38	2.34	2.41	2.41	2.40	2.50	2.48	2.42
ES700	Canarias, Islas	3.62	3.64	3.63	3.74	3.59	3.47	3.59	3.60	3.68
	ESP	**100.0**	**100.0**	**100.0**	**100.0**	**100.0**	**100.0**	**100.0**	**100.0**	**100.0**

(*continued*)

Table A3 (continued)

Code	Province	1989	1990	1991	1992	1993	1994	1995	1996	1997
ES421	Albacete	0.64	0.67	0.66	0.66	0.67	0.67	0.67	0.71	0.68
ES422	Ciudad Real	1.03	1.04	1.02	1.01	1.01	0.99	0.98	0.94	0.93
ES423	Cuenca	0.41	0.39	0.41	0.41	0.41	0.41	0.41	0.44	0.44
ES424	Guadalajara	0.52	0.49	0.48	0.48	0.48	0.47	0.41	0.39	0.40
ES425	Toledo	1.12	1.11	1.12	1.13	1.07	1.06	1.08	1.09	1.08
ES431	Badajoz	0.99	1.02	1.03	1.03	1.02	1.02	0.99	1.03	1.04
ES432	Cáceres	0.91	0.87	0.88	0.90	0.92	0.93	0.75	0.70	0.65
ES511	Barcelona	14.01	14.00	14.13	14.14	14.12	14.21	14.28	14.45	14.40
ES512	Girona	1.69	1.78	1.70	1.72	1.72	1.78	1.68	1.68	1.70
ES513	Lleida	1.13	1.10	1.09	1.15	1.14	1.13	1.08	1.13	1.13
ES514	Tarragona	2.24	2.16	2.15	2.17	2.13	2.13	1.88	1.89	1.88
ES521	Alicante/Alacant	2.96	3.02	3.03	3.02	3.04	3.02	2.99	3.16	3.16
ES522	Castellón/Castelló	1.33	1.34	1.34	1.32	1.34	1.33	1.28	1.32	1.33
ES523	Valencia/València	5.56	5.54	5.56	5.54	5.48	5.43	5.21	5.00	5.11
ES530	Balears, Illes	2.32	2.37	2.41	2.44	2.47	2.51	2.31	2.33	2.41
ES611	Almería	1.01	1.06	1.04	1.01	1.02	1.03	1.03	1.12	1.18
ES612	Cádiz	2.13	2.16	2.08	2.07	2.02	2.04	2.03	2.11	2.07
ES613	Córdoba	1.28	1.35	1.41	1.37	1.40	1.38	1.40	1.33	1.31
ES614	Granada	1.40	1.39	1.40	1.41	1.44	1.48	1.43	1.37	1.35
ES615	Huelva	1.04	1.01	0.97	0.92	0.90	0.92	0.89	0.90	0.90
ES616	Jaén	1.13	1.22	1.25	1.19	1.22	1.22	1.15	1.14	1.16
ES617	Málaga	2.30	2.31	2.30	2.25	2.24	2.22	2.26	2.25	2.27
ES618	Sevilla	3.03	3.19	3.28	3.36	3.20	3.19	3.32	3.28	3.26
ES620	Murcia	2.43	2.50	2.48	2.46	2.44	2.46	2.30	2.31	2.36
ES700	Canarias, Islas	3.57	3.50	3.49	3.58	3.73	3.74	3.83	3.83	3.86
	ESP	**100.0**	**100.0**	**100.0**	**100.0**	**100.0**	**100.0**	**100.0**	**100.0**	**100.0**

(continued)

Table A3 (continued)

Code	Province	1998	1999	2000	2001	2002	2003	2004	2005	2006
ES421	Albacete	0.69	0.68	0.66	0.67	0.69	0.67	0.67	0.67	0.66
ES422	Ciudad Real	0.92	0.91	0.93	0.91	0.91	0.94	0.94	0.91	0.91
ES423	Cuenca	0.44	0.41	0.37	0.37	0.36	0.36	0.37	0.37	0.38
ES424	Guadalajara	0.38	0.37	0.37	0.38	0.39	0.40	0.40	0.43	0.43
ES425	Toledo	1.08	1.05	1.04	1.06	1.05	1.08	1.07	1.12	1.15
ES431	Badajoz	1.05	1.04	1.03	1.02	1.01	1.01	0.99	1.02	1.00
ES432	Cáceres	0.63	0.64	0.64	0.63	0.63	0.62	0.64	0.62	0.61
ES511	Barcelona	14.30	14.39	14.32	14.26	14.09	14.07	14.01	14.08	14.01
ES512	Girona	1.69	1.67	1.68	1.73	1.77	1.79	1.81	1.82	1.88
ES513	Lleida	1.10	1.10	1.07	1.09	1.10	1.11	1.09	1.04	1.07
ES514	Tarragona	1.84	1.88	1.88	1.91	1.98	1.98	2.05	1.94	1.94
ES521	Alicante/Alacant	3.17	3.11	3.15	3.22	3.23	3.25	3.31	3.34	3.33
ES522	Castellón/Castelló	1.38	1.37	1.36	1.34	1.32	1.29	1.26	1.31	1.32
ES523	Valencia/València	5.13	5.19	5.20	5.24	5.27	5.22	5.20	5.12	5.14
ES530	Balears, Illes	2.45	2.52	2.56	2.55	2.52	2.46	2.44	2.44	2.43
ES611	Almería	1.18	1.25	1.24	1.22	1.25	1.25	1.24	1.26	1.25
ES612	Cádiz	2.03	2.01	2.08	2.06	2.05	2.04	2.08	2.06	2.05
ES613	Córdoba	1.30	1.28	1.26	1.24	1.22	1.25	1.27	1.26	1.27
ES614	Granada	1.32	1.30	1.34	1.35	1.38	1.39	1.39	1.38	1.42
ES615	Huelva	0.87	0.89	0.92	0.88	0.87	0.88	0.89	0.90	0.87
ES616	Jaén	1.15	1.06	1.04	1.04	1.01	1.09	1.06	1.01	1.00
ES617	Málaga	2.27	2.30	2.32	2.40	2.40	2.45	2.53	2.64	2.61
ES618	Sevilla	3.23	3.16	3.21	3.23	3.33	3.37	3.37	3.41	3.37
ES620	Murcia	2.38	2.37	2.44	2.45	2.49	2.53	2.53	2.57	2.58
ES700	Canarias, Islas	3.93	4.07	4.03	4.06	4.05	4.05	4.00	3.96	3.91
	ESP	**100.0**	**100.0**	**100.0**	**100.0**	**100.0**	**100.0**	**100.0**	**100.0**	**100.0**

(continued)

Table A3 (continued)

Code	Province	2007	2008	2009	2010	2011	2012	2013	2014	2015
ES421	Albacete	0.65	0.67	0.70	0.69	0.68	0.69	0.68	0.67	0.67
ES422	Ciudad Real	0.93	0.93	0.92	0.93	0.94	0.93	0.91	0.87	0.90
ES423	Cuenca	0.39	0.38	0.38	0.39	0.39	0.39	0.39	0.38	0.38
ES424	Guadalajara	0.44	0.46	0.46	0.47	0.48	0.48	0.47	0.44	0.43
ES425	Toledo	1.18	1.19	1.19	1.16	1.14	1.13	1.12	1.10	1.10
ES431	Badajoz	1.01	1.03	1.04	1.04	1.03	1.01	1.02	1.00	1.01
ES432	Cáceres	0.61	0.60	0.61	0.63	0.62	0.62	0.62	0.62	0.62
ES511	Barcelona	13.99	13.88	13.83	13.86	13.78	13.81	13.87	13.99	14.05
ES512	Girona	1.86	1.85	1.86	1.88	1.86	1.88	1.86	1.87	1.85
ES513	Lleida	1.07	1.08	1.11	1.11	1.11	1.13	1.15	1.14	1.13
ES514	Tarragona	1.96	1.98	1.99	2.03	2.02	2.02	2.01	2.03	2.07
ES521	Alicante/Alacant	3.28	3.27	3.19	3.15	3.09	3.06	3.07	3.13	3.11
ES522	Castellón/Castelló	1.27	1.24	1.23	1.23	1.25	1.21	1.21	1.21	1.23
ES523	Valencia/València	5.21	5.24	5.13	5.12	5.10	5.04	5.03	5.07	5.03
ES530	Balears, Illes	2.43	2.44	2.43	2.43	2.44	2.48	2.50	2.54	2.54
ES611	Almería	1.26	1.25	1.21	1.18	1.11	1.13	1.13	1.16	1.19
ES612	Cádiz	2.01	1.97	1.92	1.95	1.96	1.94	1.92	1.88	1.85
ES613	Córdoba	1.28	1.26	1.26	1.25	1.25	1.21	1.24	1.23	1.24
ES614	Granada	1.42	1.42	1.41	1.40	1.41	1.42	1.42	1.45	1.45
ES615	Huelva	0.85	0.85	0.81	0.84	0.88	0.88	0.83	0.82	0.84
ES616	Jaén	1.01	1.00	1.02	1.02	1.02	0.95	1.02	0.96	1.01
ES617	Málaga	2.57	2.57	2.59	2.58	2.56	2.53	2.54	2.58	2.58
ES618	Sevilla	3.40	3.36	3.39	3.36	3.38	3.41	3.35	3.38	3.33
ES620	Murcia	2.60	2.62	2.59	2.60	2.55	2.56	2.59	2.57	2.62
ES700	Canarias, Islas	3.87	3.83	3.78	3.83	3.85	3.84	3.87	3.85	3.80
	ESP	**100.0**	**100.0**	**100.0**	**100.0**	**100.0**	**100.0**	**100.0**	**100.0**	**100.0**

Table A4 Gross domestic product (%), NUTS2

Code	NUTS2	1860	1870	1880	1890	1900	1910	1920	1930
ES11	Galicia	5.6	5.4	5.3	4.9	5.7	6.3	4.9	6.1
ES12	Asturias	1.9	2.0	2.0	2.1	3.2	2.4	3.0	3.2
ES13	Cantabria	1.2	1.2	1.1	1.2	1.5	1.4	1.4	1.7
ES21	Basque Country	2.5	3.4	4.2	5.0	6.6	5.2	6.4	6.2
ES22	Navarre	2.0	2.2	2.4	1.7	1.4	1.4	1.7	1.4
ES23	La Rioja	1.0	1.1	1.1	1.0	1.1	0.8	0.6	0.7
ES24	Aragón	5.8	5.6	5.5	5.1	4.5	4.5	5.0	4.2
ES30	Madrid	5.5	6.3	6.6	6.6	6.8	6.7	8.2	10.5
ES41	Castile-Leon	11.4	11.6	11.6	11.0	10.1	9.5	8.9	7.7
ES42	Castile-La Mancha	7.5	7.3	7.0	7.3	6.4	6.0	5.6	5.0
ES43	Extremadura	3.4	3.4	3.5	3.2	3.1	3.3	2.6	2.8
ES51	Catalonia	12.2	13.4	14.7	16.0	19.5	20.1	22.5	19.8
ES52	Valencia	8.6	9.1	9.6	8.6	9.0	8.6	9.0	9.6
ES53	Balearic Islands	1.8	1.4	1.1	1.2	1.4	1.7	1.3	1.9
ES61	Andalusia	25.8	22.9	20.7	21.0	16.6	18.7	15.0	15.0
ES62	Murcia	2.5	2.7	2.9	2.7	1.9	2.1	2.1	2.4
ES70	Canary Islands	1.2	1.0	0.8	1.3	1.2	1.5	1.5	1.7
	ESP	**100.0**	**100.0**	**100.0**	**100.0**	**100.0**	**100.0**	**100.0**	**100.0**

(*continued*)

Table A4 (continued)

Code	NUTS2	1935	1940	1945	1950	1955	1957	1959	1961
ES11	Galicia	7.6	7.2	7.2	6.9	6.3	6.3	6.2	6.0
ES12	Asturias	3.6	3.8	3.7	3.6	3.5	3.5	3.5	3.4
ES13	Cantabria	1.5	1.5	1.5	1.7	1.7	1.7	1.7	1.7
ES21	Basque Country	6.0	6.0	6.4	6.7	7.3	7.2	7.1	7.3
ES22	Navarre	1.7	1.6	1.6	1.6	1.5	1.5	1.5	1.5
ES23	La Rioja	1.1	1.0	1.0	0.9	0.9	0.9	0.9	0.9
ES24	Aragón	4.2	4.2	3.9	3.9	3.7	3.8	3.7	3.7
ES30	Madrid	8.4	9.1	9.2	9.6	11.8	12.1	12.3	12.8
ES41	Castile-Leon	9.6	8.9	9.4	9.5	8.2	8.1	7.7	7.5
ES42	Castile-La Mancha	5.4	5.1	5.3	5.4	4.5	4.6	4.5	4.3
ES43	Extremadura	3.0	2.9	3.0	2.9	2.6	2.8	2.7	2.5
ES51	Catalonia	17.5	18.1	17.8	17.9	19.4	19.0	19.3	19.9
ES52	Valencia	9.0	8.9	8.8	8.4	9.2	9.2	9.4	9.2
ES53	Balearic Islands	2.0	2.2	2.0	1.8	1.9	1.8	1.9	1.9
ES61	Andalusia	14.9	15.0	14.9	14.6	13.6	13.2	13.2	13.0
ES62	Murcia	2.2	2.1	2.1	2.1	1.8	1.8	1.9	2.0
ES70	Canary Islands	2.3	2.3	2.3	2.4	2.1	2.4	2.4	2.4
	ESP	**100.0**	**100.0**	**100.0**	**100.0**	**100.0**	**100.0**	**100.0**	**100.0**

(continued)

Table A4 (continued)

Code	NUTS2	1963	1965	1967	1969	1971	1973	1975	1977	1979
ES11	Galicia	6.0	5.9	5.9	5.8	5.9	5.9	5.8	6.0	6.1
ES12	Asturias	3.3	3.2	3.3	3.2	3.1	3.0	3.1	2.9	2.9
ES13	Cantabria	1.6	1.6	1.6	1.5	1.5	1.4	1.4	1.4	1.4
ES21	Basque Country	7.5	7.7	7.6	7.8	7.6	7.5	7.6	7.2	6.8
ES22	Navarre	1.6	1.6	1.6	1.6	1.6	1.6	1.5	1.5	1.5
ES23	La Rioja	0.9	0.8	0.8	0.8	0.8	0.7	0.7	0.7	0.7
ES24	Aragón	3.7	3.6	3.5	3.5	3.4	3.3	3.3	3.3	3.3
ES30	Madrid	13.1	13.9	14.2	14.5	14.8	15.4	16.0	15.9	16.1
ES41	Castile-Leon	7.5	7.2	6.9	6.7	6.5	6.2	6.0	6.0	6.0
ES42	Castile-La Mancha	4.2	3.9	3.8	3.8	3.7	3.7	3.6	3.6	3.5
ES43	Extremadura	2.3	2.2	2.1	2.0	1.9	1.9	1.8	1.7	1.8
ES51	Catalonia	19.9	20.0	20.0	20.1	20.1	19.9	20.0	20.0	19.7
ES52	Valencia	9.1	9.0	9.1	9.1	9.2	9.4	9.4	9.7	9.8
ES53	Balearic Islands	1.9	2.0	2.1	2.2	2.2	2.2	2.2	2.3	2.4
ES61	Andalusia	12.8	12.7	12.8	12.7	12.9	12.8	12.5	12.7	12.6
ES62	Murcia	2.0	2.0	2.0	2.0	2.0	2.1	2.0	2.1	2.1
ES70	Canary Islands	2.4	2.5	2.6	2.7	3.0	3.0	2.9	3.1	3.4
	ESP	**100.0**	**100.0**	**100.0**	**100.0**	**100.0**	**100.0**	**100.0**	**100.0**	**100.0**

(continued)

Table A4 (continued)

Code	NUTS2	1980	1981	1982	1983	1984	1985	1986	1987	1988
ES11	Galicia	6.0	6.2	6.3	6.1	6.1	6.0	5.8	5.7	5.7
ES12	Asturias	2.8	2.8	2.9	2.8	2.7	2.8	2.9	2.7	2.7
ES13	Cantabria	1.5	1.5	1.5	1.5	1.5	1.4	1.3	1.3	1.4
ES21	Basque Country	7.4	7.6	7.5	7.3	7.0	7.0	6.9	6.6	6.5
ES22	Navarre	1.7	1.8	1.7	1.7	1.7	1.6	1.6	1.7	1.7
ES23	La Rioja	0.8	0.8	0.8	0.8	0.8	0.9	0.8	0.8	0.8
ES24	Aragón	3.4	3.3	3.4	3.5	3.5	3.5	3.4	3.4	3.5
ES30	Madrid	14.8	14.8	15.1	15.3	15.1	14.8	15.5	15.6	15.4
ES41	Castile-Leon	6.2	6.0	6.3	6.3	6.4	6.5	6.4	6.3	6.2
ES42	Castile-La Mancha	3.6	3.5	3.5	3.5	3.5	3.7	3.5	3.6	3.7
ES43	Extremadura	1.7	1.6	1.6	1.6	1.9	2.0	1.8	1.9	2.0
ES51	Catalonia	19.2	18.8	18.3	18.1	18.4	17.9	18.3	18.5	18.8
ES52	Valencia	10.0	10.3	10.0	10.1	10.2	10.2	9.9	9.9	9.9
ES53	Balearic Islands	2.0	2.1	2.1	2.2	2.2	2.4	2.3	2.4	2.4
ES61	Andalusia	12.8	12.8	13.0	13.1	13.0	13.4	13.3	13.6	13.5
ES62	Murcia	2.4	2.4	2.3	2.4	2.4	2.4	2.5	2.5	2.4
ES70	Canary Islands	3.6	3.6	3.6	3.7	3.6	3.5	3.6	3.6	3.7
	ESP	**100.0**	**100.0**	**100.0**	**100.0**	**100.0**	**100.0**	**100.0**	**100.0**	**100.0**

(*continued*)

Table A4 (continued)

Code	NUTS2	1989	1990	1991	1992	1993	1994	1995	1996	1997
ES11	Galicia	5.7	5.5	5.5	5.5	5.5	5.5	5.6	5.6	5.5
ES12	Asturias	2.7	2.6	2.5	2.6	2.5	2.5	2.4	2.4	2.3
ES13	Cantabria	1.4	1.3	1.3	1.3	1.3	1.3	1.3	1.2	1.2
ES21	Basque Country	6.5	6.4	6.4	6.3	6.2	6.2	6.3	6.3	6.3
ES22	Navarre	1.7	1.7	1.7	1.7	1.6	1.6	1.7	1.7	1.7
ES23	La Rioja	0.8	0.8	0.8	0.8	0.8	0.8	0.8	0.8	0.8
ES24	Aragón	3.5	3.5	3.5	3.4	3.4	3.4	3.3	3.3	3.3
ES30	Madrid	15.5	15.7	15.7	15.8	15.9	16.0	16.8	16.9	17.0
ES41	Castile-Leon	6.1	6.0	5.9	5.9	6.1	6.0	6.1	6.0	5.9
ES42	Castile-La Mancha	3.7	3.7	3.7	3.7	3.6	3.6	3.5	3.6	3.5
ES43	Extremadura	1.9	1.9	1.9	1.9	1.9	1.9	1.7	1.7	1.7
ES51	Catalonia	19.1	19.0	19.1	19.2	19.1	19.3	18.9	19.1	19.1
ES52	Valencia	9.9	9.9	9.9	9.9	9.9	9.8	9.5	9.5	9.6
ES53	Balearic Islands	2.3	2.4	2.4	2.4	2.5	2.5	2.3	2.3	2.4
ES61	Andalusia	13.3	13.7	13.7	13.6	13.4	13.5	13.5	13.5	13.5
ES62	Murcia	2.4	2.5	2.5	2.5	2.4	2.5	2.3	2.3	2.4
ES70	Canary Islands	3.6	3.5	3.5	3.6	3.7	3.7	3.8	3.8	3.9
	ESP	**100.0**	**100.0**	**100.0**	**100.0**	**100.0**	**100.0**	**100.0**	**100.0**	**100.0**

(*continued*)

Table A4 (continued)

Code	NUTS2	1998	1999	2000	2001	2002	2003	2004	2005	2006
ES11	Galicia	5.4	5.3	5.2	5.2	5.2	5.1	5.2	5.2	5.2
ES12	Asturias	2.3	2.2	2.2	2.2	2.2	2.2	2.1	2.2	2.2
ES13	Cantabria	1.2	1.2	1.2	1.2	1.2	1.2	1.2	1.2	1.2
ES21	Basque Country	6.3	6.4	6.3	6.3	6.2	6.1	6.1	6.1	6.1
ES22	Navarre	1.7	1.7	1.7	1.7	1.7	1.7	1.7	1.7	1.7
ES23	La Rioja	0.8	0.8	0.8	0.7	0.7	0.7	0.7	0.7	0.7
ES24	Aragón	3.2	3.1	3.1	3.1	3.1	3.1	3.1	3.1	3.1
ES30	Madrid	17.4	17.5	17.7	17.8	17.9	17.9	17.9	17.9	18.1
ES41	Castile-Leon	5.7	5.7	5.5	5.4	5.4	5.4	5.3	5.3	5.2
ES42	Castile-La Mancha	3.5	3.4	3.4	3.4	3.4	3.4	3.5	3.5	3.5
ES43	Extremadura	1.7	1.7	1.7	1.6	1.6	1.6	1.6	1.6	1.6
ES51	Catalonia	18.9	19.0	19.0	19.0	18.9	18.9	19.0	18.9	18.9
ES52	Valencia	9.7	9.7	9.7	9.8	9.8	9.8	9.8	9.8	9.8
ES53	Balearic Islands	2.4	2.5	2.6	2.6	2.5	2.5	2.4	2.4	2.4
ES61	Andalusia	13.3	13.2	13.4	13.4	13.5	13.7	13.8	13.9	13.8
ES62	Murcia	2.4	2.4	2.4	2.5	2.5	2.5	2.5	2.6	2.6
ES70	Canary Islands	3.9	4.1	4.0	4.1	4.1	4.1	4.0	4.0	3.9
	ESP	**100.0**	**100.0**	**100.0**	**100.0**	**100.0**	**100.0**	**100.0**	**100.0**	**100.0**

(continued)

Table A4 (continued)

Code	NUTS2	2007	2008	2009	2010	2011	2012	2013	2014	2015
ES11	Galicia	5.2	5.3	5.3	5.3	5.2	5.2	5.3	5.2	5.2
ES12	Asturias	2.2	2.2	2.1	2.1	2.1	2.1	2.0	2.0	2.0
ES13	Cantabria	1.2	1.2	1.2	1.2	1.2	1.2	1.1	1.2	1.1
ES21	Basque Country	6.0	6.1	6.0	6.1	6.1	6.2	6.1	6.2	6.2
ES22	Navarre	1.7	1.7	1.7	1.7	1.7	1.7	1.7	1.7	1.7
ES23	La Rioja	0.7	0.7	0.7	0.7	0.7	0.7	0.7	0.7	0.7
ES24	Aragón	3.2	3.2	3.2	3.2	3.2	3.1	3.2	3.2	3.1
ES30	Madrid	18.1	18.2	18.6	18.4	18.7	18.9	18.9	18.9	18.9
ES41	Castile-Leon	5.2	5.1	5.2	5.2	5.2	5.2	5.1	5.0	5.0
ES42	Castile-La Mancha	3.6	3.6	3.6	3.6	3.6	3.6	3.6	3.5	3.5
ES43	Extremadura	1.6	1.6	1.7	1.7	1.6	1.6	1.6	1.6	1.6
ES51	Catalonia	18.9	18.8	18.8	18.9	18.8	18.8	18.9	19.0	19.1
ES52	Valencia	9.8	9.8	9.6	9.5	9.4	9.3	9.3	9.4	9.4
ES53	Balearic Islands	2.4	2.4	2.4	2.4	2.4	2.5	2.5	2.5	2.5
ES61	Andalusia	13.8	13.7	13.6	13.6	13.6	13.5	13.4	13.5	13.5
ES62	Murcia	2.6	2.6	2.6	2.6	2.6	2.6	2.6	2.6	2.6
ES70	Canary Islands	3.9	3.8	3.8	3.8	3.8	3.8	3.9	3.9	3.8
	ESP	**100.0**	**100.0**	**100.0**	**100.0**	**100.0**	**100.0**	**100.0**	**100.0**	**100.0**

Table A5 Gross domestic product (%), NUTS1

Code	NUTS1	1860	1870	1880	1890	1900	1910	1920	1930
ES1	Northwest	8.7	8.6	8.4	8.3	10.4	10.0	9.4	11.0
ES2	Northeast	11.3	12.3	13.2	12.9	13.6	12.0	13.8	12.6
ES3	Madrid	5.5	6.3	6.6	6.6	6.8	6.7	8.2	10.5
ES4	Centre	22.3	22.3	22.1	21.5	19.7	18.8	17.2	15.5
ES5	East	22.7	23.9	25.4	25.8	29.9	30.3	32.8	31.3
ES6	South	28.3	25.6	23.6	23.7	18.5	20.8	17.0	17.3
ES7	Canary Islands	1.2	1.0	0.8	1.3	1.2	1.5	1.5	1.7
	ESP	**100.0**	**100.0**	**100.0**	**100.0**	**100.0**	**100.0**	**100.0**	**100.0**

Code	NUTS1	1935	1940	1945	1950	1955	1957	1959	1961
ES1	Northwest	12.7	12.5	12.4	12.2	11.4	11.5	11.3	11.1
ES2	Northeast	13.0	12.8	12.9	13.1	13.4	13.3	13.3	13.4
ES3	Madrid	8.4	9.1	9.2	9.6	11.8	12.1	12.3	12.8
ES4	Centre	18.0	16.9	17.6	17.8	15.4	15.5	14.9	14.3
ES5	East	28.6	29.3	28.6	28.1	30.4	30.1	30.6	31.0
ES6	South	17.1	17.1	17.0	16.7	15.4	15.1	15.1	15.0
ES7	Canary Islands	2.3	2.3	2.3	2.4	2.1	2.4	2.4	2.4
	ESP	**100.0**	**100.0**	**100.0**	**100.0**	**100.0**	**100.0**	**100.0**	**100.0**

Code	NUTS1	1963	1965	1967	1969	1971	1973	1975	1977	1979
ES1	Northwest	11.0	10.7	10.8	10.6	10.5	10.3	10.3	10.3	10.4
ES2	Northeast	13.7	13.8	13.6	13.6	13.3	13.1	13.2	12.8	12.3
ES3	Madrid	13.1	13.9	14.2	14.5	14.8	15.4	16.0	15.9	16.1
ES4	Centre	14.1	13.4	12.8	12.5	12.0	11.8	11.4	11.3	11.2
ES5	East	30.9	31.0	31.2	31.3	31.6	31.5	31.7	31.9	31.9
ES6	South	14.8	14.7	14.8	14.8	15.0	14.8	14.6	14.7	14.7
ES7	Canary Islands	2.4	2.5	2.6	2.7	3.0	3.0	2.9	3.1	3.4
	ESP	**100.0**	**100.0**	**100.0**	**100.0**	**100.0**	**100.0**	**100.0**	**100.0**	**100.0**

(*continued*)

Table A5 (continued)

Code	NUTS1	1980	1981	1982	1983	1984	1985	1986	1987	1988
ES1	Northwest	10.3	10.5	10.6	10.3	10.3	10.2	10.0	9.7	9.7
ES2	Northeast	13.4	13.5	13.5	13.4	13.0	13.1	12.8	12.5	12.4
ES3	Madrid	14.8	14.8	15.1	15.3	15.1	14.8	15.5	15.6	15.4
ES4	Centre	11.5	11.2	11.4	11.4	11.8	12.2	11.7	11.8	11.9
ES5	East	31.1	31.2	30.4	30.4	30.8	30.5	30.6	30.8	31.0
ES6	South	15.2	15.2	15.3	15.5	15.4	15.8	15.8	16.0	15.9
ES7	Canary Islands	3.6	3.6	3.6	3.7	3.6	3.5	3.6	3.6	3.7
	ESP	**100.0**	**100.0**	**100.0**	**100.0**	**100.0**	**100.0**	**100.0**	**100.0**	**100.0**

Code	NUTS1	1989	1990	1991	1992	1993	1994	1995	1996	1997
ES1	Northwest	9.7	9.4	9.3	9.4	9.4	9.3	9.3	9.2	9.0
ES2	Northeast	12.5	12.3	12.3	12.1	12.0	12.0	12.1	12.0	12.1
ES3	Madrid	15.5	15.7	15.7	15.8	15.9	16.0	16.8	16.9	17.0
ES4	Centre	11.7	11.6	11.5	11.5	11.6	11.5	11.4	11.3	11.1
ES5	East	31.3	31.3	31.4	31.5	31.4	31.5	30.7	31.0	31.1
ES6	South	15.7	16.2	16.2	16.0	15.9	15.9	15.8	15.8	15.9
ES7	Canary Islands	3.6	3.5	3.5	3.6	3.7	3.7	3.8	3.8	3.9
	ESP	**100.0**	**100.0**	**100.0**	**100.0**	**100.0**	**100.0**	**100.0**	**100.0**	**100.0**

Code	NUTS1	1998	1999	2000	2001	2002	2003	2004	2005	2006
ES1	Northwest	8.9	8.8	8.6	8.6	8.6	8.5	8.5	8.5	8.5
ES2	Northeast	12.0	12.0	11.9	11.8	11.8	11.7	11.6	11.6	11.6
ES3	Madrid	17.4	17.5	17.7	17.8	17.9	17.9	17.9	17.9	18.1
ES4	Centre	10.9	10.8	10.6	10.5	10.5	10.5	10.4	10.4	10.3
ES5	East	31.0	31.2	31.2	31.3	31.3	31.2	31.2	31.1	31.1
ES6	South	15.7	15.6	15.8	15.9	16.0	16.2	16.4	16.5	16.4
ES7	Canary Islands	3.9	4.1	4.0	4.1	4.1	4.1	4.0	4.0	3.9
	ESP	**100.0**	**100.0**	**100.0**	**100.0**	**100.0**	**100.0**	**100.0**	**100.0**	**100.0**

(*continued*)

Table A5 (continued)

Code	NUTS1	2007	2008	2009	2010	2011	2012	2013	2014	2015
ES1	Northwest	8.6	8.6	8.6	8.6	8.5	8.5	8.4	8.4	8.3
ES2	Northeast	11.6	11.7	11.6	11.7	11.7	11.7	11.8	11.8	11.7
ES3	Madrid	18.1	18.2	18.6	18.4	18.7	18.9	18.9	18.9	18.9
ES4	Centre	10.4	10.4	10.5	10.5	10.4	10.4	10.3	10.1	10.1
ES5	East	31.1	31.0	30.8	30.8	30.7	30.6	30.7	31.0	31.0
ES6	South	16.4	16.3	16.2	16.2	16.1	16.0	16.0	16.0	16.1
ES7	Canary Islands	3.9	3.8	3.8	3.8	3.8	3.8	3.9	3.9	3.8
	ESP	**100.0**	**100.0**	**100.0**	**100.0**	**100.0**	**100.0**	**100.0**	**100.0**	**100.0**

Table A6 Population, NUTS3

Code	Province	1860	1870	1880	1890	1900	1910	1920	1930
ES111	A Coruña	557,311	576,874	596,436	613,881	653,556	676,708	708,660	767,608
ES112	Lugo	432,516	421,663	410,810	432,165	465,386	479,965	469,705	468,619
ES113	Ourense	369,138	378,987	388,835	405,127	404,311	411,560	412,460	426,043
ES114	Pontevedra	440,259	446,103	451,946	443,385	457,262	495,356	533,419	568,011
ES120	Asturias	540,586	558,469	576,352	595,420	627,069	685,131	743,726	791,855
ES130	Cantabria	219,966	227,633	235,299	244,274	276,003	302,956	327,669	364,147
ES211	Araba/Álava	97,934	95,736	93,538	92,915	96,385	97,181	98,668	104,176
ES212	Gipuzkoa	162,547	164,877	167,207	181,845	195,850	226,684	258,557	302,329
ES213	Bizkaia	168,705	179,330	189,954	235,659	311,361	349,923	409,550	485,205
ES220	Navarra	299,654	301,919	304,184	304,122	307,669	312,235	329,875	345,883
ES230	La Rioja	175,111	174,768	174,425	181,465	189,376	188,235	192,940	203,789
ES241	Huesca	263,230	257,735	252,239	255,137	244,867	248,257	250,508	242,958
ES242	Teruel	237,276	239,721	242,165	241,865	246,001	255,491	252,096	252,785
ES243	Zaragoza	390,551	395,569	400,587	415,195	421,843	448,995	494,550	535,816
ES300	Madrid	489,332	541,763	594,194	682,644	775,034	878,641	1,067,637	1,383,951
ES411	Ávila	168,773	174,605	180,436	193,093	200,457	208,796	209,360	221,386
ES412	Burgos	337,132	334,879	332,625	338,551	338,828	346,934	336,472	355,299
ES413	León	340,244	345,227	350,210	380,637	386,083	395,430	412,417	441,908
ES414	Palencia	185,955	183,363	180,771	188,845	192,473	196,031	191,719	207,546
ES415	Salamanca	262,383	274,039	285,695	314,472	320,765	334,377	321,615	339,101
ES416	Segovia	146,292	148,172	150,052	154,443	159,243	167,747	167,081	174,158
ES417	Soria	149,549	151,601	153,652	151,530	150,462	156,354	151,595	156,207
ES418	Valladolid	246,981	247,220	247,458	267,148	278,561	284,473	280,931	301,571
ES419	Zamora	248,502	249,111	249,720	270,072	275,545	272,976	266,215	280,148
	ESP	**15,658,586**	**16,145,253**	**16,631,919**	**17,560,352**	**18,594,405**	**19,927,150**	**21,303,162**	**23,563,867**

(*continued*)

Table A6 (continued)

Code	Province	1935	1940	1945	1950	1955	1957	1959	1961
ES111	A Coruña	857,388	884,472	919,590	965,778	973,292	980,652	988,308	996,592
ES112	Lugo	524,165	528,290	482,795	518,068	496,241	490,448	484,836	478,911
ES113	Ourense	476,228	479,678	520,443	491,300	461,150	457,931	454,848	455,082
ES114	Pontevedra	645,370	664,618	683,471	710,353	676,519	678,348	685,083	701,943
ES120	Asturias	835,532	842,632	861,435	890,398	933,779	954,293	975,492	994,706
ES130	Cantabria	379,246	390,368	393,601	402,974	417,591	423,122	428,830	434,278
ES211	Araba/Álava	106,263	109,028	110,582	113,450	127,201	131,440	135,555	140,448
ES212	Gipuzkoa	304,620	314,964	339,850	368,785	418,461	439,625	461,974	483,427
ES213	Bizkaia	486,981	494,819	519,815	550,957	647,110	684,714	724,679	765,685
ES220	Navarra	351,607	353,740	365,220	381,041	392,022	395,917	400,254	408,289
ES230	La Rioja	211,972	218,086	222,644	229,616	230,174	230,219	230,322	230,709
ES241	Huesca	257,077	239,502	234,620	236,247	235,380	234,877	234,434	233,051
ES242	Teruel	249,513	238,363	237,200	241,801	226,745	222,627	218,640	214,394
ES243	Zaragoza	541,699	556,819	577,851	605,715	638,268	645,392	652,758	658,422
ES300	Madrid	1,404,565	1,525,532	1,659,293	1,812,407	2,210,435	2,348,555	2,495,903	2,661,504
ES411	Ávila	236,781	239,226	247,139	257,968	245,633	243,137	240,731	238,211
ES412	Burgos	362,486	366,576	375,193	387,704	390,249	387,062	383,986	380,695
ES413	León	475,700	492,903	517,204	547,747	563,218	571,303	579,649	584,917
ES414	Palencia	213,162	215,785	223,849	234,584	233,059	232,830	232,656	230,734
ES415	Salamanca	370,267	385,963	396,962	412,622	409,779	408,591	407,507	406,709
ES416	Segovia	185,240	188,186	194,076	202,260	199,095	197,958	196,876	195,097
ES417	Soria	161,086	160,732	161,266	163,582	154,901	152,108	149,401	146,493
ES418	Valladolid	315,948	322,650	332,421	346,084	355,135	358,267	361,517	369,075
ES419	Zamora	290,814	293,506	302,282	314,583	309,636	306,732	303,933	300,659
	ESP	**24,621,927**	**25,439,948**	**26,497,400**	**27,869,913**	**29,055,546**	**29,556,117**	**30,092,316**	**30,669,819**

(*continued*)

Table A6 (continued)

Code	Province	1963	1965	1967	1969	1971	1973	1975	1977	1979
ES111	A Coruña	1,013,609	1,033,997	1,036,216	1,034,621	1,031,814	1,039,560	1,048,351	1,061,602	1,078,726
ES112	Lugo	472,955	459,919	447,631	434,067	421,096	414,602	408,592	404,704	405,046
ES113	Ourense	461,000	463,159	458,833	449,373	439,805	435,422	431,488	429,365	428,829
ES114	Pontevedra	725,313	744,640	760,277	773,386	786,053	807,998	831,354	854,199	871,090
ES120	Asturias	1,007,034	1,020,660	1,035,365	1,046,416	1,055,158	1,071,116	1,088,345	1,106,243	1,119,494
ES130	Cantabria	440,360	448,638	457,470	464,756	470,422	477,345	484,825	493,775	503,921
ES211	Araba/Álava	148,361	160,304	174,231	188,675	202,924	216,646	230,670	243,589	251,510
ES212	Gipuzkoa	507,257	537,486	570,011	602,283	630,161	648,855	668,737	689,720	703,655
ES213	Bizkaia	813,622	870,536	932,238	994,644	1,050,505	1,090,840	1,133,780	1,179,215	1,216,677
ES220	Navarra	420,318	432,958	446,366	458,493	467,786	473,999	480,751	488,699	497,946
ES230	La Rioja	231,649	232,853	234,268	235,469	236,379	237,376	239,152	241,887	246,659
ES241	Huesca	230,505	228,544	226,802	224,242	220,617	216,688	213,027	210,779	210,152
ES242	Teruel	209,733	199,854	190,607	181,119	171,767	164,117	156,952	152,576	152,734
ES243	Zaragoza	667,291	691,450	717,108	740,981	759,727	771,360	783,909	800,339	816,649
ES300	Madrid	2,837,865	3,012,915	3,276,838	3,550,768	3,807,192	4,009,312	4,226,215	4,446,565	4,588,437
ES411	Ávila	235,521	231,082	225,524	217,948	209,215	200,703	193,740	190,490	187,749
ES412	Burgos	379,036	375,963	371,740	366,213	359,548	354,109	349,075	346,585	350,594
ES413	León	582,936	578,513	574,624	568,663	559,008	545,879	533,562	527,015	527,794
ES414	Palencia	227,516	220,664	214,210	207,180	199,666	192,971	186,671	182,339	180,111
ES415	Salamanca	405,970	399,625	393,717	386,470	377,070	366,181	355,947	350,742	354,335
ES416	Segovia	190,725	182,956	175,660	168,032	160,713	155,721	151,025	148,190	148,689
ES417	Soria	142,575	135,637	129,148	122,516	115,989	110,624	105,604	101,793	101,160
ES418	Valladolid	377,672	387,481	397,892	407,073	415,920	429,017	442,942	458,008	472,124
ES419	Zamora	295,136	285,401	276,228	266,364	255,583	244,905	234,901	227,617	226,082
	ESP	**31,295,729**	**31,945,892**	**32,721,681**	**33,442,415**	**34,067,752**	**34,693,684**	**35,405,480**	**36,252,926**	**36,985,032**

(*continued*)

Table A6 (continued)

Code	Province	1980	1981	1982	1983	1984	1985	1986	1987	1988
ES111	A Coruña	1,089,835	1,094,798	1,099,001	1,101,746	1,103,988	1,105,365	1,104,539	1,104,547	1,103,569
ES112	Lugo	406,518	405,223	404,089	402,359	400,884	399,011	396,819	394,740	392,335
ES113	Ourense	430,499	427,955	421,100	413,857	406,722	399,313	391,501	383,929	375,846
ES114	Pontevedra	876,510	884,799	889,033	892,090	894,724	896,631	897,330	898327	898,699
ES120	Asturias	1,126,215	1,130,074	1,130,287	1,129,056	1,127,303	1,124,759	1,121,039	1,117,341	1,112,177
ES130	Cantabria	510,845	514,403	517,855	520,506	522,630	524,258	525,376	526,694	527,324
ES211	Araba/Álava	254,528	258,782	261,298	263,410	265,359	267,140	268,532	269,753	270,842
ES212	Gipuzkoa	692,203	695,030	695,610	695,269	694,286	692,803	690,582	688,570	685,706
ES213	Bizkaia	1,184,216	1,190,259	1,190,741	1,190,010	1,188,095	1,185,768	1,181,962	1,177,894	1,172,862
ES220	Navarra	507,577	510,055	512,474	514,094	515,687	516,776	517,714	518,378	519,020
ES230	La Rioja	253,246	254,915	256,390	257,797	259,096	260,117	260,790	261,610	262,154
ES241	Huesca	215,398	214,940	214,908	214,500	213,906	213,188	212,317	211,547	210,639
ES242	Teruel	154,881	153,208	152,606	151,662	150,745	149,722	148,680	147,723	146,737
ES243	Zaragoza	825,462	830,041	833,442	835,605	837,431	838,929	839,087	839,882	839,921
ES300	Madrid	4,639,535	4,702,568	4,742,375	4,777,938	4,810,764	4,840,565	4,865,724	4,890,911	4,911,899
ES411	Ávila	185,230	183,451	182,983	182,325	181,616	180,942	180,029	179,049	177,869
ES412	Burgos	363,799	363,709	363,766	363,514	362,790	361,776	360,551	359,366	357,794
ES413	León	527,045	524,215	525,801	526,778	527,886	528,567	528,724	528,734	528,487
ES414	Palencia	189,156	188,561	188,701	188,705	188,796	188,721	188,301	187,959	187,442
ES415	Salamanca	365,717	364,643	365,318	365,396	365,237	364,792	364,126	363,405	362,316
ES416	Segovia	150,476	149,443	149,531	149,483	149,442	149,380	149,206	148,968	148,511
ES417	Soria	101,981	100,556	100,124	99,621	99,111	98,538	97,904	97,263	96,613
ES418	Valladolid	477,859	483,076	486,228	488,603	490,759	492,343	493,451	494,263	494,734
ES419	Zamora	230,156	227,530	226,747	225,567	224,384	223,020	221,493	220,198	218,665
	ESP	**37,374,193**	**37,645,490**	**37,867,578**	**38,040,314**	**38,204,653**	**38,345,912**	**38,450,217**	**38,560,011**	**38,641,293**

(*continued*)

Table A6 (continued)

Code	Province	1989	1990	1991	1992	1993	1994	1995	1996	1997
ES111	A Coruña	1,101,664	1,099,148	1,097,361	1,097,964	1,099,131	1,099,341	1,098,929	1,097,913	1,097,111
ES112	Lugo	389,662	386,714	383,713	381,622	379,684	377,453	375,092	372,283	369,500
ES113	Ourense	367,629	359,318	353,239	352,105	351,275	350,125	348,817	347,222	345,611
ES114	Pontevedra	898,394	897,847	897,286	898,720	900,359	901,260	901,853	901,708	901,729
ES120	Asturias	1,105,864	1,098,965	1,093,370	1,091,602	1,089,903	1,087,150	1,084,172	1,080,841	1,077,311
ES130	Cantabria	527,551	527,515	527,770	529,022	530,068	530,940	531,336	531,731	532,231
ES211	Araba/Álava	271,734	272,282	272,992	274,463	275,922	277,251	278,399	279,508	280,790
ES212	Gipuzkoa	682,538	679,076	676,401	676,097	675,876	675,470	675,044	674,589	674,067
ES213	Bizkaia	1,167,091	1,160,364	1,154,385	1,151,962	1,149,251	1,146,347	1,142,910	1,139,348	1,135,792
ES220	Navarra	519,490	519,603	520,414	523,616	526,869	530,213	533,318	536,536	539,776
ES230	La Rioja	262,664	263,233	263,861	265,075	266,217	267,480	268,518	269,629	270,841
ES241	Huesca	209,568	208,510	207,888	208,061	208,146	208,130	207,977	207,640	207,265
ES242	Teruel	145,643	144,525	143,487	142,905	142,275	141,672	140,904	140,082	139,295
ES243	Zaragoza	839,301	838,371	838,231	840,794	843,406	845,940	847,796	849,940	851,870
ES300	Madrid	4,928,968	4,942,230	4,962,889	5,006,848	5,052,504	5,096,045	5,137,372	5,178,331	5,220,731
ES411	Ávila	176,700	175,398	174,143	173,319	172,543	171,685	170,758	169,679	168,696
ES412	Burgos	356,173	354,295	352,801	352,611	352,462	352,260	351,725	351,325	350,781
ES413	León	527,706	526,720	525,056	522,244	519,215	515,883	512,424	508,814	505,280
ES414	Palencia	186,834	186,083	185,223	184,338	183,456	182,460	181,511	180,502	179,409
ES415	Salamanca	360,799	359,132	357,586	356,893	356,103	355,129	354,041	352,765	351,398
ES416	Segovia	148,138	147,576	147,184	147,455	147,567	147,623	147,670	147,705	147,825
ES417	Soria	95,903	95,098	94,435	94,088	93,798	93,513	93,086	92,702	92,304
ES418	Valladolid	494,875	494,653	494,478	495,212	495,876	496,434	496,775	496,931	497,112
ES419	Zamora	216,942	215,082	213,316	212,132	210,925	209,689	208,372	206,937	205,593
	ESP	**38,697,836**	**38,736,880**	**38,816,987**	**39,021,874**	**39,228,429**	**39,418,255**	**39,588,530**	**39,752,594**	**39,917,169**

(*continued*)

Table A6 (continued)

Code	Province	1998	1999	2000	2001	2002	2003	2004	2005	2006
ES111	A Coruña	1,096,877	1,096,195	1,095,557	1,095,711	1,097,980	1,102,327	1,106,572	1,111,830	1,117,387
ES112	Lugo	366,803	363,807	360,934	358,432	356,236	355,050	353,463	352,787	352,160
ES113	Ourense	343,941	342,090	340,322	338,882	337,424	336,597	335,217	334,415	333,386
ES114	Pontevedra	901,796	902,022	902,141	902,975	907,900	913,304	918,816	924,929	930,442
ES120	Asturias	1,073,883	1,069,742	1,066,107	1,063,676	1,062,103	1,062,196	1,062,146	1,062,559	1,063,801
ES130	Cantabria	532,691	533,044	533,568	534,572	538,550	544,887	550,972	557,962	564,188
ES211	Araba/Álava	281,968	283,217	284,445	285,906	288,500	292,440	296,305	300,724	304,299
ES212	Gipuzkoa	673,773	673,244	673,116	673,410	675,004	678,663	682,201	686,091	690,402
ES213	Bizkaia	1,132,282	1,128,773	1,125,738	1,123,233	1,123,922	1,126,222	1,129,305	1,134,194	1,139,379
ES220	Navarra	543,222	546,612	549,989	554,197	562,489	572,466	579,781	587,922	596,637
ES230	La Rioja	272,050	273,166	274,506	276,170	281,292	287,655	294,336	300,594	304,870
ES241	Huesca	207,096	206,680	206,499	206,499	207,913	210,612	212,762	215,898	218,400
ES242	Teruel	138,422	137,502	136,713	136,057	136,477	137,951	138,799	140,326	142,233
ES243	Zaragoza	853,698	855,335	857,553	860,624	873,168	882,808	892,938	907,595	922,327
ES300	Madrid	5,262,869	5,305,592	5,353,391	5,404,959	5,561,622	5,708,433	5,807,962	5,912,335	6,003,925
ES411	Ávila	167,395	166,156	164,971	163,836	163,147	163,985	165,063	166,851	168,930
ES412	Burgos	350,204	349,603	349,241	348,959	350,781	353,260	355,750	359,136	362,515
ES413	León	501,598	497,658	493,614	490,029	487,048	487,341	487,110	487,687	489,753
ES414	Palencia	178,193	176,914	175,699	174,480	173,402	172,973	172,592	172,155	172,400
ES415	Salamanca	349,950	348,402	347,045	345,887	345,222	345,685	345,839	346,204	346,862
ES416	Segovia	147,745	147,616	147,586	147,663	148,532	150,668	152,661	155,288	157,369
ES417	Soria	91,902	91,434	91,096	90,788	90,628	91,506	91,905	92,441	92,931
ES418	Valladolid	497,108	497,164	497,442	497,850	501,549	504,673	507,845	511,669	516,000
ES419	Zamora	204,233	202,542	200,991	199,547	197,733	197,338	196,508	196,102	195,839
	ESP	**40,080,079**	**40,234,615**	**40,418,177**	**40,628,543**	**41,287,208**	**42,060,103**	**42,722,946**	**43,524,070**	**44,219,305**

(*continued*)

Table A6 (continued)

Code	Province	2007	2008	2009	2010	2011	2012	2013	2014	2015
ES111	A Coruña	1,124,796	1,131,381	1,136,243	1,138,880	1,139,993	1,139,565	1,135,455	1,130,242	1,125,530
ES112	Lugo	352,358	352,170	351,628	349,925	348,524	346,057	343,053	340,108	337,169
ES113	Ourense	332,897	332,235	331,710	330,526	329,000	326,404	323,276	320,191	316,284
ES114	Pontevedra	937,033	944,201	949,561	952,419	954,133	953,721	951,446	948,790	946,108
ES120	Asturias	1,068,046	1,074,019	1,076,430	1,076,165	1,075,114	1,070,686	1,062,935	1,054,060	1,044,043
ES130	Cantabria	572,557	581,160	586,778	589,603	591,564	591,083	588,538	586,240	583,549
ES211	Araba/Álava	308,653	313,154	316,720	318,688	320,546	319,786	319,774	320,297	321,077
ES212	Gipuzkoa	696,153	701,694	704,971	706,424	707,572	708,042	707,030	707,019	707,153
ES213	Bizkaia	1,146,329	1,151,951	1,155,322	1,155,975	1,155,897	1,152,156	1,144,096	1,138,018	1,134,756
ES220	Navarra	609,776	621,976	630,109	634,983	638,581	639,374	637,020	636,003	636,253
ES230	La Rioja	312,369	318,448	319,786	319,888	321,050	320,081	316,825	314,079	312,834
ES241	Huesca	221,964	225,969	226,693	226,740	226,090	225,077	223,872	222,697	221,168
ES242	Teruel	144,754	146,142	145,630	144,466	143,538	141,852	140,303	138,538	136,698
ES243	Zaragoza	942,666	964,272	972,160	972,628	974,838	973,800	970,328	967,100	963,867
ES300	Madrid	6,152,759	6,283,747	6,354,091	6,384,358	6,409,093	6,426,229	6,392,713	6,376,749	6,401,162
ES411	Ávila	172,001	173,564	173,606	172,984	172,006	170,196	168,237	166,368	164,505
ES412	Burgos	369,175	374,053	374,302	373,338	372,676	370,367	366,989	363,756	361,129
ES413	León	492,335	494,547	494,840	494,201	493,434	490,667	486,764	481,955	477,199
ES414	Palencia	172,739	172,703	172,358	171,543	170,819	169,491	167,880	166,524	164,868
ES415	Salamanca	348,602	350,463	350,954	350,888	350,206	348,349	345,721	343,071	339,982
ES416	Segovia	161,374	163,407	163,030	163,297	163,250	161,988	160,204	158,472	157,120
ES417	Soria	93,855	94,714	94,705	94,886	94,674	94,019	93,017	92,139	91,165
ES418	Valladolid	522,298	527,430	529,614	531,184	532,280	531,821	529,885	527,800	525,831
ES419	Zamora	195,993	195,524	194,160	193,066	192,019	190,074	187,622	185,252	182,617
	ESP	**45,091,361**	**45,835,180**	**46,215,255**	**46,404,437**	**46,573,176**	**46,599,556**	**46,425,091**	**46,286,424**	**46,240,988**

(*continued*)

Table A6 (continued)

Code	Province	1860	1870	1880	1890	1900	1910	1920	1930
ES421	Albacete	206,099	212,579	219,058	229,105	237,877	264,698	291,833	332,619
ES422	Ciudad Real	247,991	254,175	260,358	292,291	321,580	379,674	427,365	491,657
ES423	Cuenca	229,514	232,884	236,253	242,462	249,696	269,634	281,628	309,526
ES424	Guadalajara	204,626	202,957	201,288	201,518	200,186	209,352	201,444	203,998
ES425	Toledo	323,782	329,410	335,038	359,562	376,814	413,217	442,933	489,396
ES431	Badajoz	403,735	418,272	432,809	481,508	520,246	593,206	644,625	702,418
ES432	Cáceres	293,672	300,133	306,594	339,793	362,164	397,785	410,032	449,756
ES511	Barcelona	726,267	781,577	836,887	902,970	1,054,541	1,141,733	1,349,282	1,800,638
ES512	Girona	311,158	305,430	299,702	306,583	299,287	319,679	325,619	325,551
ES513	Lleida	314,531	299,935	285,339	285,417	274,590	284,971	314,670	314,435
ES514	Tarragona	321,886	325,996	330,105	348,579	337,964	338,485	355,148	350,668
ES521	Alicante/Alacant	390,565	401,065	411,565	433,050	470,149	497,616	512,186	545,838
ES522	Castellón/Castelló	267,134	275,558	283,981	292,437	310,828	322,213	306,886	308,746
ES523	Valencia/València	618,032	648,539	679,046	733,978	806,556	884,298	926,442	1,042,154
ES530	Balears, Illes	269,818	279,427	289,035	312,593	311,649	326,023	338,894	365,512
ES611	Almería	315,450	332,263	349,076	339,452	359,013	380,388	358,149	341,550
ES612	Cádiz	401,700	415,453	429,206	429,872	439,390	446,185	512,608	507,972
ES613	Córdoba	358,657	372,070	385,482	420,728	455,859	498,782	565,262	668,862
ES614	Granada	444,523	461,795	479,066	484,638	492,460	522,605	573,682	643,705
ES615	Huelva	176,626	193,537	210,447	254,831	260,880	309,888	330,402	354,963
ES616	Jaén	362,466	392,746	423,025	437,842	474,490	526,718	592,297	674,415
ES617	Málaga	446,659	473,491	500,322	519,377	511,989	523,412	554,301	613,160
ES618	Sevilla	473,920	490,366	506,812	544,815	555,256	597,031	703,747	805,252
ES620	Murcia	382,812	417,237	451,661	491,436	577,987	615,105	638,639	645,449
ES700	Canarias, Islas	237,036	259,005	280,974	291,625	358,564	444,016	457,663	555,128
	ESP	**15,658,586**	**16,145,253**	**16,631,919**	**17,560,352**	**18,594,405**	**19,927,150**	**21,303,162**	**23,563,867**

(*continued*)

Table A6 (continued)

Code	Province	1935	1940	1945	1950	1955	1957	1959	1961
ES421	Albacete	349,864	367,457	380,627	398,313	385,720	380,563	375,563	371,210
ES422	Ciudad Real	500,686	520,946	541,280	569,133	575,468	578,949	582,591	579,837
ES423	Cuenca	321,413	330,368	334,618	341,957	326,938	322,935	319,061	315,040
ES424	Guadalajara	208,417	205,026	205,904	207,393	194,449	190,547	186,769	182,740
ES425	Toledo	483,902	475,238	499,818	530,434	525,650	524,562	523,598	523,097
ES431	Badajoz	711,004	723,615	763,505	812,768	825,367	829,221	833,290	829,939
ES432	Cáceres	467,732	489,559	514,128	544,948	547,814	546,961	546,242	543,790
ES511	Barcelona	1,796,686	1,875,918	2,026,226	2,202,529	2,506,420	2,637,495	2,776,100	2,917,715
ES512	Girona	330,115	314,734	315,844	320,426	338,455	343,339	348,378	355,249
ES513	Lleida	308,282	299,311	308,605	321,508	328,900	330,896	332,986	334,990
ES514	Tarragona	342,303	335,733	343,238	354,711	359,994	361,223	362,548	366,863
ES521	Alicante/Alacant	569,572	589,170	606,422	630,802	669,029	684,812	701,139	725,230
ES522	Castellón/Castelló	313,000	310,545	317,581	328,264	331,891	334,778	338,350	344,732
ES523	Valencia/València	1,133,787	1,230,165	1,275,614	1,336,253	1,386,263	1,402,903	1,420,089	1,449,831
ES530	Balears, Illes	385,697	398,570	405,549	417,096	432,185	436,512	440,993	449,364
ES611	Almería	359,894	362,159	359,198	359,586	359,471	360,201	361,021	364,205
ES612	Cádiz	547,594	571,981	623,966	689,084	752,577	776,580	800,699	815,639
ES613	Córdoba	685,345	737,731	757,004	785,473	790,524	793,954	797,597	795,211
ES614	Granada	700,278	724,296	751,943	788,551	778,028	775,434	773,033	770,122
ES615	Huelva	358,244	363,592	364,849	367,491	382,640	389,117	395,801	401,468
ES616	Jaén	710,099	737,346	754,067	776,514	753,531	747,783	742,259	736,570
ES617	Málaga	648,511	666,936	704,846	751,520	762,464	767,604	772,966	783,273
ES618	Sevilla	849,330	927,791	1,008,419	1,094,947	1,160,008	1,187,381	1,215,698	1,242,877
ES620	Murcia	678,339	708,635	725,775	751,289	777,301	786,201	795,402	803,119
ES700	Canarias, Islas	618,123	666,688	729,572	802,899	859,386	890,018	921,971	957,677
	ESP	**24,621,927**	**25,439,948**	**26,497,400**	**27,869,913**	**29,055,546**	**29,556,117**	**30,092,316**	**30,669,819**

(*continued*)

Table A6 (continued)

Code	Province	1963	1965	1967	1969	1971	1973	1975	1977	1979
ES421	Albacete	365,641	359,456	353,689	346,738	339,407	335,231	331,421	329,862	332,009
ES422	Ciudad Real	568,274	553,907	540,374	525,235	509,084	495,979	483,671	475,839	475,903
ES423	Cuenca	308,663	291,549	277,256	262,692	248,461	236,944	226,168	218,674	217,144
ES424	Guadalajara	177,779	170,616	163,269	155,666	148,641	144,484	140,576	138,742	140,204
ES425	Toledo	517,443	507,442	498,066	487,064	475,958	470,372	465,281	464,038	469,400
ES431	Badajoz	808,565	779,958	753,014	724,329	695,084	671,294	652,041	643,640	643,914
ES432	Cáceres	532,127	515,033	498,927	481,542	463,215	447,140	432,028	424,283	422,884
ES511	Barcelona	3,075,614	3,282,428	3,511,205	3,742,112	3,953,320	4,123,511	4,305,065	4,488,504	4,575,343
ES512	Girona	365,320	377,981	391,424	403,850	414,515	424,548	435,231	446,734	457,898
ES513	Lleida	337,093	340,340	343,913	346,244	346,651	345,869	345,410	347,040	350,092
ES514	Tarragona	379,127	393,533	408,841	423,181	436,902	453,680	471,549	490,382	503,847
ES521	Alicante/Alacant	763,223	804,108	847,918	890,827	932,670	979,537	1,029,727	1,081,880	1,119,571
ES522	Castellón/Castelló	352,538	361,939	371,911	380,754	388,155	396,014	404,411	413,843	423,811
ES523	Valencia/València	1,512,063	1,579,626	1,651,633	1,720,574	1,782,436	1,840,697	1,902,655	1,968,927	2,024,248
ES530	Balears, Illes	462,185	480,934	500,878	519,731	538,190	561,384	586,128	611,901	635,815
ES611	Almería	370,320	373,319	375,978	378,219	379,468	380,979	385,597	393,542	404,637
ES612	Cádiz	827,304	842,177	858,066	871,033	882,687	901,868	922,329	946,598	969,146
ES613	Córdoba	783,507	770,606	758,575	743,982	728,713	720,641	713,326	710,060	714,789
ES614	Granada	768,028	761,375	756,631	749,151	740,536	738,350	736,862	741,056	751,575
ES615	Huelva	403,566	404,239	405,267	404,804	402,675	401,037	399,773	402,245	412,890
ES616	Jaén	725,218	710,820	697,306	681,539	665,370	656,162	647,694	640,922	637,259
ES617	Málaga	797,744	813,711	830,718	844,959	858,149	879,373	901,968	925,155	955,833
ES618	Sevilla	1,264,552	1,285,678	1,308,288	1,326,401	1,338,521	1,350,188	1,363,236	1,384,029	1,427,849
ES620	Murcia	808,880	816,445	824,795	830,348	838,083	852,486	869,220	890,213	915,648
ES700	Canarias, Islas	996,996	1,033,437	1,070,735	1,111,688	1,156,743	1,210,570	1,274,498	1,338,781	1,363,160
	ESP	**31,295,729**	**31,945,892**	**32,721,681**	**33,442,415**	**34,067,752**	**34,693,684**	**35,405,480**	**36,252,926**	**36,985,032**

(*continued*)

Table A6 (continued)

Code	Province	1980	1981	1982	1983	1984	1985	1986	1987	1988
ES421	Albacete	340,034	339,788	340,862	341,581	342,288	342,667	342,584	342,855	342,966
ES422	Ciudad Real	478,109	475,547	476,552	476,852	477,434	477,640	477,536	477,419	477,258
ES423	Cuenca	218,446	215,746	215,030	214,015	213,007	211,871	210,573	209,492	208,411
ES424	Guadalajara	143,444	143,736	144,316	144,741	145,049	145,160	145,255	145,512	145,633
ES425	Toledo	475,059	475,747	478,367	480,214	482,087	483,681	484,757	486,149	487,277
ES431	Badajoz	647,537	644,119	646,455	647,582	648,949	649,771	650,181	651,057	651,384
ES432	Cáceres	424,529	421,490	421,477	420,977	420,423	419,602	418,416	417,563	416,355
ES511	Barcelona	4,586,036	4,628,087	4,641,629	4,649,628	4,655,852	4,664,425	4,668,652	4,671,609	4,671,284
ES512	Girona	463,969	468,715	473,740	478,328	482,666	486,893	490,971	495,272	499,260
ES513	Lleida	353,098	353,595	354,659	355,058	355,350	355,467	355,228	354,980	354,753
ES514	Tarragona	508,065	514,521	518,970	522,456	525,780	528,814	531,497	534,302	536,748
ES521	Alicante/Alacant	1,134,657	1,155,038	1,171,906	1,186,993	1,202,428	1,217,274	1,230,961	1,245,203	1,258,764
ES522	Castellón/Castelló	428,907	432,899	435,623	437,527	439,492	440,999	442,182	443,646	444,752
ES523	Valencia/València	2,049,593	2,070,395	2,082,208	2,090,184	2,098,116	2,104,833	2,108,907	2,113,011	2,115,079
ES530	Balears, Illes	648,208	658,350	665,347	670,989	676,773	682,576	687,649	693,001	698,140
ES611	Almería	408,370	412,418	417,674	422,535	427,586	432,202	436,269	440,674	444,899
ES612	Cádiz	982,103	992,477	1,005,168	1,016,347	1,027,501	1,037,299	1,045,748	1,054,285	1,061,906
ES613	Córdoba	722,361	722,431	727,271	731,274	735,777	739,121	742,193	745,132	748,186
ES614	Granada	758,357	760,459	765,156	769,393	773,390	777,097	780,014	783,185	785,786
ES615	Huelva	417,540	419,620	423,299	426,216	429,138	431,668	434,023	436,370	438,501
ES616	Jaén	641,186	640,252	641,404	641,442	642,292	642,196	641,851	641,635	640,586
ES617	Málaga	1,013,578	1,030,841	1,045,940	1,060,364	1,074,778	1,088,590	1,101,640	1,114,774	1,127,316
ES618	Sevilla	1,470,791	1,484,481	1,503,131	1,520,111	1,536,983	1,551,753	1,565,092	1,578,629	1,591,197
ES620	Murcia	948,490	959,392	971,262	981,301	991,269	1,000,734	1,008,975	1,017,587	1,026,052
ES700	Canarias, Islas	1,352,836	1,373,114	1,389,725	1,404,314	1,418,604	1,431,157	1,443,289	1,455,615	1,466,637
	ESP	**37,374,193**	**37,645,490**	**37,867,578**	**38,040,314**	**38,204,653**	**38,345,912**	**38,450,217**	**38,560,011**	**38,641,293**

(*continued*)

Table A6 (continued)

Code	Province	1989	1990	1991	1992	1993	1994	1995	1996	1997
ES421	Albacete	342,664	342,707	343,499	345,766	348,029	350,129	352,267	354,478	356,430
ES422	Ciudad Real	476,729	476,135	475,844	476,800	477,805	478,577	479,155	479,355	479,603
ES423	Cuenca	207,175	205,998	205,167	204,969	204,743	204,206	203,712	203,148	202,570
ES424	Guadalajara	145,693	145,663	146,425	149,018	151,628	154,140	156,783	159,388	162,089
ES425	Toledo	488,357	489,172	491,263	496,219	501,188	506,144	510,938	515,406	520,046
ES431	Badajoz	651,168	650,872	650,742	652,078	653,285	654,335	654,826	655,076	655,128
ES432	Cáceres	414,767	412,901	411,454	411,177	411,055	410,507	409,989	409,150	408,154
ES511	Barcelona	4,667,221	4,660,584	4,659,345	4,673,567	4,688,382	4,702,145	4,713,494	4,725,752	4,737,907
ES512	Girona	503,128	507,091	511,363	516,825	522,129	527,376	532,169	537,270	542,280
ES513	Lleida	354,359	353,871	353,780	354,716	355,748	356,667	357,111	357,766	358,357
ES514	Tarragona	538,823	540,726	544,084	550,363	556,685	562,958	568,859	574,861	581,101
ES521	Alicante/Alacant	1,271,823	1,284,221	1,298,069	1,314,456	1,330,756	1,346,501	1,361,545	1,376,836	1,391,756
ES522	Castellón/Castelló	445,613	446,378	447,896	451,194	454,766	458,203	461,577	464,940	468,265
ES523	Valencia/València	2,116,496	2,117,713	2,121,003	2,131,086	2,141,371	2,150,920	2,158,986	2,167,443	2,175,388
ES530	Balears, Illes	702,948	706,936	713,222	725,837	738,113	750,043	761,886	773,625	785,792
ES611	Almería	448,767	452,697	457,967	465,796	473,618	481,280	488,675	495,810	503,224
ES612	Cádiz	1,068,837	1,074,837	1,080,054	1,085,533	1,090,580	1,095,025	1,098,282	1,101,064	1,103,597
ES613	Córdoba	750,451	752,687	755,011	757,038	758,980	760,466	760,975	761,390	761,585
ES614	Granada	787,834	789,782	791,942	796,158	799,972	803,438	806,482	809,346	811,768
ES615	Huelva	440,260	442,255	444,181	446,110	448,207	450,061	452,016	453,539	455,099
ES616	Jaén	639,575	638,442	638,116	639,907	641,717	643,079	644,008	644,411	644,497
ES617	Málaga	1,139,867	1,152,062	1,164,734	1,177,234	1,189,681	1,201,316	1,212,618	1,223,635	1,234,931
ES618	Sevilla	1,602,111	1,612,717	1,623,710	1,635,655	1,647,752	1,659,153	1,669,252	1,678,312	1,687,353
ES620	Murcia	1,033,680	1,040,942	1,050,349	1,065,143	1,079,829	1,093,793	1,107,265	1,120,946	1,134,831
ES700	Canarias, Islas	1,477,658	1,487,752	1,500,257	1,520,080	1,539,581	1,558,302	1,576,858	1,594,987	1,613,099
	ESP	**38,697,836**	**38,736,880**	**38,816,987**	**39,021,874**	**39,228,429**	**39,418,255**	**39,588,530**	**39,752,594**	**39,917,169**

(*continued*)

Table A6 (continued)

Code	Province	1998	1999	2000	2001	2002	2003	2004	2005	2006
ES421	Albacete	358,367	360,112	362,061	363,991	367,705	372,603	376,565	381,393	386,095
ES422	Ciudad Real	479,406	479,045	478,946	478,894	480,811	485,588	489,893	497,390	504,642
ES423	Cuenca	201,982	201,370	200,889	200,443	199,963	202,176	203,767	206,954	209,173
ES424	Guadalajara	164,858	167,630	170,714	173,913	179,318	188,305	197,513	207,742	218,689
ES425	Toledo	524,692	529,236	534,127	539,385	550,027	566,285	582,000	601,673	622,625
ES431	Badajoz	655,046	654,522	654,430	654,535	655,059	657,837	661,210	666,168	671,310
ES432	Cáceres	406,978	405,675	404,767	403,828	402,970	404,565	405,024	405,811	406,611
ES511	Barcelona	4,750,903	4,762,884	4,778,785	4,798,670	4,898,335	5,009,660	5,092,519	5,184,895	5,256,368
ES512	Girona	547,385	552,337	557,754	563,375	580,754	605,706	630,320	658,351	681,316
ES513	Lleida	358,912	359,503	360,469	361,694	366,801	375,485	385,986	397,386	405,636
ES514	Tarragona	587,334	593,553	600,166	607,187	624,226	648,223	673,438	703,579	733,363
ES521	Alicante/Alacant	1,406,687	1,422,036	1,438,269	1,455,665	1,509,716	1,572,441	1,628,965	1,688,959	1,739,193
ES522	Castellón/Castelló	471,599	475,026	478,851	482,991	495,222	510,703	524,209	540,413	556,560
ES523	Valencia/València	2,183,309	2,191,089	2,200,917	2,212,099	2,249,383	2,298,499	2,342,930	2,395,970	2,440,925
ES530	Balears, Illes	798,319	810,526	823,401	836,907	866,087	898,642	923,983	954,612	987,203
ES611	Almería	510,592	517,927	525,752	533,823	552,637	569,447	584,675	617,802	635,564
ES612	Cádiz	1,106,100	1,108,096	1,111,079	1,114,743	1,123,919	1,136,892	1,151,630	1,168,216	1,184,864
ES613	Córdoba	761,298	760,829	761,055	761,283	763,836	768,345	772,341	778,282	783,072
ES614	Granada	813,868	815,325	817,615	820,414	825,659	837,106	847,991	864,205	877,466
ES615	Huelva	456,487	457,782	459,631	461,639	466,179	470,963	475,743	485,191	491,972
ES616	Jaén	644,474	643,999	643,917	643,780	645,254	648,376	651,269	655,081	657,787
ES617	Málaga	1,246,030	1,257,011	1,269,409	1,282,342	1,320,200	1,356,474	1,391,992	1,438,401	1,473,511
ES618	Sevilla	1,696,295	1,703,858	1,713,323	1,723,473	1,739,484	1,756,557	1,773,343	1,796,244	1,819,650
ES620	Murcia	1,148,455	1,161,774	1,176,135	1,191,814	1,224,366	1,260,716	1,291,948	1,335,288	1,367,430
ES700	Canarias, Islas	1,631,004	1,648,961	1,667,449	1,687,310	1,730,673	1,779,468	1,826,843	1,876,368	1,921,847
	ESP	**40,080,079**	**40,234,615**	**40,418,177**	**40,628,543**	**41,287,208**	**42,060,103**	**42,722,946**	**43,524,070**	**44,219,305**

(*continued*)

Table A6 (continued)

Code	Province	2007	2008	2009	2010	2011	2012	2013	2014	2015
ES421	Albacete	392,025	396,292	398,645	399,967	401,254	400,430	397,719	395,668	393,664
ES422	Ciudad Real	514,761	521,681	524,750	525,418	526,269	524,145	520,292	515,973	510,953
ES423	Cuenca	213,153	215,493	216,447	216,227	215,635	213,091	209,977	207,465	205,033
ES424	Guadalajara	231,949	241,834	248,252	252,384	256,349	257,422	255,890	254,649	254,061
ES425	Toledo	651,376	675,223	687,760	696,570	703,809	704,317	699,709	693,826	690,326
ES431	Badajoz	677,227	682,212	686,009	688,606	690,921	690,900	689,415	687,298	683,822
ES432	Cáceres	408,536	409,296	411,117	411,835	412,593	411,118	408,834	406,509	403,803
ES511	Barcelona	5,342,369	5,431,864	5,478,819	5,497,519	5,511,857	5,504,057	5,465,193	5,433,744	5,434,340
ES512	Girona	707,568	729,156	739,368	744,267	749,496	750,313	746,079	741,072	740,425
ES513	Lleida	417,241	427,956	432,727	434,853	437,306	437,075	433,779	431,200	429,600
ES514	Tarragona	765,170	788,132	796,357	800,618	805,365	804,923	798,524	793,585	791,753
ES521	Alicante/Alacant	1,793,377	1,828,487	1,837,673	1,840,159	1,847,587	1,853,643	1,850,390	1,848,498	1,839,975
ES522	Castellón/Castelló	578,042	592,164	595,415	595,086	594,524	589,792	581,478	575,440	572,229
ES523	Valencia/València	2,496,258	2,538,914	2,551,310	2,553,676	2,560,010	2,555,904	2,535,151	2,523,408	2,519,077
ES530	Balears, Illes	1,025,216	1,057,440	1,078,053	1,087,640	1,095,456	1,104,322	1,112,736	1,120,470	1,129,743
ES611	Almería	649,622	666,284	676,797	683,783	687,413	690,026	689,966	689,390	693,634
ES612	Cádiz	1,201,290	1,215,173	1,225,259	1,234,074	1,242,290	1,245,778	1,247,150	1,247,710	1,247,823
ES613	Córdoba	789,302	794,995	798,522	800,839	802,112	801,413	799,002	796,660	793,543
ES614	Granada	892,646	905,039	912,113	917,503	920,886	922,125	920,898	919,248	917,814
ES615	Huelva	501,430	507,530	512,921	516,786	519,166	520,209	521,275	521,617	521,738
ES616	Jaén	661,708	664,211	665,713	666,554	667,614	664,448	658,482	653,886	648,938
ES617	Málaga	1,510,399	1,543,169	1,559,580	1,572,991	1,588,036	1,604,584	1,613,953	1,624,647	1,635,082
ES618	Sevilla	1,846,364	1,872,245	1,893,602	1,910,388	1,925,234	1,934,552	1,936,538	1,937,694	1,939,763
ES620	Murcia	1,404,885	1,431,501	1,448,479	1,456,521	1,461,107	1,461,256	1,461,214	1,462,881	1,464,014
ES700	Canarias, Islas	1,967,966	2,009,965	2,034,165	2,053,116	2,073,985	2,092,826	2,108,462	2,118,423	2,127,770
	ESP	**45,091,361**	**45,835,180**	**46,215,255**	**46,404,437**	**46,573,176**	**46,599,556**	**46,425,091**	**46,286,424**	**46,240,988**

Table A7 Population, NUTS2

Code	NUTS2	1860	1870	1880	1890	1900	1910	1920	1930
ES11	Galicia	1,799,224	1,823,626	1,848,027	1,894,558	1,980,515	2,063,589	2,124,244	2,230,281
ES12	Asturias	540,586	558,469	576,352	595,420	627,069	685,131	743,726	791,855
ES13	Cantabria	219,966	227,633	235,299	244,274	276,003	302,956	327,669	364,147
ES21	Basque Country	429,186	439,943	450,699	510,419	603,596	673,788	766,775	891,710
ES22	Navarre	299,654	301,919	304,184	304,122	307,669	312,235	329,875	345,883
ES23	La Rioja	175,111	174,768	174,425	181,465	189,376	188,235	192,940	203,789
ES24	Aragón	891,057	893,024	894,991	912,197	912,711	952,743	997,154	1,031,559
ES30	Madrid	489,332	541,763	594,194	682,644	775,034	878,641	1,067,637	1,383,951
ES41	Castile-Leon	2,085,811	2,108,215	2,130,619	2,258,791	2,302,417	2,363,118	2,337,405	2,477,324
ES42	Castile-La Mancha	1,212,012	1,232,004	1,251,995	1,324,938	1,386,153	1,536,575	1,645,203	1,827,196
ES43	Extremadura	697,407	718,405	739,403	821,301	882,410	990,991	1,054,657	1,152,174
ES51	Catalonia	1,673,842	1,712,938	1,752,033	1,843,549	1,966,382	2,084,868	2,344,719	2,791,292
ES52	Valencia	1,275,731	1,325,162	1,374,592	1,459,465	1,587,533	1,704,127	1,745,514	1,896,738
ES53	Balearic Islands	269,818	279,427	289,035	312,593	311,649	326,023	338,894	365,512
ES61	Andalusia	2,980,001	3,131,719	3,283,436	3,431,555	3,549,337	3,805,009	4,190,448	4,609,879
ES62	Murcia	382,812	417,237	451,661	491,436	577,987	615,105	638,639	645,449
ES70	Canary Islands	237,036	259,005	280,974	291,625	358,564	444,016	457,663	555,128
	ESP	**15,658,586**	**16,145,253**	**16,631,919**	**17,560,352**	**18,594,405**	**19,927,150**	**21,303,162**	**23,563,867**

(*continued*)

Table A7 (continued)

Code	NUTS2	1935	1940	1945	1950	1955	1957	1959	1961
ES11	Galicia	2,503,151	2,557,058	2,606,299	2,685,499	2,607,202	2,607,379	2,613,075	2,632,528
ES12	Asturias	835,532	842,632	861,435	890,398	933,779	954,293	975,492	994,706
ES13	Cantabria	379,246	390,368	393,601	402,974	417,591	423,122	428,830	434,278
ES21	Basque Country	897,864	918,811	970,247	1,033,192	1,192,772	1,255,779	1,322,208	1,389,560
ES22	Navarre	351,607	353,740	365,220	381,041	392,022	395,917	400,254	408,289
ES23	La Rioja	211,972	218,086	222,644	229,616	230,174	230,219	230,322	230,709
ES24	Aragón	1,048,289	1,034,684	1,049,671	1,083,763	1,100,393	1,102,896	1,105,832	1,105,867
ES30	Madrid	1,404,565	1,525,532	1,659,293	1,812,407	2,210,435	2,348,555	2,495,903	2,661,504
ES41	Castile-Leon	2,611,484	2,665,527	2,750,392	2,867,134	2,860,705	2,857,988	2,856,256	2,852,590
ES42	Castile-La Mancha	1,864,282	1,899,035	1,962,247	2,047,230	2,008,225	1,997,556	1,987,582	1,971,924
ES43	Extremadura	1,178,736	1,213,174	1,277,633	1,357,716	1,373,181	1,376,182	1,379,532	1,373,729
ES51	Catalonia	2,777,386	2,825,696	2,993,913	3,199,174	3,533,769	3,672,953	3,820,012	3,974,817
ES52	Valencia	2,016,359	2,129,880	2,199,617	2,295,319	2,387,183	2,422,493	2,459,578	2,519,793
ES53	Balearic Islands	385,697	398,570	405,549	417,096	432,185	436,512	440,993	449,364
ES61	Andalusia	4,859,295	5,091,832	5,324,292	5,613,166	5,739,243	5,798,054	5,859,074	5,909,365
ES62	Murcia	678,339	708,635	725,775	751,289	777,301	786,201	795,402	803,119
ES70	Canary Islands	618,123	666,688	729,572	802,899	859,386	890,018	921,971	957,677
	ESP	**24,621,927**	**25,439,948**	**26,497,400**	**27,869,913**	**29,055,546**	**29,556,117**	**30,092,316**	**30,669,819**

(*continued*)

Table A7 (continued)

Code	NUTS2	1963	1965	1967	1969	1971	1973	1975	1977	1979
ES11	Galicia	2,672,877	2,701,715	2,702,957	2,691,447	2,678,768	2,697,582	2,719,785	2,749,870	2,783,691
ES12	Asturias	1,007,034	1,020,660	1,035,365	1,046,416	1,055,158	1,071,116	1,088,345	1,106,243	1,119,494
ES13	Cantabria	440,360	448,638	457,470	464,756	470,422	477,345	484,825	493,775	503,921
ES21	Basque Country	1,469,240	1,568,326	1,676,480	1,785,602	1,883,590	1,956,341	2,033,187	2,112,524	2,171,842
ES22	Navarre	420,318	432,958	446,366	458,493	467,786	473,999	480,751	488,699	497,946
ES23	La Rioja	231,649	232,853	234,268	235,469	236,379	237,376	239,152	241,887	246,659
ES24	Aragón	1,107,529	1,119,848	1,134,517	1,146,342	1,152,111	1,152,165	1,153,888	1,163,694	1,179,535
ES30	Madrid	2,837,865	3,012,915	3,276,838	3,550,768	3,807,192	4,009,312	4,226,215	4,446,565	4,588,437
ES41	Castile-Leon	2,837,087	2,797,322	2,758,743	2,710,459	2,652,712	2,600,110	2,553,467	2,532,779	2,548,638
ES42	Castile-La Mancha	1,937,800	1,882,970	1,832,654	1,777,395	1,721,551	1,683,010	1,647,117	1,627,155	1,634,660
ES43	Extremadura	1,340,692	1,294,991	1,251,941	1,205,871	1,158,299	1,118,434	1,084,069	1,067,923	1,066,798
ES51	Catalonia	4,157,154	4,394,282	4,655,383	4,915,387	5,151,388	5,347,608	5,557,255	5,772,660	5,887,180
ES52	Valencia	2,627,824	2,745,673	2,871,462	2,992,155	3,103,261	3,216,248	3,336,793	3,464,650	3,567,630
ES53	Balearic Islands	462,185	480,934	500,878	519,731	538,190	561,384	586,128	611,901	635,815
ES61	Andalusia	5,940,239	5,961,925	5,990,829	6,000,088	5,996,119	6,028,598	6,070,785	6,143,607	6,273,978
ES62	Murcia	808,880	816,445	824,795	830,348	838,083	852,486	869,220	890,213	915,648
ES70	Canary Islands	996,996	1,033,437	1,070,735	1,111,688	1,156,743	1,210,570	1,274,498	1,338,781	1,363,160
	ESP	**31,295,729**	**31,945,892**	**32,721,681**	**33,442,415**	**34,067,752**	**34,693,684**	**35,405,480**	**36,252,926**	**36,985,032**

(*continued*)

Table A7 (continued)

Code	NUTS2	1980	1981	1982	1983	1984	1985	1986	1987	1988
ES11	Galicia	2,803,363	2,812,775	2,813,223	2,810,051	2,806,318	2,800,320	2,790,188	2,781,544	2,770,449
ES12	Asturias	1,126,215	1,130,074	1,130,287	1,129,056	1,127,303	1,124,759	1,121,039	1,117,341	1,112,177
ES13	Cantabria	510,845	514,403	517,855	520,506	522,630	524,258	525,376	526,694	527,324
ES21	Basque Country	2,130,947	2,144,071	2,147,649	2,148,690	2,147,741	2,145,710	2,141,076	2,136,218	2,129,410
ES22	Navarre	507,577	510,055	512,474	514,094	515,687	516,776	517,714	518,378	519,020
ES23	La Rioja	253,246	254,915	256,390	257,797	259,096	260,117	260,790	261,610	262,154
ES24	Aragón	1,195,742	1,198,189	1,200,955	1,201,768	1,202,082	1,201,839	1,200,083	1,199,152	1,197,298
ES30	Madrid	4,639,535	4,702,568	4,742,375	4,777,938	4,810,764	4,840,565	4,865,724	4,890,911	4,911,899
ES41	Castile-Leon	2,591,420	2,585,184	2,589,200	2,589,992	2,590,021	2,588,079	2,583,784	2,579,204	2,572,432
ES42	Castile-La Mancha	1,655,092	1,650,564	1,655,126	1,657,403	1,659,864	1,661,018	1,660,706	1,661,427	1,661,545
ES43	Extremadura	1,072,065	1,065,609	1,067,932	1,068,559	1,069,372	1,069,373	1,068,597	1,068,620	1,067,739
ES51	Catalonia	5,911,167	5,964,918	5,988,997	6,005,470	6,019,649	6,035,598	6,046,348	6,056,162	6,062,045
ES52	Valencia	3,613,158	3,658,332	3,689,737	3,714,703	3,740,036	3,763,106	3,782,051	3,801,859	3,818,595
ES53	Balearic Islands	648,208	658,350	665,347	670,989	676,773	682,576	687,649	693,001	698,140
ES61	Andalusia	6,414,287	6,462,979	6,529,044	6,587,683	6,647,444	6,699,927	6,746,829	6,794,686	6,838,377
ES62	Murcia	948,490	959,392	971,262	981,301	991,269	1,000,734	1,008,975	1,017,587	1,026,052
ES70	Canary Islands	1,352,836	1,373,114	1,389,725	1,404,314	1,418,604	1,431,157	1,443,289	1,455,615	1,466,637
	ESP	**37,374,193**	**37,645,490**	**37,867,578**	**38,040,314**	**38,204,653**	**38,345,912**	**38,450,217**	**38,560,011**	**38,641,293**

(*continued*)

Table A7 (continued)

Code	NUTS2	1989	1990	1991	1992	1993	1994	1995	1996	1997
ES11	Galicia	2,757,349	2,743,027	2,731,599	2,730,411	2,730,448	2,728,179	2,724,690	2,719,127	2,713,951
ES12	Asturias	1,105,864	1,098,965	1,093,370	1,091,602	1,089,903	1,087,150	1,084,172	1,080,841	1,077,311
ES13	Cantabria	527,551	527,515	527,770	529,022	530,068	530,940	531,336	531,731	532,231
ES21	Basque Country	2,121,363	2,111,721	2,103,777	2,102,523	2,101,049	2,099,068	2,096,352	2,093,444	2,090,649
ES22	Navarre	519,490	519,603	520,414	523,616	526,869	530,213	533,318	536,536	539,776
ES23	La Rioja	262,664	263,233	263,861	265,075	266,217	267,480	268,518	269,629	270,841
ES24	Aragón	1,194,512	1,191,407	1,189,606	1,191,760	1,193,826	1,195,742	1,196,678	1,197,662	1,198,431
ES30	Madrid	4,928,968	4,942,230	4,962,889	5,006,848	5,052,504	5,096,045	5,137,372	5,178,331	5,220,731
ES41	Castile-Leon	2,564,071	2,554,038	2,544,224	2,538,293	2,531,944	2,524,677	2,516,362	2,507,360	2,498,399
ES42	Castile-La Mancha	1,660,618	1,659,674	1,662,198	1,672,773	1,683,392	1,693,196	1,702,855	1,711,775	1,720,738
ES43	Extremadura	1,065,934	1,063,773	1,062,196	1,063,254	1,064,340	1,064,842	1,064,816	1,064,226	1,063,282
ES51	Catalonia	6,063,532	6,062,271	6,068,572	6,095,471	6,122,944	6,149,145	6,171,634	6,195,649	6,219,644
ES52	Valencia	3,833,932	3,848,312	3,866,968	3,896,736	3,926,893	3,955,624	3,982,108	4,009,219	4,035,410
ES53	Balearic Islands	702,948	706,936	713,222	725,837	738,113	750,043	761,886	773,625	785,792
ES61	Andalusia	6,877,703	6,915,480	6,955,715	7,003,430	7,050,508	7,093,817	7,132,309	7,167,506	7,202,054
ES62	Murcia	1,033,680	1,040,942	1,050,349	1,065,143	1,079,829	1,093,793	1,107,265	1,120,946	1,134,831
ES70	Canary Islands	1,477,658	1,487,752	1,500,257	1,520,080	1,539,581	1,558,302	1,576,858	1,594,987	1,613,099
	ESP	**38,697,836**	**38,736,880**	**38,816,987**	**39,021,874**	**39,228,429**	**39,418,255**	**39,588,530**	**39,752,594**	**39,917,169**

(*continued*)

Table A7 (continued)

Code	NUTS2	1998	1999	2000	2001	2002	2003	2004	2005	2006
ES11	Galicia	2,709,417	2,704,113	2,698,953	2,695,999	2,699,540	2,707,278	2,714,068	2,723,961	2,733,376
ES12	Asturias	1,073,883	1,069,742	1,066,107	1,063,676	1,062,103	1,062,196	1,062,146	1,062,559	1,063,801
ES13	Cantabria	532,691	533,044	533,568	534,572	538,550	544,887	550,972	557,962	564,188
ES21	Basque Country	2,088,022	2,085,234	2,083,300	2,082,549	2,087,427	2,097,326	2,107,811	2,121,008	2,134,080
ES22	Navarre	543,222	546,612	549,989	554,197	562,489	572,466	579,781	587,922	596,637
ES23	La Rioja	272,050	273,166	274,506	276,170	281,292	287,655	294,336	300,594	304,870
ES24	Aragón	1,199,217	1,199,517	1,200,765	1,203,180	1,217,557	1,231,371	1,244,499	1,263,819	1,282,960
ES30	Madrid	5,262,869	5,305,592	5,353,391	5,404,959	5,561,622	5,708,433	5,807,962	5,912,335	6,003,925
ES41	Castile-Leon	2,488,329	2,477,489	2,467,686	2,459,039	2,458,042	2,467,429	2,475,274	2,487,533	2,502,598
ES42	Castile-La Mancha	1,729,305	1,737,393	1,746,736	1,756,627	1,777,825	1,814,956	1,849,739	1,895,152	1,941,224
ES43	Extremadura	1,062,024	1,060,197	1,059,197	1,058,363	1,058,029	1,062,402	1,066,234	1,071,980	1,077,921
ES51	Catalonia	6,244,533	6,268,277	6,297,175	6,330,927	6,470,116	6,639,074	6,782,263	6,944,211	7,076,682
ES52	Valencia	4,061,595	4,088,151	4,118,037	4,150,755	4,254,321	4,381,643	4,496,103	4,625,341	4,736,678
ES53	Balearic Islands	798,319	810,526	823,401	836,907	866,087	898,642	923,983	954,612	987,203
ES61	Andalusia	7,235,143	7,264,827	7,301,781	7,341,497	7,437,168	7,544,160	7,648,984	7,803,425	7,923,886
ES62	Murcia	1,148,455	1,161,774	1,176,135	1,191,814	1,224,366	1,260,716	1,291,948	1,335,288	1,367,430
ES70	Canary Islands	1,631,004	1,648,961	1,667,449	1,687,310	1,730,673	1,779,468	1,826,843	1,876,368	1,921,847
	ESP	**40,080,079**	**40,234,615**	**40,418,177**	**40,628,543**	**41,287,208**	**42,060,103**	**42,722,946**	**43,524,070**	**44,219,305**

(*continued*)

Table A7 (continued)

Code	NUTS2	2007	2008	2009	2010	2011	2012	2013	2014	2015
ES11	Galicia	2,747,084	2,759,988	2,769,143	2,771,750	2,771,651	2,765,747	2,753,230	2,739,332	2,725,090
ES12	Asturias	1,068,046	1,074,019	1,076,430	1,076,165	1,075,114	1,070,686	1,062,935	1,054,060	1,044,043
ES13	Cantabria	572,557	581,160	586,778	589,603	591,564	591,083	588,538	586,240	583,549
ES21	Basque Country	2,151,135	2,166,798	2,177,013	2,181,087	2,184,016	2,179,984	2,170,900	2,165,334	2,162,986
ES22	Navarre	609,776	621,976	630,109	634,983	638,581	639,374	637,020	636,003	636,253
ES23	La Rioja	312,369	318,448	319,786	319,888	321,050	320,081	316,825	314,079	312,834
ES24	Aragón	1,309,383	1,336,383	1,344,483	1,343,835	1,344,466	1,340,730	1,334,503	1,328,334	1,321,733
ES30	Madrid	6,152,759	6,283,747	6,354,091	6,384,358	6,409,093	6,426,229	6,392,713	6,376,749	6,401,162
ES41	Castile-Leon	2,528,372	2,546,405	2,547,569	2,545,387	2,541,364	2,526,973	2,506,320	2,485,335	2,464,417
ES42	Castile-La Mancha	2,003,264	2,050,524	2,075,853	2,090,566	2,103,317	2,099,405	2,083,588	2,067,580	2,054,036
ES43	Extremadura	1,085,763	1,091,508	1,097,126	1,100,441	1,103,514	1,102,017	1,098,248	1,093,807	1,087,625
ES51	Catalonia	7,232,348	7,377,107	7,447,272	7,477,257	7,504,024	7,496,369	7,443,574	7,399,601	7,396,117
ES52	Valencia	4,867,677	4,959,565	4,984,398	4,988,922	5,002,122	4,999,339	4,967,019	4,947,346	4,931,281
ES53	Balearic Islands	1,025,216	1,057,440	1,078,053	1,087,640	1,095,456	1,104,322	1,112,736	1,120,470	1,129,743
ES61	Andalusia	8,052,762	8,168,647	8,244,507	8,302,917	8,352,752	8,383,135	8,387,264	8,390,851	8,398,336
ES62	Murcia	1,404,885	1,431,501	1,448,479	1,456,521	1,461,107	1,461,256	1,461,214	1,462,881	1,464,014
ES70	Canary Islands	1,967,966	2,009,965	2,034,165	2,053,116	2,073,985	2,092,826	2,108,462	2,118,423	2,127,770
	ESP	**45,091,361**	**45,835,180**	**46,215,255**	**46,404,437**	**46,573,176**	**46,599,556**	**46,425,091**	**46,286,424**	**46,240,988**

Table A8 Population, NUTS1

Code	NUTS1	1860	1870	1880	1890	1900	1910	1920	1930
ES1	Northwest	2,559,776	2,609,727	2,659,678	2,734,252	2,883,587	3,051,676	3,195,639	3,386,283
ES2	Northeast	1,795,008	1,809,654	1,824,299	1,908,203	2,013,352	2,127,001	2,286,744	2,472,941
ES3	Madrid	489,332	541,763	594,194	682,644	775,034	878,641	1,067,637	1,383,951
ES4	Centre	3,995,230	4,058,624	4,122,017	4,405,030	4,570,980	4,890,684	5,037,265	5,456,694
ES5	East	3,219,391	3,317,526	3,415,660	3,615,607	3,865,564	4,115,018	4,429,127	5,053,542
ES6	South	3,362,813	3,548,955	3,735,097	3,922,991	4,127,324	4,420,114	4,829,087	5,255,328
ES7	Canary I.	237,036	259,005	280,974	291,625	358,564	444,016	457,663	555,128
	ESP	**15,658,586**	**16,145,253**	**16,631,919**	**17,560,352**	**18,594,405**	**19,927,150**	**21,303,162**	**23,563,867**

Code	NUTS1	1935	1940	1945	1950	1955	1957	1959	1961
ES1	Northwest	3,717,929	3,790,058	3,861,335	3,978,871	3,958,572	3,984,794	4,017,397	4,061,512
ES2	Northeast	2,509,732	2,525,321	2,607,782	2,727,612	2,915,361	2,984,811	3,058,616	3,134,425
ES3	Madrid	1,404,565	1,525,532	1,659,293	1,812,407	2,210,435	2,348,555	2,495,903	2,661,504
ES4	Centre	5,654,502	5,777,736	5,990,272	6,272,080	6,242,111	6,231,726	6,223,370	6,198,243
ES5	East	5,179,442	5,354,146	5,599,079	5,911,589	6,353,137	6,531,958	6,720,583	6,943,974
ES6	South	5,537,634	5,800,467	6,050,067	6,364,455	6,516,544	6,584,255	6,654,476	6,712,484
ES7	Canary I.	618,123	666,688	729,572	802,899	859,386	890,018	921,971	957,677
	ESP	**24,621,927**	**25,439,948**	**26,497,400**	**27,869,913**	**29,055,546**	**29,556,117**	**30,092,316**	**30,669,819**

Code	NUTS1	1963	1965	1967	1969	1971	1973	1975	1977	1979
ES1	Northwest	4,120,271	4,171,013	4,195,792	4,202,619	4,204,348	4,246,043	4,292,955	4,349,888	4,407,106
ES2	Northeast	3,228,736	3,353,985	3,491,631	3,625,906	3,739,866	3,819,881	3,906,978	4,006,804	4,095,982
ES3	Madrid	2,837,865	3,012,915	3,276,838	3,550,768	3,807,192	4,009,312	4,226,215	4,446,565	4,588,437
ES4	Centre	6,115,579	5,975,283	5,843,338	5,693,725	5,532,562	5,401,554	5,284,653	5,227,857	5,250,096
ES5	East	7,247,163	7,620,889	8,027,723	8,427,273	8,792,839	9,125,240	9,480,176	9,849,211	10,090,625
ES6	South	6,749,119	6,778,370	6,815,624	6,830,436	6,834,202	6,881,084	6,940,005	7,033,820	7,189,626
ES7	Canary I.	996,996	1,033,437	1,070,735	1,111,688	1,156,743	1,210,570	1,274,498	1,338,781	1,363,160
	ESP	**31,295,729**	**31,945,892**	**32,721,681**	**33,442,415**	**34,067,752**	**34,693,684**	**35,405,480**	**36,252,926**	**36,985,032**

(*continued*)

Table A8 (continued)

Code	NUTS1	1980	1981	1982	1983	1984	1985	1986	1987	1988
ES1	Northwest	4,440,423	4,457,252	4,461,364	4,459,613	4,456,251	4,449,337	4,436,603	4,425,579	4,409,950
ES2	Northeast	4,087,512	4,107,230	4,117,469	4,122,349	4,124,606	4,124,443	4,119,663	4,115,358	4,107,882
ES3	Madrid	4,639,535	4,702,568	4,742,375	4,777,938	4,810,764	4,840,565	4,865,724	4,890,911	4,911,899
ES4	Centre	5,318,577	5,301,357	5,312,257	5,315,954	5,319,257	5,318,470	5,313,087	5,309,252	5,301,716
ES5	East	10,172,532	10,281,599	10,344,082	10,391,163	10,436,458	10,481,280	10,516,048	10,551,023	10,578,780
ES6	South	7,362,777	7,422,371	7,500,305	7,568,984	7,638,713	7,700,660	7,755,804	7,812,272	7,864,429
ES7	Canary I.	1,352,836	1,373,114	1,389,725	1,404,314	1,418,604	1,431,157	1,443,289	1,455,615	1,466,637
	ESP	**37,374,193**	**37,645,490**	**37,867,578**	**38,040,314**	**38,204,653**	**38,345,912**	**38,450,217**	**38,560,011**	**38,641,293**

Code	NUTS1	1989	1990	1991	1992	1993	1994	1995	1996	1997
ES1	Northwest	4,390,764	4,369,507	4,352,739	4,351,035	4,350,420	4,346,268	4,340,199	4,331,699	4,323,493
ES2	Northeast	4,098,029	4,085,965	4,077,658	4,082,974	4,087,961	4,092,502	4,094,867	4,097,271	4,099,696
ES3	Madrid	4,928,968	4,942,230	4,962,889	5,006,848	5,052,504	5,096,045	5,137,372	5,178,331	5,220,731
ES4	Centre	5,290,622	5,277,485	5,268,618	5,274,320	5,279,676	5,282,715	5,284,033	5,283,361	5,282,419
ES5	East	10,600,411	10,617,519	10,648,762	10,718,044	10,787,950	10,854,812	10,915,628	10,978,493	11,040,846
ES6	South	7,911,383	7,956,422	8,006,063	8,068,572	8,130,337	8,187,610	8,239,574	8,288,452	8,336,885
ES7	Canary I.	1,477,658	1,487,752	1,500,257	1,520,080	1,539,581	1,558,302	1,576,858	1,594,987	1,613,099
	ESP	**38,697,836**	**38,736,880**	**38,816,987**	**39,021,874**	**39,228,429**	**39,418,255**	**39,588,530**	**39,752,594**	**39,917,169**

Code	NUTS1	1998	1999	2000	2001	2002	2003	2004	2005	2006
ES1	Northwest	4,315,991	4,306,899	4,298,628	4,294,247	4,300,193	4,314,361	4,327,186	4,344,483	4,361,365
ES2	Northeast	4,102,511	4,104,529	4,108,560	4,116,096	4,148,766	4,188,818	4,226,427	4,273,343	4,318,547
ES3	Madrid	5,262,869	5,305,592	5,353,391	5,404,959	5,561,622	5,708,433	5,807,962	5,912,335	6,003,925
ES4	Centre	5,279,659	5,275,079	5,273,620	5,274,029	5,293,895	5,344,787	5,391,247	5,454,665	5,521,742
ES5	East	11,104,447	11,166,954	11,238,612	11,318,589	11,590,524	11,919,359	12,202,350	12,524,164	12,800,564
ES6	South	8,383,598	8,426,601	8,477,916	8,533,312	8,661,534	8,804,876	8,940,932	9,138,712	9,291,316
ES7	Canary I.	1,631,004	1,648,961	1,667,449	1,687,310	1,730,673	1,779,468	1,826,843	1,876,368	1,921,847
	ESP	**40,080,079**	**40,234,615**	**40,418,177**	**40,628,543**	**41,287,208**	**42,060,103**	**42,722,946**	**43,524,070**	**44,219,305**

(continued)

Table A8 (continued)

Code	NUTS1	2007	2008	2009	2010	2011	2012	2013	2014	2015
ES1	Northwest	4,387,687	4,415,166	4,432,351	4,437,518	4,438,329	4,427,515	4,404,703	4,379,632	4,352,682
ES2	Northeast	4,382,664	4,443,606	4,471,390	4,479,793	4,488,113	4,480,169	4,459,249	4,443,750	4,433,805
ES3	Madrid	6,152,759	6,283,747	6,354,091	6,384,358	6,409,093	6,426,229	6,392,713	6,376,749	6,401,162
ES4	Centre	5,617,398	5,688,436	5,720,549	5,736,394	5,748,195	5,728,396	5,688,156	5,646,722	5,606,078
ES5	East	13,125,241	13,394,112	13,509,723	13,553,819	13,601,602	13,600,030	13,523,329	13,467,416	13,457,141
ES6	South	9,457,647	9,600,148	9,692,986	9,759,438	9,813,859	9,844,391	9,848,478	9,853,732	9,862,350
ES7	Canary I.	1,967,966	2,009,965	2,034,165	2,053,116	2,073,985	2,092,826	2,108,462	2,118,423	2,127,770
	ESP	**45,091,361**	**45,835,180**	**46,215,255**	**46,404,437**	**46,573,176**	**46,599,556**	**46,425,091**	**46,286,424**	**46,240,988**

Table A9 Gross domestic product per capita (Spain = 1), NUTS3

Code	Province	1860	1870	1880	1890	1900	1910	1920	1930
ES111	A Coruña	0.75	0.67	0.58	0.52	0.61	0.74	0.59	0.71
ES112	Lugo	0.21	0.26	0.31	0.31	0.41	0.48	0.55	0.68
ES113	Ourense	0.53	0.53	0.54	0.51	0.43	0.56	0.37	0.51
ES114	Pontevedra	0.37	0.40	0.42	0.45	0.66	0.59	0.40	0.61
ES120	Asturias	0.56	0.58	0.58	0.63	0.94	0.68	0.87	0.95
ES130	Cantabria	0.82	0.85	0.81	0.89	0.98	0.90	0.94	1.12
ES211	Araba/Álava	0.85	1.18	1.48	1.28	1.56	0.99	0.92	0.89
ES212	Gipuzkoa	0.89	1.26	1.71	1.78	2.45	1.88	1.25	1.58
ES213	Bizkaia	1.01	1.25	1.47	1.88	1.95	1.49	2.32	1.83
ES220	Navarra	1.05	1.19	1.29	1.00	0.83	0.87	1.13	0.98
ES230	La Rioja	0.90	0.98	1.06	0.98	1.08	0.87	0.70	0.83
ES241	Huesca	0.96	0.96	0.97	0.92	0.85	0.82	0.92	0.86
ES242	Teruel	0.94	0.88	0.81	0.83	0.80	0.73	0.69	0.59
ES243	Zaragoza	1.11	1.15	1.17	1.10	1.03	1.14	1.35	1.20
ES300	Madrid	1.77	1.86	1.83	1.70	1.63	1.52	1.64	1.80
ES411	Ávila	0.88	0.88	0.87	0.89	0.75	0.83	0.69	0.69
ES412	Burgos	0.80	0.89	0.95	0.81	0.92	0.79	0.95	0.72
ES413	León	0.50	0.51	0.50	0.45	0.47	0.57	0.78	0.69
ES414	Palencia	1.06	1.08	1.09	0.96	0.96	0.83	0.75	0.77
ES415	Salamanca	0.88	1.05	1.20	0.91	1.05	1.03	0.92	0.77
ES416	Segovia	1.08	1.00	0.94	0.92	0.81	0.74	0.69	0.78
ES417	Soria	0.79	0.83	0.88	1.00	0.76	0.83	0.70	0.69
ES418	Valladolid	1.10	1.11	1.10	1.05	0.99	0.98	0.91	0.83
ES419	Zamora	0.86	0.81	0.77	0.95	0.73	0.69	0.75	0.64
	ESP	**1.00**	**1.00**	**1.00**	**1.00**	**1.00**	**1.00**	**1.00**	**1.00**

(*continued*)

Table A9 (continued)

Code	Province	1935	1940	1945	1950	1955	1957	1959	1961
ES111	A Coruña	0.86	0.82	0.82	0.80	0.74	0.73	0.74	0.73
ES112	Lugo	0.65	0.62	0.63	0.61	0.63	0.67	0.68	0.65
ES113	Ourense	0.58	0.57	0.59	0.61	0.57	0.56	0.56	0.56
ES114	Pontevedra	0.80	0.77	0.77	0.76	0.78	0.80	0.80	0.78
ES120	Asturias	1.05	1.14	1.13	1.13	1.09	1.10	1.08	1.06
ES130	Cantabria	0.98	0.97	1.04	1.15	1.15	1.16	1.19	1.17
ES211	Araba/Álava	1.40	1.39	1.42	1.28	1.39	1.36	1.37	1.42
ES212	Gipuzkoa	2.04	2.02	2.07	1.93	1.72	1.64	1.58	1.55
ES213	Bizkaia	1.46	1.50	1.59	1.84	1.88	1.78	1.71	1.67
ES220	Navarra	1.18	1.14	1.15	1.17	1.14	1.14	1.16	1.16
ES230	La Rioja	1.22	1.22	1.20	1.12	1.09	1.11	1.13	1.13
ES241	Huesca	0.89	0.93	0.94	0.95	0.96	1.02	1.06	1.08
ES242	Teruel	0.68	0.62	0.64	0.65	0.74	0.77	0.74	0.72
ES243	Zaragoza	1.18	1.24	1.17	1.16	1.07	1.09	1.10	1.12
ES300	Madrid	1.48	1.52	1.47	1.48	1.56	1.53	1.49	1.48
ES411	Ávila	0.77	0.75	0.76	0.75	0.58	0.61	0.60	0.59
ES412	Burgos	1.13	1.02	1.03	1.00	0.90	0.91	0.89	0.87
ES413	León	0.82	0.76	0.81	0.90	0.83	0.85	0.82	0.80
ES414	Palencia	1.11	1.02	1.11	1.14	0.90	0.86	0.86	0.84
ES415	Salamanca	0.83	0.78	0.88	0.88	0.79	0.80	0.81	0.81
ES416	Segovia	0.89	0.79	0.93	1.03	0.93	0.94	0.89	0.83
ES417	Soria	0.93	0.91	0.92	0.89	0.78	0.81	0.75	0.74
ES418	Valladolid	1.01	0.95	1.00	1.01	1.00	0.97	0.94	0.93
ES419	Zamora	0.70	0.71	0.76	0.76	0.72	0.71	0.70	0.69
	ESP	**1.00**	**1.00**	**1.00**	**1.00**	**1.00**	**1.00**	**1.00**	**1.00**

(continued)

Table A9 (continued)

Code	Province	1963	1965	1967	1969	1971	1973	1975	1977	1979
ES111	A Coruña	0.73	0.72	0.74	0.76	0.79	0.80	0.81	0.85	0.86
ES112	Lugo	0.65	0.64	0.67	0.66	0.64	0.63	0.63	0.67	0.71
ES113	Ourense	0.57	0.56	0.54	0.57	0.58	0.60	0.59	0.59	0.61
ES114	Pontevedra	0.79	0.79	0.82	0.81	0.84	0.84	0.85	0.87	0.88
ES120	Asturias	1.03	1.02	1.03	1.03	0.99	0.98	0.99	0.95	0.95
ES130	Cantabria	1.16	1.13	1.12	1.11	1.09	1.03	1.02	1.03	1.03
ES211	Araba/Álava	1.50	1.59	1.54	1.57	1.49	1.46	1.46	1.42	1.38
ES212	Gipuzkoa	1.56	1.59	1.51	1.48	1.44	1.40	1.39	1.31	1.22
ES213	Bizkaia	1.64	1.57	1.47	1.41	1.31	1.28	1.26	1.17	1.06
ES220	Navarra	1.21	1.17	1.17	1.14	1.14	1.14	1.14	1.13	1.12
ES230	La Rioja	1.16	1.14	1.13	1.10	1.08	1.06	1.04	1.06	1.10
ES241	Huesca	1.10	1.05	1.04	1.06	1.10	1.05	1.15	1.14	1.17
ES242	Teruel	0.75	0.74	0.76	0.83	0.78	0.79	0.83	0.88	0.88
ES243	Zaragoza	1.14	1.11	1.08	1.06	1.02	1.02	1.01	1.02	1.03
ES300	Madrid	1.44	1.48	1.42	1.36	1.32	1.33	1.34	1.30	1.30
ES411	Ávila	0.61	0.58	0.57	0.61	0.60	0.61	0.64	0.65	0.68
ES412	Burgos	0.92	0.94	0.94	0.95	0.94	0.94	0.97	1.01	0.99
ES413	León	0.81	0.81	0.81	0.77	0.78	0.75	0.75	0.76	0.80
ES414	Palencia	0.87	0.87	0.84	0.87	0.85	0.83	0.87	0.95	0.99
ES415	Salamanca	0.81	0.78	0.77	0.78	0.78	0.75	0.76	0.78	0.79
ES416	Segovia	0.82	0.79	0.81	0.84	0.85	0.86	0.87	0.88	0.87
ES417	Soria	0.76	0.77	0.77	0.81	0.80	0.80	0.81	0.81	0.79
ES418	Valladolid	0.99	1.01	1.02	1.06	1.06	1.07	1.07	1.07	1.04
ES419	Zamora	0.72	0.73	0.70	0.67	0.67	0.67	0.66	0.68	0.68
	ESP	**1.00**	**1.00**	**1.00**	**1.00**	**1.00**	**1.00**	**1.00**	**1.00**	**1.00**

(*continued*)

Table A9 (continued)

Code	Province	1980	1981	1982	1983	1984	1985	1986	1987	1988
ES111	A Coruña	0.87	0.89	0.93	0.89	0.87	0.86	0.85	0.84	0.82
ES112	Lugo	0.79	0.82	0.84	0.88	0.91	0.82	0.76	0.76	0.80
ES113	Ourense	0.63	0.67	0.68	0.65	0.70	0.74	0.70	0.71	0.75
ES114	Pontevedra	0.81	0.82	0.81	0.80	0.79	0.81	0.79	0.77	0.78
ES120	Asturias	0.93	0.94	0.96	0.94	0.93	0.97	0.98	0.94	0.93
ES130	Cantabria	1.08	1.11	1.08	1.07	1.07	1.02	0.96	0.95	0.99
ES211	Araba/Álava	1.61	1.69	1.68	1.64	1.50	1.49	1.47	1.39	1.38
ES212	Gipuzkoa	1.32	1.33	1.31	1.29	1.21	1.26	1.23	1.23	1.23
ES213	Bizkaia	1.23	1.25	1.26	1.23	1.21	1.20	1.20	1.13	1.10
ES220	Navarra	1.28	1.32	1.28	1.26	1.24	1.22	1.22	1.27	1.24
ES230	La Rioja	1.16	1.18	1.19	1.22	1.22	1.33	1.18	1.12	1.12
ES241	Huesca	1.15	1.04	1.08	1.03	1.11	1.23	1.17	1.10	1.15
ES242	Teruel	1.12	1.22	1.26	1.24	1.33	1.06	1.06	1.00	1.07
ES243	Zaragoza	1.04	1.02	1.03	1.11	1.09	1.09	1.10	1.12	1.15
ES300	Madrid	1.19	1.19	1.21	1.22	1.20	1.17	1.22	1.23	1.21
ES411	Ávila	0.82	0.78	0.73	0.75	0.76	0.78	0.79	0.78	0.80
ES412	Burgos	1.06	1.05	1.07	1.08	1.10	1.16	1.15	1.19	1.13
ES413	León	0.83	0.86	0.89	0.91	0.95	0.94	0.91	0.87	0.82
ES414	Palencia	1.06	0.98	0.96	1.06	1.07	0.98	0.94	1.02	0.99
ES415	Salamanca	0.76	0.73	0.80	0.81	0.82	0.86	0.84	0.83	0.85
ES416	Segovia	0.90	0.87	0.98	0.94	0.91	1.00	1.00	0.97	0.98
ES417	Soria	0.90	0.86	0.97	0.95	1.04	1.04	1.05	1.00	1.06
ES418	Valladolid	1.01	0.97	1.03	1.00	0.98	1.01	1.03	1.02	1.04
ES419	Zamora	0.74	0.68	0.71	0.71	0.76	0.85	0.79	0.79	0.81
	ESP	**1.00**	**1.00**	**1.00**	**1.00**	**1.00**	**1.00**	**1.00**	**1.00**	**1.00**

(continued)

Table A9 (continued)

Code	Province	1989	1990	1991	1992	1993	1994	1995	1996	1997
ES111	A Coruña	0.84	0.81	0.81	0.82	0.83	0.82	0.88	0.86	0.85
ES112	Lugo	0.76	0.75	0.74	0.73	0.75	0.74	0.80	0.79	0.76
ES113	Ourense	0.73	0.73	0.74	0.76	0.79	0.78	0.76	0.73	0.72
ES114	Pontevedra	0.78	0.78	0.78	0.78	0.77	0.78	0.78	0.79	0.80
ES120	Asturias	0.93	0.91	0.90	0.92	0.91	0.92	0.89	0.87	0.85
ES130	Cantabria	1.01	0.98	0.96	0.98	0.97	0.97	0.93	0.92	0.92
ES211	Araba/Álava	1.34	1.30	1.31	1.27	1.26	1.26	1.34	1.39	1.40
ES212	Gipuzkoa	1.25	1.24	1.21	1.19	1.20	1.22	1.23	1.24	1.24
ES213	Bizkaia	1.12	1.12	1.13	1.12	1.13	1.12	1.14	1.11	1.12
ES220	Navarra	1.28	1.24	1.24	1.23	1.21	1.21	1.27	1.28	1.29
ES230	La Rioja	1.11	1.11	1.12	1.12	1.11	1.12	1.13	1.13	1.13
ES241	Huesca	1.10	1.12	1.10	1.09	1.14	1.14	1.06	1.04	1.02
ES242	Teruel	1.16	1.05	1.12	1.09	1.08	1.07	1.07	1.07	1.08
ES243	Zaragoza	1.15	1.14	1.14	1.14	1.13	1.13	1.10	1.11	1.11
ES300	Madrid	1.21	1.23	1.23	1.23	1.23	1.23	1.29	1.29	1.30
ES411	Ávila	0.82	0.82	0.83	0.82	0.86	0.85	0.84	0.83	0.78
ES412	Burgos	1.09	1.07	1.05	1.05	1.07	1.07	1.17	1.19	1.17
ES413	León	0.85	0.81	0.80	0.81	0.83	0.83	0.88	0.85	0.85
ES414	Palencia	0.95	0.94	0.94	0.92	0.99	0.92	0.98	0.98	0.95
ES415	Salamanca	0.84	0.85	0.85	0.84	0.89	0.92	0.85	0.86	0.83
ES416	Segovia	0.96	0.96	0.97	0.96	0.98	0.99	1.03	0.95	0.97
ES417	Soria	1.06	1.01	1.01	0.99	1.06	1.01	1.06	1.06	1.08
ES418	Valladolid	0.99	0.96	0.99	1.01	1.02	0.99	1.08	1.08	1.05
ES419	Zamora	0.79	0.77	0.76	0.79	0.83	0.80	0.77	0.75	0.70
	ESP	**1.00**	**1.00**	**1.00**	**1.00**	**1.00**	**1.00**	**1.00**	**1.00**	**1.00**

(continued)

Table A9 (continued)

Code	Province	1998	1999	2000	2001	2002	2003	2004	2005	2006
ES111	A Coruña	0.85	0.83	0.80	0.79	0.82	0.83	0.85	0.87	0.87
ES112	Lugo	0.74	0.71	0.74	0.75	0.74	0.75	0.76	0.80	0.81
ES113	Ourense	0.70	0.71	0.70	0.72	0.75	0.75	0.75	0.76	0.77
ES114	Pontevedra	0.80	0.81	0.79	0.79	0.78	0.80	0.82	0.82	0.84
ES120	Asturias	0.86	0.83	0.84	0.84	0.85	0.85	0.86	0.88	0.90
ES130	Cantabria	0.93	0.93	0.93	0.94	0.94	0.94	0.93	0.94	0.93
ES211	Araba/Álava	1.43	1.44	1.39	1.39	1.42	1.42	1.43	1.45	1.49
ES212	Gipuzkoa	1.25	1.25	1.26	1.28	1.27	1.25	1.26	1.27	1.30
ES213	Bizkaia	1.14	1.16	1.17	1.14	1.14	1.16	1.16	1.18	1.17
ES220	Navarra	1.28	1.27	1.27	1.25	1.25	1.25	1.25	1.25	1.24
ES230	La Rioja	1.13	1.12	1.12	1.10	1.09	1.09	1.08	1.07	1.07
ES241	Huesca	0.98	1.00	1.01	1.03	1.05	1.06	1.05	1.03	1.03
ES242	Teruel	1.05	1.02	1.05	1.05	1.06	1.03	1.03	1.05	1.04
ES243	Zaragoza	1.10	1.07	1.06	1.05	1.07	1.08	1.08	1.09	1.09
ES300	Madrid	1.33	1.33	1.34	1.34	1.33	1.32	1.32	1.32	1.33
ES411	Ávila	0.79	0.78	0.79	0.77	0.75	0.75	0.77	0.75	0.75
ES412	Burgos	1.17	1.12	1.11	1.08	1.08	1.10	1.11	1.11	1.09
ES413	León	0.83	0.86	0.82	0.83	0.83	0.83	0.82	0.85	0.85
ES414	Palencia	0.95	0.94	0.91	0.91	0.96	0.98	0.99	1.00	0.99
ES415	Salamanca	0.82	0.77	0.79	0.82	0.82	0.85	0.84	0.83	0.83
ES416	Segovia	0.95	1.00	1.00	0.96	0.98	0.98	0.97	0.98	0.97
ES417	Soria	1.05	1.00	0.99	0.95	0.99	0.99	1.01	0.96	0.96
ES418	Valladolid	1.02	1.03	1.01	1.00	1.00	0.99	0.99	1.01	1.00
ES419	Zamora	0.68	0.73	0.70	0.70	0.71	0.72	0.74	0.72	0.74
	ESP	**1.00**	**1.00**	**1.00**	**1.00**	**1.00**	**1.00**	**1.00**	**1.00**	**1.00**

(continued)

Table A9 (continued)

Code	Province	2007	2008	2009	2010	2011	2012	2013	2014	2015
ES111	A Coruña	0.90	0.92	0.94	0.95	0.94	0.93	0.94	0.93	0.92
ES112	Lugo	0.81	0.80	0.81	0.84	0.85	0.86	0.87	0.89	0.90
ES113	Ourense	0.77	0.80	0.79	0.82	0.84	0.86	0.86	0.83	0.85
ES114	Pontevedra	0.86	0.88	0.87	0.85	0.83	0.83	0.84	0.85	0.85
ES120	Asturias	0.91	0.92	0.91	0.92	0.91	0.90	0.88	0.87	0.88
ES130	Cantabria	0.94	0.94	0.94	0.94	0.93	0.92	0.91	0.89	0.91
ES211	Araba/Álava	1.52	1.55	1.49	1.47	1.49	1.50	1.53	1.54	1.54
ES212	Gipuzkoa	1.31	1.30	1.29	1.32	1.33	1.35	1.33	1.33	1.32
ES213	Bizkaia	1.17	1.20	1.22	1.24	1.23	1.25	1.24	1.26	1.26
ES220	Navarra	1.23	1.24	1.24	1.24	1.25	1.24	1.25	1.26	1.25
ES230	La Rioja	1.07	1.07	1.07	1.08	1.08	1.08	1.08	1.08	1.09
ES241	Huesca	1.07	1.12	1.10	1.12	1.13	1.11	1.16	1.08	1.13
ES242	Teruel	1.04	1.07	1.05	1.06	1.06	1.08	1.11	1.03	1.11
ES243	Zaragoza	1.11	1.10	1.10	1.11	1.10	1.09	1.10	1.09	1.10
ES300	Madrid	1.32	1.32	1.35	1.34	1.36	1.37	1.37	1.37	1.36
ES411	Ávila	0.77	0.78	0.79	0.79	0.80	0.82	0.80	0.78	0.80
ES412	Burgos	1.10	1.11	1.11	1.12	1.14	1.16	1.14	1.10	1.13
ES413	León	0.86	0.86	0.88	0.88	0.88	0.89	0.87	0.84	0.86
ES414	Palencia	1.03	1.04	1.04	1.03	1.06	1.04	1.04	1.03	1.03
ES415	Salamanca	0.82	0.83	0.86	0.83	0.83	0.84	0.82	0.83	0.83
ES416	Segovia	0.95	0.92	0.92	0.92	0.92	0.91	0.90	0.90	0.91
ES417	Soria	0.97	0.97	0.96	1.00	1.02	1.00	1.02	1.02	1.04
ES418	Valladolid	1.00	0.98	0.99	1.01	1.01	1.00	1.00	1.01	1.01
ES419	Zamora	0.75	0.75	0.77	0.79	0.81	0.84	0.82	0.79	0.81
	ESP	**1.00**	**1.00**	**1.00**	**1.00**	**1.00**	**1.00**	**1.00**	**1.00**	**1.00**

(*continued*)

Table A9 (continued)

Code	Province	1860	1870	1880	1890	1900	1910	1920	1930
ES421	Albacete	1.02	1.16	1.33	1.23	1.08	0.92	0.93	0.94
ES422	Ciudad Real	1.09	1.03	0.92	1.00	0.83	0.82	0.72	0.60
ES423	Cuenca	0.84	0.73	0.62	0.75	0.74	0.57	0.56	0.52
ES424	Guadalajara	1.00	0.91	0.79	0.79	0.77	0.68	0.59	0.63
ES425	Toledo	0.93	0.94	0.97	1.05	0.88	0.82	0.77	0.59
ES431	Badajoz	0.80	0.80	0.81	0.71	0.72	0.70	0.58	0.61
ES432	Cáceres	0.69	0.73	0.78	0.66	0.57	0.59	0.45	0.54
ES511	Barcelona	1.49	1.67	1.84	2.06	2.54	2.55	2.81	2.05
ES512	Girona	0.89	0.96	1.05	1.05	1.07	1.51	0.86	0.97
ES513	Lleida	0.79	0.86	0.96	0.92	0.83	0.90	0.88	0.81
ES514	Tarragona	0.95	0.95	0.97	1.03	1.18	1.09	1.24	1.13
ES521	Alicante/Alacant	0.95	0.94	0.93	0.91	0.86	0.88	0.95	1.12
ES522	Castellón/Castelló	0.98	1.00	1.05	1.02	1.04	0.89	0.95	1.07
ES523	Valencia/València	1.16	1.25	1.35	1.12	1.17	1.11	1.24	1.28
ES530	Balears, Illes	1.05	0.82	0.62	0.66	0.82	1.01	0.82	1.23
ES611	Almería	1.08	0.91	0.84	0.72	0.72	0.66	0.69	0.66
ES612	Cádiz	1.80	1.61	1.43	1.50	1.17	1.56	0.84	0.94
ES613	Córdoba	0.93	0.83	0.77	0.94	0.73	0.75	0.74	0.70
ES614	Granada	1.66	1.37	1.13	0.99	0.78	1.01	0.92	0.77
ES615	Huelva	0.94	0.88	0.93	1.12	0.89	0.85	0.57	0.81
ES616	Jaén	0.98	0.84	0.72	0.87	0.74	0.74	0.58	0.48
ES617	Málaga	1.56	1.30	1.09	1.09	0.77	1.01	0.64	0.81
ES618	Sevilla	1.45	1.37	1.28	1.26	1.10	1.15	0.96	0.92
ES620	Murcia	1.03	1.05	1.05	0.97	0.62	0.67	0.69	0.86
ES700	Canarias, Islas	0.79	0.63	0.47	0.78	0.61	0.65	0.72	0.71
	ESP	**1.00**	**1.00**	**1.00**	**1.00**	**1.00**	**1.00**	**1.00**	**1.00**

(*continued*)

Table A9 (continued)

Code	Province	1935	1940	1945	1950	1955	1957	1959	1961
ES421	Albacete	0.67	0.62	0.69	0.68	0.61	0.65	0.64	0.65
ES422	Ciudad Real	0.70	0.66	0.70	0.73	0.67	0.65	0.64	0.66
ES423	Cuenca	0.65	0.66	0.68	0.71	0.64	0.71	0.70	0.66
ES424	Guadalajara	0.72	0.73	0.74	0.74	0.73	0.81	0.81	0.75
ES425	Toledo	0.79	0.75	0.77	0.81	0.67	0.70	0.70	0.67
ES431	Badajoz	0.67	0.63	0.65	0.63	0.57	0.62	0.62	0.59
ES432	Cáceres	0.58	0.56	0.56	0.54	0.54	0.55	0.55	0.54
ES511	Barcelona	1.72	1.82	1.73	1.72	1.79	1.68	1.64	1.64
ES512	Girona	1.27	1.28	1.32	1.40	1.31	1.27	1.31	1.39
ES513	Lleida	1.17	1.18	1.18	1.07	0.88	0.97	1.00	1.11
ES514	Tarragona	1.33	1.29	1.25	1.16	1.16	1.19	1.23	1.24
ES521	Alicante/Alacant	1.03	0.99	1.00	0.96	1.01	0.98	0.99	1.00
ES522	Castellón/Castelló	0.85	0.92	0.94	0.91	1.07	1.11	1.14	1.09
ES523	Valencia/València	1.20	1.14	1.12	1.08	1.18	1.21	1.23	1.19
ES530	Balears, Illes	1.29	1.41	1.31	1.21	1.25	1.24	1.30	1.30
ES611	Almería	0.48	0.55	0.56	0.58	0.53	0.55	0.57	0.57
ES612	Cádiz	0.90	0.90	0.90	0.81	0.74	0.71	0.72	0.72
ES613	Córdoba	0.66	0.69	0.68	0.69	0.72	0.69	0.71	0.67
ES614	Granada	0.63	0.56	0.56	0.53	0.54	0.53	0.53	0.54
ES615	Huelva	0.83	0.80	0.84	0.85	0.78	0.76	0.72	0.69
ES616	Jaén	0.62	0.64	0.58	0.55	0.54	0.55	0.59	0.58
ES617	Málaga	0.69	0.69	0.70	0.69	0.65	0.66	0.67	0.70
ES618	Sevilla	1.09	1.03	1.00	0.99	0.86	0.83	0.81	0.81
ES620	Murcia	0.79	0.75	0.77	0.77	0.69	0.69	0.71	0.75
ES700	Canarias, Islas	0.91	0.89	0.85	0.83	0.72	0.79	0.78	0.76
	ESP	**1.00**	**1.00**	**1.00**	**1.00**	**1.00**	**1.00**	**1.00**	**1.00**

(*continued*)

Table A9 (continued)

Code	Province	1963	1965	1967	1969	1971	1973	1975	1977	1979
ES421	Albacete	0.68	0.65	0.64	0.65	0.67	0.66	0.67	0.71	0.72
ES422	Ciudad Real	0.68	0.68	0.66	0.70	0.68	0.74	0.75	0.76	0.74
ES423	Cuenca	0.66	0.64	0.65	0.63	0.64	0.73	0.76	0.78	0.77
ES424	Guadalajara	0.78	0.78	0.83	0.90	0.95	1.01	0.99	1.03	1.03
ES425	Toledo	0.67	0.65	0.68	0.75	0.78	0.84	0.83	0.84	0.83
ES431	Badajoz	0.55	0.55	0.54	0.54	0.56	0.58	0.57	0.57	0.58
ES432	Cáceres	0.54	0.53	0.55	0.56	0.57	0.59	0.59	0.62	0.65
ES511	Barcelona	1.58	1.53	1.48	1.41	1.37	1.32	1.29	1.26	1.24
ES512	Girona	1.41	1.36	1.32	1.33	1.31	1.28	1.29	1.32	1.32
ES513	Lleida	1.16	1.11	1.06	1.14	1.13	1.13	1.10	1.08	1.08
ES514	Tarragona	1.21	1.18	1.19	1.21	1.16	1.17	1.27	1.25	1.23
ES521	Alicante/Alacant	1.01	1.00	1.00	0.98	0.97	0.97	0.96	0.96	0.98
ES522	Castellón/Castelló	1.05	0.99	0.99	0.98	0.99	1.00	1.02	1.04	1.05
ES523	Valencia/València	1.13	1.09	1.06	1.04	1.04	1.03	1.02	1.04	1.03
ES530	Balears, Illes	1.30	1.31	1.36	1.39	1.41	1.38	1.34	1.34	1.37
ES611	Almería	0.57	0.55	0.58	0.59	0.64	0.69	0.71	0.80	0.76
ES612	Cádiz	0.71	0.71	0.74	0.77	0.79	0.76	0.76	0.79	0.78
ES613	Córdoba	0.66	0.67	0.66	0.67	0.68	0.67	0.66	0.68	0.70
ES614	Granada	0.55	0.55	0.56	0.58	0.59	0.59	0.58	0.60	0.61
ES615	Huelva	0.69	0.68	0.68	0.73	0.82	0.89	0.94	0.91	0.86
ES616	Jaén	0.57	0.58	0.59	0.59	0.59	0.60	0.59	0.61	0.63
ES617	Málaga	0.72	0.76	0.78	0.78	0.81	0.81	0.79	0.80	0.81
ES618	Sevilla	0.80	0.80	0.82	0.81	0.83	0.82	0.80	0.80	0.79
ES620	Murcia	0.77	0.77	0.80	0.82	0.83	0.84	0.83	0.84	0.85
ES700	Canarias, Islas	0.76	0.76	0.80	0.82	0.87	0.86	0.81	0.83	0.92
	ESP	**1.00**	**1.00**	**1.00**	**1.00**	**1.00**	**1.00**	**1.00**	**1.00**	**1.00**

(continued)

Table A9 (continued)

Code	Province	1980	1981	1982	1983	1984	1985	1986	1987	1988
ES421	Albacete	0.75	0.71	0.73	0.72	0.73	0.78	0.70	0.71	0.72
ES422	Ciudad Real	0.80	0.79	0.79	0.81	0.82	0.83	0.84	0.87	0.86
ES423	Cuenca	0.77	0.72	0.78	0.73	0.74	0.78	0.76	0.73	0.74
ES424	Guadalajara	1.06	1.04	1.05	1.03	1.08	1.15	1.09	1.10	1.24
ES425	Toledo	0.83	0.86	0.82	0.80	0.80	0.87	0.81	0.86	0.88
ES431	Badajoz	0.56	0.55	0.55	0.53	0.60	0.59	0.57	0.59	0.59
ES432	Cáceres	0.61	0.61	0.63	0.65	0.82	0.87	0.82	0.84	0.89
ES511	Barcelona	1.17	1.14	1.11	1.08	1.10	1.06	1.09	1.11	1.13
ES512	Girona	1.30	1.29	1.24	1.25	1.29	1.29	1.32	1.32	1.32
ES513	Lleida	1.28	1.27	1.27	1.29	1.31	1.26	1.24	1.26	1.26
ES514	Tarragona	1.47	1.44	1.49	1.54	1.50	1.60	1.66	1.56	1.59
ES521	Alicante/Alacant	1.05	1.05	1.01	1.02	1.00	1.00	0.93	0.93	0.92
ES522	Castellón/Castelló	1.17	1.17	1.15	1.16	1.12	1.15	1.20	1.17	1.14
ES523	Valencia/València	1.00	1.04	1.01	1.01	1.04	1.04	1.01	1.01	1.01
ES530	Balears, Illes	1.14	1.18	1.21	1.23	1.26	1.35	1.31	1.32	1.32
ES611	Almería	0.76	0.83	0.81	0.79	0.84	0.80	0.82	0.86	0.82
ES612	Cádiz	0.83	0.82	0.85	0.82	0.79	0.81	0.84	0.82	0.81
ES613	Córdoba	0.68	0.67	0.70	0.71	0.68	0.70	0.65	0.69	0.68
ES614	Granada	0.66	0.67	0.67	0.68	0.70	0.65	0.65	0.68	0.69
ES615	Huelva	0.92	0.88	0.86	0.88	0.92	0.92	0.98	0.90	0.89
ES616	Jaén	0.70	0.71	0.69	0.77	0.70	0.75	0.71	0.70	0.74
ES617	Málaga	0.76	0.75	0.78	0.79	0.78	0.81	0.79	0.82	0.80
ES618	Sevilla	0.73	0.72	0.72	0.70	0.70	0.75	0.73	0.75	0.75
ES620	Murcia	0.95	0.94	0.91	0.93	0.93	0.92	0.95	0.94	0.91
ES700	Canarias, Islas	1.00	1.00	0.99	1.01	0.97	0.93	0.96	0.95	0.97
	ESP	**1.00**	**1.00**	**1.00**	**1.00**	**1.00**	**1.00**	**1.00**	**1.00**	**1.00**

(continued)

Table A9 (continued)

Code	Province	1989	1990	1991	1992	1993	1994	1995	1996	1997
ES421	Albacete	0.72	0.75	0.74	0.74	0.75	0.75	0.75	0.79	0.76
ES422	Ciudad Real	0.84	0.85	0.83	0.83	0.83	0.81	0.81	0.78	0.77
ES423	Cuenca	0.77	0.74	0.78	0.79	0.79	0.80	0.79	0.86	0.86
ES424	Guadalajara	1.38	1.31	1.28	1.25	1.23	1.19	1.05	0.96	0.98
ES425	Toledo	0.88	0.88	0.88	0.89	0.84	0.82	0.84	0.84	0.83
ES431	Badajoz	0.59	0.61	0.62	0.62	0.61	0.61	0.60	0.62	0.64
ES432	Cáceres	0.85	0.82	0.83	0.85	0.87	0.89	0.72	0.68	0.64
ES511	Barcelona	1.16	1.16	1.18	1.18	1.18	1.19	1.20	1.22	1.21
ES512	Girona	1.30	1.36	1.29	1.30	1.29	1.33	1.25	1.24	1.25
ES513	Lleida	1.24	1.21	1.20	1.27	1.25	1.25	1.19	1.25	1.26
ES514	Tarragona	1.61	1.55	1.54	1.54	1.50	1.49	1.31	1.31	1.29
ES521	Alicante/Alacant	0.90	0.91	0.91	0.90	0.90	0.88	0.87	0.91	0.91
ES522	Castellón/Castelló	1.16	1.17	1.17	1.14	1.15	1.15	1.10	1.13	1.13
ES523	Valencia/València	1.02	1.01	1.02	1.01	1.00	0.99	0.96	0.92	0.94
ES530	Balears, Illes	1.28	1.30	1.31	1.31	1.31	1.32	1.20	1.20	1.23
ES611	Almería	0.87	0.91	0.88	0.85	0.84	0.85	0.83	0.90	0.94
ES612	Cádiz	0.77	0.78	0.75	0.74	0.73	0.73	0.73	0.76	0.75
ES613	Córdoba	0.66	0.69	0.73	0.71	0.72	0.72	0.73	0.69	0.68
ES614	Granada	0.69	0.68	0.69	0.69	0.71	0.72	0.70	0.67	0.66
ES615	Huelva	0.91	0.89	0.85	0.81	0.79	0.80	0.78	0.79	0.79
ES616	Jaén	0.68	0.74	0.76	0.72	0.74	0.75	0.71	0.70	0.72
ES617	Málaga	0.78	0.78	0.77	0.75	0.74	0.73	0.74	0.73	0.73
ES618	Sevilla	0.73	0.77	0.78	0.80	0.76	0.76	0.79	0.78	0.77
ES620	Murcia	0.91	0.93	0.91	0.90	0.89	0.89	0.82	0.82	0.83
ES700	Canarias, Islas	0.93	0.91	0.90	0.92	0.95	0.95	0.96	0.95	0.96
	ESP	**1.00**	**1.00**	**1.00**	**1.00**	**1.00**	**1.00**	**1.00**	**1.00**	**1.00**

(*continued*)

Table A9 (continued)

Code	Province	1998	1999	2000	2001	2002	2003	2004	2005	2006
ES421	Albacete	0.77	0.76	0.74	0.75	0.77	0.75	0.76	0.76	0.76
ES422	Ciudad Real	0.77	0.77	0.78	0.77	0.79	0.81	0.82	0.80	0.80
ES423	Cuenca	0.88	0.83	0.75	0.74	0.75	0.75	0.79	0.79	0.80
ES424	Guadalajara	0.93	0.90	0.87	0.89	0.90	0.89	0.87	0.89	0.87
ES425	Toledo	0.83	0.80	0.79	0.80	0.79	0.80	0.78	0.81	0.82
ES431	Badajoz	0.64	0.64	0.64	0.63	0.64	0.65	0.64	0.67	0.66
ES432	Cáceres	0.62	0.64	0.63	0.63	0.64	0.65	0.68	0.66	0.67
ES511	Barcelona	1.21	1.22	1.21	1.21	1.19	1.18	1.18	1.18	1.18
ES512	Girona	1.23	1.22	1.22	1.24	1.26	1.24	1.23	1.20	1.22
ES513	Lleida	1.23	1.23	1.20	1.22	1.24	1.24	1.21	1.14	1.16
ES514	Tarragona	1.25	1.27	1.27	1.28	1.31	1.28	1.30	1.20	1.17
ES521	Alicante/Alacant	0.90	0.88	0.88	0.90	0.88	0.87	0.87	0.86	0.85
ES522	Castellón/Castelló	1.17	1.16	1.15	1.13	1.10	1.07	1.03	1.05	1.05
ES523	Valencia/València	0.94	0.95	0.96	0.96	0.97	0.96	0.95	0.93	0.93
ES530	Balears, Illes	1.23	1.25	1.26	1.24	1.20	1.15	1.13	1.11	1.09
ES611	Almería	0.92	0.97	0.95	0.93	0.93	0.92	0.90	0.89	0.87
ES612	Cádiz	0.74	0.73	0.76	0.75	0.75	0.75	0.77	0.77	0.77
ES613	Córdoba	0.68	0.68	0.67	0.66	0.66	0.69	0.70	0.70	0.72
ES614	Granada	0.65	0.64	0.66	0.67	0.69	0.70	0.70	0.69	0.72
ES615	Huelva	0.76	0.78	0.81	0.77	0.77	0.78	0.80	0.81	0.78
ES616	Jaén	0.72	0.66	0.65	0.65	0.65	0.70	0.69	0.67	0.68
ES617	Málaga	0.73	0.74	0.74	0.76	0.75	0.76	0.78	0.80	0.78
ES618	Sevilla	0.76	0.75	0.76	0.76	0.79	0.81	0.81	0.83	0.82
ES620	Murcia	0.83	0.82	0.84	0.84	0.84	0.84	0.84	0.84	0.83
ES700	Canarias, Islas	0.97	0.99	0.98	0.98	0.97	0.96	0.93	0.92	0.90
	ESP	**1.00**	**1.00**	**1.00**	**1.00**	**1.00**	**1.00**	**1.00**	**1.00**	**1.00**

(*continued*)

Table A9 (continued)

Code	Province	2007	2008	2009	2010	2011	2012	2013	2014	2015
ES421	Albacete	0.75	0.77	0.81	0.80	0.79	0.80	0.80	0.79	0.78
ES422	Ciudad Real	0.81	0.82	0.81	0.83	0.83	0.83	0.81	0.81	0.79
ES423	Cuenca	0.82	0.80	0.81	0.83	0.85	0.86	0.86	0.84	0.85
ES424	Guadalajara	0.86	0.87	0.86	0.87	0.87	0.87	0.86	0.77	0.81
ES425	Toledo	0.82	0.81	0.80	0.77	0.76	0.74	0.75	0.73	0.74
ES431	Badajoz	0.67	0.69	0.70	0.70	0.70	0.68	0.69	0.68	0.67
ES432	Cáceres	0.67	0.67	0.69	0.71	0.70	0.71	0.71	0.70	0.71
ES511	Barcelona	1.18	1.17	1.17	1.17	1.16	1.17	1.18	1.20	1.19
ES512	Girona	1.19	1.16	1.16	1.17	1.16	1.17	1.16	1.16	1.16
ES513	Lleida	1.16	1.16	1.18	1.18	1.18	1.20	1.23	1.22	1.22
ES514	Tarragona	1.16	1.15	1.15	1.18	1.17	1.17	1.17	1.21	1.19
ES521	Alicante/Alacant	0.83	0.82	0.80	0.80	0.78	0.77	0.77	0.78	0.79
ES522	Castellón/Castelló	0.99	0.96	0.95	0.96	0.98	0.96	0.97	0.99	0.97
ES523	Valencia/València	0.94	0.95	0.93	0.93	0.93	0.92	0.92	0.92	0.93
ES530	Balears, Illes	1.07	1.06	1.04	1.04	1.04	1.04	1.04	1.05	1.04
ES611	Almería	0.87	0.86	0.82	0.80	0.75	0.76	0.76	0.80	0.77
ES612	Cádiz	0.76	0.74	0.73	0.73	0.73	0.73	0.71	0.69	0.69
ES613	Córdoba	0.73	0.73	0.73	0.72	0.72	0.71	0.72	0.72	0.72
ES614	Granada	0.72	0.72	0.71	0.71	0.71	0.72	0.72	0.73	0.73
ES615	Huelva	0.76	0.77	0.73	0.75	0.79	0.79	0.74	0.74	0.73
ES616	Jaén	0.69	0.69	0.71	0.71	0.71	0.66	0.72	0.71	0.68
ES617	Málaga	0.77	0.76	0.77	0.76	0.75	0.74	0.73	0.73	0.73
ES618	Sevilla	0.83	0.82	0.83	0.82	0.82	0.82	0.80	0.80	0.81
ES620	Murcia	0.83	0.84	0.82	0.83	0.81	0.82	0.82	0.83	0.81
ES700	Canarias, Islas	0.89	0.87	0.86	0.87	0.86	0.86	0.85	0.83	0.85
	ESP	**1.00**	**1.00**	**1.00**	**1.00**	**1.00**	**1.00**	**1.00**	**1.00**	**1.00**

Table A10 Gross domestic product per capita (Spain = 1), NUTS2

Code	NUTS2	1860	1870	1880	1890	1900	1910	1920	1930
ES11	Galicia	0.48	0.48	0.47	0.45	0.54	0.61	0.49	0.64
ES12	Asturias	0.56	0.58	0.58	0.63	0.94	0.68	0.87	0.95
ES13	Cantabria	0.82	0.85	0.81	0.89	0.98	0.90	0.94	1.12
ES21	Basque Country	0.93	1.24	1.56	1.74	2.05	1.55	1.78	1.64
ES22	Navarre	1.05	1.19	1.29	1.00	0.83	0.87	1.13	0.98
ES23	La Rioja	0.90	0.98	1.06	0.98	1.08	0.87	0.70	0.83
ES24	Aragón	1.02	1.02	1.02	0.98	0.92	0.95	1.08	0.97
ES30	Madrid	1.77	1.86	1.83	1.70	1.63	1.52	1.64	1.80
ES41	Castile-Leon	0.85	0.88	0.91	0.85	0.82	0.80	0.81	0.73
ES42	Castile-La Mancha	0.97	0.95	0.93	0.97	0.86	0.78	0.72	0.65
ES43	Extremadura	0.75	0.77	0.80	0.69	0.66	0.66	0.53	0.58
ES51	Catalonia	1.14	1.26	1.40	1.52	1.84	1.93	2.04	1.67
ES52	Valencia	1.06	1.10	1.16	1.04	1.05	1.00	1.10	1.20
ES53	Balearic Islands	1.05	0.82	0.62	0.66	0.82	1.01	0.82	1.23
ES61	Andalusia	1.36	1.18	1.05	1.07	0.87	0.98	0.76	0.77
ES62	Murcia	1.03	1.05	1.05	0.97	0.62	0.67	0.69	0.86
ES70	Canary Islands	0.79	0.63	0.47	0.78	0.61	0.65	0.72	0.71
	ESP	**1.00**	**1.00**	**1.00**	**1.00**	**1.00**	**1.00**	**1.00**	**1.00**

(continued)

Table A10 (continued)

Code	NUTS2	1935	1940	1945	1950	1955	1957	1959	1961
ES11	Galicia	0.75	0.72	0.73	0.72	0.70	0.71	0.71	0.70
ES12	Asturias	1.05	1.14	1.13	1.13	1.09	1.10	1.08	1.06
ES13	Cantabria	0.98	0.97	1.04	1.15	1.15	1.16	1.19	1.17
ES21	Basque Country	1.65	1.66	1.74	1.81	1.77	1.69	1.63	1.60
ES22	Navarre	1.18	1.14	1.15	1.17	1.14	1.14	1.16	1.16
ES23	La Rioja	1.22	1.22	1.20	1.12	1.09	1.11	1.13	1.13
ES24	Aragón	0.99	1.03	1.00	1.00	0.98	1.01	1.02	1.03
ES30	Madrid	1.48	1.52	1.47	1.48	1.56	1.53	1.49	1.48
ES41	Castile-Leon	0.91	0.85	0.90	0.92	0.83	0.84	0.82	0.80
ES42	Castile-La Mancha	0.71	0.68	0.72	0.74	0.66	0.69	0.68	0.67
ES43	Extremadura	0.63	0.60	0.61	0.60	0.56	0.59	0.59	0.57
ES51	Catalonia	1.55	1.63	1.58	1.56	1.60	1.53	1.52	1.54
ES52	Valencia	1.10	1.07	1.06	1.02	1.12	1.13	1.15	1.12
ES53	Balearic Islands	1.29	1.41	1.31	1.21	1.25	1.24	1.30	1.30
ES61	Andalusia	0.76	0.75	0.74	0.72	0.69	0.67	0.68	0.68
ES62	Murcia	0.79	0.75	0.77	0.77	0.69	0.69	0.71	0.75
ES70	Canary Islands	0.91	0.89	0.85	0.83	0.72	0.79	0.78	0.76
	ESP	**1.00**	**1.00**	**1.00**	**1.00**	**1.00**	**1.00**	**1.00**	**1.00**

(*continued*)

Table A10 (continued)

Code	NUTS2	1963	1965	1967	1969	1971	1973	1975	1977	1979
ES11	Galicia	0.70	0.70	0.72	0.73	0.75	0.75	0.76	0.79	0.81
ES12	Asturias	1.03	1.02	1.03	1.03	0.99	0.98	0.99	0.95	0.95
ES13	Cantabria	1.16	1.13	1.12	1.11	1.09	1.03	1.02	1.03	1.03
ES21	Basque Country	1.60	1.58	1.49	1.45	1.37	1.34	1.33	1.24	1.15
ES22	Navarre	1.21	1.17	1.17	1.14	1.14	1.14	1.14	1.13	1.12
ES23	La Rioja	1.16	1.14	1.13	1.10	1.08	1.06	1.04	1.06	1.10
ES24	Aragón	1.06	1.03	1.02	1.03	1.00	0.99	1.01	1.03	1.04
ES30	Madrid	1.44	1.48	1.42	1.36	1.32	1.33	1.34	1.30	1.30
ES41	Castile-Leon	0.83	0.83	0.82	0.83	0.83	0.83	0.84	0.86	0.87
ES42	Castile-La Mancha	0.68	0.67	0.68	0.71	0.73	0.77	0.78	0.80	0.79
ES43	Extremadura	0.55	0.54	0.55	0.55	0.56	0.59	0.58	0.59	0.61
ES51	Catalonia	1.50	1.45	1.41	1.37	1.33	1.29	1.28	1.25	1.24
ES52	Valencia	1.09	1.05	1.03	1.02	1.01	1.01	1.00	1.01	1.02
ES53	Balearic Islands	1.30	1.31	1.36	1.39	1.41	1.38	1.34	1.34	1.37
ES61	Andalusia	0.68	0.68	0.70	0.71	0.73	0.74	0.73	0.75	0.74
ES62	Murcia	0.77	0.77	0.80	0.82	0.83	0.84	0.83	0.84	0.85
ES70	Canary Islands	0.76	0.76	0.80	0.82	0.87	0.86	0.81	0.83	0.92
	ESP	**1.00**	**1.00**	**1.00**	**1.00**	**1.00**	**1.00**	**1.00**	**1.00**	**1.00**

(continued)

Table A10 (continued)

Code	NUTS2	1980	1981	1982	1983	1984	1985	1986	1987	1988
ES11	Galicia	0.80	0.82	0.84	0.82	0.83	0.82	0.80	0.79	0.79
ES12	Asturias	0.93	0.94	0.96	0.94	0.93	0.97	0.98	0.94	0.93
ES13	Cantabria	1.08	1.11	1.08	1.07	1.07	1.02	0.96	0.95	0.99
ES21	Basque Country	1.31	1.33	1.33	1.30	1.25	1.26	1.24	1.19	1.18
ES22	Navarre	1.28	1.32	1.28	1.26	1.24	1.22	1.22	1.27	1.24
ES23	La Rioja	1.16	1.18	1.19	1.22	1.22	1.33	1.18	1.12	1.12
ES24	Aragón	1.07	1.05	1.07	1.11	1.13	1.11	1.10	1.10	1.14
ES30	Madrid	1.19	1.19	1.21	1.22	1.20	1.17	1.22	1.23	1.21
ES41	Castile-Leon	0.90	0.88	0.92	0.92	0.94	0.96	0.95	0.95	0.94
ES42	Castile-La Mancha	0.82	0.81	0.81	0.80	0.81	0.85	0.81	0.84	0.85
ES43	Extremadura	0.58	0.58	0.58	0.58	0.68	0.70	0.67	0.68	0.71
ES51	Catalonia	1.21	1.19	1.16	1.15	1.16	1.13	1.16	1.18	1.20
ES52	Valencia	1.03	1.06	1.02	1.03	1.04	1.04	1.01	1.01	1.00
ES53	Balearic Islands	1.14	1.18	1.21	1.23	1.26	1.35	1.31	1.32	1.32
ES61	Andalusia	0.75	0.74	0.75	0.76	0.75	0.77	0.76	0.77	0.76
ES62	Murcia	0.95	0.94	0.91	0.93	0.93	0.92	0.95	0.94	0.91
ES70	Canary Islands	1.00	1.00	0.99	1.01	0.97	0.93	0.96	0.95	0.97
	ESP	**1.00**	**1.00**	**1.00**	**1.00**	**1.00**	**1.00**	**1.00**	**1.00**	**1.00**

(*continued*)

Table A10 (continued)

Code	NUTS2	1989	1990	1991	1992	1993	1994	1995	1996	1997
ES11	Galicia	0.79	0.78	0.78	0.79	0.80	0.79	0.82	0.81	0.81
ES12	Asturias	0.93	0.91	0.90	0.92	0.91	0.92	0.89	0.87	0.85
ES13	Cantabria	1.01	0.98	0.96	0.98	0.97	0.97	0.93	0.92	0.92
ES21	Basque Country	1.19	1.18	1.18	1.16	1.17	1.17	1.19	1.19	1.20
ES22	Navarre	1.28	1.24	1.24	1.23	1.21	1.21	1.27	1.28	1.29
ES23	La Rioja	1.11	1.11	1.12	1.12	1.11	1.12	1.13	1.13	1.13
ES24	Aragón	1.14	1.13	1.13	1.12	1.12	1.12	1.09	1.09	1.09
ES30	Madrid	1.21	1.23	1.23	1.23	1.23	1.23	1.29	1.29	1.30
ES41	Castile-Leon	0.92	0.90	0.91	0.91	0.94	0.93	0.97	0.96	0.94
ES42	Castile-La Mancha	0.87	0.86	0.86	0.86	0.85	0.84	0.83	0.83	0.82
ES43	Extremadura	0.69	0.69	0.70	0.71	0.71	0.72	0.65	0.64	0.64
ES51	Catalonia	1.22	1.22	1.22	1.23	1.22	1.23	1.21	1.23	1.23
ES52	Valencia	1.00	1.00	1.00	0.99	0.98	0.97	0.94	0.94	0.95
ES53	Balearic Islands	1.28	1.30	1.31	1.31	1.31	1.32	1.20	1.20	1.23
ES61	Andalusia	0.75	0.77	0.77	0.76	0.75	0.75	0.75	0.75	0.75
ES62	Murcia	0.91	0.93	0.91	0.90	0.89	0.89	0.82	0.82	0.83
ES70	Canary Islands	0.93	0.91	0.90	0.92	0.95	0.95	0.96	0.95	0.96
	ESP	**1.00**	**1.00**	**1.00**	**1.00**	**1.00**	**1.00**	**1.00**	**1.00**	**1.00**

(*continued*)

Table A10 (continued)

Code	NUTS2	1998	1999	2000	2001	2002	2003	2004	2005	2006
ES11	Galicia	0.80	0.79	0.78	0.78	0.79	0.80	0.81	0.83	0.84
ES12	Asturias	0.86	0.83	0.84	0.84	0.85	0.85	0.86	0.88	0.90
ES13	Cantabria	0.93	0.93	0.93	0.94	0.94	0.94	0.93	0.94	0.93
ES21	Basque Country	1.22	1.23	1.23	1.22	1.22	1.22	1.23	1.24	1.26
ES22	Navarre	1.28	1.27	1.27	1.25	1.25	1.25	1.25	1.25	1.24
ES23	La Rioja	1.13	1.12	1.12	1.10	1.09	1.09	1.08	1.07	1.07
ES24	Aragón	1.07	1.05	1.05	1.04	1.06	1.07	1.07	1.07	1.08
ES30	Madrid	1.33	1.33	1.34	1.34	1.33	1.32	1.32	1.32	1.33
ES41	Castile-Leon	0.92	0.92	0.91	0.90	0.91	0.91	0.92	0.92	0.92
ES42	Castile-La Mancha	0.81	0.80	0.78	0.78	0.79	0.80	0.80	0.80	0.80
ES43	Extremadura	0.63	0.64	0.64	0.63	0.64	0.65	0.65	0.67	0.66
ES51	Catalonia	1.21	1.22	1.22	1.22	1.21	1.20	1.19	1.18	1.18
ES52	Valencia	0.95	0.95	0.95	0.96	0.95	0.94	0.93	0.92	0.91
ES53	Balearic Islands	1.23	1.25	1.26	1.24	1.20	1.15	1.13	1.11	1.09
ES61	Andalusia	0.74	0.73	0.74	0.74	0.75	0.76	0.77	0.78	0.77
ES62	Murcia	0.83	0.82	0.84	0.84	0.84	0.84	0.84	0.84	0.83
ES70	Canary Islands	0.97	0.99	0.98	0.98	0.97	0.96	0.93	0.92	0.90
	ESP	**1.00**	**1.00**	**1.00**	**1.00**	**1.00**	**1.00**	**1.00**	**1.00**	**1.00**

(continued)

Table A10 (continued)

Code	NUTS2	2007	2008	2009	2010	2011	2012	2013	2014	2015
ES11	Galicia	0.86	0.87	0.88	0.89	0.88	0.88	0.89	0.88	0.89
ES12	Asturias	0.91	0.92	0.91	0.92	0.91	0.90	0.88	0.87	0.88
ES13	Cantabria	0.94	0.94	0.94	0.94	0.93	0.92	0.91	0.89	0.91
ES21	Basque Country	1.27	1.29	1.28	1.30	1.30	1.32	1.31	1.32	1.32
ES22	Navarre	1.23	1.24	1.24	1.24	1.25	1.24	1.25	1.26	1.25
ES23	La Rioja	1.07	1.07	1.07	1.08	1.08	1.08	1.08	1.08	1.09
ES24	Aragón	1.09	1.10	1.09	1.10	1.10	1.09	1.11	1.08	1.11
ES30	Madrid	1.32	1.32	1.35	1.34	1.36	1.37	1.37	1.37	1.36
ES41	Castile-Leon	0.92	0.92	0.94	0.94	0.95	0.95	0.94	0.93	0.94
ES42	Castile-La Mancha	0.81	0.81	0.81	0.81	0.81	0.80	0.80	0.78	0.78
ES43	Extremadura	0.67	0.69	0.70	0.71	0.70	0.69	0.69	0.69	0.69
ES51	Catalonia	1.18	1.17	1.17	1.17	1.17	1.17	1.18	1.19	1.19
ES52	Valencia	0.90	0.90	0.89	0.88	0.88	0.87	0.87	0.88	0.88
ES53	Balearic Islands	1.07	1.06	1.04	1.04	1.04	1.04	1.04	1.05	1.04
ES61	Andalusia	0.77	0.77	0.76	0.76	0.76	0.75	0.74	0.74	0.74
ES62	Murcia	0.83	0.84	0.82	0.83	0.81	0.82	0.82	0.83	0.81
ES70	Canary Islands	0.89	0.87	0.86	0.87	0.86	0.86	0.85	0.83	0.85
	ESP	**1.00**	**1.00**	**1.00**	**1.00**	**1.00**	**1.00**	**1.00**	**1.00**	**1.00**

Table A11 Gross domestic product per capita (Spain=1), NUTS1

Code	NUTS1	1860	1870	1880	1890	1900	1910	1920	1930
ES1	Northwest	0.53	0.53	0.53	0.53	0.67	0.65	0.63	0.77
ES2	Northeast	0.99	1.10	1.20	1.18	1.26	1.12	1.29	1.20
ES3	Madrid	1.77	1.86	1.83	1.70	1.63	1.52	1.64	1.80
ES4	Centre	0.87	0.88	0.89	0.86	0.80	0.76	0.73	0.67
ES5	East	1.10	1.16	1.24	1.25	1.44	1.47	1.58	1.46
ES6	South	1.32	1.17	1.05	1.06	0.83	0.93	0.75	0.78
ES7	Canary Islands	0.79	0.63	0.47	0.78	0.61	0.65	0.72	0.71
	ESP	**1.00**	**1.00**	**1.00**	**1.00**	**1.00**	**1.00**	**1.00**	**1.00**

Code	NUTS1	1935	1940	1945	1950	1955	1957	1959	1961
ES1	Northwest	0.84	0.84	0.85	0.85	0.84	0.85	0.85	0.84
ES2	Northeast	1.27	1.29	1.31	1.34	1.33	1.32	1.31	1.31
ES3	Madrid	1.48	1.52	1.47	1.48	1.56	1.53	1.49	1.48
ES4	Centre	0.78	0.74	0.78	0.79	0.72	0.73	0.72	0.71
ES5	East	1.36	1.39	1.35	1.33	1.39	1.36	1.37	1.37
ES6	South	0.76	0.75	0.74	0.73	0.69	0.68	0.68	0.68
ES7	Canary Islands	0.91	0.89	0.85	0.83	0.72	0.79	0.78	0.76
	ESP	**1.00**	**1.00**	**1.00**	**1.00**	**1.00**	**1.00**	**1.00**	**1.00**

Code	NUTS1	1963	1965	1967	1969	1971	1973	1975	1977	1979
ES1	Northwest	0.83	0.82	0.84	0.84	0.85	0.84	0.85	0.86	0.87
ES2	Northeast	1.33	1.31	1.27	1.26	1.21	1.19	1.19	1.16	1.11
ES3	Madrid	1.44	1.48	1.42	1.36	1.32	1.33	1.34	1.30	1.30
ES4	Centre	0.72	0.72	0.72	0.73	0.74	0.76	0.77	0.79	0.79
ES5	East	1.33	1.30	1.27	1.24	1.22	1.20	1.18	1.17	1.17
ES6	South	0.69	0.69	0.71	0.72	0.75	0.75	0.74	0.76	0.76
ES7	Canary Islands	0.76	0.76	0.80	0.82	0.87	0.86	0.81	0.83	0.92
	ESP	**1.00**	**1.00**	**1.00**	**1.00**	**1.00**	**1.00**	**1.00**	**1.00**	**1.00**

(continued)

Table A11 (continued)

Code	NUTS1	1980	1981	1982	1983	1984	1985	1986	1987	1988
ES1	Northwest	0.87	0.89	0.90	0.88	0.88	0.88	0.86	0.84	0.85
ES2	Northeast	1.23	1.24	1.24	1.23	1.21	1.22	1.20	1.17	1.17
ES3	Madrid	1.19	1.19	1.21	1.22	1.20	1.17	1.22	1.23	1.21
ES4	Centre	0.81	0.80	0.81	0.81	0.85	0.88	0.85	0.86	0.87
ES5	East	1.14	1.14	1.12	1.11	1.13	1.11	1.12	1.12	1.13
ES6	South	0.77	0.77	0.77	0.78	0.77	0.79	0.78	0.79	0.78
ES7	Canary Islands	1.00	1.00	0.99	1.01	0.96	0.93	0.95	0.95	0.97
	ESP	**1.00**	**1.00**	**1.00**	**1.00**	**1.00**	**1.00**	**1.00**	**1.00**	**1.00**

Code	NUTS1	1989	1990	1991	1992	1993	1994	1995	1996	1997
ES1	Northwest	0.85	0.84	0.83	0.84	0.85	0.85	0.85	0.84	0.83
ES2	Northeast	1.18	1.17	1.17	1.16	1.16	1.16	1.17	1.17	1.17
ES3	Madrid	1.21	1.23	1.23	1.23	1.23	1.24	1.29	1.30	1.30
ES4	Centre	0.86	0.85	0.85	0.85	0.87	0.86	0.86	0.85	0.84
ES5	East	1.14	1.14	1.15	1.15	1.14	1.14	1.11	1.12	1.13
ES6	South	0.77	0.79	0.78	0.77	0.77	0.77	0.76	0.76	0.76
ES7	Canary Islands	0.93	0.91	0.90	0.92	0.95	0.95	0.96	0.96	0.95
	ESP	**1.00**	**1.00**	**1.00**	**1.00**	**1.00**	**1.00**	**1.00**	**1.00**	**1.00**

Code	NUTS1	1998	1999	2000	2001	2002	2003	2004	2005	2006
ES1	Northwest	0.83	0.82	0.81	0.81	0.82	0.83	0.84	0.86	0.87
ES2	Northeast	1.18	1.18	1.17	1.16	1.17	1.17	1.18	1.18	1.19
ES3	Madrid	1.32	1.33	1.34	1.34	1.33	1.32	1.32	1.32	1.33
ES4	Centre	0.83	0.82	0.81	0.81	0.82	0.82	0.82	0.83	0.83
ES5	East	1.12	1.12	1.13	1.13	1.11	1.10	1.09	1.08	1.08
ES6	South	0.75	0.75	0.75	0.76	0.76	0.78	0.78	0.78	0.78
ES7	Canary Islands	0.97	0.99	0.98	0.98	0.97	0.96	0.93	0.92	0.90
	ESP	**1.00**	**1.00**	**1.00**	**1.00**	**1.00**	**1.00**	**1.00**	**1.00**	**1.00**

(continued)

Table A11 (continued)

Code	NUTS1	2007	2008	2009	2010	2011	2012	2013	2014	2015
ES1	Northwest	0.88	0.89	0.89	0.90	0.89	0.89	0.89	0.88	0.89
ES2	Northeast	1.20	1.21	1.20	1.22	1.22	1.22	1.22	1.22	1.23
ES3	Madrid	1.32	1.32	1.35	1.34	1.36	1.37	1.37	1.37	1.36
ES4	Centre	0.83	0.84	0.84	0.85	0.85	0.85	0.84	0.83	0.83
ES5	East	1.07	1.06	1.05	1.05	1.05	1.05	1.06	1.06	1.06
ES6	South	0.78	0.78	0.77	0.77	0.77	0.76	0.76	0.76	0.75
ES7	Canary Islands	0.89	0.87	0.86	0.87	0.86	0.86	0.85	0.83	0.85
	ESP	**1.00**	**1.00**	**1.00**	**1.00**	**1.00**	**1.00**	**1.00**	**1.00**	**1.00**

Index[1]

[1]Note: Page numbers followed by 'n' refer to notes.

A. Díez-Minguela et al., *Regional Inequality in Spain*, Palgrave Studies in Economic History, https://doi.org/10.1007/978-3-319-96110-1

The manufacturer's authorised representative in the EU is Springer Nature Customer Service Centre GmbH, Europaplatz 3, 69115 Heidelberg, Germany. If you have any concerns regarding our products, please contact ProductSafety@springernature.com

Printed and bound by CPI Group (UK) Ltd, Croydon, CR0 4YY
30/09/2026
02225434-0006